Victory at Mortain

Victory at Mortain

Stopping Hitler's Panzer Counteroffensive

Mark J. Reardon

 University Press of Kansas

Published by the University Press of Kansas (Lawrence, Kansas 66049), which was organized by the Kansas Board of Regents and is operated and funded by Emporia State University, Fort Hays State University, Kansas State University, Pittsburg State University, the
University of Kansas, and Wichita State University

Library of Congress Cataloging-in-Publication Data

Reardon, Mark J., 1957 Oct. 22–
    Victory at Mortain : stopping Hitler's panzer counteroffensive /
Mark J. Reardon.
        p. cm. — (Modern war studies)
    Includes bibliographical references and index.
    ISBN 0-7006-1158-4 (cloth: alk. paper)
        1. World War, 1939–1945—Campaigns—France—Mortain. 2. World War,
    1939–1945—Campaigns—France—Normandy. 3. United States. Army.
    Infantry Division, 30th—History. 4. World War, 1939–1945—Regimental
    histories—United States. I. Title. II. Series.
    D762.M56 R43 2002
    940.54'21421—dc21
                            2001005179

British Library Cataloguing in Publication Data is available.

Printed in the United States of America

10 9 8 7 6 5 4 3 2 1

The paper used in this publication meets the minimum requirements of the American
National Standard for Permanence of Paper for Printed Library Materials Z39.48-1984.

Contents

Illustrations

MAPS

A Key to Tactical Unit Map Symbols appears on page xv.

Preface

Despite the fact that fifty-five years has elapsed, we can still find crucial campaigns of World War II that have been overlooked by historians, readers, and participants alike. The sheer scope of that conflict provides us with one reason for this phenomenon. Another factor may lie in the difficulty encountered when researching unevenly recorded events. In other instances, a multitude of peripheral works has obscured the surprising fact that a specific campaign or battle has been overlooked.

Amazingly enough, the campaign in Normandy falls into this category. Discounting books that focus on D-Day itself, there are distressingly few accounts that focus on the American army in Normandy. Joseph Balkoski's *Beyond the Beachhead: The 29th Infantry Division in Normandy* provides its readers with a detailed tactical account of a single infantry division from Omaha Beach on D-Day to the fall of St.-Lô. Detailed discussion of the American breakout in Normandy, which changed the complexion of the entire campaign, can be found only in James Jay Carafano's superlative *After D-Day: Operation Cobra and the Normandy Breakout.* An examination of the pivotal battle of Mortain, which arguably set the stage for the culmination of the Normandy campaign, is limited to Alwyn Featherston's *Saving the Breakout: The 30th Division's Heroic Stand at Mortain, 7–12 August 1944.*

Normandy provides us with an insight into the process by which the U.S. Army matured into a smoothly running juggernaut that fought its way to victory in Europe. However, the vast majority of the American divisions that landed in Normandy had never seen combat before. The same can be said for senior American commanders at army group, army, corps, and division levels. The Norman hedgerows provided the Americans with a traumatic introduction to warfare against implacable, well-equipped, and tactically proficient German opponents. Stumbling occasionally but learning from its mistakes, the American army quickly matured into an organization that displayed an unparalleled ability to master any situation it encountered on European battlefields during 1944–1945. This book chronicles the first attempt by the Germans to decisively influence the course of the war in western Europe following D-Day. On 7 August, five panzer divisions launched an assault against a single American infantry division defending the small French town of Mortain. By examining the reasons why this battle took place, *Victory at Mortain* provides the reader with crucial insights into the relationship between combat at the tactical level, operational maneuver, and decisionmaking by senior commanders.

Although this account is not intended as a comprehensive analysis of the German and American armies in Normandy, it will provide readers with an opportunity to gauge the performance of the U.S. Army at a key transition point. For the first time since D-Day, American small-unit leaders were remaining alive long enough to learn their trade. By examining the fighting that took place, one can discern how the U.S. Army was beginning to evolve into the proven and professional military machine that went on to win the war in Europe.

I have chosen to analyze Mortain because it was the first large-scale German counteroffensive against the American army on the European continent. In effect, a miniature Battle of the Bulge occurred in and around that picturesque Norman town in August 1944. It is no exaggeration to liken Mortain to the Ardennes offensive, as the scale and objectives of each are roughly comparable. Both operations featured massed panzer units designed to smash rapidly through thinly held American lines to seize critical objectives. Mortain ultimately involved elements of six German panzer and panzergrenadier divisions racing to seize two bridges twenty miles from their line of departure. In comparison, the attacking force in the Ardennes included the equivalent of thirteen panzer and panzergrenadier divisions heading for Antwerp, approximately one hundred miles from their starting point. In both instances, the Germans hoped that success would regain the strategic initiative for them while dealing a serious military setback to the Allies.

Events that occurred as a result of the fighting at Mortain are also examined. Historians have spent countless hours arguing over what might have happened if the Falaise Pocket had been closed sooner. Too little effort has been expended to analyze how the opportunity to destroy an entire German army at Falaise appeared in the first place. For instance, a number of books have highlighted how the British drew the bulk of the German armor away from the Americans throughout much of the Normandy campaign, thus permitting Lieutenant General Omar Bradley's First Army to break out of the hedgerows in late July. Yet these same historians overlook the fact that General Bernard Montgomery was able to launch his first successful offensive only after the Germans sent five panzer divisions to attack the Americans at Mortain. Lacking armored reserves to restore their shattered lines, the Germans were unable to prevent Montgomery's troops from joining with Patton's Third Army at Falaise.

Similarly, while much has also been made of Lieutenant General George Patton's sweeping advance through southeastern France immediately following the breakout, to accept this operation at face value overlooks the fact that the Germans refrained from employing the panzers against Patton's advancing troops because they were defeated at Mortain. The Normandy battlefield was a very dynamic place, with action and reaction taking place as a result of decisions made by both armies. With the bulk of the German armor committed to the operation to recapture Avranches, Patton's troops initially were just opposed by *Panzer Division 9* as they moved south. Faced with only a hodgepodge of German infantry and security troops, Third Army's armored spearheads could not have failed to gain the momentum that carried them to Falaise and beyond.

In preparing for their assault against Avranches, the Germans secretly assembled elements of six panzer and panzergrenadier divisions. Hoping to sever Patton's main supply route where it passed through a narrow corridor south of Avranches. the Germans had to destroy two bridges, one at Avranches and the other at Pontaubault, in order to achieve this goal. Both bridges were located less than twenty miles from the front lines. All of the elements necessary for a closely fought and dramatic encounter were present, yet to date only Alwyn Featherston has attempted to produce a full-length account of the Battle of Mortain, albeit from the limited perspective of the 30th Infantry Division's participants.

One of the reasons why Mortain has been overlooked is that even key participants have often devoted only a few pages to this battle. Eisenhower, Bradley, and Patton all intimate that the German counteroffensive could not have succeeded. German accounts echo these sentiments by claiming that Hitler's attempts to mandate every detail of the counterattack deprived the panzer divisions of a reasonable chance of success. This line of reasoning tends to minimize Mortain's importance by labeling it as an incidental or insignificant battle within the overall Normandy campaign.

Sandwiched between Operation COBRA and the Battle of the Falaise Pocket, the German counteroffensive against Avranches, code-named *Unternehmen Lüt-tich,* has largely been lost to history. However, the fact that a number of American and British historians have not chosen to dwell on *Unternehmen Lüttich* at length does not diminish its importance. It represents, in actuality, the first Battle of the Bulge scenario on the Western Front in which Hitler hoped to launch a surprise attack designed to decisively redress a rapidly deteriorating strategic situation. Like the offensive of December 1944, the attackers achieved almost complete surprise.

Only by painstakingly weaving together a wide variety of materials, including World War II official records, postwar German accounts, and interviews with American veterans, have I been able to compile a detailed narrative of events. This book is intended to put into proper perspective the achievements of the soldiers who fought the Battle of Mortain.

In piecing together what happened at Mortain more than a half century ago, interviews with veterans proved particularly valuable as primary sources, since records such as unit journals and after-action reports normally do not contain extensive accounts of small-unit actions. Statements by local residents have captured the experiences of the unwilling participants of the battle, the civilian population. Contemporary regional maps, supplemented by a battlefield walking tour by the author, did much to identify the proper place names as well as to clarify the relationship of terrain to the tactics used in 1944.

Finally, this book does not overlook the common soldier when examining the actions of high-ranking generals and large-scale battles. Capturing the individual soldier's experiences is necessary to understand the events that occurred at Mortain and during World War II as a whole. To overlook this viewpoint is to ignore that warfare is an intensely personal affair. A visit to one of the many German and American cemeteries in France will remind the reader of this fact; they contain thousands of soldiers who are forever young. It is my hope that the men who fought at Mortain, whose extraordinary efforts have not previously been appreciated in the scope of World War II historiography, will now receive the recognition they deserve.

Acknowledgments

Although many people provided invaluable assistance to me in the course of writing this book, only two individuals endured this project on a daily basis: namely, my lovely wife, Kimberly, and our daughter, Summer. Not only did they suffer in silence when I was totally immersed in this work, but Kimberly also rendered invaluable advice and welcome assistance as my "editor in chief at home."

Since this work is largely based on primary sources, I owe a tremendous debt to those individuals who repeatedly have delved into obscure files to provide me with information. These dedicated professionals include Thomas Jenkins from the National Archives at College Park; Jim Layerzapf at the Dwight D. Eisenhower Presidential Library; Dave Keogh from the U.S. Army Military History Institute; Bill Eigelsbach at the University of Tennessee–Knoxville Library Special Collections; Germaine Pavlova at the Fort Benning Donovan Technical Library; Lieutenant Colonel Gilberto Villahermosa at the U.S. Army Center of Military History; and Rusty Rafferty from the Fort Leavenworth Combined Arms Research Library.

Equally important to this account were the contributions by the veterans themselves. Although a complete list of contributors is found in the bibliography, I would be remiss if I did not single out the following individuals for special recognition: Jack Sabata, Hank Morgan, and Sam Belk of the 35th Infantry Division; and Charles Corbin, Colonel (retired) Sam Hogan, Emmett Tripp, Thomas Magness, Belton Y. Cooper, Frank Plezia, Haynes Dugan, and Thomas Tousey of the 3d Armored Division. I also consider myself very fortunate to have been provided with an extremely well-written manuscript of Tousey's experiences during World War II.

Veterans of the 30th Infantry Division who graciously provided me with interviews as well as written input include Stanley R. Weber, Robert Weiss, Delmont Byrn, Joseph Reaser, John O'Hare, Frank Pruitt, John Hanratty, and Frank

E. Moody. From the 12th Infantry Regiment, Charles Jackson, Colonel (retired) Kenneth Lindner, Alton Pearson, and Marc Dillard helped immensely with the preparation of this book. Thomas Springfield, Colonel (retired) Thompson Raney, Robert C. Clark, George Simmons, and George Greene of the 823d Tank Destroyer Battalion contributed invaluable insights into the crucial opening hours of the German counteroffensive. From the 39th Infantry Regiment, Charlie Scheffel, Brigadier General (retired) Frank Gunn, Jack Dunlap, Dr. William Butler, and Colonel (retired) H. Price Tucker unhesitatingly filled in many of the voids in accounts of the fighting that took place at Cherence le Roussel.

The contributions of separate General Headquarters (GHQ) tank battalions operating in support of infantry units during World War II largely have been overshadowed by the exploits of American armored divisions. This book will provide its readers with dramatic examples of the selfless service rendered by the 70th, 737th, 743d, and 746th Tank Battalions. In particular, veterans of the 737th Tank Battalion, including Harry Haines, Ben Hackman, Junior K. Lambert, and Leo Showfety, made significant contributions to this manuscript by providing me with accounts of the ill-fated attack on 10 August. Robert Hamilton also assisted my research efforts by sending information on C/746th Tank Battalion at Cherence le Roussel.

The completed manuscript benefited from the informed scrutiny of several key individuals, including Niklas Zetterling and longtime friend John Stawasz of Killeen, Texas. Zetterling's comments were especially useful because he provided unique insights into the German perspective using primary documents from both the Bundesarchiv and Captured Records section of the National Archives. *Oberstleutnant* Gunther Guderian cheerfully assisted me by clarifying certain terms found in German military terminology that no longer exist today. Last, but certainly not least, I must belatedly thank Gerhard Boettger for his invaluable assistance in translating many of the German language accounts. Boettger, a veteran of the *Kriegsmarine* during World War II, passed away before this manuscript was completed. I sorely miss his support and friendship.

Of course, I accept sole responsibility for any errors, omissions, or misinterpretations found within this book.

Types of Units

⊠	Armored Infantry or *Panzergrenadier*	
⊘	Cavalry or Reconnaissance, and *Panzeraufklärungs*	
◯	Armored or *Panzer*	
◉	Armored Artillery or *Panzerartillerie*	
▢	Artillery or Cannon, and *Artillerie*	
▽	Tank Destroyer or *Panzerjäger*	
▽	Antitank	
MORT	Mortar	
MG	Machine gun	

Sizes of Units

•	Squad
• •	Section
• • •	Platoon
I	Company
I I	Battalion
I I I	Regiment
X	Combat Command
XX	Division
XXX	Corps
XXXX	Army
XXXXX	Army Group

A Key to Tactical Unit Map Symbols

1

The Second Front Opens in Normandy

Preoccupied with events in Russia and Italy, Adolf Hitler regarded an Allied invasion of France as a distant threat prior to 1944.[1] Because of his perception, most German divisions stationed in the west consisted of static defense units or infantry and panzer divisions recuperating from combat in Russia. When the Germans finally began to accelerate defensive preparations in France, a string of Soviet successes during the first half of 1944 wrought havoc on their ability to allocate sufficient resources to defeat an Allied invasion force sailing from England. With each mile of territory regained by Soviet troops, Hitler diverted troops and equipment to the Eastern Front as he tried to retain a foothold in Russia and prop up his faltering Balkan alliances.[2]

Although the Germans possessed extremely limited means of collecting information on Allied invasion preparations, there were many signs of an imminent landing by early 1944. Hitler was convinced that an Allied landing in northern France would occur that summer. Despite continued Soviet successes and a deteriorating situation in Italy, he grudgingly gave priority to the Western Front. Although an entire *SS-Panzer Korps* was transferred to Russia in April, German troop strength in the west increased from forty-six to fifty-eight divisions between March and June 1944.

The Germans did not know precisely where the Allies would land, which meant that thirty-three of the fifty-eight divisions consisted of static units manning fixed fortifications spread along the length of the entire French coast. Frantic efforts to improve fortifications protecting French beaches, although statistically impressive in overall terms of concrete pillboxes built and mines emplaced, proved to be too little and too late. The core of the German defensive effort, therefore, rested with mobile divisions capable of carrying out the full range of offensive and defensive operations. By June 1944, no fewer than thirteen infantry divisions, two parachute divisions, six army

1

panzer divisions, and four *SS* panzer or panzergrenadier divisions were stationed in the west.

The defending German forces were organized into two army groups, *Heeresgruppe B* and *Armeegruppe G*, which were further subdivided into four numbered armies: *1*, *7*, *15*, and *19 Armee*. *Generalfeldmarschall* Erwin Rommel's *Heeresgruppe B*, consisting of *7* and *15 Armee*, was assigned the mission of defending northern France. *Generaloberst* Johannes von Blaskowitz's *Armeegruppe G*, which commanded *1* and *19 Armee*, defended the Bay of Biscay and southern France. *Generalfeldmarschall* Gerd von Rundstedt's *Oberbefehlshaber West* (*OB West*) coordinated the operations of both *Armeegruppen*. As the overall theater commander, von Rundstedt reported directly to Berlin.

Generaloberst Hans von Salmuth's *15 Armee* controlled the bulk of the divisions allocated to *Heeresgruppe B* and was responsible for protecting Pas de Calais, located thirty miles across the channel from England. Because the Germans considered Pas de Calais as the most likely objective for an invading force, they concentrated the bulk of their troops and fortifications in that area. Von Salmuth controlled eighteen divisions distributed among four corps. *Generaloberst* Friedrich Dollman's *7 Armee*, which was located south of Pas de Calais with the mission of defending Normandy, numbered fourteen divisions organized into four corps.

The defensive plan developed by Hitler's generals was founded upon the integrated employment of obstacles, indirect fire, and organic infantry weapons to stop the Allies on the beaches. Mobile forces would be used to counterattack Allied troops who succeeded in overwhelming the coastal defenses. A special armored staff, designated *Panzer Gruppe West*, was formed to oversee the training and employment of the panzer and panzergrenadier divisions stationed in France. The Germans also transferred one of their most experienced panzer corps staffs from Russia to France to coordinate and launch the planned armored counterattack.[3]

Preparations for the defense of France, however, were marred by quarrels between Rommel and von Rundstedt. Although both believed the Allies intended to land at Pas de Calais, they disagreed on the precise tactics that should be used to destroy the invaders. Specifically, both *Generalfeldmarschall* disagreed on how the decisive counterattack would be conducted. Von Rundstedt believed that the panzers should be held further back from the coast to execute a powerful counterattack once the Allies were established ashore. Rommel, on the other hand, felt that the panzers should be stationed close to threatened coastal regions in order to counterattack while the Allies were trying to get off the beaches. Hitler, who refused to make a decision, compromised by splitting the available panzers into a local and strategic reserve. The strategic reserve, consisting of four panzer divisions, was answerable only to Hitler.[4]

In this instance, Hitler can be credited with a clearer sense of the battlefield than his senior commanders. Von Rundstedt and Rommel discussed the employment of the panzer divisions as if all of those units were fully combat ready. In reality, only *Panzer Lehr, SS-Panzer Division 12, Panzer Division 2,* and *Panzer Division 21* possessed sufficient serviceable panzers and wheeled transport to enable them to be committed as a complete division. The remaining divisions suffered from serious shortages of panzers, wheeled and tracked transports, and other vital equipment. Whereas portions of the other panzer divisions in France were capable of being committed soon after the invasion occurred, it would take time for their main body to arrive at the battlefront.

While his generals squabbled over the positioning of tactical panzer reserves, Hitler viewed the question of an Allied invasion through a wider perspective. The Russians had just concluded a series of offensives from January through mid-April 1944 that returned a tremendous amount of territory to their control. German troops besieging Leningrad in the north were pushed back one hundred miles while Soviet tank and infantry spearheads were nearing the Polish border.

Only the presence of German troops in Romania, Hungary, and Bulgaria was keeping Hitler's Balkan allies faithful. In Italy, the Allied force trapped at Anzio since January had broken out and was approaching Rome. Intermediate defensive lines in France were nonexistent, and the Siegfried Line protecting the western border of Germany had fallen into disrepair. The west, Hitler reasoned, would become the decisive theater of the war when the Allies invaded France.[5]

Hitler considered numerous options dealing with potential German responses to an Anglo-American landing in France. He could heed Rommel's advice and counterattack immediately. However, this course of action would expose the attacking panzer divisions to a tremendous barrage of Allied air and naval gunfire. Von Rundstedt's plan offered a more deliberate approach, permitting Hitler sufficient time to determine if the landings represented the Allied main effort or were simply intended as a diversion. Hitler knew he could not afford to commit the bulk of his mobile forces against a diversionary effort, since this would undoubtedly ensure that the panzers would be out of position to confront the main Allied landings.

Hitler believed that, in the long run, the destruction of a few assault divisions would not suffice to provide him with the strategic breathing space necessary to regain the initiative on the Eastern Front. In order to indefinitely cripple Allied follow-on efforts, it would be preferable to allow the invaders to land ten to fifteen divisions before launching the decisive counterattack to destroy the lodgment. An additional advantage to be gained by confining the Anglo-Americans' lodgment for several months was that the planned German counterattack would take place under fall weather conditions adverse to the employment of tactical close air support. The delay would also permit the Germans to build up sufficient air and sea power to seriously attrit the Allied invasion fleet.

Accepting temporary stalemate in order to gain strategic advantage with the onset of autumn weather appeared to offer many advantages to the defenders. Several key conditions, however, had to be met before Hitler could expect this course of action to produce the desired results. First, German troops had to retain control of seaports to deny the Allies a protected anchorage and cargo handling facilities. By confining the Anglo-Americans to unprotected beaches, their logistical system would become very vulnerable to bad weather as the summer wore on. Second, the Allied main effort had to be established. Third, the decisive panzer counterattack would only be launched when it possessed a favorable opportunity to destroy a substantial number of Allied divisions.[6]

The Anglo-Americans gathered three dozen infantry, airborne, and armored divisions to oppose the formidable array of German troops in France. The 4,226 landing craft and ships allotted to the invasion force carried a total of 174,320 men and 20,108 vehicles in the first wave. It would require three days to disembark the initial assault echelon. Allied naval commanders were therefore held to a strict timetable to ensure that sufficient combat power was available ashore to retain the lodgment in the face of expected German counterattacks.[7] Limited shipping, logistics support, beaches, and maneuver space all conspired to require several months to transport these divisions from England to France. Because they were only able to achieve overall numerical parity with the defenders, the Allies depended heavily on airpower and deception to significantly delay the flow of German reinforcements.

The Allies chose Normandy as the site for the invasion rather than Pas de Calais, which was much closer to England. Although a landing in the Pas de Calais region would facilitate shipping turnaround and construction of a cross-channel pipeline for gasoline and oil, it was the most strongly defended area of the French coast and the pivot of the German coastal defense system. The only four beaches suitable for the landing of assault divisions lay astride Boulogne, between Cap Gris Nez and the Canche River. Although suitable for landing large numbers of troops, these beaches were exposed to the prevailing wind, were backed by extensive sand dunes, and were dominated south of Boulogne by high ground. Exits from the beaches were generally limited to stream or river valleys. Moreover, numerous obstacles, such as concrete walls, minefields, and antitank ditches, blocked all exits.

It was estimated that the exit limitations would prevent the landing of more than one assault division on D-Day. However, two German coastal divisions normally held the sector between Gravelines and the Somme River, which included Boulogne. A portion of the German armored reserve in the west also was customarily located north of the Seine River behind the Pas de Calais and Belgian coast. Moreover, Pas de Calais could be reinforced more easily than Normandy, either from the interior of France or from Germany.

Additionally, the main ports in the area, Boulogne and Calais, were believed capable of maintaining only nine to twelve Allied divisions by D+90 (D-Day plus ninety days). In order to obtain the required port facilities, it would be necessary to expand the Pas de Calais beachhead eastward to include the ports from Boulogne to Antwerp inclusive or southwestward to include the ports from Calais to Le Havre and Rouen inclusive.[8] Pas de Calais was discarded as a potential landing site. However, the Allies were not about to let the Germans know that.

The Normandy beaches between the Orne River and the Carentan Estuary and the east coast of the Cotentin Peninsula in the vicinity of St.-Mere-Eglise were selected as the sites for the amphibious assaults. Assault landing craft were provided to transport three British divisions with attached commando units and two American divisions (one of which was composite) with attached ranger units. Landing craft and ships for two additional divisions afloat were to be provided for follow-up on the second tide of D-Day. The plan provided for airborne landings by one British division near Caen and by two American divisions in the Carentan area about six hours in advance of the amphibious assaults in the two areas. Heavy air and naval bombardment of targets in rear areas and German installations on the beaches would precede the amphibious assault.

The choice of landing beaches, with the British in the north and Americans to the south, was largely due to the location of British and American forces in England. British troops had occupied the eastern coast of England since 1940 in anticipation of a German invasion. As American troops arrived, they were billeted in southern and western England. Confusion was avoided by ensuring that American convoys sailing from ports in southern and western England were confined to southerly routes. Thus, the Americans were landed in the most inhospitable section of Normandy while the British conducted operations in the less heavily vegetated region near the city of Caen.

No one believed that the Allies could avoid a German counterattack by landing in Normandy. However, the Allies would be able to rapidly build up a strong defensive perimeter by exploiting the natural terrain features unique to that region. The compartmented terrain and marshes, which severely limited vehicular trafficability, would serve to confine counterattacking panzers to easily defensible avenues of advance. Another point in favor of choosing Normandy was that the German defenses were not as well established as they were in the Pas de Calais. Finally, early acquisition of the port of Cherbourg was highly desirable to enhance the rate at which troops and supplies could be delivered to the beachhead.[9]

The Allied ground assault force was under the overall command of General Bernard Montgomery, commanding 21st Army Group. The Second British Army, commanded by Lieutenant General Miles Dempsey, in cooperation with the Eastern Naval Task Force, would assault the British zone on the left. Five brigades would land between Asnelles sur Mer and Ouistreham while two airborne brigades dropped east of the Orne River. Three and one-third British infantry divisions were slated to be ashore by the evening of D-Day. The mission of the British forces would be the development of the beachhead south of the St.-Lô–Caen line and southeast of Caen to secure airfield sites as well as the protection of the First U.S. Army's left flank while the latter captured Cherbourg.

Lieutenant General Omar N. Bradley's First U.S. Army, in cooperation with the Western Naval Task Force, would land immediately to the west of the British zone of operations. One regimental combat team would assault Varreville and the Carentan Estuary on Utah Beach, while two other combat teams would attack between Vierville and Colleville sur Mer on Omaha Beach. Two airborne divisions would drop in the area behind Utah and Omaha Beaches. Two and two-thirds American infantry divisions were to be ashore by the evening of D-Day, and additional airborne troops would land via glider late on D-Day or early on D+1.

The single most important strategic objective was the early capture and development of a major port, or ports, for the use of American forces. In order to build up sufficient forces and supplies with which eventually to force a crossing of the Seine River, the OVERLORD plan estimated that the most probable Allied line of action, after the seizure of Cherbourg, would be the capture of the Brittany ports. The plan visualized a rapid advance inland and, in the west, the early capture of Cherbourg; an eastern expansion of the beachhead to the Eure River from Dreux to Rouen, thence along the lower Seine to the sea; and the simultaneous seizure of Chartres, Orleans, and Tours.

At the same time, American troops were to drive south and cut off the Brittany peninsula to pave the way for the opening of the Brittany ports and the development of Quiberon Bay as a major logistical site. The lodgment area would be cleared of Germans as far south as the Loire River before an advance was made beyond Paris and the Seine ports. It was anticipated that it would require three months to obtain all of these objectives.[10]

The opening stages of the campaign for Normandy unfolded in an unexpected manner for both the Allies and the Germans. Although the Americans suffered heavy casualties on Omaha Beach, the Allied landings were uniformly successful. The British succeeded in fending off halfhearted German attempts to destroy the invasion force as it consolidated ashore in the wake of the landings. *SS-Panzer Division 12* and *Panzer Division 21* both launched assaults against the British beaches, but they were repulsed. Faced with maintenance and equipment shortages, difficult terrain, naval gunfire, and Allied airpower, the Germans were never able to assemble a massive force of panzers to counterattack the initial Allied lodgment.

In the air and at sea, the Germans also met with failure. Their naval and aerial attacks failed to achieve significant results against the invasion fleet. An umbrella of Allied fighters kept the *Luftwaffe* away from the beaches, and Allied aircraft sank most *Kriegsmarine* surface craft based in France before the invasion began. The surviving light craft that sortied from their bases to attack the transport ships were normally deflected from that task by the immense screen of Allied escort vessels. Until additional German naval and air assets could be assembled in the west, Hitler would have to depend on poor weather to disrupt the flow of Allied reinforcements and supplies.

The Allies had counted heavily on airpower to prevent the Germans from utilizing the excellent French rail and road facilities to their advantage. The

Allied aerial interdiction efforts, however, met with mixed success. While pre-invasion airstrikes succeeded in reducing rail traffic by 60 percent between 1 March and 6 June, the Germans were able to reinforce their forces in France during that period with twelve additional divisions.[11] The transfer of additional divisions, however, was accomplished at the expense of German logistical sustainment. By devoting scarce transportation resources to the movement of reinforcements, the Germans were unable to efficiently distribute fuel and ammunition already located within the theater of operations.[12]

The Allied deception plan, code-named Operation FORTITUDE, met with greater success. Designed to convince Hitler that the initial landing in Normandy was a feint and that the main effort would be made against Pas de Calais six weeks after D-Day, the plan worked better than the Allies had hoped for. As late as mid-July the German high command remained undecided on the Normandy landings. Fearing a second landing, Hitler held *15 Armee* in place to guard Pas de Calais. The German divisions designated as a counterattack force were employed instead in a defensive role.

By transitioning to the defensive instead of unleashing an immediate and massive counterattack against the beaches, the Germans inadvertently succeeded in disrupting the OVERLORD plan. The Allies had hoped to secure a decisive victory by defeating the German counterattack force. Once the Allies defeated the German divisions concentrated against the landing, they logically anticipated that the Germans would fall back with the main body of their forces to cover Paris while delaying along the Seine River.

Hitler's decision to defend every inch of Normandy resulted in unanticipated challenges for the Allies. By driving inland on D-Day, Montgomery hoped to unhinge German attempts to establish a defensive line by seizing Caen. However, the vital crossroads city did not fall as planned. The Germans were able to retain control of Caen until early July. Bradley's First Army was tasked to seize the port of Cherbourg by 21 June, or D+15. In fact, the last German defender did not surrender until 1 July. The Americans were also expected to quickly establish a defensive line running roughly from Lessay–Periers–St.-Lô prior to launching an offensive to secure Avranches and Domfront at the base of the Brittany peninsula by D+20. None of these objectives was accomplished as scheduled.

The OVERLORD plan seemed to have been based on the assumption that the Germans would offer themselves up for defeat in a desperate series of attacks designed to erase the beachhead. Lieutenant General George Patton, for example, had been briefed on 1 June that the Germans would oppose the landings with eighteen hundred tanks by D+1.[13] Instead, the Germans transitioned to a deliberate defense.[14]

The Americans clearly did not expect their opponents to dig in rather than counterattack. Lieutenant General Bradley's aide quoted him on 15 June as stating that "the corps commanders are all full of piss and vinegar. They all wanted to go like hell. I've got to stop them, get them solid and dug in. He's [the Germans] going to hit us hard and I don't want a breakthrough." The First Army staff also expressed amazement "at the slight reaction of the German to our beach head. We expected him to be throwing everything now. Certainly a counterattack of several divisions."[15]

The topography of Normandy had unexpectedly influenced the plans of both Allied and German commanders. Hedgerow country, which began ten miles inland from the Normandy beaches, extended from Caumont to the western edge of the Cotentin Peninsula. Sturdy embankments consisting of half hedge and half earth crowned with vines, trees, and bushes, the hedgerows were intended to act as boundary fences, to keep in cattle, and to prevent erosion. Consequently, a wide swath of Normandy was broken up into irregularly shaped walled enclosures connected only by farm trails and openings protected by gates. Vegetation grew in profusion along the base and top of the hedgerows, which ranged from three to fifteen feet in height.

The Norman terrain did not come as a total surprise to either combatant. The Germans had been training in that area since 1940. Allied planners had commissioned a comprehensive study entitled "Notes on the Topography of Lower Normandy and the Cotentin." This report described the terrain as "nothing but criss-crossed hedges, meadows full of trees that would seem an immense forest, only cleared here and there, covering it all with its green mantle. From close by, the illusion is dissipated—trees are everywhere and forests are nowhere . . . the roads, artificial creation of a suspicious government, run straight, far from the villages, over the countryside without revealing their secrets."

The study also revealed that the French revolutionary government had fought a guerrilla war against the peasants in Normandy during the early nineteenth century. The peasants, who were "ranged against the revolution to defend their faith and their ancestral habits, found in their country their most precious allies." The French revolutionary forces soon discovered that they could not "get the upper hand in these dark combats where the adversary was always invisible, where pursuit was broken against hedges or brooks." Even after the French revolutionaries triumphed over the aristocracy, the Norman peasants remained undefeated. After a peace agreement was eventually concluded with them, the newly installed revolutionary government placed great emphasis on the construction of "wide main roads [to] open the countryside and allow rapid transport of troops."[16]

Each of the attacking American corps had also analyzed the Normandy terrain. Both of the assault forces, V and VII Corps, concluded that the hedgerows were a terrain obstacle that would be incorporated into an antiarmor defense against counterattacking German panzers. Follow-on forces, such as VIII and XIX Corps, were more concerned about the hedgerows as a significant impediment to *movement*. XIX Corps noted that "the country is in general covered with orchards, woodlands, and hedged or stone-walled pastures, which together with the valleys would severely restrict the deployment of vehicles from the roads."[17] This assessment might indicate that some American planners optimistically believed the Germans would shift their defensive effort beyond the range of naval gunfire once the Atlantic Wall defenses were breached.

The limited fields of vision characteristic of hedgerow country made it very difficult to navigate or identify landmarks. The lack of recognizable terrain posed a particularly serious challenge. In a region dominated by sunken lanes, small orchards, and endless, irregularly shaped fields surrounded by earthen hedgerows known in the local parlance as *bocage,* it often proved impossible to anticipate what type of terrain a unit might encounter while moving. Hemmed in by the earthen embankments topped by bushes and trees, the combatants experienced significant difficulty identifying their own location, let alone pinpointing their opponents. The German defenders gained some relief by occupying commanding terrain and church steeples affording them a superior view of the local battlefield.[18]

The earthen hedgerows materially aided attempts to fortify defensive lines and protect equipment. The Germans were provided with sufficient time to improve these natural defenses when the Americans attacked Cherbourg rather than immediately pushing south toward St.-Lô. Tree-crowned hedgerows, small wooded areas, abundant undergrowth, and scattered orchards provided good concealment, and the Germans were able to easily construct shelters and firing positions along the base of a hedgerow or earthen bank of a sunken road. With defensive positions rendered almost invisible by natural cover and concealment, the effectiveness of fire support available to an attacking force was often severely curtailed.

While the hedgerows certainly proved to be one factor that enhanced the Germans' defensive capabilities, they also proved to be an obstacle. One great disadvantage associated with defending in the *bocage* was that it required many men just to maintain observation, which forced the Germans to have more soldiers forward than they normally would have wanted. This had two effects. First, it exposed more men to Allied artillery fire, thereby increasing casualties. Second, it made it more difficult to create reserves. If the Germans found hilltops or similar terrain features, they could get some observation for indirect fire, but it still was not comparable to open terrain. American artillery could be aided by observation from aircraft, a technique that was impossible for the Germans, given the Allied air superiority.

The defending Germans also were loath to employ their technologically superior armored fighting vehicles in the *bocage.* The German Panther and Tiger tanks were designed for operations on the featureless plains of Russia. The densely clustered Norman hedgerows, however, would permit American tanks mounting less capable guns to effectively engage better armed and armored opponents at extremely short ranges. Additionally, the narrow sunken lanes were ill suited for use by large vehicles such as the Panther and Tiger tanks. The hedgerow terrain was considered such poor tank country that the defenders chose not to deploy any of their heavy tank battalions against the Americans. Although the German assault guns were lighter and more maneuverable, their low silhouette made it difficult to obtain a good field of fire in the *bocage.*

Because the hedgerows were so forbidding, the Germans chose to concentrate the preponderance of their panzer divisions against the British. Not only was the open terrain better suited for heavier panzers such as the Tiger and Panther, but it also provided the Germans with a fairly open avenue of approach favoring the employment of massed panzers against the Allied lodgment. In order to support the use of panzers in open terrain, the Germans deployed an entire flak corps to the Caen front.

In addition to the tactical difficulties encountered by the Germans, the hedgerows also influenced the operational complexion of their defense in Normandy. By mid-July, the Germans sent 410,000 men in divisions and nondivisional combat units to Normandy, more than half of which faced the British. To this figure can be added another 80,000 men in corps and army service units. German casualties from 6 June–23 July amounted to 116,863 men, while only 10,078 replacements arrived. The fighting in the hedgerow country was characterized by infantry combat at short range, which produced high casualties on both sides. German infantry units facing the Americans sustained most of the losses suffered during this period, which meant that the number of German troops facing the First Army was steadily diminishing at an unsupportable rate.

Severe losses, coupled with the compartmentalization of the hedgerow terrain, drove the Germans to employ battalion and regimental *Kampfgruppen* rather than entire divisions. While these tactics sufficed as long as the Americans attacked on a narrow front, it would later prove less effective against an assault on a broad front.

However, hedgerows were not the sole reason for disappointing progress on the part of the Allies. The British conducted major operations in both the *bocage* and open terrain along the Caen-Falaise corridor. It did not seem as if the open terrain was more advantageous to the attackers compared to the *bocage*. In particular, British armor received its worst losses when attacking against longer ranging German tank and antitank guns in the open.

One reason that the hedgerows were proving to be such a difficult problem was that many American units were new to combat. When the commanding general of the American First Army, Lieutenant General Omar N. Bradley, received reports of the difficulties encountered by some American units advancing inland, he exclaimed, "Isn't this the damnedest country you ever saw? Collins says it is as bad as some of the stuff he hit on Guadal[canal]. Heavy underbrush with thick hedges. German in position under the hedges and it is necessary to root him out when he persists in sticking as he frequently does."[19]

Lieutenant General Courtney Hodges, then deputy commanding general of First Army, was tasked by Bradley to visit new divisions to deliver a pep talk on hedgerows. In a meeting with officers and men from the 3d Armored Division, Hodges stated that "hedgerows are becoming a greater psychological hazard than was merited by their defensive worth. He [Hodges] had seen tanks in action against obstacles far tougher and he knew what they could do."[20]

Only a few American divisions, namely the 1st and 9th Infantry Divisions, 2d Armored Division, and 82d Airborne Division, had experienced combat before Normandy. While the hedgerows proved to be a problem even for veteran troops, they could concentrate on devising specific tactics to overcome the German defenses anchored amidst the rough Norman terrain. Divisions new to combat had to learn the business of warfare before they could develop the sophistication necessary to rapidly adjust to changing combat situations and environments. Existing doctrine and stateside training were sound, but new units were still learning how to put that knowledge into practice.

One of the most serious shortfalls encountered by inexperienced units was their inability to successfully coordinate tank-infantry operations in the hedgerows. Although foot soldiers were well suited for difficult terrain such as Normandy, the offensive power of an infantry unit "decreases appreciably when . . . freedom of maneuver is limited or when . . . confronted by an organized defensive position. Under these conditions or against a force of combined arms, the limited firepower of infantry must be reinforced adequately by the support of artillery, tanks, and other arms."[21]

American service schools and manuals stressed the importance of the infantry-tank-artillery team; however, more attention was given to the infantry-artillery combination in actual training. The doctrines and techniques of the infantry-artillery team were firmly established prior to World War II. Combined training was carried on until infantry and artillery became thoroughly indoctrinated in the operational procedures necessary to coordinate their actions on the battlefield.[22] American doctrine also emphasized the employment of tanks in support of infantry assaulting organized positions. However, artillery and armor were viewed in separate and distinct supporting roles, which invariably failed to take into account the requirement to coordinate the employment of all three components in order to operate effectively on the battlefield.

The commanding general of the 90th Infantry Division, when questioned regarding the failure of his troops to advance, attributed his lack of success primarily to "tank-infantry coordination [that] left much to be desired."[23] The problem of poor tank-infantry cooperation, however, was not limited to infantry divisions who were allocated a single General Headquarters (GHQ) tank battalion for support. In early June, tankers belonging to the 2d Armored Division's veteran 66th Armored Regiment discovered that "most attempts at coordination with the task force's own 41st Armored Infantry were frustrating. The [armored] infantry [was] reluctant to accompany the tanks through the difficult hedgerows even though infantry support was badly needed."[24]

By early July, attempts to refine American tank-infantry teamwork began to gain tangible results. To attain the expertise needed to overcome the terrain, the Americans improved combined arms cooperation, developed better communications, and instilled a sense of mutual trust between tankers and foot soldiers. Separate tank battalions were habitually attached to the same infantry division to foster development of cohesion and trust. Tanks were also fitted with external telephones or provided with infantry radios to aid in communications.

The most effective method of attack proved to be the combined action of infantry, artillery, tanks, and engineers with some tanks equipped with bulldozer blades or large teeth in front to punch holes through the hedgerows. Frontages had to be assigned according to specific fields and hedgerows instead of yardage. Reduced distances and intervals between tactical formations also became necessary, with cross-hedgerows acting as phase lines to control movement. The rifle company usually moved in a box formation with two assault platoons in the lead followed by a support platoon and weapons platoon. The tanks moved with the leading infantry elements along with engineer demolition crews. During the advance, fire from mortars, grenades, automatic weapons, and tank guns was directed against the hedges, especially the hedgerow corners. Some supporting tanks moved along the hedgerows parallel to the direction of the attack. As the tanks crossed each row, the leading wave of infantry and combat engineers protected the vehicles against German antitank teams, while the supporting wave of infantry mopped up in the rear and eliminated snipers.

The artillery was concentrated in close support of the infantry-tank-engineer team, firing on hedgerows in advance to destroy German defensive positions and to keep down antitank fire. Close air support was also used in addition to the artillery to disorganize German positions in the path of the advancing infantry and tanks. The newly refined tactics clearly stressed the need to have tanks and infantry advance together, each protecting the other as they moved forward. The armored vehicles suppressed the opposing machine guns until attacking GIs crawled close enough to toss grenades into the German positions. In return, the American foot soldiers stuck close to their supporting tanks to protect them from *Panzerfaust* teams and antitank guns. Although these tactics permitted U.S. troops to advance with fewer casualties, the Americans were not content with the limited success they brought.

Greater success was also being achieved by the Americans in refining the use of close air support provided by fighter-bombers to frontline units. The habitual association of tactical air force with ground units resulted in the effective use of fighter-bombers against pinpoint targets. The execution of close air support was facilitated by very high frequency radio, permitting direct radio contact between the aircraft, the fighter-bomber control center, and the forward ground controller. During the early phases of the Normandy campaign, the Americans developed "horsefly" and "armored column cover" tactics. Horsefly tactics featured liaison aircraft equipped with a high frequency radio directing the activities of high performance fighters operating against close-in targets or targets of opportunity in direct support of ground units. Armored column cover involved similar techniques worked out by fighter-bombers and tank teams with the mission of providing close air support for rapidly moving armored units.

While inexperienced American units were learning how to fight in the hedgerows, their commanding general also was learning his trade. Lieutenant

General Omar Bradley was a competent field commander, typical of American generals with an infantry background, but he was not known as a visionary or a risk-taker. Bradley's willingness to perform as a team player was the primary reason why General Dwight D. Eisenhower recommended him for command of First Army. During the Tunisian and Sicilian campaigns, Eisenhower had grown weary of dealing with unruly prima donnas such as Montgomery and Patton. He justified his decision to General George C. Marshall by explaining that Bradley was "the best rounded in all aspects, counting experience, and *he has the great characteristic of never giving his commander one moment of worry.*"[25]

Omar Bradley's professional background, which consisted primarily of staff and academic assignments rather than troop duty, reflected on his initial performance as an army commander. His first assignment was with the 14th Infantry Regiment stationed in Washington State. Although his regiment was briefly deployed to Arizona following General Pershing's punitive expedition in 1916, a sorely disappointed Bradley missed being sent to France during World War I. He was assigned as an ROTC instructor at the Brookings Institute followed by a stint on the faculty of West Point. After graduating second in his Infantry Officer Advance Course at Fort Benning, Georgia, Bradley was sent to the 27th Infantry Regiment in Hawaii.[26]

Requesting a return to stateside duty, Bradley was ordered to Fort Leavenworth, Kansas, where he attended the Command and General Staff College. At the conclusion of his schooling, Bradley found himself assigned to the Infantry School at Fort Benning. Here he made a favorable impression on the assistant commandant, Colonel George C. Marshall. Several years later, Bradley found himself assigned as deputy assistant to Marshall when the latter assumed the duties of Army Chief of Staff in 1939. Success in this high visibility position led to Bradley's promotion to brigadier general and command of the Infantry School in March 1941.

Bradley did not remain at Fort Benning for very long, as he was assigned to command the newly activated 82d Infantry Division soon after the attack on Pearl Harbor. He excelled as an individual and small-unit trainer, which resulted in his being transferred in June 1942 to take over the 28th Infantry Division, a troubled National Guard unit from Pennsylvania. Bradley's troop-leading mettle, however, was not tested by participation in one of the series of armywide maneuvers. His experience as a division commander was limited to teaching his officers and men basic soldiering skills, staffwork, and small-unit tactics.

On the eve of the 28th Infantry Division's final training exercises in February 1943, Bradley received new orders. He had expected to take command of X Corps but instead found himself transferred to Tunisia. Upon arrival, Bradley was informed that he would act as Supreme Allied Commander Dwight D. Eisenhower's "eyes and ears" on the battlefield. Although Bradley, who had been a friend of Eisenhower's at West Point, did not like his new assignment, he did not protest. After a short stint as Eisenhower's assistant, he was assigned to II Corps as deputy commander under George S. Patton. Eisenhower also promised Bradley that he would assume command of II Corps if he performed well as Patton's deputy.

Bradley performed competently as the corps deputy, assuming command of II Corps on 15 April 1943. The Tunisian campaign, however, only lasted another three weeks, so he would have to wait until the invasion of Sicily to get his first real taste of combat. During the Sicilian invasion, Bradley served once more under Patton, who had been promoted to command Seventh Army, and performed well as a corps commander.

In his debut as First Army commander, it was apparent that Bradley was still in the process of learning the ropes at army level. He turned down a British offer to supply his assault troops with specialized armor on D-Day, resulting in heavy casualties on Omaha Beach, and disregarded advice from army amphibious warfare experts sent to Europe. Having never commanded an army in combat, Bradley's grasp of operational art was at best purely theoretical, and he initially exhibited a tendency to attack everywhere rather than concentrate his forces against a decisive point. Bradley also failed to anticipate that the Germans would reinforce *7 Armee* during a lengthy period of rainy weather in late June.[27]

With St.-Lô finally in American hands, he began preparing to execute the next phase of OVERLORD. At a meeting of his corps commanders on 12 July, Bradley unveiled his concept for an offensive designed to pave the way for entry into the Brittany peninsula. In order to build sufficient forces and supplies necessary to force a crossing of the Seine River, the OVERLORD planners estimated that the most probable line of Allied action, after the capture of Cherbourg, would be the seizure of the Brittany ports.[28]

Bradley's plan, which was code-named COBRA, centered on a single reinforced corps as the main effort. In the first phase, two infantry divisions supported by heavy bombers would open a hole in the German defenses. In the second phase, two armored divisions, accompanied by a motorized infantry division, passed through the hole in order to encircle the city of Coutances on the west coast of the Cotentin Peninsula. Once the German troops in Coutances were isolated, another corps would attack south along the coast to destroy the surrounded defenders. The seizure of Coutances would serve to break the German hold on the Atlantic coast of Normandy as well as secure a springboard for subsequent operations on the Brittany peninsula.[29]

Ineffective leadership at the tactical level, which resulted in five division commanders and countless regimental commanders being replaced, had proven to be a factor in the lackluster performance by some American units earlier in the campaign. To ensure that Operation COBRA would prove to be a success, Bradley chose his best corps commander, Major General J. Lawton Collins, to lead the troops designated to take part in the assault. Born in Algiers, Louisiana, in 1896, Collins was commissioned from West Point in 1917. Although he missed combat during World War I, Collins was assigned to occupation duty in Germany

Major General J. Lawton Collins in trenchcoat and goggles. (Dwight D. Eisenhower Library)

from 1919 to 1921. A stint as an instructor at Fort Benning during 1927–1931 brought him into close contact with then Colonel George C. Marshall and Major Omar N. Bradley.

After a variety of staff and troop assignments, Collins took command of the 25th Infantry Division, which he led in combat on Guadalcanal. It was in the Pacific Theater that he came to light as a leader of some ability, demonstrating traits of aggressiveness and tactical excellence that won him corps command in Europe. Under Collins's leadership in Normandy, VII Corps built up a well-deserved reputation for accomplishing difficult missions, which included storming the D-Day beaches and the capture of Cherbourg.

Shortly after announcing his intention to conduct Operation COBRA, Lieutenant General Bradley asked Major General Collins for his initial impression of the proposed plan of attack. Collins visited Bradley's headquarters on 15 July, impressing the First Army staff as "a smooth operator with a powerful gift of persuasion . . . people are already predicting great things for him in this operation. [We are] glad to know that Collins is carrying the ball. Everyone has great confidence in him and is certain that if anyone can execute the plan, he can."[30]

After examining COBRA in detail, Collins discussed making some changes to the plan with the First Army commander. He was concerned about the prospect of providing the Germans with time to establish another defensive line protecting the entrance to the Brittany peninsula. Collins suggested a broader operation that would disrupt the German defenses west of the Vire River and facilitate rapid exploitation to the south by VIII Corps once the Germans in Coutances were destroyed.

The First Army plan had originally allocated two infantry divisions to the opening phase of the attack. The commanding general of VII Corps felt that an additional infantry division was necessary to rapidly punch a hole in the German defenses. Collins asked permission to use the 4th Infantry Division, in addition to the 9th and 30th Infantry Divisions, during the initial phase. Once a gap had been opened in the opposing lines, VII Corps planned to commit the 2d and 3d Armored Divisions as well as the motorized 1st Infantry Division to accomplish the second phase. In addition to encircling Coutances, the armored divisions would establish blocking positions to prevent the Germans from interfering with VIII Corps moving toward Brittany. With the addition of the 4th Infantry Division, VII Corps controlled an assault force that amounted to nearly half of the divisions assigned to First Army.[31]

Bradley was also thinking along the same lines. He made several alterations to the original COBRA plan that assuaged some of Collins's concerns. Both V and XIX Corps would make supporting attacks to pin down German forces when VII Corps commenced its assault, while VIII Corps would wait twenty-four hours before it began its attack along the coast. *Generalmajor* Fritz Bayerlain's *Panzer Lehr Division,* situated opposite the attackers, was the target of over 3,370 tons of bombs to be delivered by 1,496 four-engine bombers. In addition to the strategic bombers, the Americans would also pummel Bayerlain's troops with 550 fighter-bombers and 380 medium bombers.[32]

Bradley's desire to incorporate an overwhelming amount of aerial firepower into Operation COBRA was understandable. American commanders normally sought to utilize all of the firepower they could obtain against their German opponents. The destructive force of aerial bombs had been proven time and again in previous operations. However, the rather low degree of accuracy associated with strategic aerial bombardment proved to be a sobering deterrent to more extensive use of air support for the immediate assistance of ground units. To secure the best results, air bombardment had to be close enough to be followed by artillery fire covering the advance of the infantry, thus keeping the German positions continually under fire during the entire approach to the position.

The procedures governing the use of strategic bombers in support of ground troops, however, had not been fully refined by the Americans in July 1944. Use of massed heavy bombers emphasized the utmost in coordination and cooperation between air and ground commanders. Unfortunately, this level of expertise was somewhat lacking during the planning of preparatory aerial bombardment in support of COBRA. Bradley had requested that the planes fly parallel to the American front lines to reduce the possibility of bombing errors causing friendly casualties. The air force did not want to fly the route proposed by Bradley, citing that it would expose the bombers to greater amounts of antiaircraft fire and decrease the number of planes that could simultaneously fly over the target. Rather than resolve the matter, both ground and air commanders skirted around the dispute during coordination meetings.

At battalion and regimental levels, the Americans intended to utilize new tactics during COBRA that they had learned previously at great expense. American infantry commanders realized that the key to success lay in developing practical means allowing their units to fight as fully integrated combat teams without fear of disruption by the terrain or defenders. A memorandum published by VII Corps noted that "experience in the present campaign have [sic] further demonstrated that proper coordination is essential for the successful execution of an attack by infantry supported by tanks."[33] Tactical innovation, however, came largely because of trial and error on the battlefield. Each division or corps tried to accelerate the learning process by distributing lessons learned by other units to their subordinate elements.[34]

With Bradley counting so heavily on aerial support, it is no wonder that COBRA was canceled several times due to inclement weather. Originally set to take place on 18 July, the attack was postponed three times because of poor flying conditions.[35] The planes were finally given the order to attack on the morning of 24 July, and at 1130 hours, the first wave of fighter-bombers arrived on station. After delivering their ordnance, the fighter-bombers were followed by the medium and heavy bombers. The seemingly endless flights of four-engine aircraft flew directly over American troops as they headed toward the target area, providing onlookers with both a terrifying and impressive spectacle. With the appearance of the airplanes, however, came reports of fighter-bombers accidentally hitting friendly units. The lingering clouds and low-lying haze apparently had affected the accuracy of the initial air strikes. Rather than risk having the heavy bombers accidentally hit friendly units, the attack was called off.

Approximately three hundred of the bombers dropped their loads before they received word that the mission had been canceled. Before turning back, however, at least one formation inadvertently salvoed their bombs directly onto the waiting assault troops. The riflemen of the 2/120th Infantry were caught by a deluge of high explosive, accounting for the majority of the 24 killed and 128 wounded lost by the 30th Infantry Division that day. The aerial assault was rescheduled for the next day at 1100 hours.

Despite all precautions, the aerial bombardment on the following day proved even more deadly to the soldiers of VII Corps. Again, the aircraft flew directly over the U.S. troops before releasing their loads, resulting in a number of misdropped bombs that impacted within friendly lines: 111 Americans were killed and 490 wounded by errant fire.[36] The intended targets of the airstrike, *Fallschirmjäger Regiment 14, Kampfgruppe Heinz,* and *Panzer Lehr,* suffered about the same number of casualties.[37]

Despite the massive bombing attack, the German defenses did not collapse immediately. Some German strongholds were obliterated while adjacent units remained untouched. The 4th Infantry Division, for example, encountered this curious situation as one assault battalion advanced against scattered resistance while other units were held up for most of the day by stubborn defenders. The capture of the crossroads towns of Marigny and St.-Gilles, which would have signaled commitment of the follow-on echelon, did not occur that day. The 9th Infantry Division was far short of Marigny, while the 30th Infantry Division had just entered the outskirts of St.-Gilles.

Despite the fact that the leading infantry units had not secured Marigny and St.-Gilles, Major General Collins hoped that the German defenses were critically weakened by the combination of aerial and infantry attacks. Accordingly, he decided to commit his tanks at first light on 26 July. The Shermans of 2d Armored Division's Combat Command A (CCA), led by Brigadier General Maurice Rose, began passing through the 30th Infantry Division that morning. The tankers quickly captured St.-Gilles before continuing on to Canisy, which also fell after a brief struggle. With the 22d Infantry Regiment in support, Brigadier General Rose headed for the high ground three miles beyond Canisy. Despite the arrival of darkness, CCA continued moving until it completely secured its final objective by midday on 27 July.

The other prong of Collins's armored thrust consisted of Major General Clarence Huebner's 1st Infantry Division, reinforced by the tanks of 3d Armored Division's Combat Command B (CCB). The 1st Infantry and accompanying tankers quickly ran into a number of panzers defending Marigny. After an inconclusive battle lasting all day, the 1st Infantry Division took up defensive positions outside of the town. A daylight attack by the 18th Infantry Regiment on 27 July finally cleared the Germans from Marigny.

On 27 July, German counterattacks also hampered VII Corps's efforts to consolidate its hold on the shoulders of the penetration. Fierce fighting by the defenders limited the 9th Infantry Division to gains of less than two miles that day. In the 4th Infantry Division sector, however, elements of the 8th Infantry Regiment had pushed forward three miles, overrunning a portion of *Infanterie Division 353* and forcing elements of *Panzer Lehr* to displace. The 30th Infantry Division experienced the most success, advancing three miles by midday to cut the Coutances–St.-Lô highway. By late afternoon, Collins instructed his division commanders to continue their attacks through the night to prevent the Germans from interfering with the exploitation force.[38]

On 26 July, Major General Troy Middleton's VIII Corps launched its own assault designed to temporarily fix in place the German troops to their front while VII Corps seized Coutances. The 8th, 83d, and 90th Infantry Divisions were limited to slight gains that day, losing 1,150 men while capturing only a small amount of terrain and fewer than 100 prisoners.[39] Reports of success in the adjoining VII Corps sector, however, encouraged Middleton to plan another attack at first light on 27 July. Soon after the assault began, it became apparent that the Germans had withdrawn during the night, leaving behind mines and booby traps to delay the Americans. After engineers replaced a bridge at Lessay on 28 July, VIII Corps advanced ten miles to the outskirts of Coutances. With the 1st Infantry Division stalled by fierce resistance east of the city, VIII Corps entered Coutances only to discover the Germans had escaped encirclement.

On the morning of 28 July, Lieutenant General Omar Bradley took stock of the situation. After weeks of slowly advancing across the hedgerow country, First Army had achieved almost all of its designated objectives within seventy-two hours. A week before, the British had launched an offensive near Caen, code-named GOODWOOD and almost identical to Operation COBRA in concept and execution. However, counterattacks by *Panzer Gruppe West* resulted in the destruction of over three hundred attacking tanks, forcing the British to suspend operations. During Operation COBRA, the defenders clearly had not anticipated that the Americans would change their tactics.

First Army employed heavy bombers not only as a means to destroy the defending troops but also to prevent the Germans from reacting effectively against VII Corps in the initial stages of Operation COBRA. By disrupting the German units opposing VII Corps, the Americans were able to gain forward momentum in the opening hours of their assault. First Army was able to sustain this momentum by exploiting favorable weather that permitted the employment of artillery-spotting aircraft and fighter-bombers operating in close support of the attacking troops. German attempts to reorganize their defenses under cover of darkness were also nullified when VII Corps continued its attack during the night of 26 July.

Operation COBRA had also benefited from the unfavorable situation facing the Germans arrayed against First Army. With steadily diminishing troop strength, the Germans were unable to create significant reserves and were forced to employ small formations of panzers scattered throughout frontline positions to bolster the defending infantry long after the Americans had devised tactics to overcome that type of defense. Instead of absorbing the initial shock with infantry units, which would have permitted the creation of an armored reserve capable of counterattacking, most of the panzers assigned to *7 Armee* were scattered across the battlefield in small packets.

The Germans were unable to stem Operation COBRA because they did not have the resources to mount a large-scale counterattack until they received two panzer divisions from *Panzer Gruppe West*. Even after the panzer divisions transferred from the Caen sector had arrived, the Germans still found themselves fighting at a severe disadvantage. Forced to fight in the open during daylight hours where its units were visible to the prying eyes of Allied fighter-bombers, *7 Armee* was unable to halt the American offensive.

Although the elements of *LXXXIV Armee Korps* in the Coutances sector succeeded in escaping, Operation COBRA realized even greater success than Major

Tanks of the 4th Armored Division pass through the heavily damaged town of Avranches on 31 July 1944. (National Archives)

General Collins imagined by disrupting the German defensive line west of Vire. Situation reports clearly indicated to Bradley that the success of COBRA warranted a continuation of the attack. Accordingly, he decided to exploit the gains made by VII and VIII Corps by attacking with all of the troops at his disposal. With First Army assessing the "destruction of *LXXXIV Korps* at hand and the destruction of *II Fallschirmjäger Korps* a distinct possibility," Lieutenant General Bradley ordered his subordinates to maintain unrelenting pressure on *7 Armee*.[40]

With this latest set of instructions, First Army sought to shatter *7 Armee* while it was reeling in the wake of COBRA. XIX Corps was instructed to seize the crossroads town of Vire to the east while VII Corps continued south toward Brecey. V Corps would support by maintaining contact with the British along an axis running from Caumont–Le Foret D' Eveque–Vire. With each mile gained by First Army, correspondingly larger segments of the road network came under control of the Americans. The loss of these roads had a significant negative impact on the ability of the Germans to respond to the American advance by committing their panzers. On the other hand, First Army would enjoy a correspondingly superior ability to employ its own armor in exploitation operations designed to hasten the destruction of *7 Armee*.

II Fallschirmjäger Korps, pressured by frontal attacks launched by V and XIX Corps and with its flank threatened by Brigadier Maurice Rose's CCA, began retreating toward Vire. German rear guards frantically sought to buy time for their parent unit to escape destruction at the hands of the relentlessly attacking Americans. *7 Armee* appeals for assistance finally resulted in the transfer of two panzer divisions from *Panzer Gruppe West.* With additional armor at their disposal, the Germans were able to shore up the northern portion of their crumbling defensive line. Fierce fighting took place in the vicinity of the crossroad towns of Villabuadon, Percy, and Villedieu les Poeles as the panzers also sought to buy time for *LXXXIV Armee Korps* to escape.

Although the tactical situation in Normandy had changed significantly because of Operation COBRA, a significant victory would become possible only after Avranches was captured. The Germans were attempting to reestablish a defensive line along the high ground running between Vire and Avranches. Once the Americans were halted, *7 Armee* could concentrate on bringing up reinforcements to flesh out its shattered ranks. Most of the German units in Brittany, however, had already been transferred to other sectors in Normandy. This meant that while the Germans could restore their lines in the north by using troops from the Caen sector, they lacked ready access to the men and material necessary to anchor the southern end of that line along the Brittany coast. If the Americans captured Avranches, they could threaten the entire *7 Armee* with encirclement.

The worst fears of the Germans were realized as VIII Corps prepared to launch two armored divisions against Avranches. With Coutances firmly in his possession, Major General Middleton passed the 4th and 6th Armored Divisions forward through his infantry. Middleton wanted to move south before the Germans could reorganize. With fighter-bombers providing overhead cover, both armored divisions began advancing on 29 July. The 6th Armored Division rapidly captured the coastal towns of Brehal and Granville, while the 4th Armored made spectacular progress against scattered opposition as it lunged toward Avranches.

On 30 July, CCB of the 4th Armored Division entered the city to seize two critical bridges spanning the See River. However, several German units hoping to escape capture by VII Corps also entered Avranches from the north. Intense combat seesawed back and forth during the night of 30 July as the 4th Armored Division sought to retain its hold on the city. As dawn broke on 31 July, however, the Americans remained in possession of Avranches.

The seizure of the bridges at Avranches, as well as an adjacent bridge in the town of Tirepied, prevented the Germans from using the See River as a defensive line. The seizure of these spans, however, would not prove sufficient to support a large-scale advance into Brittany. Just to the south of Avranches lay the Selune River. Eager to gain a foothold on the southern bank of the Selune, Major General Middleton ordered the 4th Armored Division to capture the bridge at Pontaubault. The tankers also had the mission of expanding the VIII Corps's foothold in Brit-

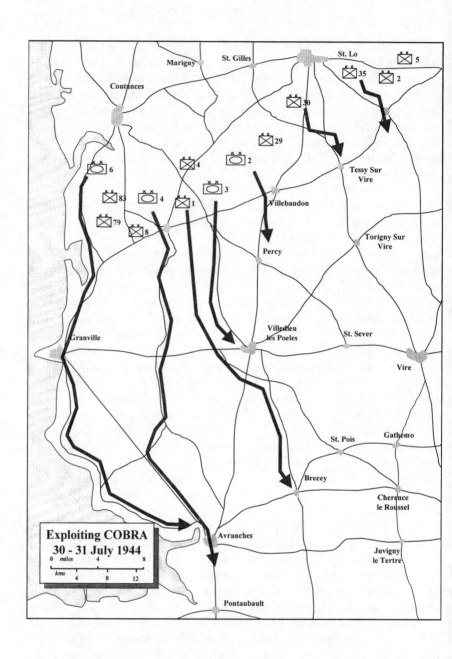

Exploiting COBRA
30 - 31 July 1944

tany, a task that entailed securing the high ground to the south and southeast of Avranches as well as gaining additional crossing sites on the Selune River.

The 4th Armored Division fanned out to the south and southeast to seize intact the Pontaubault Bridge over the Selune River. The Germans remained unaware for some time that the bridges at Avranches and Pontaubault had been captured. At 1845 hours on 31 July, *XXV Armee Korps* in Brittany reported to *OB West* that "two tanks crossed bridge at Pontaubault . . . the bridge was then destroyed by fighterbombers."[41] Not only were the bridges undamaged, but elements of several American armored divisions were pouring over them.

CONCLUSIONS

Operation COBRA demonstrated conclusively that the difficulty of combat in the hedgerows had actually worked to the advantage of First Army. Despite heavy losses, the intensity of the fighting served to rapidly weld together green American units. As a result of this experience, the American commanders who survived that terrible experience grew increasingly competent, assured, and expert in their trade. Tanks, artillery, infantry, and close air support worked together with an ease and effectiveness they had not exhibited in early June and July.

The capture of Avranches significantly altered the operational balance in Normandy. The Germans could no longer hope to confine the Americans to the hedgerow country, which clearly favored the defender. With the last natural obstacle barring the path to Brittany removed, the only viable course of action for the Germans was to launch a counteroffensive to restore the situation. Ironically, the Germans found themselves in the same predicament as the Allies had been earlier in the campaign. With *7 Armee* remaining predominantly on the defensive for six weeks, German regimental and divisional commanders were afforded few opportunities to hone their offensive skills amidst the hedgerows. Since *7 Armee* primarily consisted of infantry formations suited to defensive action, the Germans also had to transfer additional panzers from *Panzer Gruppe West*. In doing so, they would have to accept the risk that the British would not take advantage of their absence by launching another offensive south of Caen.

In a strategic sense, the excellence at which the German soldier conducted defensive operations in the hedgerows served to work against the *Wehrmacht* by fostering Hitler's belief that success in France could be gained by confining the Americans to Normandy for an indefinite period. Hitler also failed to recognize that American combined arms employment and leadership had fundamentally improved. Instead, he attributed the Allied success to heavy bombers, faulty dispositions of *LXXXIV Armee Korps,* and subsequent mistakes on the part of the *7 Armee* staff.

Hitler reacted to Operation COBRA by dismissing a number of high-ranking officers. He also continued to deny permission for the construction of fixed defenses east of Normandy. The only positive aspect of Operation COBRA, in the viewpoint of the German military, was that it persuaded Hitler to accelerate the transfer of troops from Pas de Calais and southern France to Normandy. However, he continued to insist on defending every inch of French soil despite the rapidly deteriorating situation. His stubborn stance would have a decisive influence on German operational decisionmaking for the next few crucial days.

2

The Third Army Moves into Brittany

In the immediate wake of Operation COBRA, significant changes were taking place within the American command structure. Eisenhower envisioned the creation of an American 12th Army Group following the capture of Coutances, thus putting Bradley on an equal footing with Montgomery. However, VIII Corps succeeded in securing Coutances before these plans could be implemented. Preparations to activate the Army Group headquarters accelerated as Bradley sought to fully exploit the opportunities presented by Operation COBRA. The capture of Avranches placed the entire Brittany peninsula within reach. Coalition politics notwithstanding, the capture of Brittany would expand the American sector by threefold, rendering a single army headquarters woefully inadequate to direct combat operations over such a wide expanse of terrain.

The 12th Army Group headquarters was activated on 1 August. That same day Bradley relinquished command of First Army to his deputy, Lieutenant General Courtney H. Hodges.[1] The 12th Army Group was composed of both First Army and the newly activated Third Army. Third Army, which was commanded by Lieutenant General George S. Patton, consisted of VIII, XII, XV, and XX Corps. With the exception of VIII Corps, which arrived in France on 14 June, all of the other corps headquarters were new arrivals. XV Corps, which arrived on 11 July, and XX Corps, which disembarked on 24 July, were still assembling north of Avranches. XV and XX Corps were slated to follow VIII Corps through Avranches into Brittany. XII Corps, which was assigned the task of receiving and staging new units arriving from England, would follow the remainder of Third Army at an unspecified future date.[2]

One of the first actions of 12th Army Group was to direct the transfer of six infantry and two armored divisions, numerous artillery groups, antiaircraft battalions, tank destroyer battalions, tank battalions, and a host of service units necessary to form the Third Army and 12th Army Group reserve. The fighting divisions and their support units headed south toward Avranches on a course that took them directly across First Army's eastward advance.

As Third Army developed plans to seize Brittany, First Army was encountering stiffening resistance as the Germans recovered from Operation COBRA. The sheer mechanics involved in creating 12th Army Group, combined with the defensible terrain that the Germans now occupied, served to provide *7 Armee* with a brief respite.[3] Not only did First Army provide a number of divisions to Third Army, but many of these units had been actively engaged in combat immediately prior to the transfer. The First Army zone of operations was also compressed into an area between Vire and Mayenne, which reduced Hodges's opportunity for maneuver. The British Second Army closing on Vire from the north was in the process of pinching out V Corps, while the traffic priority accorded to Patton's Third Army reduced the ability of First Army to extend its lines southward. Hodges's options were largely confined to frontal attacks against a recovering German defense anchored on wooded ridgelines that dominated the surrounding terrain.

As his newly activated Third Army prepared to go into battle, Lieutenant General George S. Patton was grateful for another opportunity to command troops in combat. He had wanted to lead an army in battle since childhood. When he graduated from West Point in 1909 as a second lieutenant of cavalry, Patton inscribed "qualities of a good general: tactically aggressive (loves a fight)" on the back of one of his textbooks. Those words mirrored his ensuing military career. Patton was an outspoken maverick widely renowned for his combativeness. He fought the Germans in two world wars and his own military establishment between the wars.

The new Third Army commander backed up his words with considerable troop leading experience. Patton commanded the 1st Tank Brigade in 1918, the Western Task Force during the Torch Invasion in November 1942, II Corps in Tunisia in 1943, and Seventh Army during the invasion of Sicily. On 1 January 1944, however, he was relieved of command of Seventh Army. After achieving victory in every battle he had fought, George S. Patton met defeat after he slapped two shell-shocked soldiers in Sicily.

When Eisenhower had returned to the United States to consult with Army Chief of Staff George C. Marshall in January 1944, Patton's eventual fate was still unresolved. After a lengthy debate with Marshall, Eisenhower chose Patton as the future commander of Third Army. Patton was immensely pleased at being reinstated to command, however, he soon found himself in trouble again when he inadvertently snubbed the Russians in a speech at the opening of a British Welcome Club in Knutsford, England, on 25 April 1944. His offhand remarks found their way into the newspapers, raising congressional ire in the United States as well as the hackles of the American public. Eisenhower, recognizing that Patton's abilities could prove crucial in the upcoming invasion of France, smoothed over ruffled feelings once more. However, he also issued Patton a letter of reprimand warning him that his next transgression would be his last.[4]

The Third Army advance into Brittany was predominantly based on pre-invasion logistics estimates. Growing Allied concern about the capability of their logistics infrastructure was not entirely without merit, as British and American troop strength in France was growing on a daily basis. On 18 June, there were twenty British and American divisions in Normandy. Five weeks later, this figure had grown to twenty-nine, with no appreciable increase in logistics capability. By 1 August, there were thirty-seven Allied divisions fighting in France, requiring a total of twenty-six thousand tons of supplies per day to sustain their needs. To meet their supply demands, the Allies constructed two artificial harbors, one British and one American, to handle additional reinforcements and supplies landing on the invasion beaches. The American artificial harbor, however, was severely damaged by a storm in late June. Despite this setback, the artificial harbors had proven sufficient in the near term, although Allied logisticians predicted that they would soon be inadequate to meet daily needs.

The Allies sought to remedy the projected disparity between supply and demand through the acquisition of French port facilities. Cherbourg, which had been secured on 29 June, had been severely damaged by the Germans before it was captured. By the first week of August, repairs on the port were not complete. As a result, Cherbourg was only capable of handling 266,000 tons per month, far short of the 780,000 tons required on a monthly basis to support the growing number of Allied troops in France. For the time being, the artificial harbors would have to make up the shortfalls in Cherbourg's cargo handling capacity. However, given the potential damage that unpredictable Atlantic gales could inflict on the artificial harbors, the logistical picture for the Allies looked bleak.[5]

Coalition politics had also proven to be another factor that influenced Bradley's decision to divert troops into Brittany. The British, headed by Winston Churchill, were still lobbying against an invasion of southern France, an operation code-named DRAGOON. Rather than commit ten Allied divisions to DRAGOON, the British proposed to transfer them to Normandy. With Cherbourg largely in ruins, the Brittany seaports seemed to provide an ideal place to receive the divisions released from DRAGOON. Despite Eisenhower's firm stance on the necessity of DRAGOON, his planning staff was still working as late as 6 August on studies designed to refute British claims that Breton ports could be usefully employed by troops diverted from the operation in southern France.

Supreme Headquarters Allied Expeditionary Forces (SHAEF) planners pointed out that even if DRAGOON forces were sent to reinforce OVERLORD, the impending logistics crisis made it doubtful that they could be adequately supplied once they had arrived on the continent. At best, two divisions could be expected to pass through Brittany by mid-September or early October.[6] Although Eisenhower had always resisted pressure from the British prime minister to cancel DRAGOON, the final decision to go ahead with the landings in southern France was not made until the first week of August.[7]

Bradley initially met with Patton on 30 July to discuss the Brittany operation in detail. Patton noted that "Bradley came up by air at 1400 and told me his plans. They are getting more ambitious, but are just what I intended to do, as I set down the other day, so I am very happy." While agreeing on the overall aims of the Brittany operation, Patton was not impressed with the tempo of operations suggested by Bradley. After a second meeting the following day, Patton recorded that "General Bradley simply wants a bridgehead over the Selune River. What I want, and intend to get, is Brest and Angers."[8]

Patton intended to conduct a rapid armored thrust along the length of the Brittany peninsula in an attempt to gain his assigned objectives before the Germans could establish a coherent defense or demolish the port facilities. Bradley, on the other hand, envisioned a more deliberate advance in Brittany, a concept that was also held by the commander of VIII Corps, Major General Middleton.

It may appear that Patton was willing to acquiesce to Bradley's wishes rather than wage his own unique brand of mobile warfare.[9] Nothing could have been further from the truth. There are no indications in Patton's diary that he believed Bradley had any part in his reinstatement as Third Army commander. Events would later show that Patton did not hesitate to "ask for forgiveness rather than permission" as he fought in accordance with his own vision of the battle. However, it is clear that Patton supported Bradley's decision to send Third Army into Brittany since it was in accord with his own intent.

Patton tackled his newly assigned mission with characteristic energy and aggressiveness, issuing verbal orders at 1200 hours on 1 August to secure the Brittany ports. The Third Army's mission, as envisioned by Patton, was to "drive south and southwest to cut off and capture Brittany and open [the] Brittany ports."[10] Patton discussed operational boundaries with Bradley at 1500 hours, noting they were "rather cramped so far as Third Army is concerned, as we have to slide through a very narrow bottleneck between Avranches and St. Hilaire . . . Bradley is worried about a counterattack west from Mortain. Personally, I do not give much credence to this, but by moving the 90th Division I can get it forward and also cover the exposed flank."[11]

Limited road space between Coutances and Avranches would restrict Third Army to committing its troops into battle sequentially. Only one corps at a time could move through the Avranches corridor. The battle-tested VIII Corps led the advance simply because it was the first unit to reach Avranches. Patton planned to send the 4th Armored Division, trailed by the 8th Infantry Division, to capture the city of Rennes. The 6th Armored Division, accompanied by the 79th Infantry Division, would seize the cities of Pontorson, Dol-de-Bretagne, and Dinan. Once these objectives were secured the 4th Armored Division would surround Lorient while the 6th Armored Division secured the port of St.-Malo.[12] The armored units would contain the Germans until additional forces could be spared to launch a determined attack against the ports.[13]

On 1 August, Major General John S. Wood's 4th Armored Division headed toward Rennes, located halfway between Quiberon Bay and Avranches. Rennes

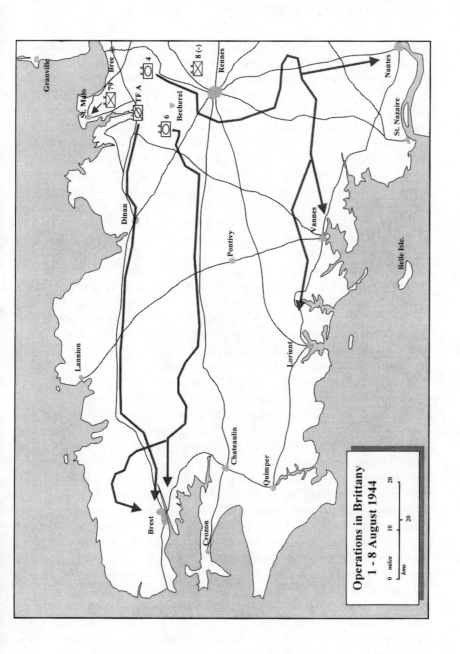

**Operations in Brittany
1 - 8 August 1944**

Granville

Brée

St. Malo

79

TF A

4

6

Becherel

Rennes

8 (-)

Nantes

St. Nazaire

Dinan

Pontivy

Vannes

Belle Isle.

Lannion

Chateaulin

Quimper

Lorient

Brest

Crozon

0   miles   10   20

kms   20

formed the hub of an extensive road network linking Brittany with the interior of France. The tankers quickly covered the forty miles from Pontaubault to Rennes, reaching the outskirts of the city at dusk. However, a hasty attack by CCB that was launched against a *Luftwaffe* airfield on the outskirts resulted in the loss of eleven Sherman tanks. Realizing the city was held in greater strength than previously thought, the 4th Armored withdrew to await reinforcements.

As his 6th Armored Division was moving south on 1 August, Major General Robert Grow was approached by Patton while directing traffic at a crossroads in Avranches. Patton told Grow that he expected the 6th Armored to arrive at Brest within the next five days; the objectives assigned to it by VIII Corps were no longer valid. Patton then visited the VIII Corps headquarters to inform Middleton of the guidance he had given to Grow. By 1600 hours that afternoon, VIII Corps published a new field order designating Brest as the 6th Armored Division's primary objective.[14]

The 6th Armored Division headed south on the afternoon of 1 August only to run into an ambush outside of the town of Bree. Continuing on despite heavy fire, the tankers rolled into Pontorson, seizing intact the span over the Cousenon River. The following morning, CCB passed through Pontorson heading toward Dinan. When the Americans came into possession of a marked map showing that Dinan was strongly defended, Major General Grow decided to bypass the city rather than get involved in a protracted fight. As night fell on 2 August, the 6th Armored occupied assembly areas near the small town of Bécherel.

Despite the resistance encountered at Rennes and Dinan, the push into Brittany progressed so rapidly that Middleton soon lost contact with his lead elements. VIII Corps was stretched over such a vast area and moving so rapidly that signal communications, which had already been severely strained by the move from Coutances to Avranches, broke down almost completely. Wire was impossible to install or maintain over such distances, and radio proved undependable. As Major General Middleton later commented, "The expensive signal equipment at the disposal of the corps was never designed apparently for a penetration and pursuit of the magnitude of the Brittany operation."[15] VIII Corps used light planes to locate the two armored divisions before sending out couriers bearing new orders and updated intelligence information.[16]

When Major General Middleton learned of the delay suffered by the 4th Armored Division, he sent the 13th Infantry Regiment to assist the tankers in securing Rennes. Piling aboard four quartermaster truck companies provided by Third Army, the 13th departed that evening. Upon learning that the infantry was en route, the 4th Armored's commanding general decided to bypass Rennes. Middleton, however, was convinced that the 4th Armored had to seize Rennes before continuing on, not only to eliminate a threat to its rear but also to open up a supply line to the western coast of Brittany. Accordingly, he ordered the division to capture Rennes before continuing its advance.[17]

Hurrying to Rennes, the 13th Infantry Regiment reached the outskirts of the city on 3 August. Complying with an order from the 4th Armored Division to launch an immediate attack, a battalion of the 13th forced its way into the northeastern outskirts. With their perimeter almost completely encircled by tanks and with American infantry working their way deeper into the city, the defenders of Rennes received permission to abandon their defensive positions. The 13th Infantry Regiment, followed soon afterward by the remainder of the 8th Infantry Division, occupied Rennes without a fight on the morning of 4 August. The seizure of Rennes struck a particularly significant blow against *7 Armee,* as it contained no less than four major support installations, including ammunition, fuel, supply, and equipment depots.[18]

Despite the lack of organized opposition faced by VIII Corps, Bradley was still convinced that the Germans posed a significant threat to Third Army. Although he supported sending VIII Corps deeper into Brittany, Bradley desired Patton to position the XV Corps in such a manner as to protect Middleton's push toward Lorient and Brest from interference by *7 Armee.* On 2 August, 12th Army Group published a directive amending the original intent to secure Brittany using the entire Third Army. Hodges's First Army was ordered to take Vire and Mortain while Third Army established a defensive line running from St.-Hilaire-du-Harcouet–Fougeres–Rennes. The directive noted that "in order to take full advantage of this bridgehead [in Brittany], we must make it secure by pushing our attack vigorously until we secure the road center at Vire, Mortain, and Fougeres as the main German threat will be from the east and southeast."[19]

Conforming to Bradley's directive, Lieutenant General Hodges ordered XIX Corps to capture Vire, while VII Corps was instructed to seize Mortain. Hodges transferred the 2d Armored Division from VII Corps to support Major General Charles Corlett's XIX Corps's push toward Vire. Corlett secured the outlying town of Tessy, but his troops encountered stiffening resistance as they neared Vire. With the British converging on Vire from the north, First Army was forced to stop V Corps for lack of maneuver space. To the south of Vire, VII Corps was bogged down outside the town of St.-Pois. Only in the extreme southernmost portion of the First Army sector was significant progress made. VII Corps, led by the tanks of 3d Armored Division, brushed aside scattered detachments of German troops to seize the town of Brecey on 1 August.

In compliance with the 12th Army Group directive, Patton assigned Major General Wade Haislip's XV Corps the mission of establishing a defensive line running from St.-Hilaire-du-Harcouet–Fougeres–Rennes. Haislip's corps consisted of the 83d and 90th Infantry Divisions and 5th Armored Division. Displacing his divisions in successive bounds, Haislip had taken great care to avoid entangling his units among the trailing elements of VIII Corps. In an effort to widen the Avranches bottleneck, however, Patton directed XV Corps to pass the 90th Infantry Division through the VII Corps's zone of action west of Avranches in an effort to secure additional crossings over the Selune River for the Third Army's use.[20]

Lieutenant General George S. Patton (left) meets with Lieutenant General Omar Bradley to discuss strategy during the first week of August 1944. (National Archives)

At 1500 hours on 2 August, Lieutenant General Patton passed on a new set of orders to Major General Haislip. Patton instructed Haislip to occupy a defensive line between St.-Hilaire-du-Harcouet and Reffuveille using the 90th Infantry Division. After this was accomplished, XV Corps would dispatch the 5th Armored Division south from Periers through Avranches to secure the town of Fougeres. As soon as the 83d Infantry Division was able to assume responsibility for the defense of Fougeres, XV Corps would send the 5th Armored Division to secure the city of Laval.[21]

The 12th Army Group commander remained concerned that *7 Armee* would launch a counterattack into the exposed flank of Third Army. When Bradley visited the VIII Corps command post, he told Major General Middleton that "some people are more concerned with headlines and the news they'll make rather than the soundness of their tactics. I don't care if we get Brest tomorrow or ten days later. If we cut the peninsula, we'll get it sooner or later. But we can't risk a loose hinge."

Bradley decided to redirect the 79th Infantry Division to Fougeres in anticipation of a multidivision German counterattack. Outlining the rationale for his decision to Middleton, Bradley explained that if "the Germans hit us with three divisions there . . . it'll make us look follish [*sic*]. It would be very embarrassing to George. George is used to an attack from a single division. He's buttoned up well enough for that. But he's not used to having three or four German divisions hit him. He doesn't know what it means yet."[22]

Bradley countermanded Patton's orders to Haislip. The 12th Army Group commander explained to Patton that he had "just left VIII Corps. I am worried about the possibilities of the enemy launching an attack from the east or southeast through Fougeres. I wish you would move with the least practicable delay the 79th Infantry Division on Fougeres, with the mission of occupying and securing the line from Fougeres to Louvigne du Desert." As soon as his meeting with Bradley concluded, Patton visited the 79th Infantry Division command post where he met with the division commander and Major General Middleton. Discussing the change in mission with Middleton, Patton emphasized that he wanted to send the 79th to Fougeres as soon as possible.[23]

In an effort to avert any confusion that might arise due to his previous instructions to Major General Haislip, Patton dispatched an aide to inform XV Corps that the 79th Infantry Division now had responsibility for the occupation and defense of Fougeres. The 5th Armored was to halt in place, clear the roads, and prepare to resume movement at daylight on 3 August. In the event that the 5th Armored Division was already in Fougeres, Patton told his aide to instruct the tankers to pull back to an assembly area west of Louvigne du Desert as soon as the 79th Infantry arrived to relieve them.[24]

Major General Ira Wyche's 79th Infantry Division began moving toward Fougeres during the evening of 2 August. Led by the 79th Cavalry Reconnaissance troop, the Americans occupied Fougeres without opposition on the morning of 3 August, establishing contact with the 90th Infantry Division to the north.[25] Bradley's concern that the Germans might gather sufficient forces to seriously dispute Third Army's lodgment south of Avranches dissipated with the news that Fougeres had been secured.[26] XV Corps was now firmly situated to defend VIII Corps from counterattack.

The events of the previous twenty-four hours served to convince Bradley that the Germans were in greater disarray than he had previously imagined. News of the lightning advance of VIII and XV Corps sparked growing optimism extending even to the highest level of the Allied command structure. As the 12th Army Group G-2 noted, "The rapid progress of our advance through Avranches to the base of the Brittany peninsula invited serious consideration of a turn to the east."[27] Bradley began to visualize a grand envelopment in which Patton's spearheads turned toward Paris.

Bradley decided to privately share his concept with his friend and superior, General Dwight D. Eisenhower. After listening to Bradley explain his idea, an optimistic Eisenhower immediately drafted a letter to Army Chief of Staff General George C. Marshall, which stated that "in 2–3 days time Bradley will so manhandle the western flank of the enemy forces that he will create virtually an open flank." Eisenhower confidently predicted that Bradley would have almost complete freedom in selecting the next move, making it "unnecessary to detach any large forces for the conquest of Brittany and instead allow him to devote the great bulk of the forces to the task of completing the destruction of the German Army, at least that portion west of the Orne, and *exploiting beyond that as far as possible.*"[28]

Although Bradley and Eisenhower continued to view the eventual acquisition of the Brittany ports as crucial to sustaining the logistical buildup in France, they were willing to put that priority aside for a brief period. Speed, deception, the thinning of the defending garrison during the preceding months, and aid from French resistance fighters resulted in a sizable portion of Brittany falling into American hands by 2 August. While the reduction of the peninsula was far from complete, VIII Corps was positioned astride all of the vital routes of communication leading from the ports.

A review of the overall operational situation in Normandy appeared to favor adoption of Bradley's proposal. Three armored divisions and three infantry divisions belonging to Third Army were readily available. The convergent advance of 21st Army Group and Third Army, which was resulting in a progressive narrowing of the First Army front, would also permit the release of additional infantry divisions for employment in Brittany. Once these units could relieve the armored divisions of VIII Corps, the additional tanks could be employed to reinforce the drive toward Paris. The armored divisions assigned to First Army also could be sideslipped into the Third Army zone to join the attacking force. Last, the impending invasion of southern France would serve to pin down German forces south of the Loire River, effectively preventing them from interfering with Bradley's plans.[29]

Although the 12th Army Group commander confided his vision to Eisenhower, he continued to work out the details of the plan in private. As Bradley fleshed out his concept, which had not been revealed to his own staff, he envisioned that Patton's Third Army, minus one corps in Brittany, and Hodges's First Army would occupy a line running from Vire to Le Mans. Once sufficient supplies were moved south of Avranches, both American armies would take part in an offensive, spearheaded by six armored divisions, designed to swing around Paris, back to the Seine River, then north to the coast at Dieppe. At the same time, the British and Canadians would attack from Caen to fix the Germans in place, preventing them from reacting against the Americans. Bradley was sure his plan would produce a "war winning drive" leading directly to the heart of Hitler's Germany."[30]

Bradley's concept bore a striking resemblance to a version of the SHAEF plan entitled Lucky Strike which was premised on the possible acceleration of OVERLORD timing. Plan B of Lucky Strike was based on few, if any, German forces left in Brittany or in the area between the Loire River and Laval–Le Mans –Chartres. It also postulated that the Germans would not have any strong mobile forces south of the Loire River. In brief, the plan was based on the assumption that a virtually open flank had been created.

Lucky Strike B called for a drive to the east by 21st Army Group and a portion of the American troops as well as a simultaneous wide sweep by a strong U.S. armored force along the north bank of the Loire to block the Paris-Orleans gap and thereafter cooperate with the other armies in the destruction of the German armies west of the Seine River. Operations in Brittany would be conducted with a minimum of troops. Bradley's concept differed from Lucky Strike B in one regard: namely, that the U.S. armored forces would hook around Paris before proceeding north to Dieppe.[31]

Certain that developments in Normandy warranted the adoption of his new plan, Bradley began to set up the conditions for launching his bold offensive. Telephoning Montgomery, Bradley explained that Patton was facing light resistance in Brittany. Rather than commit the remainder of Third Army, Bradley asked for permission to employ a minimum of forces to seize the Brittany ports. Montgomery, who readily agreed with Bradley's assessment, instructed his own staff to review Lucky Strike B with the intent of taking advantage of the rapidly changing situation in the American sector.

The 21st Army Group planners predicted that the American advance to the southeast would result in the Germans being pushed against the lower reaches of the Seine River. Since most of the bridges in that area had been destroyed by air attacks designed to isolate the Normandy battlefield, the Germans would find themselves unable to continue their retreat to the east. Hemmed in between the Americans and the British, with their line of retreat blocked by the Seine, the 21st Army Group staff concluded that the Germans would be left with only two alternatives: surrender or death.[32]

Montgomery's own appreciation of the situation led him to conclude that the only logical choice for the Germans was to begin retreating to the east. As the threat posed by Patton's Third Army increased, the German timetable for withdrawal would undoubtedly accelerate. Rather than pause while Bradley established the supply dumps necessary to support his planned envelopment, Montgomery decided to immediately launch the British and Canadians in an offensive against Falaise.

As Montgomery began preparing for an assault against Falaise, Bradley published Letter of Instruction No. 2 on 3 August. The new directive stated that "while maintaining relentless pressure on the enemy [12th Army Group] will continue to clear the BRITTANY Peninsula and secure ports thereon and will initiate a drive to the east to secure the lodgment area." Third Army was directed to "complete the securing of BRITTANY ports and the clearance of the Peninsula with a minimum of forces. Secure crossings across the MAYENNE River in zone as far south as CHATEAU GONTIER (inclusive) prepared for further action with strong armored forces to the east and southeast."[33]

The 12th Army Group directive also established a solid foundation for the grand plan Bradley was hoping to execute. The language left no doubt that he intended to launch a decisive operation using American troops aimed at bringing about an Allied victory in France. Organizing a strong armored force within the Third Army zone of operations was consistent with his concept calling for a large mechanized spearhead aimed at Paris.[34]

General Montgomery's 21st Army Group also issued new orders on 4 August outlining a revised concept for the employment of Allied forces in Normandy. The directive instructed the First Canadian Army to attack toward Falaise "as early as possible and in any case not later than 8 August." The British Second Army would support the Canadians by capturing Argentan. Bradley's 12th Army Group was to make its main effort on the right flank by advancing to the east and northeast toward Paris and the Seine River.[35] Montgomery intended to use the Americans as an anvil upon which the British-Canadian hammer smashed Hitler's forces in Normandy.

When the new 12th Army Group directive arrived, Patton immediately shifted Third Army's main effort from Middleton's VIII Corps in Brittany to XV Corps southeast of Avranches. Major General Haislip was hurriedly summoned to the town of Gavray where he met with Patton at 2115 hours.[36] Patton instructed Haislip to secure Mayenne and Laval, as well as other crossing sites along the Mayenne River, no later than 5 August. Patton also cautioned Haislip to be prepared to move quickly north or northeast as soon as Mayenne and Laval were secured.[37]

At 2300 hours, Haislip assembled the commanding generals of the 79th and 90th Infantry Divisions and 5th Armored Division at his command post near Ducey. The XV Corps attack, he explained, would begin at 0800 hours on 5 August. The 90th Infantry would seize Mayenne and secure crossing sites on the Mayenne River, while the 79th would secure crossings on the Mayenne River between Chateau Gontier and Laval. The advance of each infantry division would be led by elements of the 106th Cavalry Group. The 5th Armored was directed by Haislip to guard against German units in Brittany launching a counterattack against the 79th Infantry. The 5th Armored was also ordered to unload fuel and lubricants from a hundred trucks, which would be employed to motorize the two infantry divisions.

The advance guard of the 90th Infantry Division consisted of a task force commanded by Brigadier General William G. Weaver. Task Force Weaver was composed of the 357th Infantry Regiment, 343d Field Artillery Battalion, 90th Reconnaissance Troop, 712th Tank Battalion, one company of the 607th Tank Destroyer (TD) Battalion, and A/315th Engineer Battalion. Despite the fact that one infantry company of the leading battalion took a wrong turn, the soldiers of the 90th Infantry Division reached Mayenne shortly before 1400 hours on 5 August.

Entering the western section of the city, the Americans were taken under fire by German defenders from positions on the opposite bank of the Mayenne River. The 357th Infantry Regiment responded by placing an artillery barrage on the defenders before launching an assault across the sole remaining span over the Mayenne River. By 2030 hours, the 90th Infantry Division had secured the city as well as an intact bridge across the Mayenne River.[38]

Major General Ira T. Wyche's 79th Infantry Division, spearheaded by a motorized task force built around the 313th Infantry Regiment, launched its attack against Laval at 0800 hours on 5 August. Led by the 106th Cavalry Group, the Americans encountered a strong roadblock halfway to their objective. It required several hours of hard fighting by the 313th Infantry Regiment to reduce the road-block, resulting in a delay that prevented the leading troops of the 79th Infantry Division from approaching Laval prior to midnight on 5 August. With immediate access to the western half of the city blocked by destroyed bridges, the Americans settled down to prepare for a full-scale assault the following morning.

During the night, Major General Wyche consolidated the remainder of his division in the vicinity of Laval. Patrols soon discovered that the Germans had evacuated the city. At dawn, the 79th Infantry sent two battalions across the Mayenne River over a hurriedly constructed engineer footbridge. A third infantry battalion crossed single file over a nearby dam. Securing the city before noon, the 79th rushed to expand its slender bridgehead. Two additional battalions crossed that afternoon using assault boats. Wyche's engineers quickly began working on a bridge over the Mayenne River capable of supporting vehicular traffic.[39]

As the 79th and 90th Infantry Divisions secured their objectives, Lieutenant General Patton met with Bradley at the First Army command post of Lieutenant General Hodges. During the conference, Patton received instructions confirming his mission to seize a bridgehead at Mayenne until relieved by First Army and to secure other crossings on the Mayenne River to the south, including Laval. However, Bradley also wanted Third Army to push on to Le Mans.[40] Patton was satisfied with the results of the meeting. He succeeded in convincing Bradley to alter the boundary between First and Third Armies, which resulted in Patton "getting the boundary Brecey–St.-Hilaire–Mayenne–Le Mansall . . . this is exactly the boundary I desire as it keeps me on the outside—on the running end."[41]

Only the 5th Armored Division, however, was in position to advance on Le Mans. The 4th and 6th Armored Divisions were still committed to securing ports in Brittany, and the French 2d Armored Division would not begin moving south from Utah Beach until the evening of 6 August.[42] Patton's instructions to Third Army upon his return from the meeting reiterated the requirement for XV Corps to seize Mayenne and Laval. Major General Walton Walker's XX Corps, which was preparing to pass through Avranches, was directed to move south and east on army order to secure crossings on the Mayenne River in the vicinity of Chateau Gontier.[43] Instead of moving east to Le Mans, XX Corps was preparing to deploy south of XV Corps.

Patton hesitated to recall either the 4th or 6th Armored Division from Brittany while there was still a chance of obtaining a port without a prolonged struggle. The 6th Armored temporarily halted its advance on 3 August after a courier arrived from VIII Corps bearing orders to attack Dinan instead of Brest. The entire division would have to turn around and head back east. Major General Grow tried to persuade Middleton to change the order, but the poor communications prevented him from receiving a prompt response. Middleton had already changed his mind once he learned where Grow's tanks were located, but he could not get word to the 6th Armored Division that the order to attack Dinan was rescinded.

Major General Grow was preparing to attack Dinan when Patton arrived at his division command post at 1100 hours on 4 August. The division staff noticed the Third Army commander was controlling his anger with some difficulty as he walked toward the operations tent. Major General Grow gave Patton the message from Middleton that had halted the 6th Armored Division's advance. Patton read the note and smiled before putting it in his pocket. He told Grow, "I'll see Middleton, you go ahead where I told you to go."[44]

Meanwhile, the 4th Armored Division found itself almost out of gasoline at Rennes. Supply trucks that could carry gasoline had been used to bring the 13th Infantry Regiment forward to assist the tankers in capturing the city. The 4th Armored did not receive sufficient gasoline to resume its advance before late afternoon on 4 August. CCA drove seventy miles to the city of Vannes on the morning of 5 August, entering the city by 2300 hours. The capture of Vannes cut off the Brittany peninsula at its base, thus sealing off the German troops defending the ports.

On the evening of 6 August, Major General Wood sent Patton a message informing him that "[we] have Vannes, will have Lorient this evening. Vannes, intact, hope Lorient the same. Trust we can turn around and get headed in the right direction soon."[45] The announcement that 4th Armored Division would soon have Lorient turned out to be premature. CCB did not arrive outside of the port until 7 August, where it was greeted with a storm of artillery fire that inflicted 105 casualties and destroyed fifteen vehicles. The tankers quickly pulled back out of range of Lorient's defenses.

These losses must have seemed especially useless to Wood, who had never accepted the necessity of capturing the Brittany ports. Wood, focusing on the tactical objective, believed that immediate steps to ensure the destruction of *7 Armee* took precedence over an operation seeking to secure port facilities needed to support future operations. When Major General Middleton visited the 4th Armored Division command post on 4 August, Wood exclaimed in frustration that "they [meaning Bradley and Eisenhower] are winning the war the wrong way." Wood clearly held an opinion, however, that was not shared by his superiors.

Patton probably felt some of Wood's frustrations, but for different reasons. Not only did it seem that Third Army would fail to seize a seaport without a prolonged battle, but Haislip's XV Corps also lacked the resources necessary to conduct an extended advance to the east or southeast. Logistical considerations and traffic congestion continued to have a significant impact on the rate at which

Third Army entered the fray. Both 5th and 6th Armored Divisions, for example, were facing severe gasoline shortages. Troops moving through the Avranches corridor were limited to transiting "two narrow, winding routes, filled with rubble, dead animals, and wrecked vehicles."[46]

Between 1 and 4 August, three armored (4th, 5th, and 6th) and three infantry (8th, 79th, and 83d) divisions managed to squeeze through or past the Avranches bottleneck. A seventh division, the 90th Infantry, was able to avoid the congestion by moving through the VII Corps zone of operations.[47] During a period of ninety-six hours, approximately thirteen thousand trucks, tanks, jeeps, half-tracks, and howitzers crossed over the Pontaubault Bridge, averaging one vehicle every thirty seconds. However, over half of Third Army headed into Brittany instead of turning north to savage the exposed flank of 7 Armee.

Although the movement of so many troops through Avranches represented a considerable feat, it also paradoxically meant that conditions might get worse before they got better. Each division possessed numerous logistics vehicles that delivered ammunition and fuel to combat units. As additional divisions passed to the south, more supply vehicles would be making the daily round trip through Avranches, clogging the roads with two-way traffic. The supply vehicles were forced to make this trip because most of Patton's supply dumps were still sited north of Avranches. When Third Army relocated these stockpiles south of Avranches, it would mean that even larger numbers of logistics vehicles would temporarily congest the road network. With increasing amounts of two-way supply traffic, XX Corps and XII Corps could potentially face even greater difficulties passing through Avranches.

The coastal road that bore the Third Army ran from Coutances to the town of Pontaubault, a distance of thirty-two miles. Between Coutances and Avranches, two parallel roads carried traffic, but they converged at the bridge over the See River. South of Avranches, Third Army engineers were in the process of building a second road leading to Pontaubault. When that project was completed, it only alleviated some of the congestion because the newly constructed road and coastal route still converged at the bridge over the Selune River in Pontaubault. Third Army did not gain any relief until units passed south of Pontaubault, where the road network branched out toward St.-Malo, Dinan, Rennes, Fougeres, and St.-Hilaire-du-Harcouet.

The roads leading into Brittany, both French and American built, were also carrying a far greater amount of traffic than anyone had ever envisioned. Empty logistical vehicles belonging to Third Army, VIII Corps, and XV Corps headed north to obtain new loads from supply dumps that were still located north of St.-Lô. Combat units and logistical columns from Third Army and XV Corps continued to flow to the south. The divisions reassigned to Third Army from First Army were forced to move across the latter's lines of communication before arriving in Villedieu les Poeles. From Villedieu the convoys turned southwest toward Avranches, where they joined the flow moving along the coastal roads.

By 5 August, the leading echelons of XX Corps appeared on the route.[48] In addition, First Army convoys contributed to the congestion in a vain attempt to avoid VII Corps traffic traveling along secondary routes between Brecey and St.-Hilaire-du-Harcouet.

The situation proved so confused that 12th Army Group was forced to issue another letter of instruction on 3 August devoted solely to clarifying the boundaries between First Army and Third Army. The letter also directed that "all First Army troops in the Third Army area driving to the southeast will clear Third Army zone without delay and assist in every way possible the advance of the Third Army."[49]

Even with the help of 12th Army Group, Third Army attempts to regulate traffic met with mixed success. Combat units moving into Brittany were permitted to move only during daylight. At dusk, the units had to pull into assembly areas to allow supply vehicles unimpeded access to the roads. Divisions were divided into smaller columns that would move through Avranches interspersed with convoys of other divisions. Disregarding air attacks or traffic jams, the vehicles from a particular division would head to a prearranged assembly area south of Pontaubault, where they waited until the remaining convoys arrived. While this technique allowed Third Army to simultaneously pass several divisions through the bottleneck, it also took considerable time. The 8th Infantry Division, for example, required two days to move its regimental combat teams to an assembly area south of Avranches.

Despite strict measures, the sheer number of vehicles often overwhelmed Military Police assigned to control traffic. Unable to maintain order when confronted by convoy commanders, the MPs quickly found themselves replaced by senior officers. The conditions were so hectic and the situation changed so frequently that one disgusted liaison officer from XX Corps reported that "Military Police are hopelessly befuddled and no definite information available along entire route . . . a general just in from Avranches route says very crowded . . . four divisions trying to cross on one bridge at same time."[50] Division commanders were not immune from a stint of traffic control duty if they wanted their units to pass expeditiously through the bottleneck.

The growing number of American troops moving into southeastern France had not gone unnoticed. With Patton's Third Army confined to a limited road network, the Germans intended to employ the *Luftwaffe* to delay the southward movement of American troops and supplies. *Jagdkorps 2* ordered all German fighters in France to concentrate their efforts against convoys in the Avranches sector. About 225 sorties of specially fitted ground attack Fw-190 and Me-109 fighters would be available per day to attack ground targets.[51]

Patton was very aware of the lucrative target that his convoys presented to the Germans. He noted that "these truck movements of large numbers of infantry are very dangerous and might be almost fatal if the Germans should spot them, particularly if there is a traffic jam." Patton took drastic steps to avoid congestion on the roads, ordering all of his available staff officers to man traffic control points. He was not reticent about issuing the same instructions to senior officers, as exemplified by his orders to Major General Haislip to personally control the flow of traffic moving through Avranches in order to guarantee that the 90th Infantry Division moved south with minimum disruption.[52]

The Germans hoped that an aerial assault on Third Army as it moved through Avranches would significantly reduce the rate at which Patton could build up forces to support the expansion of the Brittany lodgment. By delaying Patton's buildup, the Germans hoped to extend the window of opportunity they might gain for organizing a counteroffensive against the Americans. The efforts of the *Luftwaffe* resulted in a dramatic upswing in daylight aerial attacks against American troops.

VIII Corps noted that German "air activity, which had been confined to night operations, not only increased during darkness, but enemy planes ventured forth during the daylight hours to strafe and bomb our columns. This was particularly true of the roads leading in and out of Avranches and the town of Avranches itself. Here the enemy concentrated his night bombing attacks to get the bridges on the crowded approaches to the town."[53]

Patton was also impressed by the frequency of *Luftwaffe* attacks. On 2 August, he counted "over a hundred bomb hits, some quite near." The following day, Patton noted that "the bombing last night hit some road intersections near here and also the bridge at Avranches, without destroying it. However, we are having engineers construct an extra crossing at Avranches."[54]

Distinctive targets such as engineer bridging units attracted marauding German fighter-bombers. The 990th Engineer Treadway Company, for example, was attacked three times on 1 August, followed by three more attacks the following day.[55] The *Luftwaffe* did not intend to pass up any target that appeared even remotely worth their attention, strafing the XV Corps command post on 2 August.[56] Although the aggressiveness of the German pilots was noteworthy, their skill at attacking ground targets was not. With rare exceptions, the American units suffered only minor casualties from the low-flying intruders.

The *Luftwaffe* fighter pilots flying over Avranches used tactics developed during the opening stages of the Normandy campaign to combat Allied air superiority. The Germans had discovered that formations of forty to sixty aircraft could consistently penetrate American fighter cover. The sight of large numbers of German fighters often persuaded smaller American flights to avoid combat. The *Luftwaffe* paid a price, however, by adopting these methods. Not all American fighter pilots were deterred by large numbers of Germans planes. When aerial combat ensued, the Germans often got in each other's way. This tactic also required extensive coordination and considerable effort to assemble large formations, which reduced the time spent over the target area as well as the daily number of sorties.

American antiaircraft defenses posed a significant threat to the *Luftwaffe*. As it prepared for war in 1940, the U.S. Army watched newsreels of Stuka dive-bombers screaming down on French and British troops. The German propaganda footage resulted in the Americans deploying far more antiaircraft to Europe than they would ever need. In this instance, however, the precautions taken by the Americans paid off handsomely. Anticipating the use of German airpower in the constricted Avranches corridor, Third Army deployed antiaircraft artillery (AAA) along the routes used by vehicles moving south. The presence of these antiaircraft units significantly decreased the effectiveness of German aerial attacks.

Luftwaffe fighter-bombers quickly learned to approach American artillery with caution. An entire AAA battalion, for example, was allocated to each artillery group in VIII Corps. The German fighters also avoided striking columns consisting primarily of heavily armored tanks mounting antiaircraft machine guns. When a viable target was sighted, the German planes restricted themselves to hurried passes to avoid being effectively engaged by the defending guns.

Even fixed targets such as the bridges proved to be a difficult target for the Germans. By 1944, the *Luftwaffe* in France consisted primarily of daylight fighters. There were only limited numbers of bombers available, and even fewer pilots possessed the skill necessary to hit point targets during darkness. Recognizing the importance of the Pontaubault and Avranches bridges, Third Army massed an entire AAA battalion to protect each span. The intensity of the aerial onslaught against the bridges can be gauged by American claims of eighteen planes downed over a two-day period.[57] It remained to be seen, however, if the sacrifices made by the *Luftwaffe* could stem the flood of Americans pouring into southeastern France.

CONCLUSIONS

The merits of launching VIII Corps into Brittany instead of attacking the exposed southern flank of *7 Armee* have been frequently debated. However, at the time that the decision was made, all of the senior American commanders supported Bradley. As commander of the newly formed 12th Army Group, he was focused on separating the First and Third Armies. Bradley did not consider sending Third Army north because this would have placed Patton on a collision course with First Army advancing to the east. The 12th Army Group commander felt that Hodges's First Army possessed sufficient resources to defeat Hausser's *7 Armee* without assistance from Third Army. Even Patton, who thirsted for a decisive battle, believed that Brittany proved a more worthwhile objective for Third Army than aiding Hodges in finishing off *7 Armee*.

Arguments concerning the merits of whether the Americans should have ignored Brittany fail to consider that Bradley's decision also served to convince the Germans that they had gained an opportunity to significantly alter the operational balance in Normandy. The often overlooked impact of Bradley's decision was that it also served to convince the Germans that a counteroffensive against

Avranches was now a realistic possibility. The Germans did not believe that the narrow Avranches corridor could support a simultaneous thrust into Brittany and southeastern France. When the Americans entered Brittany, the Germans believed that they could accept risk on the southern flank of *7 Armee* while assembling a counterattack force to recapture Avranches.

3

German Preparations for a Counteroffensive

Despite continued pressure from First Army, Hausser's *7 Armee* managed to reestablish a defensive line stretching from Vire to the town of Barenton by 1 August. There was no guarantee, however, that this line could be maintained without significant reinforcements. To the north, *II Fallschirmjäger Korps* defended the vital road junction of Vire while *XLVII Panzer Korps* held the sector between Vire and the Foret-de-St.-Sever. To the south of *XLVII Panzer Korps,* the shattered remnants of *LXXXIV Armee Korps,* reinforced by *Panzer Division 116,* were stretched between the Foret-de-St.-Sever and Barenton.

XLVII Panzer Korps, which consisted of *Panzer Division 2* and *SS-Panzer Division 2,* was a relative newcomer to *7 Armee,* having been transferred from *Panzer Gruppe West* the previous week. On July 28 and 29, *7 Armee* committed *XLVII Panzer Korps* against American troops advancing on the road junctions of Villedieu les Poeles, Tessy, and Percy. Although the German panzers could not stop the Americans, the appearance of *XLVII Panzer Korps* temporarily stabilized the situation long enough for *7 Armee* to reestablish a defensive line.

When *7 Armee* committed *XLVII Panzer Korps* north of Avranches, the loss of that key city was inevitable. The capture of Avranches, which served to anchor the southern flank of *7 Armee,* meant that the Allies had succeeded in forcing open an unobstructed corridor through the Norman hedgerows. The Germans had to mount a counteroffensive to recapture Avranches before the Americans could consolidate their gains. By reestablishing an unbroken defensive line, the Germans could return to the semistatic positional warfare that allowed them to previously contain the Allied lodgment in Normandy. The recapture of Avranches would also erase the immediate threat to the Brittany ports and the southern flank of *7 Armee.*

Although the capture of Avranches meant that their defensive line was outflanked, the Germans did not consider retreat as a viable option. The Seine River to the east, with its numerous twists and curves, did not offer as distinct a defensive advantage as the hedgerows. Since the Allies would undoubtedly pursue, a withdrawal to the Seine might result in the Germans being caught up in mobile warfare, an unfavorable proposition at best given the Anglo-American command of the air. If Normandy could not be held, then the only other area offering a reasonable chance of success was the West Wall. The loss of France, however, was strategically unacceptable to Hitler; the German Army would continue to defend Normandy.

Remaining on the defensive, however, would not bring about a solution to the unfavorable situation currently facing the Germans. By recapturing Avranches, they would be able to isolate a large number of American troops while restoring the southern flank of *7 Armee*. Stabilizing the entire battlefront would also prove much easier in the wake of a stinging defeat inflicted upon Bradley's 12th Army Group. With the southern portion of the Normandy front restored, the Germans could begin in-depth preparations of long neglected defenses designed to protect the approaches to the Reich.

Time would prove to be the key factor needed to stabilize the Normandy battlefront. Fortunately for *OB West,* the Americans seemed more intent on gaining the Brittany ports than threatening the exposed southern flank of *7 Armee*. This situation had several benefits, primary among them the fact that *7 Armee* could not defend against simultaneous threats from several directions. By moving into Brittany, the Americans were providing *7 Armee* with sufficient time to extend its existing defensive line to the southeast until it could link up with *Armeegruppe G*. Every American unit bound for Brittany also consumed precious supplies that would have been used to attack *7 Armee* or support an advance into southeastern France.

With *7 Armee* fully absorbed in the defense of Vire, the Germans did not have any local reserves to employ in a counteroffensive against Avranches. *LXXXIV Armee Korps,* which held the sector north and east of Avranches, lacked any sort of offensive capability. *LXXXIV Armee Korps,* which was directly in the path of VII Corps during Operation COBRA, had suffered tremendous losses in the past week. By 1 August, it consisted of only *Panzer Division 116,* which had been recently detached from *XLVII Panzer Korps*, and a number of fragmented units formed into ad hoc *Kampfgruppen* (battlegroups). To make matters worse, *LXXXIV Armee Korps* found itself under a new commander unfamiliar with the tactical situation. His predecessor had been relieved for failing to halt the American breakthrough.

The *XXV Armee Korps,* positioned south of Avranches, also lacked sufficient troops. Over the past months, it had been systematically stripped of personnel and equipment sent to reinforce units fighting in Normandy. Lacking the combat power necessary to oppose the American tanks, *XXV Armee Korps* retreated into the prepared defenses of the coastal ports, abandoning the interior of the Brittany peninsula to the Americans. As long as *XXV Armee Korps* retained control of the

Brittany ports, however, it could assist *7 Armee* by tying down a considerable number of American units.

OB West attempted to relieve some of the burden on *7 Armee* by ordering *Armeegruppe G* to assume responsibility for the defense of Orleans and Nantes while simultaneously extending the latter's zone of operations northward from the Biscay coast to the Loire River. *Armeegruppe G* would continue to retain responsibility for defending southern France. *OB West,* recognizing that *7 Armee* would require additional troops to protect its southern flank, transferred *LXXXI Armee Korps* from *15 Armee*.[1] *Armeegruppe G* was also directed to provide one panzer division, an infantry division, and an assault gun brigade to *LXXXI Armee Korps*.[2]

In an effort to quickly gather the troops necessary for a counteroffensive, the Germans began examining the other portions of the Normandy front. Excepting the loss of Avranches, the overall situation was not hopeless. Of the four corps assigned to *General der Panzertruppen* Hans Eberbach's *Panzer Gruppe West,* only *SS-Panzer Korps II* was actively engaged against the British. Eberbach's other corps were reporting only normal activity in their respective sectors.

Another bright spot was the fact that Berlin finally granted *OB West* permission to shift troops from *15 Armee* and *Armeegruppe G* to reinforce Hausser's battered *7 Armee*. Between 27 July and 1 August, six infantry divisions and one panzer division were dispatched to Normandy. *Panzer Division 9* and *Infanterie Division 708,* transferred from southern France, would be assigned to *LXXXI Armee Korps* as soon as that headquarters arrived from Pas de Calais. *LXXXIV Armee Korps* was slated to receive *Infanterie Divisionen 84, 331,* and *363. Panzer Gruppe West,* which transferred *XLVII Panzer Korps* to *7 Armee,* would be compensated with *Infanterie Divisionen 85* and *89*.[3]

Since the Americans swerved west into Brittany rather than attack *7 Armee, Generalfeldmarschall* Guenther von Kluge decided that the circumstances were ripe for a counteroffensive aimed at Avranches. To his credit, von Kluge reacted quickly after discovering he had been misinformed as to the magnitude of the crisis facing *7 Armee*. Von Kluge originally received a telephone call from *XXV Armee Korps* on 31 July reporting that Allied fighter-bombers had destroyed the Pontaubault Bridge.[4] By the next day, however, he discovered the bridge had not been knocked out. In fact, American tanks were crossing over it in large numbers as they streamed into Brittany.

At 1100 hours on 1 August, von Kluge telephoned Hitler's headquarters to report that "the situation in Avranches had become considerably aggravated and that our troops had to be withdrawn behind the sector at Pontaubault . . . the area east of Avranches is now wide open." However, he was convinced that "the breakthrough could be averted if other fronts were stripped to the utmost."[5]

Von Kluge's next telephone call was to *Oberstgruppenführer und General der Waffen SS* Paul Hausser, commanding *7 Armee,* requesting an immediate meeting to discuss plans for a counteroffensive against Avranches. The pair agreed to hold the planning conference at the manor of la Mageantiere in the town of Bion, located south of Mortain.[6] Von Kluge set the agenda for the conference by presenting Hausser with a directive stating that *7 Armee* had the mission of blocking the American breakthrough east of Avranches by concentrating all available forces for a counteroffensive in that sector. *Generalfeldmarschall* von Kluge explained that "it was of the greatest importance to carry out the counterattack against Avranches with the highest speed and greatest striking power in order to block the break and reestablish the situation."[7]

Von Kluge explained to Hausser that since the Allies were currently confining their efforts to securing the Brittany peninsula, *7 Armee* had an unparalleled opportunity to strike while their adversaries were occupied elsewhere. The American lines of communication, which ran from north to south through Avranches, were extremely vulnerable to a German counteroffensive from the east. Von Kluge instructed Hausser to employ *XLVII Panzer Korps,* which would consist of *Panzer Division 2, SS-Panzer Division 2,* and *Panzer Division 116,* to conduct the proposed counteroffensive.

Von Kluge softened the request by promising Hausser that he would seek Hitler's permission to straighten out the defensive line in Normandy to free up several infantry divisions belonging to *Panzer Gruppe West.* These infantry divisions would then be transferred to *7 Armee* to replace the panzers as they were pulled out of the line. The transfer of forces would allow Hausser to reconstitute *LXXXIV Armee Korps* and reinforce *II Fallschirmjäger Korps* using the infantry divisions en route from other areas in France.

After glancing over the directive, *Oberstgruppenführer und General der Waffen SS* Hausser noted that the designated units, with the exception of *Panzer Division 116,* were depleted by recent losses. While he agreed that the counteroffensive had to be launched as soon as possible, Hausser requested a delay until additional panzers were available. Von Kluge was aware that Hausser was exaggerating. Reports forwarded to *Heeresgruppe B* indicated that in addition to *Panzer Division 116,* both *Panzer Division 2* and *SS-Panzer Division 2* were still rated as *Kampfwert I,* which meant that they were capable of conducting the full range of offensive and defensive missions. Deferring to Hausser's concerns, von Kluge promised to reinforce *7 Armee* with panzer divisions from *SS Panzer Korps I and II,* as well as *Panzer Division 9* and the *LVIII Panzer Korps* headquarters. He also promised to send additional artillery battalions and mortar brigades.

Von Kluge suggested that Hausser utilize *Infanterie Divisionen 331, 363,* and *708* to retain Avranches after it was recaptured. By employing the infantry divisions in a defensive role, *7 Armee* would be free to employ its panzer divisions to meet the inevitable American counterattack. *Infanterie Division 708,* however, would be temporarily assigned to *LXXXI Armee Korps* until the situation in the south of Mayenne was stabilized. Von Kluge then sweetened the pot by intimating that Hausser would also receive *Fallschirmjäger Division 6* as soon as Hitler authorized its release.

Although he was impressed with von Kluge's apparent sincerity, Hausser realized that the timing of the counteroffensive would depend on the arrival of promised reinforcements. Shifting large bodies of troops would be extremely difficult due to Allied air superiority. Complicating the matter was the fact that most of the promised units did not belong to *7 Armee*. *Armeegruppe G* still had to contend with the possibility of an Allied landing along the Mediterranean coast of France, while to the north, *Panzer Gruppe West* faced the potentiality of a renewed Canadian offensive in the Caen sector. *Generalfeldmarschall* von Kluge, however, gave Hausser his personal guarantee that the troops would be released in time to take part in the counteroffensive.[8]

As he departed the meeting with Hausser, von Kluge realized that he had a lot more at stake than merely his professional reputation. The penalty for failure almost certainly would cost him his life. Having been aware of the failed assassination attempt against Hitler before it took place on 20 July, von Kluge was certain that his every move was being watched and that it would only be a matter of time before his complicity was discovered. As long as German troops could continue to contain the Allied beachhead in Normandy, von Kluge felt that he was safe from Hitler's wrath. He also knew that if he offered Hitler the slightest pretext to recall him to Berlin, it probably would mean his death. The success of Operation COBRA, followed closely by the loss of Avranches, could provide Hitler with a pretext to dismiss him. Von Kluge had to recapture Avranches or face dire consequences.

Beginning his career as an artillery officer in the First World War, von Kluge rose to command a *Reichswehr* corps by the 1930s. He was nicknamed "Kluger Hans" (the German word for smart or clever is "kluge") in recognition of his ability to curry political favor if it would lead to rapid promotion. He was rewarded in 1939 with command of *4 Armee,* which he led in Poland, France, and Russia. Following the relief in December 1941 of *Generalfeldmarschalls* Fedor von Bock and Gerd von Runstedt for sanctioning a withdrawal in defiance of Hitler's explicit orders, von Kluge was named commander of *Heeresgruppe Mitte* in Russia. Injured in an automobile accident in October 1943, von Kluge was sent back to Germany to recuperate, where he remained on the inactive list until the Allied landings.

Hitler personally sent von Kluge to France in early July 1944, where he replaced *Generalfeldmarschall* von Runstedt as commander in chief West. *Generalfeldmarschall* Rommel, with the approval of von Rundstedt, had circulated a proposal calling for German troops to pull back along a line running from the Orne River to Caumont. This move would confer two immediate benefits: it put the German troops out of the range of Allied naval firepower while offering a shorter defensive line that would facilitate the creation of a large armored reserve. When word got back to Berlin that von Rundstedt had sanctioned these proposals, Hitler summarily ordered his dismissal.

When a strafing attack left *Generalfeldmarschall* Rommel severely wounded, von Kluge also took command of *Heeresgruppe B*. Never content to stay in his headquarters, *Generalfeldmarschall* von Kluge was constantly on the road. His inspection tours provided firsthand evidence of the deteriorating situation, and he discovered that every senior commander in France agreed with Rommel's proposal to withdrawal. He was also amazed at the impact that Allied airpower had on ground operations. Von Kluge concluded that Rommel may have been abrasive and pushy, but he was not a defeatist nor had he exaggerated Allied military capabilities. Unfortunately for von Kluge, he was sure there was no way to convince Hitler of the true situation.

One reason von Kluge found himself on shaky ground with *Oberkommand Wehrmacht* in Berlin was because of Hitler's long-standing feud with the leadership of the German army over his tendency to promote *SS* generals whom he prized for their unswerving personal loyalty and belief in eventual triumph. After Cherbourg fell, Hitler relieved the *7 Armee* commander, *Generaloberst* Friedrich Dollman, with *Oberstgruppenführer und General der Waffen SS* Paul Hausser, who transferred from *SS-Panzer Korps II* to take command. The *SS* general's qualifications for higher command seemed impressive: he was a courageous and untiring officer who possessed considerable combat experience. Perhaps more important, at least from Hitler's perspective, Hausser was an ardent Nazi. However, von Kluge believed that Hausser lacked strategic perspective, a function of the *SS* general's limited experience at higher level command.

Von Kluge was extremely dissatisfied with Hausser's reaction in the wake of Operation COBRA. When Collins's VII Corps succeeded in breaking through the forward defenses of *7 Armee,* von Kluge anticipated that the next phase in the American plan called for the capture of Coutances. Once Coutances fell, the Americans would be in a position to outflank *7 Armee* while simultaneously opening up a route leading into Brittany. Hausser played into American hands by ordering his troops to move away from the coast in an effort to escape encirclement rather than attempt to retain Coutances and block the approaches to Brittany as von Kluge wished.

In a memorandum dated 29 July, *Generalfeldmarschall* von Kluge criticized Hausser's actions, noting that a gap would be created in the already weak German defenses covering Avranches. Von Kluge recorded that Hausser, focused exclusively on preserving the tactical integrity of his forces, had inadvertently provided the Americans with a golden opportunity to outflank the entire *7 Armee.*[9] Von Kluge ordered Hausser to revoke his original orders, directing him instead to hold Avranches and Villedieu les Poeles at all costs. If either town were lost, *7 Armee* was directed to recapture them immediately.

The operational situation had already changed by the time von Kluge's directive arrived at the *7 Armee* command post. With its command and control network significantly degraded, *7 Armee* had to resort to using couriers to deliver orders to subordinate units. German messengers, however, found it extremely difficult to travel in daylight due to Allied air activity. Consequently, orders drafted by *7 Armee* were usually rendered obsolete before they could be delivered. The opposing Americans even noted that "it was only necessary for the First Army to take advantage of the disorganized state of the enemy."[10]

The countermeasures employed by Hausser against the attacking Americans ultimately proved to be uncoordinated and ineffective. Although most German units escaped encirclement, *LXXXIV Armee Korps* was severely mauled during Operation COBRA. Since *7 Armee* lacked an armored reserve to conduct counterattacks, von Kluge reinforced Hausser with *XLVII Panzer Korps,* hurriedly transferred from *Panzer Gruppe West,* in an attempt to halt the American advance. While *XLVII Panzer Korps* achieved some local success, it was unable to restore the German defensive line between St.-Lô and Coutances. Despite the fact that von Kluge had reinforced Hausser with a panzer corps, Avranches and Villedieu les Poeles were captured by the Americans.

Following the American breakout, von Kluge sought to deflect Hitler's anger by selectively conducting a purge of senior German officers. Unable to touch Hausser, von Kluge instead ousted the *7 Armee* chief of staff. He also sacked the commander of the *LXXXIV Armee Korps*. However, Hitler disclosed to *Generalfeldmarschall* Alfred Jodl on 1 August that he had proof of Rommel and von Kluge's complicity in the July assassination plot. He went on to say that he was looking for a new commander in chief West. [11] Once the Avranches situation was dealt with, Hitler remarked, von Kluge would go.

The *7 Armee* staff was too absorbed in fending off attacks by the American First Army while simultaneously preparing for a counteroffensive against Avranches to spend much time discussing political ideology. Armed with guidance from the meeting, Hausser's staff began preparing a detailed plan for the counteroffensive. With the bulk of the American troops in Normandy threatening Vire, Hausser chose to launch his counteroffensive in a more lightly defended sector south of the See River. Running parallel to the proposed avenue of advance, the river itself represented a natural obstacle to any American force attempting to threaten the flank of the German counteroffensive. The terrain between Vire and the See River consisted of hedgerow country, which offered little opportunity to American commanders seeking to deploy large formations of armor against the German counteroffensive. Additionally, the high ground along the southern bank of the See would afford German artillery observers a good view of any attempt to cross the river.

A suitable road network was also available south of the See River. Hard surface roads capable of supporting the movement of the panzers ran directly through Juvigny le Tertre and Mortain to Avranches. The panzer divisions participating in the counteroffensive would also be able to assemble in secrecy within forested tracts near Sourdeval and Mortain. The town of Mortain, however, had to remain in German hands to ensure that the proposed plan stood a reasonable chance of success. If the Americans occupied the high ground to the east of Mortain, possession of this dominating terrain, combined with the presence of a deep valley to the west, would drastically retard the initial momentum of the counteroffensive.

Hausser designated *General der Panzertruppen* Hans von Funck's *XLVII Panzer Korps* as the headquarters for the counteroffensive. Von Funck had considerable experience in armored warfare, having served in motorized units since 1919. He was chosen to command *Panzer Regiment 5* in 1940, an assignment that was followed by a two-year stint as commanding general of *Panzer Division 7*. Successful active service during the Russian campaign had resulted in von Funck being appointed as commander of *XXIII Armee Korps* in December 1943, and soon afterward, he assumed command of *XLVII Panzer Korps*. Transferred from Russia to Normandy, he performed credibly against the British at Caen.[12] Despite glowing professional credentials, however, his subordinates described von Funck as "brutal and ruthless, much disliked by officers and men, never goes to the front line, and hounds his men to death."[13]

Von Kluge clearly realized that the potential for success was directly related to the number of panzers he could assemble. Because *7 Armee* had never possessed many panzers, von Kluge would be forced to transfer units from *Panzer Gruppe West*. Once this was accomplished, however, von Kluge risked defeat on two fronts should the operation against Avranches fail while he fatally weakened *Panzer Gruppe West* in the process. Exacerbating this dilemma was the fact that *General der Panzertruppen* Hans Eberbach, commanding *Panzer Gruppe West*, would probably argue strongly against losing any of his assigned panzer units on the eve of an impending Canadian offensive against Falaise.

Despite the known risks, von Kluge threw himself into the task of collecting the divisions needed for the counteroffensive, now code-named *Unternehmen Lüttich* (Operation LIEGE). When initially queried about the possibility of sending five panzer divisions to *7 Armee*, the commander of *Panzer Gruppe West* bluntly informed von Kluge that *SS-Panzer Korps II* would not be able to participate in *Unternehmen Lüttich*. *General der Panzertruppen* Eberbach explained that while the British had failed to make significant headway against a stubborn defense offered by the *SS* panzers following an attack on 30 July, the assault showed no signs of abating. If *SS-Panzer Korps II* were transferred to *7 Armee*, Eberbach could not guarantee that the sector would hold. As a compromise, he proposed to delay the movement of *SS-Panzer Divisions 9* and *10* for at least three to four days. At that time, *Panzer Gruppe West* could part with one or both divisions.[14]

When von Kluge mentioned that *SS-Panzer Korps I* could contribute the required panzers, Eberbach replied that *Panzer Gruppe West* could transfer both of the panzer divisions assigned to *SS-Panzer Korps I*, but it would be left with only two infantry divisions to block any British offensive aimed at Falaise. Eberbach suggested another compromise solution: *SS-Panzer Division 1* (also known as *Leibstandarte*) would be transferred to *7 Armee*, providing that von Kluge replaced it with *Infanterie Division 89*, and *SS-Panzer Division 12* would be pulled out of line to form a strong reserve for *SS-Panzer Korps I*. Eberbach's recommendation also required von Kluge to gain permission from Berlin for a limited withdrawal by a portion of *Panzer Gruppe West*.

After agreeing with Eberbach, von Kluge promised to obtain permission for a limited withdrawal. At 1100 hours on 3 August, von Kluge reported to *Oberkommand Wehrmacht (OKW)*, the High Command headquarters in Berlin, that ongoing offensive operations by British troops would prevent *Panzer Gruppe West* from transferring *SS-Panzer Korps II* or *Panzer Division 21* to *7 Armee*.[15] However, *SS-Panzer Division 1* would be available to participate in *Unternehmen Lüttich*. After explaining the situation to Berlin, von Kluge received authorization to withdraw *Panzer Gruppe West* (soon to be renamed *Panzerarmee 5*) to a line running generally from Thury-Harcourt to Vire. The movement would take place during the night of 3 August.

Eberbach had insisted on retaining *SS-Panzer Division 12* in reserve because there was some risk involved when replacing experienced panzer troops with a yet unproven infantry unit. Allied intelligence officers considered *Infanterie Division 89* as a "low-category" unit. It had been formed only four months previously in Norway and contained a significant percentage of non-Germans as well as ethnic Germans under eighteen and over forty years of age. Although stronger in foot soldiers, *Infanterie Division 89* was ill suited to take over the sector held by *SS-Panzer Division 1*.

The *SS* panzers had opted for a thin front line backed by a strong mobile reserve. *Infanterie Division 89,* however, did not possess a fraction of the armor protection, mobility, or firepower of *SS-Panzer Division 1*. The divisional reserve of the incoming unit consisted of two infantry battalions sited to protect supporting artillery. The remaining troops occupied the villages of Tilly, La Hogue, and May-Sur-Orne as well as positions on Verrieres Ridge. With its defense anchored on immobile strongholds, *Infanterie Division 89* would prove more vulnerable to a British armored attack than *Leibstandarte* had.[16]

Although the core of *Oberstgruppenführer und General der Waffen SS* Josef "Sepp" Dietrich's *SS-Panzer Korps I* now consisted of *Infanterie Divisionen 89* and *272*, Eberbach was not overly concerned with Dietrich's ability to hold his assigned sector. With the departure of *Leibstandarte*, Dietrich complied with orders to place *SS-Panzer Division 12* in reserve. If the British launched an offensive, he intended to employ *SS-Panzer Division 12* to seal off any gap opened by the Allies. The bulk of the *Nebelwerfer* batteries assigned to *SS-Panzer Division 1*—eight combat-ready Tigers from *Schwere SS-Panzer Abteilung 101,* elements of *III Flak Korps*, and *Werfer Brigade 83*—were positioned to support the defending infantry. Despite the transfer of *Leibstandarte, SS-Panzer Korps I* still possessed 126 panzers, 100 artillery pieces, and approximately 100 88mm and 75mm antitank guns, sited in depth along its defensive sector.[17]

The short summer nights coupled with pressure exerted by the opposing Canadians conspired to delay the movement of *SS-Panzer Division 1*. *Leibstandarte* was only able to pull out two panzer battalions, two panzer grenadier battalions, one self-propelled artillery battalion, and one engineer company as well as its flak and reconnaissance battalions during the night of 4 August. Before the rest of *SS-*

Panzer Division 1 was able to depart, it was forced to endure an additional day of local attacks by Canadian units seeking to capture the village of La Hogue.[18]

The piecemeal withdrawal meant that a number of *Leibstandarte* units would not arrive in time to participate in the opening phase of *Unternehmen Lüttich*. Instead of arriving as a complete division, the participation of *Leibstandarte* would be limited to battalion- and regiment-sized components. Von Funck was aware that the delay might have a significant negative impact on the initial momentum of the counteroffensive. The situation grew worse as Hausser began to siphon off units to assist the hard-pressed *LXXXIV Armee Korps*. *Kampfgruppe Schiller,* consisting of the headquarters of *SS-Panzergrenadier Regiment 1*, a composite battalion of panzergrenadiers, an artillery battalion, a *Nebelwerfer* battery, and a platoon of assault guns, had already been diverted to reinforce *Infanterie Division 84* south of Vire.

Although he had promised Hausser that *SS-Panzer Korps I* and *II* would participate in the counteroffensive against Avranches, von Kluge realized that he would have to find panzer divisions from other sources and briefly considered substituting units from *Armeegruppe G*.[19] Departing southern France on 30 July, *Panzer Division 9* would require eight to nine days to reach Normandy instead of the four days usually allotted.[20] The delay was attributable to Allied air attacks that left the French rail system in a shambles. Since *Panzer Division 9* was not expected to reach the front before the night of 7 August, von Kluge discarded the possibility that it could be employed in the opening phases of *Unternehmen Lüttich*.

Von Kluge also discovered that the same situation existed for the infantry divisions deployed to Normandy from other sectors in France. *Infanterie Division 708* departed Royan on 30 July via rail for Samur, where it was forced to transfer personnel and equipment into motor convoys before continuing. Its leading element, *Infanterie Regiment 728,* was not slated to arrive in Mayenne prior to the evening of 7 August.[21] *Sturmgeschütz Brigade 341* departed for the front on 29 July; however, it had been diverted to Avranches in an attempt to slow the American advance into Brittany. Although it had arrived prior to the main body of *LXXXI Armee Korps,* there was no guarantee that the assault gun brigade would remain capable of sustained combat if the fighting at Avranches went badly.[22]

When von Kluge learned that the Americans were advancing toward Laval and Mayenne, he realized that a crisis was developing on the extreme southern flank of *7 Armee*. The requirement to protect Hausser's exposed flank far outweighed von Kluge's desire to employ *LXXXI Armee Korps* in support of the counteroffensive against Avranches. *Panzer Lehr* was instructed to deploy its remaining troops between Barenton and Mayenne while awaiting the arrival of *Panzer Division 9* and *Infanterie Division 708*.

With such a large sector to defend, *LXXXI Armee Korps* planned on fighting a mobile defense against Patton's Third Army. Since *Infanterie Division 708* consisted primarily of dismounted infantry, it was augmented with approximately fifty armored fighting vehicles. In addition to *Sturmgeschütz Brigade 341, Infanterie Division 708* could count on the support of the tank destroyer battalion from *SS-Panzergrenadier Division 17* as well as a *Kampfgruppe* consisting of the *Panzer Lehr* engineer battalion reinforced with Panther tanks.

Despite the realization that he could provide *7 Armee* with only a fraction of the promised resources, von Kluge instructed Hausser to continue with the preparations for the counteroffensive. *XLVII Panzer Korps* would comprise the bulk of the forces taking part in the operation. Since von Funck's troops were already committed against the Americans, *XLVII Panzer Korps* would have to pull out of the front lines prior to assembling for the counteroffensive. Hausser received permission to conduct a limited withdrawal to free up sufficient infantry to replace the departing panzers. Once the panzers were pulled out of the front lines, *II Fallschirmjäger Korps* and *LXXXIV Armee Korps* would extend their frontages to assume responsibility for the *XLVII Panzer Korps* sector. However, *LXXXIV Armee Korps* would have to wait until *Infanterie Divisionen 84* and *363* arrived, which meant that the rearward movement of the panzers would require a phased withdrawal spread over three successive nights.

This course of action promised immediate relief while incurring long-term risk. Although it would prove feasible to employ reinforcements assigned to *LXXXIV Armee Korps* to replace troops from *XLVII Panzer Korps, 7 Armee* was committing infantry divisions that had been earmarked to secure Avranches once it was recaptured. Hausser was also replacing *XLVII Panzer Korps* with inexperienced troops. The battleworthiness of *Infanterie Division 84* was particularly in question; it clearly lacked the training, equipment, and experience necessary to stand up against the Americans.[23] Additionally, this decision meant that *7 Armee* would find it difficult to reposition its panzers once the initial operation was completed. Once the panzers were committed to the defense of Avranches, they would no longer be readily available to counterattack American penetrations in other portions of the *7 Armee* defensive line.

Despite the numerous problems it had encountered, *7 Armee* completed detailed planning for the counteroffensive by 4 August. The participating units included *Panzer Division 2, Panzer Division 116,* and *SS-Panzer Division 1,* as well as a composite formation made up of *SS-Panzer Division 2* and *SS-Panzergrenadier Division 17.* The inventory of serviceable panzers in each division, however, varied considerably. The inventory of *SS-Panzer Division 2,* for example, was reduced from seventy-six panzers and thirty-six assault guns in mid-July to twenty-six panzers and ten assault guns, while *Panzer Division 116* still possessed thirty Pzkfw IVs, thirty-two Panthers, fifteen assault guns, and seventeen self-propelled antitank guns.

Panzer Division 2 possessed thirty-two Pzkfw IVs, six Panthers, and fifteen assault guns as well as sixteen 88mm dual-purpose guns. *SS-Panzer Division 1* boasted forty-three Panthers, fifty-five Pzkfw IVs (medium tanks), and twenty-nine assault guns; however, *7 Armee* had already ordered one company of *Leib-*

standarte Pzkfw IVs to be sent to Domfront. Despite Hausser's continued willingness to divert units assigned to the counteroffensive to other sectors, approximately three hundred serviceable panzers and assault guns were available to participate in *Unternehmen Lüttich*.[24]

What the assembled panzer divisions might have lacked in numbers, they made up for in combat experience. *Panzer Division 2* had perhaps the most impressive lineage. Formed in October 1935, its first commander was then *Oberst* Heinz Guderian, father of modern-day blitzkrieg tactics. The division first saw combat at 0445 hours on 1 September 1939, when the guns of *Panzer Artillerie Regiment 74* opened fire on Polish border defenses. It subsequently took part in the French campaign and the invasion of Yugoslavia and Greece, as well as the attack against Russia. Sent to France for rest and recuperation after several years of combat on the Eastern Front, the division received a new commander, *Generalleutnant* Freiherr von Luettwitz, on 1 February 1944.

Baron Diepold Georg Heinrich von Luettwitz was born in Silesia in 1896. His military career began in 1914 when he enlisted in the Imperial Army. Serving as an enlisted soldier for a short period, von Luettwitz was commissioned as an infantry lieutenant in 1915. He fought until the end of the war, choosing to remain in the military following Germany's defeat. Von Luettwitz served in the *Reichswehr*'s 8th Cavalry Regiment for many years before joining the panzer force in 1935. While leading the 1st Reconnaissance Battalion in Poland, he was severely wounded. His unit remained in Poland after the 1939 campaign, missing out on the invasion of France and Greece.

Transferred to Russia as a replacement officer, von Luettwitz's career was resurrected when he was given command of an infantry regiment in *Panzer Division 20*. He went on to distinguish himself, successively commanding *Grenadier Brigade 20, Panzer Division 20,* and then *Panzer Division 2*. Placed under *XLVII Panzer Korps* in mid-June, von Luettwitz continued to lead his division with distinction against British troops near Caen. Of the four panzer divisions opposing the Americans during Operation COBRA, *Panzer Division 2* suffered the fewest casualties, losing 57 men killed, 251 wounded, and 39 missing during the last week of July.[25] As noted previously, *Panzer Division 2* was rated at *Kampfwert I*. Both panzergrenadier regiments still fielded at least 1,000 riflemen, while the reconnaissance and engineer battalions counted 350–450 men apiece.[26] Transferring men from the divisional replacement battalion had filled many of the personnel casualties suffered by *Panzer Division 2* during June and July.[27]

Panzer Division 116 was also slated to take part in the counteroffensive. It was formed in the spring of 1944 by combining the remnants of *Panzergrenadier Division 16* with the cadre from *Reserve Panzer Division 179*. Despite its lack of seasoning, *Panzer Division 116* was imbued with an enormous sense of esprit de corps. Nicknamed the *Windhund* (Greyhound) division, it was rated by *OB West* as an excellent unit, largely due to the organizational skills of the division's commander, *Generalleutnaut* Gerhard Graf von Schwerin, who believed in realistic prebattle training. Morale in *Panzer Division 116* was considered on par with the elite *SS-Panzers.*

Gerhard Graf von Schwerin began the war as an intelligence officer in the English section of *OKW.* After wangling his way to a troop assignment, von Schwerin participated as a regimental commander in the crossing of the Meuse River and Amiens breakthrough during the French campaign of 1940. In 1941, he was transferred to Libya, where he served with *Leichte Division 5.* Von Schwerin was given command of a motorized infantry division after being promoted to *Generalmajor* in October 1942. He fought in Russia throughout 1943 and into the spring of 1944 before bringing the survivors of his shattered division to France for rest and recuperation. Awarded the Knight's Cross with Oakleaves and Swords in late 1943, von Schwerin was reputedly known as "a brilliant officer."[28]

When the Normandy invasion took place, *Panzer Division 116* remained on guard against a second landing and was not transferred until early July, where it was placed in *Heeresgruppe B* reserve near Airan–St.-Sylvain. The division, which numbered 14,358 officers and men on 1 July, remained in reserve until it was committed south of St.-Lô. Hurriedly flung against the rapidly advancing Americans, *Panzer Division 116* spasmodically attacked in one direction, only to shift emphasis to another sector the following day. Despite its rude introduction to combat, the division was fortunate to have lost only 89 killed, 370 wounded, and 57 missing between 28 July and 1 August.[29] On 30 July, it still possessed an overall rating of *Kampfwert I,* which meant that its subordinate maneuver battalions were considered strong and the division's overall mobility stood at 80 percent.[30]

Although *General der Panzertruppen* von Funck of *XLVII Panzer Korps* may have been glad to acquire *Panzer Division 116,* he quickly came into conflict with the mercurial von Schwerin. Von Funck felt that von Schwerin continually questioned his orders, and stories of shouting matches between the two generals quickly became public knowledge among senior German officers. *Generalmajor der Waffen-SS* Fritz Kraemer, chief of staff of the neighboring *SS-Panzer Korps I,* was of the opinion that von Schwerin's formidable intellect was largely to blame for the poor relationship between the commanders of *Panzer Division 116* and *XLVII Panzer Korps.* Although von Schwerin was arguably smarter than his corps commander, Kraemer felt that this advantage could actually prove to be a handicap during combat.[31]

An intense personal dislike had developed between von Schwerin and von Funck because of the savage handling received by *Panzer Division 116* during Operation COBRA. When the American breakthrough at St.-Lô occurred, von Schwerin's division was rushed south on 28 July. Moving up under the cover of darkness and overcast skies, *Panzer Division 116* was ordered to join *II Fallschirmjäger Korps* near Percy. Soon after it arrived, von Schwerin's division found itself attached instead to *XLVII Panzer Korps.*

Von Schwerin's first mission was to link up with *SS-Panzer Division 2* near

Coutances. Von Funck radioed *Panzer Division 116* to countermand those orders, explaining that *Panzer Division 2* had already established itself astride the St.-Lô –Percy road at la Denisiere, where it succeeded in briefly stemming the American advance toward Coutances. With a respite granted by this success, von Funck hoped that the commitment of *Panzer Division 116* would prove decisive, so he ordered the division to block an American advance from the northeast. A short while later, von Funck ordered von Schwerin to counterattack toward Villebaudon, north of Percy. Frustrated with rapidly changing directives as well the prospect of carrying out an attack in broad daylight, von Schwerin loudly protested his third set of orders.

A bitter argument took place between von Funck and von Schwerin, with the latter citing unfavorable terrain, the fact that his reconnaissance units had already departed to carry out their original mission, and that his division was oriented in a totally different direction. Readjusting his troops would take time, which von Funck admitted was true, but the *XLVII Panzer Korps* commander continued to insist that *Panzer Division 116* carry out the attack as ordered. The latest set of orders stood, despite von Schwerin's objections.

This heated disagreement resulted in a very poor beginning for the professional relationship between the two generals. Both men openly expressed doubts concerning the loyalty and competence of the other. When von Funck questioning his division's battleworthiness, the aristocratic von Schwerin was tremendously insulted. He also felt that von Funck had made derogatory statements about *Panzer Division 116* to *7 Armee* simply for the purpose of deflecting future blame from *XLVII Panzer Korps*. Little did von Schwerin realize how quickly this would turn out to be true.[32]

During the evening of 30 July, the pair clashed again at von Schwerin's divisional command post. Von Schwerin characterized this argument as "an open rupture between the Corps commander and the division commander, when the former insulted the honor of the division."[33] In the aftermath of this argument, von Funck began to let emotions get the better of him as far as von Schwerin was concerned.

By the following day, the disagreement had seeped into official communiqués when von Funck bluntly reported that *Panzer Division 116* continually failed to clear up American penetrations made in its sector. None of the normal extenuating circumstances, such as strong fighter-bomber activity or artillery fire, were given. Although the admission of failure in itself was rarely seen in official reports, what is even more damning is that no reason for the failure was given. One could assume that von Funck wished *7 Armee* headquarters to regard *Panzer Division 116* as unreliable.[34] If anything went wrong during *Unternehmen Lüttich,* von Schwerin was sure that the *XLVII Panzer Korps* commander would blame him at the first available opportunity for any failures.

Fortunately, not all of the participating division commanders were on such poor personal terms with von Funck. Both of the chosen *Waffen-SS* divisions, *SS-*

Panzer Division 1 and *SS-Panzer Division 2,* boasted battlefield credentials equal to von Luettwitz's *Panzer Division 2.* The two *SS* units were originally formed as motorized infantry regiments, although *SS-Panzer Division 2* (also known as *Das Reich*) was soon expanded in size to a division. Both units saw combat in Poland, France, and Greece before taking part in the Russian campaign. Superb performance by *SS-Panzer Division 1* (also known as *Leibstandarte*) in Russia led Hitler to also authorize its expansion from a motorized regiment to an over-strength panzer division. After two and a half years of hard combat against the Red Army, both *Das Reich* and *Leibstandarte* were sent to France in the spring of 1944 for a period of rest and refitting.

Commanded by *SS-Brigadeführer* Theodor (Teddy) Wisch, *Leibstandarte* found itself thrust once more into the fray. A member of Hitler's elite bodyguard company formed in 1933, Wisch was born in Schleswig-Holstein in 1907 and first saw combat in Poland as a panzergrenadier company commander. Winner of the Iron Cross 1st and 2d Class, German Cross, and Knight's Cross, he had commanded *Leibstandarte* in combat since 21 March 1943 with only a short break for medical leave in May 1944.

Leibstandarte had been suffering from serious equipment shortfalls when the invasion began. In addition to significant deficiencies in wheeled transport and half-tracks, the division had to await deliveries of additional panzers before it could be considered combat ready. On 17 June, elements of *Leibstandarte* finally began loading onto trains bound for Normandy following the delivery of fifty-three Pzkfw IVs and fourteen new Panthers. After the trains were unloaded a week later at marshaling yards west of Paris and in the vicinity of Rouen, *SS-Panzer Division 1* began road-marching to the battlefront.

The first operation conducted by *SS-Panzer Division 1* consisted of a regimental assault, under the control of *SS-Panzer Division 12,* against the village of Mouen on 28 June. The assault was only partially successful, because British counterattacks forced the *Leibstandarte* units to pull back from their newly won gains. When the remainder of *SS-Panzer Division 1* arrived to join *I SS-Panzer Korps,* it took part in fierce fighting as the British launched two major offensives (respectively code-named Operations EPSOM and CHARNWOOD) between late June and mid-July. *SS-Panzer Division 1* was relieved by *Infanterie Division 272* on 15 July. The respite proved to be brief, since *Leibstandarte* was again committed to battle when Montgomery launched Operation GOODWOOD on 18 July. *Leibstandarte* continued to man frontline defenses until it received orders to join *7 Armee.*

The other *Waffen-SS* panzer division participating in *Unternehmen Lüttich* had undergone a similar experience. Commanded by *Brigadeführer* Heinz Lammerding, *Das Reich* was not sent to Normandy as a complete unit due to severe equipment shortages. Of the 3,000 authorized trucks, only 617 were in running order on 1 June. *SS-Panzer Division 2* also lacked thirty-six Pzkfw IVs and thirty-three Panthers. On 11 June, those portions of the division capable of road-marching to Normandy were ordered to deploy to the battlefront. However, at least two panzergrenadier battalions as well as elements of the division's reconnaissance, engineer, and artillery components remained in their original assembly area until the late June-July time frame.

Rommel initially placed *SS-Panzer Division 2* in reserve, but within a few days, British attacks against various points on the front lines led to its piecemeal commitment. A *Kampfgruppe* from *Das Reich* under the command of *XLVII Panzer Korps* was committed against the Americans near Caumont, while a second *Kampfgruppe* was sent to plug a gap in the west flank of *Panzer Lehr*. During this period, Lammerding was wounded in an air attack.

On 30 June, *SS-Panzer Division 2* was transferred to *XLVII Panzer Korps*. Within a few days, however, elements of its panzer regiment were sent to defend St.-Lô against the American 30th Infantry Division and 3d Armored Division. Advancing from Periers toward Sainteny, *Das Reich* panzer crews claimed ninety-eight opposing tanks over an eight-day period. When the COBRA breakthrough occurred, the division was ordered to buy time for *LXXXIV Armee Korps* to retreat. Although the *SS* panzers saved their infantry brethren from being overrun, *Das Reich* incurred significant casualties in the process, including its second division commander, who was killed by a patrol from B/41st Armored Infantry Regiment on 28 July.

Das Reich lost 193 killed, 541 wounded, and 112 missing during the fighting that took place in late July. Although it had been rated *Kampfwert I* as late as 23 July, it had suffered heavily during COBRA. Late arrivals to the Normandy battlefront, however, made up for some of those losses. *SS-Panzer Division 2* may have lacked a significant percentage of its authorized panzers, artillery pieces, and antiaircraft guns, but it was still theoretically capable of fielding 14,500 soldiers.[35]

Standartenführer Otto Baum took command of *Das Reich* in the midst of Operation COBRA. Baum was a talented infantry officer who had served with distinction in Poland, France, and Russia. After spending several months serving as a lecturer at various *SS* schools in Germany, he originally was sent to Normandy in June 1944 to take command of *SS-Panzergrenadier Division 17,* also known as *Götz von Berlichingen* or *GVB,* when its commander was wounded. Due to a shortage of experienced *SS* commanders, Baum was transferred to *Das Reich* after it lost its commander on 28 July.

The *GVB* artillery regiment commander, *Standartenführer* Otto Binge, was chosen as temporary division commander in Baum's absence. However, Binge was rated by previous commanders as exhibiting somewhat tactically ponderous regimental leadership during the Normandy campaign since it was very different from the type of combat he had experienced in Russia. Rather than allow Binge free rein with uncertain results, *Standartenführer* Baum remained in command of both *SS* divisions.[36]

SS-Panzergrenadier Division 17 was originally activated in November 1943, but after eight months it still was not considered fully ready for combat.

Although there was a surplus of 741 enlisted soldiers at the beginning of June, *Götz von Berlichingen* lacked 40 percent of its authorized strength in officers and non-commissioned officers. Additionally, it only possessed 257 of 1,441 authorized trucks. Despite these deficiencies, *GVB* was one of the first divisions to arrive in Normandy after the Allied invasion took place on 6 June.[37]

Tough fighting against American troops resulted in the loss of 539 killed, 3,469 wounded, and 1,655 missing between 13 June and late July. Shortfalls in personnel and equipment were exacerbated by the fact that *SS-Panzergrenadier Division 17* originally lacked its engineer battalion, tank destroyer battalion, and portions of its flak battalion. Heavy losses among its infantry formations finally forced *GVB* to consolidate its panzergrenadier regiments into a single unit under *Sturmbannführer* Jakob "Jupp" Fick.[38]

During Operation COBRA, a sizable portion of *SS-Panzergrenadier Division 17* was surrounded at Coutances but eventually succeeded in breaking out despite the loss of considerable amounts of equipment. By August, *Götz von Berlichingen* was rated *Kampfwert IV*—capable only of limited defensive missions—which resulted in it being attached to *SS-Panzer Division 2*. Although its engineer battalion had rejoined in mid-July, the division still lacked an 88mm flak battery and its organic tank destroyer battalion, which was in the process of being formed at Laval in early August.[39] Soon after Baum moved over to command *Das Reich,* he ordered *SS-Panzer Division 2* to formally absorb the remnants of *SS-Panzergrenadier Division 17*.

Once the divisions slated to participate in *Unternehmen Lüttich* were chosen, the *XLVII Panzer Korps* staff began assigning each unit a specific mission. *Panzer Divisionen 2* and *116* composed the lead echelon. *Generalleutuant* von Luettwitz's division would remain south of the See River with von Schwerin's division echeloned to his right rear. Von Luettwitz originally planned to attack in two columns, with his own *Panzergrenadier Regiment 304,* augmented by *Sturmgeschütz Brigade 394,* in the north. To the south, *Panzergrenadier Regiment 2* formed the second attacking group of *Panzer Division 2*. Von Luettwitz's *Panzer Regiment 3* would support both columns, and elements of his engineer and antitank battalions would accompany each column.[40]

The terrain in the sector of *Panzer Division 116* complicated von Schwerin's mission. Le Mont Furgon, a commanding height southeast of Sourdeval, split his divisional zone of operations neatly in two. Accordingly, he planned to employ his *Panzergrenadier Regiment 60* north of le Mont Furgon while *Panzergrenadier Regiment 156* operated to the south. The tanks of von Schwerin's *Panzer Regiment 16* as well as self-propelled guns, engineers, and artillery would support both panzergrenadier regiments.

Success or failure for *Unternehmen Lüttich* would largely be determined by the ability of the leading panzer divisions to punch a hole through the American defenses. *SS-Panzer Division 1,* which would constitute the main effort of the counteroffensive, would initially remain in reserve until a gap was created. Once this occurred, *Leibstandarte* would pass through the leading echelon before proceeding west to seize the bridges at Pontaubault and Avranches.

SS-Panzer Division 2, reinforced by elements of *SS-Panzergrenadier Division 17*, would follow *Leibstandarte* as far west as St.-Hilaire-du-Harcouet. The primary mission of *Das Reich* was to capture Mortain and the surrounding high ground before moving on to seize St.-Hilaire-du-Harcouet.[41] Once it achieved that goal, *Das Reich* would orient south to protect the left flank of *SS-Panzer Division 1*.

After some deliberation, Hausser chose 1800 hours on 6 August as the start time for the counteroffensive. Although it did not become completely dark until 2300 hours, air to ground visibility decreased dramatically after 2000 hours. Hausser counted on the inability of the Allies to commit significant numbers of fighter-bombers before it became too difficult to identify targets on the ground. Given the relatively small number of American defenders opposing the panzers, he was sure *XLVII Panzer Korps* would cover most of the distance to Avranches before the following morning. Mixed in among American rear echelon units and artillery, the attacking panzers would prove difficult targets for Allied fliers. Further study by the *7 Armee* staff concluded that all of the participating panzer divisions, barring unforeseen delays, would reach their assembly areas prior to the designated start time.[42] Ultimate success, however, hinged upon von Luettwitz seizing the crossroads at Juvigny le Tertre before daybreak.

The capture of Avranches would not signal the end of the operation, for success also depended on the ability of *7 Armee* to hold the territory it had gained. Once the lines of communications for Patton's Third Army were severed, the attacking panzers would be reinforced with all available reserves to establish a strong defensive line along the See River. Hausser was sure that the American First Army would fling itself against the See River in an effort to free their trapped comrades.

XLVII Panzer Korps would also have to contend with counterattacks by Patton's Third Army. Hausser knew it would require several days of hard combat before the Third Army exhausted its available supplies within the pocket. Once the Americans had been rendered immobile by lack of gasoline, halting the Third Army drive into Brittany and southeastern France would prove to be a much more realistic task for Hausser's *7 Armee*.

The process of assembling the panzers proved to be a difficult one. Because of the lingering uncertainty about which divisions would actually participate in the counteroffensive, *7 Armee* was unable to issue orders until 4 August, which meant that *Panzer Divisionen 2* and *116* as well as *Das Reich* would have precious little time to reconnoiter the terrain or work out details such as traffic control. Most of the initial planning effort went into coordinating the relief in place that had to occur before the panzers would be able to move to their designated assembly areas. (A relief in place occurs when one military unit replaces another; however, the newly arrived unit will always occupy the same positions held by the unit it is relieving.) During the night of 4 August, *Infanterie Division 363* would replace *SS-Panzer Division 2* as well as von Luettwitz's *Panzergrenadier Regiment 304.*[43] *Panzer Division 116* was scheduled to turn over responsibility for its sector to *Infanterie Division 84.*

Other problems, infinitely more serious, also began to crop up as *7 Armee* assembled the striking force. When the initial planning for the counteroffensive began, German troops were positioned within seven miles of Avranches. By 5 August, however, *LXXXIV Armee Korps* had been pushed twenty kilometers further to the east. The attacking panzers now had to travel three times as far from their line of departure to the objective. The American advance to the east also forced *XLVII Panzer Korps* to fight for its assembly areas. *General der Panzertruppen* von Funck did not have the option of retreating to avoid a fight: *Oberst* Rudolf Christoff von Gersdorff, Hausser's chief of staff, specifically instructed von Funck to push westward rather than let the Americans overrun the *Unternehmen Lüttich* assembly areas.

In a conversation between Hausser and von Kluge on the night of 5 August, the *7 Armee* commander noted that "the aforementioned penetrations will make it more difficult to carry out the intentions of the 7th Army." Pessimism also began to seep into the *7 Armee* staff. Although *Oberst* von Gersdorff reported to *OB West* that "despite the changed condition, we are retaining the plan 'Lüttich' even though changes may be called for," he believed that a counteroffensive would not be possible if another American division was committed south of Vire.[44]

Pressure exerted on the inexperienced *Infanterie Division 84* by the American 4th and 9th Infantry Divisions forced von Funck to send *Panzer Division 116* back into the fray. Von Schwerin's division had just begun assembling near Gathemo when it received instructions to help *Infanterie Division 84.* *XLVII Panzer Korps* was also required to significantly adjust its plan to account for the unexpected commitment of *Panzer Division 116.* Plans were altered once more when *Sturmgeschütz Brigade 394* was diverted by *7 Armee* to defend supply depots located in the Foret-de-St.-Sever.[45] To compensate for this change, von Funck ordered *Panzer Division 116* to send its Panther battalion and a company of self-propelled antitank guns to reinforce von Luettwitz.

Rather than allow the tremendous offensive capability of *SS-Panzer Division 1* to remain idle during the opening phase of the counteroffensive, von Funck instructed *Leibstandarte* to send its Panther battalion, a half-track–mounted panzergrenadier battalion, and its reconnaissance battalion to reinforce *Panzer Division 2.* Von Luettwitz attached the *SS* Panthers and panzergrenadiers to his southern attack column. The *Leibstandarte* reconnaissance battalion, along with the Panthers and self-propelled antitank guns detached from *Panzer Division 116,* were used to reinforce his northern attack column.[46]

The evolving operational situation was not the only source of last-minute changes to the counteroffensive plan, as the commanding general of *7 Armee* continued to divert troops from *XLVII Panzer Korps*. In addition to siphoning off units from *Leibstandarte* and *Sturmgeschütz Brigade 394*, Hausser permitted *II Fallschirmjäger Korps* to withhold motorized artillery from *XLVII Panzer Korps*.[47] Hausser's actions exasperated von Kluge, prompting him to reexamine *Unternehmen Lüttich*. After noting that the area around Mortain was very hilly, von Kluge allowed himself to be convinced that *XLVII Panzer Korps* should avoid the avenue of approach chosen by *7 Armee*.

Based on this reassessment, von Kluge asked Hausser to consider the possibility of attacking from a position southwest of Mortain rather than to the north as planned. The *7 Armee* operations staff, who had worked closely with *XLVII Panzer Korps* to refine the scheme of maneuver, pointed out that the terrain southwest of Mortain was constricted by hedgerows and had a poor road network. The best route, which already had been agreed upon by all parties concerned, consisted of the most direct approach to the objective. It took all the persuasive powers of *Oberst* von Gersdorff to reassure von Kluge that the plan should not be changed at the last minute.[48]

In contrast to von Kluge's shifting mood, Hausser still believed that the counteroffensive had a good chance of success.[49] *Luftwaffe* representatives reassured him that three hundred fighters would provide air cover for the advancing panzers, and he was convinced that *XLVII Panzer Korps* possessed sufficient strength to overcome anticipated American resistance as it traversed the thirty kilometers to Avranches.

Furthermore, Hausser was sure the Americans would be surprised by the scope and timing of the attack. The strictest security measures were observed during the planning stages of the operation, including a total ban on radio traffic. All of the directives related to *Unternehmen Lüttich* had been delivered by messenger or sent over secure telephone lines. The supply situation was better than expected, with ample amounts of ammunition available from depots in the Foret de Mortain. In fact, Hausser was sure that the most difficult part of the operation would be holding on to Avranches once it had been captured.

CONCLUSIONS

With the attention of *7 Armee* diverted by the First Army assault on Vire, preparations for *Unternehmen Lüttich* lagged significantly behind the rapidly evolving operational situation. Consequently, the Germans were not fully prepared to conduct such a complex offensive operation on short notice. It is no wonder that motorized artillery was not dispatched to reinforce von Funck, that divisions transferred from *Panzer Gruppe West* encountered traffic jams, and that the *Luftwaffe* misunderstood their battlefield support tasks on the day the counteroffensive began.

The Avranches counteroffensive was also marked by tensions between Berlin and *OB West*. Although Hitler offered several suggestions during the planning process for *Unternehmen Lüttich,* he did not openly interfere with von Kluge's preparation for the counteroffensive. Von Kluge, however, was aware that his own concept of operations differed markedly from Hitler's, who envisioned a much larger effort involving eight of the nine panzer divisions in Normandy as well as the panzer division deploying from southern France. Von Kluge would only be able to successfully champion his own vision as long as he could guarantee that it would produce victory.

Von Kluge was painfully aware that Hitler would assume complete control if the plan developed by *OB West* failed. Convinced that his own operational abilities were superior to Hitler's, von Kluge risked placing his armies in even greater jeopardy by failing to foresee what would happen if the counteroffensive did not achieve its objectives. Not only would the Americans be alerted to German intentions, but Hitler also would undoubtedly demand that von Kluge implement the plan developed by *OKW.* Whether von Kluge could safely shift sufficient panzer divisions from the Caen sector to accommodate Hitler's concept remained to be seen.

4
First Army Moves East

As Patton's Third Army raced for distant ports on the western tip of Brittany, First Army pursued objectives closer at hand: the critical road junctions of Vire and Mortain. Vire, an ancient fortified city of approximately eight thousand inhabitants, was the center of several converging roads. Built atop high ground surrounded by farmland crisscrossed with hedgerows, the town overlooked the Vire River as well as a smaller tributary known as the Vaux de Vire. There was no doubt that the Germans intended to retain the town, and *II Fallschirmjäger Korps* feverishly prepared for house-to-house fighting as the Americans approached. On the outskirts of Vire, the Germans sited roadblocks protected by antitank guns, while artillery observers manned prominent observation points on nearby hilltops.

Mortain, a smaller town of only thirteen hundred inhabitants, represented a very different proposition for the combatants. Located on the southern flank of *LXXXIV Armee Korps,* only a few German troops were available for its defense. Detachments of *Infanterie Division 275,* augmented by a few armored vehicles from *Panzer Lehr,* manned outposts extending south to the small town of Barenton. Mortain itself was nestled at the foot of Mont Joie, known in military parlance as Hill 314. An imposing stone church, la Collegial Saint Evoult, sat squarely in the middle of the town.

The military significance of Mortain, however, was not derived from the shops, market stalls, or hotels lining the Grand Rue or from the railroad nestled in the Cance River valley. As a market and mining center, Mortain connected Vire, Sourdeval, Flers, and Domfront with the coastal city of Avranches. The road network surrounding Mortain acted as a magnet, irresistibly drawing the Americans toward the otherwise nondescript town.

Mortain was designated as the primary objective of VII Corps, which paused briefly on 31 July to reorganize in the wake of Operation COBRA. VII Corps now

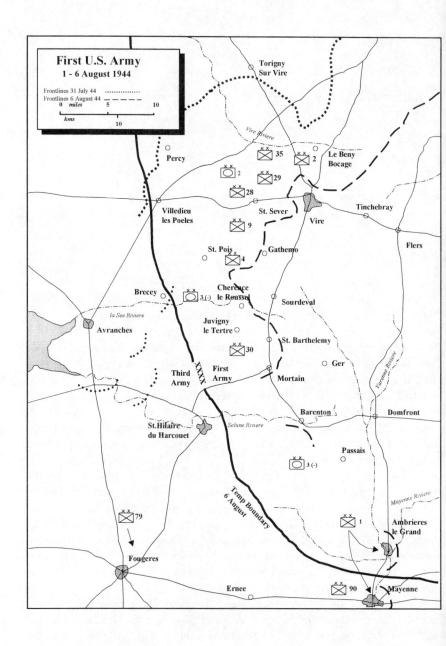

First U.S. Army
1 - 6 August 1944

Frontlines 31 July 44 ....
Frontlines 6 August 44 — — — —
0   miles   5   10
kms   10

Torigny
Sur Vire

Vire Riviere

Percy

35

2

29

28

Le Beny
Bocage

2

Tinchebray

Villedieu
les Poeles

St. Sever

9

Vire

St. Pois

4

Gathemo

Flers

Brecey

3 (-)

Cherence
le Roussel

Sourdeval

la See Riviere

Juvigny
le Tertre

St. Barthelemy

Avranches

30

Ger

Vayenne Riviere

Third
Army

First
Army

Mortain

St.Hilaire
du Harcouet

Selune Riviere

Barenton

Domfront

Passais

3 (-)

Temp Boundary
6 August

Mayenne Riviere

79

1

Ambrieres
le Grand

Fougeres

Ernee

90

Mayenne

consisted of the 1st, 4th, and 9th Infantry Divisions as well as the 3d Armored Division. The 30th Infantry Division had been detached to V Corps and the 2d Armored Division to XIX Corps. On 1 August, Collins instructed Major General Clarence Huebner's 1st Infantry Division to seize the high ground and road centers west of Mortain, while Major General Raymond O. Barton's 4th Division secured St.-Pois and the road junction at Cherence le Roussel. The 9th Division, commanded by Major General Manton S. Eddy, would attack within its zone of action to seize the high ground and road centers in the vicinity of Gathemo–Perriers-en-Beauficel–Le Mons D'Eron. Major General Leroy Watson's 3d Armored Division would provide CCA to support 1st Infantry Division and CCB to the 4th Infantry Division.[1]

The advance of the 4th and 9th Infantry Divisions would eliminate the threat of a German counterattack against Brecey while shielding Huebner's 1st Division as it moved toward Mortain. Collins had consciously weighted his main effort to the south in an effort to take full advantage of the fluid situation that existed south of Vire. After Mortain was secured, the 1st Infantry Division would be in a good position to gain contact with Third Army to the south.

The 4th Infantry Division resumed its advance to the east on 2 August, clashing with *Panzer Division 116* north of St.-Pois. Major General Barton, seeking to bypass the stubborn panzers, directed his troops to seize several hills dominating the town. The 12th Infantry Regiment was assigned the mission of capturing Hill 232 to the northeast, while the 22d Infantry Regiment attacked the town itself, supported by elements of the 8th Infantry Regiment. The remainder of the 8th Infantry was tasked to seize Hill 211 to the southeast, and CCB of the 3d Armored Division supported the assault by attacking from the south. Despite the commitment of a reinforced infantry division, however, it would take VII Corps three days to secure St.-Pois.[2]

The 9th Infantry Division advanced ten miles toward the town of Gathemo before encountering stiff resistance offered by *LXXXIV Korps* on 3 August. *Infanterie Division 353*, aided by remnants of *Infanterie Division 352* and *Fallschirmjäger Regiment 6*, slowed Major General Eddy's advance to a crawl. When the 9th Infantry threatened to overrun several supply bases located within the Foret-de-St.-Sever, the Germans reinforced *Infanterie Division 353* with the newly arrived *Sturmgeschütz Brigade 394*, diverted from its original mission of supporting *Panzer Division 2* during *Unternehmen Lüttich*.[3]

In sharp contrast to the resistance met by the remainder of VII Corps, the 1st Infantry Division encountered only scattered opposition as it headed southeast from Brecey on 2 August. Attacking with the 16th Infantry Regiment on the left and the 26th Infantry Regiment on the right, the 1st Infantry slowly made its way along narrow winding roads. Fierce fighting broke out near the village of Cuves, located five miles southeast of Brecey, when a patrol of the 26th Infantry was engaged by German troops. Supporting tanks from CCA moved forward but halted after coming under artillery fire while trying to cross a bridge over the See River.

Elements of *Sturmgeschütz Brigade 394* and *Panzer Division 116* fought hard in a vain attempt to halt the 1st Infantry Division's advance. Not until 1850 hours was CCA able to push through to the village of Juvigny le Tertre. Two miles to the east, the 18th Infantry, which had been moved up from reserve, encountered German panzers at Reffuveille. Despite skirmishing that flared up during the night, the 1st Division was firmly established astride the road running from Juvigny le Tertre to Avranches by 2300 hours on 2 August.

Early the following morning, the 1st Infantry Division began advancing once more. By 1007 hours, the 18th Infantry Regiment occupied Hill 285, located a mile due west of Mortain. To their rear, however, elements of *Panzer Division 116* reoccupied the village of Juvigny le Tertre. Several Shermans were destroyed as the 3d Armored Division tankers supported a coordinated attack by the 1/18th Infantry to retake the village.[4] When the Americans encountered stiff resistance, 3/18th was committed to reinforce the assault against Juvigny le Tertre.

By 1145 hours, the Germans in the village had been killed, captured, or driven off. The 3/18th Infantry moved east along the road connecting St.-Barthelemy with Juvigny le Tertre to occupy positions along the high ground to the northwest by 1715 hours. Although VII Corps ordered the 1st Infantry Division to hold fast at Juvigny le Tertre, Major General Huebner continued to press toward Mortain, reporting to Major General Collins at 2305 hours that his division had at least one battalion occupying Hill 314.[5]

Late the next morning, reconnaissance elements of the 1st Infantry Division entered Mortain. Moving through Mortain, the Americans clashed briefly with reconnaissance troops from *Infanterie Division 84* before securing the town. The 18th Infantry also consolidated its hold on Hill 314 with the coming of daylight. Recognizing that the imposing bulk of Mont Joie dominated the terrain for miles in every direction, Major General Collins reminded Huebner of its military significance when he told the commanding general of 1st Infantry Division, "Ralph, be sure to take Hill 314." Major General Huebner grinned before replying, "Joe, I already have it."[6]

Huebner directed Colonel George Smith's 18th Infantry Regiment to garrison Hill 314 with a reinforced battalion. The remainder of the 18th defended the town of Mortain itself as well as the high ground to the west. Because of the relatively slow progress of the neighboring 4th Infantry Division, the capture of Mortain had resulted in a salient protruding forward of the remainder of VII Corps. To guard against a counterattack from Sourdeval or Vire, Huebner positioned most of his combat power to the north and northeast. CCA and the 16th Infantry Regiment occupied positions near Reffuveille, while the 26th Infantry defended St.-Barthelemy against a German thrust from the northeast.

To safeguard his exposed right flank from German reinforcements known to be en route from southern France, Huebner instructed the 4th Cavalry Group at 1300 hours on 4 August to send one squadron to secure Barenton and le Teilleul. The 4th Cavalry Group directed the 4th Cavalry Squadron to send A Troop to

Barenton while committing the remainder of the squadron against le Teilleul. Troop A advanced toward Barenton but was stopped approximately two miles west of its objective by intense small arms fire. During a brief skirmish, the American cavalry troop took twenty Germans prisoner before withdrawing. The remainder of the 4th Cavalry Squadron, employing C Troop as an assault element, seized le Teilleul by 2230 hours after defeating a mixed German force consisting of foot soldiers from *Infanterie Division 275* supported by two tanks belonging to *Panzer Lehr*.[7]

Several hours later, Huebner ordered the 4th Cavalry Group to dispatch its remaining element, the 24th Cavalry Squadron, to seize the village of Buais, located southwest of Mortain. The 3/16th Infantry was also ordered to reinforce the cavalry in the event that they encountered serious resistance. Both American units entered the town unopposed at 1530 hours. With Buais secured, the 24th Cavalry began reconnoitering east along the Buais–le Teilleul road in an effort to gain contact with the 4th Cavalry. Later that evening, mounted patrols from both squadrons were able to make contact, successfully establishing a screen designed to protect the southern flank of the 1st Infantry Division.

Major General Collins intended to extend the southern flank of VII Corps in order to gain contact with Haislip's XV Corps in the vicinity of Mayenne. Accordingly, he provided Major General Huebner with sufficient resources to fill the gap developing between First Army and Third Army. By the evening of 4 August, the 1st Infantry Division had been reinforced to the point where it virtually amounted to a miniature corps. In addition to CCA, Major General Collins also attached Colonel Truman E. Boudinot's CCB to Huebner. The 1st Infantry Division controlled the 4th Cavalry Group, 188th Field Artillery (FA) Group, two tank destroyer battalions, and a separate tank battalion. A combat team (CT) from 9th Infantry Division would also be assigned to the 1st Division effective at 2000 hours that evening.[8] The steady stream of attachments resulted in the positioning of twelve infantry battalions, seven tank battalions, three tank destroyer battalions, three cavalry squadrons, and ten artillery battalions to defend Mortain.

With the 9th Infantry Division's drive on Gathemo temporarily stalled, Collins ordered Eddy to send his reserve regiment south to seize high ground in the vicinity of Cherence le Roussel. The regiment would then pivot to the north, threatening the Germans in the St.-Sever–Gathemo area with encirclement. By placing a regiment on their southern flank, Collins intended to force the Germans facing the 4th and 9th Infantry Divisions to retreat. His action would also serve to augment the precautions taken by Huebner to prevent a German counterattack against the northern flank of the salient at Mortain. Accordingly, Major General Eddy notified the commander of the 39th Infantry Regiment to prepare his men for a motor march to an assembly area near Juvigny le Tertre.[9] Major General Huebner, tasked by VII Corps to support the commitment of Eddy's reserve regiment, ordered CCB, 3d Armored Division, to secure the 39th's probable line of departure.[10]

The commander of the 39th Infantry Regiment, Lieutenant Colonel Van H. Bond, was a thirty-six-year-old graduate of the West Point class of 1931 who had served as the operations officer for the 9th Infantry Division until reassigned as the executive officer of the 39th in 1943. He commanded the 3/39th Infantry in Sicily, where he was awarded the Silver Star and Purple Heart. Prior to the invasion of Normandy, Bond had resumed his duties as the regimental executive officer. He took command of the regiment in July 1944 when Colonel Paddy Flint was killed in action. A "thoughtful, soft-spoken man in his 30's well versed in his profession," Bond was respected throughout his regiment.[11]

After receiving instructions to move south from Major General Eddy, Lieutenant Colonel Bond ordered his regiment to load onto borrowed quartermaster trucks. Caught up in traffic snarls, the lead elements of the 39th did not arrive at Juvigny le Tertre until 0015 hours on 5 August. By 0040 hours, however, Lieutenant Colonel Bond had successfully established radio communications with the 1st Infantry Division. Over the next several hours, Bond's remaining troops, including all three of his rifle battalions as well as the supporting 26th Field Artillery, had also shown up.[12]

Calling for a conference with his battalion commanders, Lieutenant Colonel Bond quickly issued his orders. The 39th Infantry Regiment would seize the high ground to the northeast of Juvigny le Tertre before continuing toward Sourdeval and Gathemo. Seizure of the high ground would permit Bond's supporting artillery to accurately direct fire against any German unit attempting to block the 39th's advance to the north. The key terrain feature in the regiment's zone of operations was a low hill named le Mont Furgon. The 1/39th Infantry, commanded by Lieutenant Colonel H. Price Tucker, was tasked to seize le Mont Furgon, while the 2d and 3d Battalions would secure the high ground further to the north. Departing Bond's command post, Tucker mentally prepared himself for a tough uphill fight, as he was sure the Germans had already prepared a deliberate defense atop le Mont Furgon.

Tucker gave specific directions to his company commanders upon his return. Company A, commanded by Lieutenant Ralph A. Edgar, would seize the northern half of le Mont Furgon. He would be supported by the 1st Platoon, A Company, 899th Tank Destroyer (TD) Battalion, as well as a section of heavy machine guns from D/39th Infantry. Lieutenant Charles Scheffel's C/39th Infantry would occupy the southern portion of the battalion objective. The 1st Platoon of C Company, 746th Tank Battalion, and a platoon of heavy machine guns accompanied Scheffel. Lieutenant Jack Dunlap's Company B trailed in support of the leading units.

At precisely 0800 hours on 5 August, the 1/39th Infantry began moving through the positions of CCB, 3d Armored Division, south of Cherence le Roussel. The Americans moved steadily until the leading elements reached the road running east from le Mesnil Tove to Grand Dove. Company C lost radio communications with Tucker and, unbeknownst to anyone, began veering east. As Lieutenant Scheffel's company reached a small group of stone houses known as la Helandiere, the Americans ran into a German unit moving west. C Company immediately halted as scattered shots were exchanged.

By this time, A Company had reached the eastern outskirts of Cherence le Roussel, while B Company was crossing the stream southeast of the village. Lieutenant Colonel Tucker, attracted to the sound of firing, arrived soon afterward at C Company. Quickly realizing the situation had been altered by Scheffel's chance contact, Tucker instructed Company A to halt its advance. Lieutenant Edgar's new mission would be to assume a defensive position to protect the battalion's left flank (Company A had earlier outpaced Scheffel's company, as it had faced almost no opposition).

As Lieutenant Colonel Tucker completed his reconnaissance, he realized le Mont Furgon was virtually unoccupied. In addition, C Company had obviously hit something much larger than an outpost. Tucker decided he had to scrap his original plan; a whole new approach was needed since the Germans were located east of his positions rather than to the north. Tucker quickly issued new orders to all of his company commanders: Lieutenant Dunlap's company would fill in the gap between A Company and C Company. Once B Company came on line with Company C, both would attack the German force blocking Scheffel's advance.

Meanwhile, Lieutenant Scheffel met with his attached tank platoon leader, Lieutenant Coy O. Parker. Both officers decided that the best course of action would be a combined attack. Scheffel suggested that Parker should lead off since the Germans did not seem to have any heavy weapons. The tanks would advance in a wedge formation followed by one of Scheffel's platoons, and the remaining rifle platoons would provide covering fire. Scheffel would follow on foot behind Parker's tank, directing the fire of the buttoned-up Shermans using a sound-powered phone. His intent was to overpower the Germans with a heavy volume of direct fire, driving them off the position they occupied.

On a hand signal from Scheffel, the attacking riflemen advanced at a brisk pace, firing from the hip, while 60mm mortars began dropping rounds on the German positions. The defenders initially replied to the American fire rather vigorously, but as the tanks and riflemen drew closer, their response decreased. Emboldened by the faltering return fire, Company C increased its pace of advance. Soon the Americans reached a point where it was farther to their jump-off positions than it was to their objective. There was no turning back. Rebel yells and shouting broke out as the riflemen of Company C broke into a trot.

Lieutenant Parker's platoon began pumping 75mm rounds into any position that looked as if it would offer substantial resistance to the advancing American infantry. The fire of the tanks was personally directed by Scheffel initially, then the line running from the field phone attached to the platoon leader's tank broke. By this time, however, the Germans had suffered numerous losses and began to pull back as the Americans drew closer. Lieutenant Scheffel's company overran the enemy position at the cost of only one man killed. Judging by the bodies scattered about, the Germans had suffered several dozen casualties.

Lieutenant Charles Scheffel, commander of C/39th Infantry at Cherence le Roussel. (Charles Scheffel)

Even as Company C was removing the German unit blocking their path, Company B, led by Lieutenant Dunlap, was moving up to reinforce Scheffel. When Tucker gave Company B their new orders, Dunlap's men were deployed in an approach march formation in a valley just southwest of Company C. Dunlap immediately began moving toward the sound of small arms fire. Company B came up through a wooded area on Scheffel's right flank, joining in with the attack until the Germans pulled back. As Lieutenant Scheffel consolidated his newly won gains, Lieutenant Dunlap held fast, awaiting additional guidance from his battalion commander.

C Company had advanced to a point much farther east than the rest of the 1st Battalion, and Lieutenant Colonel Tucker realized that Scheffel's company was exposed to counterattack. Although Scheffel had not made contact with the Germans, artillery observation planes could see indications of activity just north of Sourdeval. The pilots informed their parent unit, the 26th Field Artillery (FA) Battalion, that a counterattack was developing against the 1/39th Infantry. The 26th FA also asked for support in repelling the attacking Germans. The 1st Infantry Division dedicated the 957th FA Battalion to provide direct support to the 26th, while the division's remaining FA battalions also began preparing to support the 39th Infantry Regiment as needed.[13] Three missions were fired by the 26th FA and one by the 957th, dispersing several of the German units forming up to attack Tucker's battalion.[14] The 26th FA fired eleven more missions on targets that included dug-in troops, strongholds, mortars, and tanks.

The 2/39th and 3/39th Infantry had also encountered severe resistance. Attacking with I and L Companies abreast, the 3d Battalion was pinned down by fire from high ground located to its right front by 1340 hours. G Company had also received a considerable amount of tank and machine-gun fire. At 1610 hours, the 2/39th Infantry ran into a company-sized element of German parachutists.[15] By late afternoon, Lieutenant Colonel Bond's entire regiment, as well as the 4th Infantry Division to the north, were in contact with elements of *Panzer Divisionen 2* and *116*. Both von Luettwitz's and von Schwerin's troops had hastily been summoned to protect the *Unternehmen Lüttich* assembly areas from the unexpected American assault.

By 1725 hours, the 3/39th Infantry faced an assault by twenty to thirty panzers, while *Luftwaffe* fighters strafed the 2/39th command post. Low-lying cloud cover, however, delayed the employment of close air support requested by the 39th Infantry Regiment. When American planes appeared at 1955 hours, they bombed the 2/39th command post by mistake, and Bond hurriedly requested a halt to the supporting air strikes. Faced with elements of a panzer division holding the high ground northeast of Cherence le Roussel, Lieutenant Colonel Bond issued orders to consolidate in a night defensive position rather than continue the assault. Despite the significant resistance encountered during the course of the day, Bond decided to renew the assault again at daylight on 6 August.[16]

Even as Bond prepared his regiment for action, significant progress was also being made in the Vire sector. The 29th Infantry Division, supported by CCA, 2d Armored Division, had advanced along the Tessy-Vire highway to the village of Martilly, where German artillery knocked out fourteen Shermans attempting to cross a nearby bridge over the Vire River. Other elements of CCA proved more successful, however, seizing Hill 219 overlooking the center of Vire. With this initial foothold firmly secured, XIX Corps committed the green 28th Infantry Division to the fight. With Vire predicted to fall within forty-eight hours, Lieutenant General Hodges published Field Order No. 5 on 5 August calling for "First US Army to shift its advance at once from the Mortain-Vire area to secure the area Domfront–Ambrieres le Grand, relieving elements of the Third Army in the Mayenne area, and [to] be prepared for action further to the east."[17]

Lieutenant General Hodges directed XIX Corps to send Major General Edward H. Brooks's 2d Armored Division, minus CCA, on an enveloping maneuver designed to secure a line running from Ambrieres le Grand to Domfront. CCA would remain behind to support the 28th Infantry Division once the rest of 2d Armored departed. To reach Domfront, however, the 2d Armored Division would have to pass through the zone of operations of VII Corps.

First Army's Field Order No. 5 also directed VII Corps to extend south until it physically linked up with the northernmost elements of Third Army. Because the 90th Infantry Division was originally in a position to quickly seize Mayenne, Lieutenant General Bradley agreed to a temporary boundary change placing the city within the Third Army's zone. However, First Army would be required to send troops to relieve the 90th Infantry Division. As soon as this could occur, the 90th would rejoin XV Corps for the attack on Le Mans.[18] Huebner's 1st Infantry Division was the logical choice to relieve the 90th Division. Since the remaining divisions of VII Corps were still heavily engaged, First Army ordered V Corps to send the 30th Infantry Division south to relieve the 1st Division at Mortain.[19]

At 2005 hours on 5 August, VII Corps alerted the 1st Infantry Division for a move to Mayenne.[20] The order from Collins came as a surprise to Major General Huebner. While coordinating the movement of the 90th Infantry Division through his area of operations the previous day, Huebner had mentioned casually to Major General Haislip that he expected to remain in Mortain for several days.[21] Huebner had given permission for CCB, 3d Armored Division, to conduct extensive maintenance on its vehicles, and many of its tanks and half-tracks were completely disassembled. Although the order came somewhat unexpectedly, the veteran 1st Infantry Division quickly began preparing to carry out its new mission.

The relief in place between the 1st and 30th Infantry Divisions would also impact on the move of the 2d Armored Division to Domfront. The 30th would begin moving south during the afternoon of 5 August, with the move ending by the evening of 6 August. However, Lieutenant General Hodges was aware that the roads linking Vire with Mortain would not support the simultaneous movement of an armored division and an infantry division. Concerned that the Germans might gain an advantage from delaying the movement of Brooks's armor to Domfront, Hodges asked Major General Collins to consider sending a regimental combat team from either the 1st or 30th Infantry Division to hold the city until the 2d Armored arrived.

On a positive note, the 1st Infantry Division had already dispatched a task force to secure the town of Barenton. With Barenton in American hands, the 2d Armored Division would have a clear path leading to Domfront. Major General Heubner had instructed CCA to send a battalion to seize the town when the 4th Cavalry had failed to do so the previous day. Brigadier General Doyle Hickey sent Battlegroup 2, a battalion-sized element from Task Force X, to accomplish the mission. Consisting of a rifle company from Lieutenant Colonel Carlton P. Russell's 3/36th Armored Infantry Regiment (AIR) reinforced with tanks, TDs, artillery, and engineers, Battlegroup 2 departed from Reffuveille at 1630 hours on 5 August. Russell, a thirty-four-year-old graduate of Mississippi State College ROTC, had commanded the 3/36th AIR since it landed in France.

Russell's battlegroup did not make contact with German troops until it arrived at Barenton. The leading medium tank had just rounded the last curve in the road leading into town when it was fired upon. The driver of the Sherman, transferred from a tank knocked out a few days previously, reversed so quickly that his vehicle commander was thrown against the turret hatch. Clutching broken ribs, the tank commander reported that he had encountered resistance as he guided the Sherman into a concealed position just off the road.[22]

After making a quick reconnaissance, Lieutenant Colonel Russell reported to CCA that Barenton was held by one hundred German troops armed with *Panzerfaust* and supported by a self-propelled 75mm gun as well as five armored cars. A marshy streambed also lay between Battlegroup 2 and town, limiting access to a small road bridge. Convinced that the Germans had emplaced antitank guns to cover the bridge, Russell decided to wait until dark before conducting an assault on the town.[23] Brigadier General Hickey, however, did not concur and badgered Russell all afternoon about his decision. What was not apparent to Russell was the fact that Hickey was under pressure to seize Barenton quickly in order to secure the 1st Infantry Division's flank as it moved to Mayenne.

Acceding to Hickey's demands, Russell ordered his armored infantry to clear the southern approaches to Barenton before night fell. The lead rifle platoon moved out single file toward the bridge, keeping in the lengthening shadows as they advanced down the road. Lieutenant Colonel Russell accompanied his troops as they began checking the bridge for mines. A German antitank gun, spotting movement at the bridge, opened fire on the Americans at the far end. Russell watched as a shell hit in front of him, striking sparks from the blacktop road. It exploded, sending one fragment slicing through the muscle of his upper right arm. Another metal shard almost sheared off the barrel of the .45-caliber pistol in his holster. Several other men were also wounded.[24]

Russell painfully made his way back to his command post, clutching his arm to stem the flow of blood. As the medics treated his wounds, Russell briefed his executive officer and headquarters company commander on the situation. By this time, all of the other wounded had been loaded into an ambulance. Russell was placed next to the driver, who quickly made it evident that he did not know how to get back to the field hospital. Clutching a map provided by the medics, Russell guided the ambulance to the evacuation hospital, arriving just as dawn broke on 6 August.[25]

With Russell's departure, his headquarters company commander, Captain Thomas Tousey, made his way forward to the bridge. The armored infantry company commander clearly did not want to force his way into Barenton, citing the darkness, lack of information on the terrain, and uncertain situation. Although the initial probe by Battlegroup 2 had been repulsed, both men believed that Barenton would prove lightly held. They quickly decided to wait until daylight in order to fully utilize their attached tank company.[26]

Tousey returned to the command post where the executive officer of Battlegroup 2 agreed with the decision to wait until daylight. The 3/36th AIR battalion reconnaissance officer, however, suggested sending a patrol into Barenton from the west. Tousey concurred. While maintaining continuous communication via a handheld radio, the patrol entered Barenton without incident at 0700 hours, reporting that they were at a cafe in the middle of town drinking wine with three French World War I veterans. The Germans, it seemed, had pulled out during the night. Battlegroup 2, however, was unable to notify CCA that Barenton had been secured. The only radio traffic they could hear was someone talking faintly about rations.[27]

The attention of the 1st Infantry Division had been focused elsewhere as Battlegroup 2 secured Barenton. Not only was Major General Huebner required to orchestrate his division's movement to Mayenne, but he also would coordinate the relief in place with the 30th Infantry Division. In addition, the 26th Infantry Regiment and attached elements of CCA had experienced heavy artillery and mortar fire throughout the day. The activity on 5 August can be gauged by the fact that the 1st Infantry Division's artillery fired sixty-six missions, expending 1,730 rounds of ammunition. In addition to supporting the 39th Infantry, the division's guns wiped out a German convoy, knocking out twenty-three vehicles and several artillery pieces. The *Luftwaffe* was also active over Mortain that evening. Although the planes inflicted few casualties, B/1st Engineer Battalion was kept busy repairing road craters and fighting fires.

Despite intermittent interference from the Germans, the 1st Infantry Division planned on moving south at first light on 6 August. The movement to Mayenne, led by elements of CCA and the 1st Reconnaissance Troop, would take place sequentially as regiments were relieved by their counterparts from the 30th Infantry Division. Since the 16th Infantry Regiment was not occupying frontline positions, it was prepared to depart at 0600 hours. A rifle battalion from the 18th Infantry would head for Ambrieres le Grand one hour later, while the remainder of the regiment followed soon afterward. Because Major General Huebner felt that the 26th Infantry Regiment would prove to be the most difficult of his units to disengage, it would trail the remainder of the division to Mayenne. Upon arrival, however, the 26th Infantry Regiment was tasked to immediately conduct a crossing of the Mayenne River to establish a bridgehead on the east bank.[28]

As the 1st Infantry Division began moving to Mayenne on 6 August, the 39th Infantry Regiment renewed the contest for le Mont Furgon. Lieutenant Colonel Bond telephoned his battalion commanders, who dispatched runners to each company with orders to attack at 0800 hours. In the 1st Battalion sector, A and C Companies, would lead the assault while B Company remained in reserve. The assault, however, encountered a tremendous amount of direct and indirect fire almost as soon as it began.

At 0810 hours, Lieutenant Colonel Tucker radioed Bond that his men had started forward but almost immediately were pinned down.[29] C Company advanced only a short distance before the Germans forced Lieutenant Scheffel's men to seek cover. After placing four tanks on line to mass their firepower against the German defenders, Scheffel was able to seize one group of stone houses but failed to make any headway trying to gain a second cluster of buildings located further up the slope of le Mont Furgon.[30]

By 0837 hours, the 3/39th Infantry immediately to the north of Tucker's battalion also halted its advance after encountering significant resistance. *Panzer Division 116* committed *Major* Kuno von Meyer's *I Abteilung, Panzer Regiment 24,* against the attacking Americans. *Hauptmann* Klaus Hossenfelder's *Panzer Pioniere Abteilung 675* supported von Meyer's Panthers.[31] The newly arrived panzers quickly made their presence felt in the 3d Battalion sector, and several were able to edge up to a position just one hedgerow in front of the leading rifle companies before opening fire.

At 0955 hours, Lieutenant Colonel Frank Gunn's 2d Battalion reported that it could observe eight panzers in its sector.[32] Lieutenant Colonel Gunn called for artillery support before sending his attached TDs forward. A/899th TD dispatched its 2d Platoon and one section of the 3d Platoon against the German vehicles. After a ten-minute firefight, the TDs destroyed two Panthers and two Pzkfw IVs, forcing the surviving panzers to retreat.[33] None of the TDs were lost in the engagement. The 2/39th and 3/39th Infantry were both able to exploit this success by edging forward slightly.

Despite the success enjoyed by the TDs, Lieutenant Colonel Bond made the decision to halt his regiment's attack. It was obvious that his troops would not be able to secure le Mont Furgon, let alone their final objective, as long as they were opposed by elements of a German panzer division. The 3d Battalion command post was hit repeatedly by German shelling, and Company L continued to receive direct fire from the defending panzers. C Company alone had suffered three killed and twenty-three wounded. To complicate matters further, German artillery began landing in the rear of the attacking rifle battalions. Low clouds and competing priorities kept Allied airpower from the fight. Only eight P-47Ds of the 50th Fighter Group appeared that afternoon, attacking a small group of German vehicles before returning to base.[34]

The 30th Infantry Division was in reserve near Tessy-sur-Vire on 5 August when it received a memorandum from First Army stating "effective immediately,

30th Div (823d TD Bn, 743d Tk Bn, and 531st AA AW Bn atchd) is attached to VII Corps." Six truck companies would be provided by First Army to aid in moving the three rifle regiments. As soon as the trucks arrived, one regiment would move immediately. A second regiment would move during the night of 5 August, while the remainder of the 30th shifted south on 6 August. The convoys would be met by representatives from VII Corps at Percy, who would lead the 30th Division troops to Mortain.[35]

The First Army order issued on 5 August also directed that the movement to Mortain would begin no later than 1100 hours that morning. Because American infantry divisions required external assistance to conduct a motor march, the movement had to be delayed until additional trucks could be dispatched. For the movement to Mortain, each of the division's infantry regiments would require augmentation by two quartermaster truck companies. Once the movement was complete, the trucks would return to First Army control.[36]

The commanding general of the 30th Infantry Division, Major General Leland S. Hobbs, dispatched his assistant division commander to VII Corps headquarters to obtain more information on the situation at Mortain. Hobbs was a stocky, long-serving regular with closely cropped hair and a piercing glance. Commissioned in the infantry from West Point in 1915, the fifty-two-year-old Hobbs had lettered in football, basketball, and baseball. His friends at West Point included Eisenhower and Bradley. Prior to Normandy, his combat experience had been limited to a skirmish with Mexican troops at Nogales in November 1915. Although ordered to France during World War I, his overseas service had been limited to a postwar assignment with the American Expeditionary Force advanced school detachment.

Hobbs's troop leading experience was extremely limited. Between the wars, he had served primarily as an aide-de-camp to several generals, an instructor at West Point, chief of personnel in the Office of the Chief of Infantry between 1928 and 1932, as well as a brief stint as the Third Army Chief of Staff. Promoted to brigadier general in 1942, Hobbs was briefly assigned to the 80th Infantry Division as the assistant division commander. In September of that same year, he was elevated in rank to major general and given command of the 30th Division.

Brigadier General William K. Harrison, serving as the 30th Infantry Division's assistant division commander, did not get along well with Hobbs. Harrison had been commissioned at West Point in 1917 as a second lieutenant of cavalry, but their alma mater was the only thing that the two generals had in common. Major General Hobbs preferred to direct operations via telephone from the division command post. He also was prone to berate rather than encourage subordinates whom he perceived as failing to carry out an assigned mission. Harrison constantly toured the front lines to gain firsthand information and to show the soldiers that he was willing to share the dangers they faced. He would quietly counsel an officer or soldier who erred, pointing out the right way to accomplish the task. Although a fair amount of friction existed between the two general

Major General Leland Hobbs (left) with Brigadier General William K. Harrison in early 1945.
(Dwight D. Eisenhower Library)

officers, their sharply contrasting leadership traits combined to mold a division that quickly garnered a reputation for accomplishing any mission, no matter how difficult.

Small, slight, and quiet, Harrison had not participated in athletics at West Point prior to his graduation. After leaving the Military Academy, he spent World War I in both California and Texas. Assigned to the War Plans Department when war broke out, Harrison fought hard to ensure that he would not miss this conflict. He was given his brigadier's star in June 1942 and appointed as the assistant division commander of the 78th Infantry Division. At Hobbs's insistence, Harrison was reluctantly transferred to the 30th Division late in 1942.

As the 30th Infantry Division prepared to move from Tessy to Mortain, Major General Hobbs personally visited Huebner's command post to gain some insight on the terrain and tactical situation. Mindful of Huebner's need to quickly relieve the 90th Division at Mayenne, Hobbs agreed to have his division in place as soon as possible on 6 August. Although doctrine recommended that a relief should take place at night, Hobbs and Huebner agreed that the Germans opposite the 1st Division were incapable of interfering with a daylight operation.

Traffic congestion, however, resulted in the move of the 30th Infantry Division being delayed. The first convoys did not depart until 0130 hours on 6 August. Observers from XX Corps, monitoring the roads in anticipation of their own corps's movement south, had reported that "column moving south at 3 miles per hour. [Vehicles are] parked at side [of] road and moving by fits and starts. Traffic totally stopped at Brecey for periods as long as 30 minutes. Military Police at Brecey state they have orders to give priority to 30th Division until they are cleared, thereafter to give priority to 35th Division troops."[37] With convoys slowed to a crawl by the tremendous amount of American military traffic, it took an average of twelve hours to move the forty miles to Mortain.

Colonel Hammond D. Birks's 120th Infantry Regiment arrived in Mortain at 1000 hours. Birks originally enlisted in the army in 1917 during his third year at the University of Chicago. Serving in France for eighteen month, he saw extensive combat at Alsace, Die, and St.-Mihiel. After taking a competitive examination, Birks was commissioned as an infantry second lieutenant. His postwar assignments were limited to staff or teaching positions, with the exception of a year as the commander of 2/21st Infantry at Schofield Barracks and an assignment as the Fort Custer Reception Center commander in 1941. Birks, whom Harrison considered a "top-notch" commander, had led the 120th Infantry since June 1942.

Colonel Birks drove ahead of his slow-moving convoy to meet with Colonel George Smith at the 18th Infantry Regiment command post.[38] Smith informed Birks that it had been relatively quiet in the Mortain area for the past several days, with enemy activity limited to several patrol actions on the eastern slope of Hill 314. Although the Germans occasionally lobbed artillery into the town, the most notable attack occurred when *Luftwaffe* planes scattered a number of bombs on the town during the night of 5 August. The remainder of Birks's staff arrived soon afterward, establishing their own command post adjacent to Smith's.

Lieutenant Colonel Paul W. McCollum's 3/120th Infantry, serving as the regimental reserve, occupied a bivouac site near the colocated regimental command posts. As the 3d Battalion dismounted from their trucks, McCollum informed the commander of K/120th Infantry, Lieutenant Joseph Reaser, that his company was being attached to the 2/120th. Reaser's men were trucked back to Mortain, where they replaced a rifle company from the 3/18th Infantry that was occupying a wooded area on the northern slope of Hill 314.[39]

Lieutenant Colonel William S. Bradford's 1/120th Infantry occupied Hill 285, which was located immediately to the west of Mortain. Bradford was one of the two replacement battalion commanders new to the 120th Infantry. The 2/18th Infantry, previously responsible for defending Hill 285, had already departed for Mayenne. The 1st Infantry Division unit, however, had left behind several officers to orient the newly arrived battalion from the 30th Division. Bradford instructed Lieutenant Milton Smith's Company A to occupy positions on the northeastern portion of the hill. Lieutenant Murray S. Pulver's B Company, oriented southeast toward Mortain, was located south of A Company. C Company, commanded by Lieutenant Albert A. Smith, was echeloned to the rear and oriented to the southwest.

Lieutenant Pulver had the opportunity to chat with officers from the 2/18th Infantry as he surveyed his new position. They told him that even though they had not seen any German ground troops for several days, the *Luftwaffe* remained very active.[40] Lieutenant Pulver decided to use many of the emplacements constructed by the 2/18th, although he found it necessary to order additional foxholes dug in a few locations. However, Pulver felt that the farmhouse used as a command post by the departing 1st Infantry Division was too obvious a place for his own headquarters, so he told his men to establish a company command post one hedgerow behind the building.

Lieutenant Colonel Eads J. Hardaway's 2/120th Infantry was tasked with the defense of Hill 314 and the town of Mortain. Hardaway, a quiet and immensely likable man, had only recently taken command of the 2d Battalion. The trucks bearing his men halted in front of the Hotel de la Poste near the center of town, where the battalion dismounted in preparation for a steep climb up the high ground looming over Mortain. Each of the 2/120th Infantry's rifle companies assumed positions occupied by elements of the 1st Division. Lieutenant Ronal E. Woody's G Company replaced B/18th Infantry, which had been protecting an improved road that entered Mortain from the east. Lieutenant Ralph A. Kerley's E/120th Infantry relieved A/18th on the southeastern slope of Hill 314. Captain Delmont K. Byrn's Company H, laden with heavy machine guns and 81mm mortars, exchanged places with D/18th Infantry.

Lieutenant Colonel Hardaway directed F/120th Infantry, commanded by Captain Reynold Erichson, to take over roadblocks established by C/18th on the outskirts of Mortain. Captain Erichson's 1st Platoon, commanded by Lieutenant Tom F. H. Andrew, occupied a position near the monastery of L'Abbaye Blanche. The 2d Platoon, commanded by Lieutenant George A. Stewart, took over several houses vacated by a platoon from C/18th Infantry. Erichson's 3d Platoon, commanded by Lieutenant John O'Connor, headed toward la Croix des Sept Coeurs, a road junction south of Mortain.

Lieutenant O'Connor's men had perhaps the most difficult task of any element of 2/120th Infantry. Spread thin to begin with, their job was made even more difficult when the 3d Platoon was also directed to protect two 57mm anti-

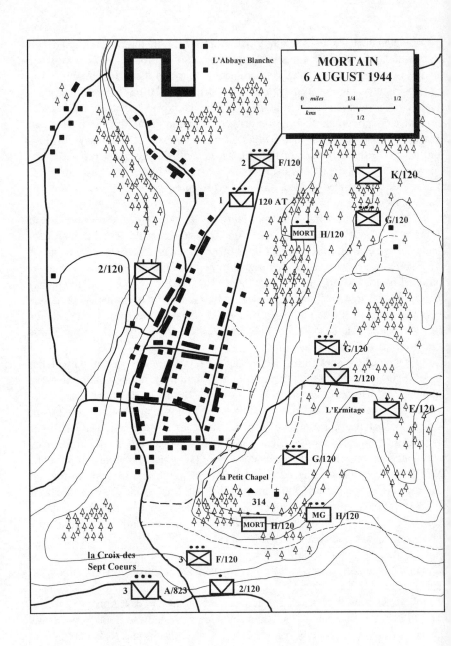

L'Abbaye Blanche

**MORTAIN
6 AUGUST 1944**

0   miles   1/4   1/2

kms   1/2

2 ⊠ F/120

⊠ K/120

1 ⊠ 120 AT

⊠ G/120

MORT H/120

2/120

⊠

⊠ G/120

⊠ 2/120

L'Ermitage ⊠ E/120

⊠ G/120

la Petit Chapel

▲ 314

MORT H/120

MG H/120

la Croix des
Sept Coeurs

3 ⊠ F/120

3 ⊠ A/823

⊠ 2/120

tank guns. Ordered to safeguard the southern approaches to Mortain as well as provide security for the battalion antitank guns, O'Connor's men were split up into squad-sized outposts. Captain Erichson did not expect his 3d Platoon to accomplish anything except provide warning of an impending attack. There were too few men available to do anything else.

Lieutenant Robert L. Weiss, a forward observer from B Battery, 230th FA Battalion, drove his jeep to the summit of Hill 314. When he arrived atop Mont Joie, he was met by Lieutenant Michael J. Walsh of the 32d FA Battalion who showed him around, pointing out several potential observation posts, including one that provided Weiss with a view of the east-west road running over the crest of Hill 314.[41] Lieutenant Walsh commented that directing fire was simple given the excellent visibility. Only the small trails that connected the main roads were hidden from view. Walsh advised Weiss to concentrate on threats originating from the east, since the view to the north was not as good.[42]

The 2/120th Infantry's headquarters company dismounted in front of the Hotel de la Poste, which served as the 1/18th's command post. Lieutenant Colonel Hardaway remarked to Lieutenant Guy B. Hagen, the battalion communications officer, that the 1st Division soldiers "sure seemed to be in a hurry to pull out."[43] The 1/18th Infantry had established their message center in the nearby la Collegial Saint Evoult. As they prepared to leave, the 1st Division troops took their switchboard and telephones but left behind the telephone wires laid to the rifle companies on Hill 314. When Lieutenant Hagen inspected the wire network, he concluded that the 1/18th might as well have taken it with them. The telephone lines were in such bad shape that Hagen knew he would have to send out wire teams to check all the connections.

As the 120th Infantry assumed responsibility for the defense of Mortain, other elements of the 30th Division began to arrive. The lead convoy of the 117th Infantry Regiment appeared in Juvigny le Tertre at 1230 hours, prepared to conduct a relief in place with the 26th Infantry. Lieutenant Colonel Walter M. Johnson commanded the 117th Infantry Regiment. A National Guard officer, Johnson had served as the regimental executive officer prior to assuming command in mid-July. Although it was rumored by some that Hobbs did not particularly care for National Guard officers, he apparently changed his mind upon discovering that few Regular Army officers could do a better job than Johnson did.

The 26th Infantry Regiment occupied a rough triangular formation, with the 1/26th occupying St.-Barthelemy, 2/26th located to the southwest where it had been tied in with the 2/18th on Hill 285, and 3/26th defending Juvigny le Tertre against an attack from the northeast. Lieutenant Colonel Robert Frankland's 1/117th Infantry would relieve the 1/26th. The 2/117th Infantry, led by Lieutenant Colonel James W. Lockett, was slated to take over the positions vacated by the 2/26th. Instead of assuming responsibility for the positions held by the 3/26th, Johnson sited Lieutenant Colonel Samuel T. MacDowell's 3/117th Infantry on high ground to the east.

Lieutenant Colonel MacDowell felt that his position was too exposed, and he was not in immediate contact with any friendly units to the north. His concerns were heightened when a local inhabitant, claiming to be the mayor of le Mesnil Tove, was brought to the 3/117th Infantry command post early that evening. The man told MacDowell that a large number of Germans were assembling in a wooded area in nearby Bellefontaine. The German unit apparently included several panzers. MacDowell passed the information up to his regimental headquarters and soon afterward received a call from division headquarters ordering him to stop spreading rumors.[44]

The men of the 1/117th Infantry marched three miles to St.-Barthelemy after dismounting from their trucks at Juvigny le Tertre. The relief went smoothly and quickly. An officer from 1/26th Infantry told Lieutenant Robert O. Murray, the 1st Platoon leader of A/117th, that "we had no trouble taking this place. You're lucky to be sent up to hold a position already taken." Captain Walter L. Schoener's C Company protected the southern approaches to the village, while Lieutenant Myrl N. MacArthur's A Company occupied the center of the battalion sector. Captain Fredolph Hendrickson's B Company was sited six hundred yards to the northwest, protecting the crossroads of la Foutelaye. Lieutenant Colonel Frankland's forward command post was located in St.-Barthelemy.

Frankland ordered each of his companies to establish a roadblock to provide warning of a German advance. One squad from A Company occupied a roadblock near the small hamlet of la Sablonniere, a thousand yards south of St.-Barthelemy. Captain Hendrickson sent his 3d Platoon, along with two 57mm guns, to the crossroads near Bois du Parc, five hundred yards northeast of la Foutelaye. C Company dispatched a squad armed with bazookas to Grande la Dainie, a collection of farmhouses near la Tête de Femme, a junction where the roads connecting Sourdeval and St.-Barthelemy with Mortain joined together.

Colonel Edwin M. Sutherland's 119th Infantry Regiment arrived at le Mesnil Adelee at 1330 hours that afternoon. A short and rather humorless officer, Sutherland had graduated from West Point in 1919. He was a Regular Army officer who served in Alaska from 1924 to 1927 and in China from 1931 to 1939. Unlike the other regimental commanders in the 30th Infantry Division, however, Sutherland had seen combat before Normandy, having spent a total of two years in the China-Burma-India Theater and the Aleutians. However, he had only commanded the 119th Infantry since 14 July.

The 119th Infantry was greeted by a small party of guides from the 16th Infantry, which had already left for Mayenne. Because the 3/16th had moved to le Teilluel several days earlier, Colonel Sutherland's regiment would only be required to occupy positions already vacated by the 1st and 2d Battalions of the 16th Infantry. This did not cause a problem, however, since the 119th also lacked a rifle battalion, having sent away the 2/119th Infantry several days previously to support the 2d Armored Division at Vire.

Colonel Sutherland positioned Major Robert Herlong's 1/119th Infantry near the small hamlet of la Blarie, a short distance from the tanks of CCB conducting maintenance outside Reffuveille. Lieutenant Colonel Courtney P. Brown's 3d Battalion settled down two miles west of Juvigny le Tertre near a tiny collection of houses known as L'Oiseliere. The forty-one-year-old Brown was the most experienced battalion commander in the 30th Division, having served in North Africa with the 1st Division. A temporary assembly area was also chosen for Lieutenant Colonel Edwin E. Wallis's 2/119th Infantry, which was expected to return within the next twenty-four hours.

Each of the rifle regiments of the 30th Infantry Division possessed a company of towed three-inch guns of the 823d Tank Destroyer Battalion. The 823d was unique in that it represented a curious step backward in American organizational development during the Second World War. The poor showing on the part of the half-track–mounted 75mm gun in North Africa, compared with the successes gained by the British who employed towed six-pounders, had convinced the Americans in late 1943 to convert twenty self-propelled TD battalions to towed guns. The towed guns were issued on a basis of one battalion per infantry division, while the self-propelled TD battalions were allocated to corps and army.

Soon after the invasion took place, it became apparent that the hedgerows, small fields, and apple orchards made Normandy a vastly different place to fight in comparison to the wide-open desert spaces of North Africa. Additionally, infantry units discovered that their organic antitank weapons, the 57mm gun and M1A1 rocket launcher, would not effectively protect them from German panzers. The 57mm gun in particular lacked the penetrating power necessary to destroy German tanks at combat ranges. Although the bazooka was capable of knocking out an opposing panzer, in the hands of unseasoned troops it often proved ineffective.

Consequently, towed TD's gravitated toward the front lines, taking over the responsibilities of divisional antitank weapons. When towed tank destroyers were employed in the front lines, their unprotected crews suffered heavy personnel losses. Towed guns also were frequently abandoned when their supporting infantry was forced to retire. The large front covered by infantry divisions normally required the deployment of all supporting TDs, which restricted antitank coverage to a thin line lacking depth. At any given point, the most that could be expected was the mutually supporting fire of two guns.

Against small attacks these tactics proved satisfactory. German armor had normally been employed only in small numbers against First Army to date, which meant that American antitank defenses in Normandy had yet to undergo a severe test. However, a postwar report noted that the lack of centralized control and defense in depth was inadequate "against the employment of large scale attacks . . . had the enemy been willing to accept losses, a fast moving hard hitting attack could have penetrated our lines at will."[45]

Captain Bruce Crissinger's A/823d TD Battalion accompanied the 120th Infantry Regiment to Mortain. Lieutenant Thomas Springfield's 1st Platoon and

Lieutenant Elmer Miller's 3d Platoon were both sent to defend the road junction known as la Croix des Sept Coeurs. Captain Crissinger's 2d Platoon, commanded by Lieutenant Francis J. Connors, was instructed to establish firing positions in support of the 1/120th Infantry on Hill 285. All three of Crissinger's TD platoons were supposed to occupy positions vacated by M-10 self-propelled guns from the 634th TD Battalion.

After looking over his assigned area, Lieutenant Springfield persuaded Lieutenant Colonel Hardaway that Lieutenant Miller's 3d Platoon would suffice to protect la Croix des Sept Coeurs. Impressed by Springfield's initiative and logic, Hardaway concurred when the TD lieutenant recommended shifting his platoon of three-inch guns to defend L'Abbaye Blanche.[46] Displacing to the north, Lieutenant Springfield's TDs halted outside L'Abbaye Blanche while their platoon leader reconnoitered the area. Although he would be required to dig in his guns, Springfield was satisfied with his new location.

B Company of the 823d TD Battalion, commanded by Captain Frank Wilts, supported the 117th Infantry Regiment. Wilts was preparing to send Lieutenant George I. Greene's 3d Platoon into St.-Barthelemy when he received orders not to move any vehicles forward of the regimental command post. The 1st Platoon of B/823d, led by Lieutenant Lawson Neel, had already occupied firing positions in support of the 2/117th Infantry. After questioning several infantry officers, Wilts learned that the Germans were dropping mortar barrages onto the road connecting Juvigny le Tertre and St.-Barthelemy. In addition to the mortar fire, two Fw-190s machine-gunned the 1st Battalion and regimental command posts. In the wake of the strafing and mortar barrages, Lieutenant Colonel Johnson made it clear that he did not want his supporting TDs knocked out while trying to enter St.-Barthelemy during daylight.

Lieutenant Greene, however, had already departed to locate positions for his tank destroyers. Although he had avoided the main road, German gunners dropped several mortar rounds near his jeep. Greene parked his jeep under cover near la Grande Dainie until the mortaring ceased. After a short pause, he directed his driver to creep along a sunken road in low gear, following it until he reached St.-Barthelemy. He was dismayed to discover that none of the positions occupied by the M-10s supporting the 1/26th Infantry would suffice for his towed TDs. Lieutenant Greene's platoon would have to remove sections of intervening hedgerows if they hoped to obtain adequate fields of fire.[47]

One example of the inflexibility that sometimes arose when organizing assets in support of infantry regiments was the attachment of C/823d TD Battalion to the 119th Infantry Regiment. Even though Colonel Sutherland's unit occupied a position far behind the front lines, Captain Samuel D. Swanson's C/823d TD was sited to cover routes leading into the 119th's assembly area. The 1st Platoon of C/823d TD was located at Reffuveille with firing positions covering the main highway running from Juvigny le Tertre, while the 2d and 3d Platoons protected its command post and headquarters company near la Derais. As a result,

Captain Swanson's TD company would be unable to provide an immediate defense against attack by German panzers.

As each infantry regiment of the 30th Division arrived, its supporting FA Battalion exchanged positions with their counterpart from the 1st Division. Although a significant portion of VII Corps artillery accompanied the 1st Infantry Division to Mayenne, the 142d FA Group, consisting of one battalion of towed 155mm howitzers, one battalion of self-propelled 155mm guns, and one battery of eight-inch howitzers, remained behind. The 30th Division also assumed control of the 26th FA Battalion supporting the 39th Infantry. Whether or not the 30th Division could effectively coordinate the use of the VII Corps FA battalions remained in the hands of wire crews who worked through the night to fix faulty telephone lines.[48]

Before the 30th Infantry Division could begin improving positions or repairing telephone lines, Major General Hobbs received a phone call from Major General Collins. The VII Corps commander was thinking of sending an infantry regiment to Passais. He also intended to transfer the 47th Infantry of the 9th Division south of Mortain where it would relieve the 4th Cavalry Group. When Collins asked Hobbs if the 30th Division could spare a regiment to send to Passais, Hobbs replied that the 119th, less its 2d Battalion, was available.

The pair then ironed out the details of the move, agreeing that the 120th Infantry would secure Mortain and Barenton while the 117th, less one rifle battalion, held St.-Barthelemy. The 2/117th Infantry would move to le Teilleul as soon as possible using transportation organic to Hobbs's division, and the 3/120th would depart for Barenton. At 0200 hours, two truck companies would meet Colonel Sutherland's 119th Infantry at Reffuveille. After the regiment loaded onto the vehicles, it would conduct a motor march to Passais. Collins expected the 119th to secure Passais no later than the afternoon of 7 August.

Major General Collins's decision to send a rifle battalion from the 30th Division to Barenton was based on inaccurate reporting. VII Corps originally reported to First Army G-2 at 1410 hours on 6 August that "our forces have outpost in town of Barenton, and enemy is maintaining an out-post just east of the town."[49] Several hours later, a liaison officer from the 6th Tank Destroyer Group informed VII Corps that Battlegroup 2 had been driven out of Barenton. In reality, Captain Tousey's unit still held the town.

Colonel Birks summoned Lieutenant Colonel McCollum to his regimental command post, where he informed him of the 3/120th Infantry's new mission. Birks told McCollum that the 30th Reconnaissance Troop would guide his battalion to Barenton. The 3d Platoon of the 120th's antitank company and Company B of the 743d Tank Battalion would also be attached to the 3/120th Infantry. Birks instructed McCollum to make sure that an advance party arrived outside Barenton before darkness. As soon as the remainder of the battalion arrived, McCollum would drive out the Germans and secure the town.

Colonel Birks had little or no information to pass on concerning the strength or disposition of the 3d Armored Division units in the Barenton area. Since he would lose his regimental reserve when the 3d Battalion departed, he directed the 1/120th Infantry to provide a rifle company to replace the 3/120th Infantry. Lieutenant Colonel Bradford chose C/120th Infantry, which departed Hill 285 to take up positions near Colonel Birks's headquarters.

Upon leaving the regimental command post, McCollum ordered his battalion operations officer to lead a small advance party to Barenton. McCollum also informed his operations officer that the remainder of the 3d Battalion, less Lieutenant Reaser's Company K, would follow the lead element within the next two hours. The advance party would consist of the 30th Reconnaissance Troop, 1/120th Infantry, and the 120th's regimental intelligence and reconnaissance (I&R) platoon. The 230th FA Battalion would provide transportation for the rifle company. As soon as the rifle company finished boarding their trucks, the advance party left for Barenton.[50]

By 2000 hours, the 3d Battalion advance party began moving to Barenton. Thirty minutes later, however, nine German fighters strafed the American vehicles. Rockets screamed earthward, destroying four trucks and damaging several others. The attack killed five soldiers and wounded forty-eight others. The 1st Infantry Division also drew the attention of the *Luftwaffe* to the Mortain area. At 1600 hours, thirty to fifty *Luftwaffe* fighters attacked several 1st Division convoys. Accompanying antiaircraft units claimed five German fighters shot down.[51]

The delay created by the strafing attack did have one bright spot: the Shermans of Lieutenant Frederick Fleming's B/743d Tank Battalion were able to link up with the advance party as it was reorganizing. The convoy finally began moving again, arriving outside Barenton at 2300 hours, where they were surprised to discover the Headquarters Company of 3/36th AIR. The 3d Armored Division troops, however, were unable to provide the new arrivals with a clear picture of the situation. Lacking such information, Lieutenant Colonel McCollum still assumed he would have to fight for Barenton.

At 0130 hours, the trucks carrying L/120th Infantry arrived. Lieutenant Colonel McCollum had decided to isolate Barenton before attacking the town with his attached tanks. The rifle companies would establish roadblocks to the east and west of town. Both companies began moving out at 0300 hours, with Company L encountering only slight resistance as it moved to its objective. A platoon from Company I, however, was involved in a prolonged firefight with German troops who finally pulled back at dawn, leaving behind numerous casualties.

At 0600 hours, the remainder of 3/120th Infantry, spearheaded by B/743d Tank Battalion, attacked Barenton from the south. The tanks of Lieutenant Peter Henderson's 2d Platoon, accompanied by engineers, led the assault. Henderson's tanks moved forward until they encountered a makeshift obstacle blocking a fording site south of town. The engineers dismounted, inspected the logs forming the barrier, and then returned to inform Henderson that the roadblock did not appear to be mined.

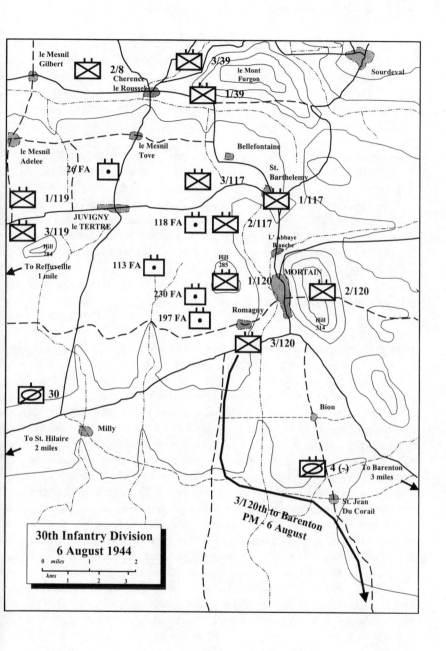

le Mesnil
Gilbert

2/8

Cherence
le Rousselay

3/39

le Mont
Furgon

Sourdeval

1/39

le Mesnil
Adelee

le Mesnil
Tove

Bellefontaine

26 FA

St.
Barthelemy

3/117

1/119

1/117

JUVIGNY
le TERTRE

118 FA

2/117

L' Abbaye
Blanche

3/119

Hill
284

113 FA

Hill
285

To Reffuvelle
1 mile

MORTAIN

1/120

2/120

230 FA

197 FA

Romagny

Hill
314

3/120

30

Bion

To St. Hilaire
2 miles

Milly

4 (-)

To Barenton
3 miles

St. Jean
Du Corail

3/120th to Barenton
PM - 6 August

30th Infantry Division
6 August 1944

0   miles   1   2

kms   1   2   3

Lieutenant Henderson's tank moved forward, pushing the logs aside. The second tank in Henderson's platoon bypassed the demolished obstacle before starting up a dirt trail. There was a terrific crash as four mines exploded simultaneously under the Sherman, severing both tracks and cracking the hull. Henderson, agitated to find mines where he had been assured none were located, ordered the engineers to sweep the road again. Six more mines were defused before the tanks could resume their advance.

Lieutenant Colonel McCollum, frustrated by the delay encountered by B/743d Tank Battalion, ordered both of his rifle companies to immediately send a platoon into town. As the U.S. troops made their way cautiously into the center of Barenton, they captured several German stragglers. When B/743d Tank Battalion finally breached the obstacle, the Shermans surged into the town square to meet the waiting infantry, where Lieutenant Colonel McCollum ordered Lieutenant Fleming to send a platoon of Shermans to reinforce each infantry company.

Lieutenant Henderson's platoon continued moving slowly north until it reached the edge of Barenton. On the outskirts of town, Henderson's tank ran into a German Pzkfw IV from *Panzer Lehr.* Both vehicles exchanged fire at a range of not more than thirty yards. Startled by a target that completely filled their respective sights, both gunners missed. Henderson quickly backed down the road, pulling into a sunken lane. The Pzkfw IV also retreated, with its crew tossing antitank mines that had been piled on the front fender into the road. Reporting his encounter to Lieutenant Colonel McCollum, Henderson was ordered to establish a roadblock. McCollum also promised him assistance in the form of an 81mm mortar section, a 60mm mortar section, and a heavy machine-gun section.

Soon afterward, Lieutenant Henderson heard trucks driving toward town. Although the vehicles were hidden from view, he could distinctly hear the sounds of their motors. Each truck halted for a moment or two before the clashing of gears could be heard as they crossed a field to the west of Henderson's position. Henderson ordered the mortar section supporting his tanks to engage the Germans while he sent a runner back to find an artillery observer.

Drawn by the noise of the mortar fire, an observer from the self-propelled howitzer battery supporting Battlegroup 2 appeared. After receiving an update from Henderson, the forward observer directed several volleys at the German troops.[52] The German unit, disorganized by accurate shelling, hurriedly pulled back. Oddly enough, both American units occupying Barenton continued to ignore the presence of the other. The town would remain in American hands for the time being, but in Mortain that same issue would soon be very much in doubt.

CONCLUSIONS

First Army had done a credible job maintaining pressure on the Germans as Patton's troops surged through Avranches. Intent on widening the Avranches corridor, VII Corps in particular had significantly disturbed German preparations as it moved eastward. Elements of the 9th Infantry Division, for example, forced *XLVII Panzer Korps* to commit troops in defense of the *Unternehmen Lüttich* assembly areas. Although the Germans eventually halted VII Corps, they only did so after surrendering a significant amount of territory and suffering considerable casualties. VII Corps also gained key terrain astride the German line of departure when it captured the town of Mortain.

However, First Army had failed to unhinge the defensive line reestablished by *7 Armee*. With the situation temporarily stabilized, the Germans were able to successfully shift a number of panzer units to conduct a counteroffensive aimed at the juncture of the First and Third Armies. Allocating sufficient panzers to the operation, however, came at a tremendous cost in tactical and operational flexibility. Any opportunity for *7 Armee* to create tactical reserves vanished when *XLVII Panzer Korps* was pulled out of the line. Although they were seeking to achieve a decisive victory, the Germans inadvertently created the same precarious tactical situation that existed in the *7 Armee* prior to Operation COBRA: the lack of sufficient reserves to counter an American penetration of their defensive line.

Hausser had to achieve success at Avranches in order to force First Army to divert a significant portion of its combat power from the weakening front held by *LXXXIV Armee Korps* south of Vire. If the Avranches counteroffensive failed, Hausser could expect to find himself threatened with an American breakthrough north of Mortain. The panzer divisions massed to recapture Avranches could find themselves too far out of position to quickly react if this worst-case scenario occurred.

5

The Counteroffensive Begins

By evening of 6 August, *XLVII Panzer Korps* was still unable to assemble the units designated to take part in the counteroffensive, due to the unspectacular, yet unrelenting, advance of Hodges's First Army. Under strong pressure from the Americans, *II Fallschirmjäger Korps* refused to detach motorized artillery to *XLVII Panzer Korps*, feeling that the situation at Vire was too serious. Although *Panzer Divisionen 2* and *116* disengaged as planned, both units were forced to recommit their troops against the 39th Infantry Regiment at Cherence le Roussel.

Von Kluge also experienced great difficulty providing Hausser with troops and equipment from outside *7 Armee*. Allied aerial interdiction significantly delayed troop movements from other sectors in France. Von Kluge originally hoped to include *Panzer Division 9* in the counteroffensive against Avranches. However, its lead regiment encountered Huebner's 1st Infantry Division at Mayenne shortly after midnight on 6 August. The realization that a German panzer division was nearing Mayenne attracted the attention of Haislip's XV Corps. *Panzer Division 9*, along with the remainder of *LXXXI Armee Korps*, was quickly involved in intense fighting.

Units shifted from *Panzer Gruppe West* also encountered significant problems. *SS-Panzer Division 1* was held up by heavy traffic as it tried to link up with *XLVII Panzer Korps*. The SS panzers were forced to compete for road space and assembly areas with logistical convoys, medical units, and other combat elements of *7 Armee*. By 1630 hours, *SS-Brigadeführer* Theodor Wisch was forced to report that his Panther battalion, a company of Pzkfw IVs, and the divisional reconnaissance would be a few hours late; however, they would arrive that evening. The Panthers would require maintenance and refueling at the completion of the seventy-kilometer road march. The rest of his division would not arrive until the night of 7 August.[1]

General der Panzertruppen von Funck grew angrier as more problems arose.

In addition to the tardy appearance of *SS-Panzer Division 1,* von Luettwitz telephoned *XLVII Panzer Korps* to complain that he had not received von Schwerin's Panther battalion. This claim was based on inaccurate information, but von Funck accepted it without question. In reality, the Panthers had arrived at *Panzer Division 2* late that afternoon.[2] Von Funck telephoned Hausser to ask permission to relieve von Schwerin.[3] Although Hausser sympathized, he was unwilling to make another change in a plan at literally the eleventh hour. Hausser's only concession was to grant von Funck permission to delay the counteroffensive by two hours to ensure that the Panthers of *SS-Panzer Division 1* had sufficient time to perform maintenance.

Hausser tried to reassure von Funck by noting that the loss of time that evening could be made up by foggy conditions the following morning. In spite of the delays and missing units, *Unternehmen Lüttich* would be executed. As for the matter of von Schwerin's alleged disobedience, the matter was dropped for the time being. This incident, however, served to illustrate the depth to which paranoia and fear of Hitler had permeated the senior leadership of the German army.

At 2200 hours, Hausser received another phone call from von Funck, who stated that he wanted to postpone the entire attack. Hausser exclaimed that this was "utter madness" and reminded von Funck that it was approaching H-hour even as they spoke. Von Funck went on to explain that the lead elements of *SS-Panzer Division 1* were still six miles short of the start line; only its divisional reconnaissance battalion and one company of Pzkfw IVs had arrived. Furthermore, the *Leibstandarte* Panther battalion would appear even later than originally thought due to "mistakes by the lower command . . . [it] would not be ready for action before 2400 hours."[4]

When the Panthers finally arrived, they created a traffic jam that affected vehicles from *Panzer Division 2* and *SS-Panzer Division 2* moving out of their assembly areas in preparation for the attack. Between the traffic snarls and maintenance requirements for the Panthers, the advance of the southern column of *Panzer Division 2* was held up for five hours. The northernmost elements of *SS-Panzer Division 2* experienced similar delays. Concerned that the sound of tank engines might carry over to the American lines, von Luettwitz ordered his artillery to mask the noise of milling panzers by shelling St.-Barthelemy.

The Allied top-secret signal intercept and decoding facility—ULTRA, located at Bletchley Park in England—was unable to provide early warning of the German counteroffensive. The sophisticated decoding machines provided a wealth of important data that paid significant dividends in Normandy, but on this occasion German security measures, including complete radio silence, effectively prevented the Allies from learning about *Unternehmen Lüttich* until too late.

The Americans only gained their first clue of the impending assault after *SS-Panzer Division 2* violated radio security. *Das Reich* sent out several requests for air support on 6 August before the counteroffensive actually took place. The first message, dated 1400 hours, requested "night fighter operations for protection of own attack over area Saint Clement to Saint Hilaire and day fighters on seventh over same area." The second specifically mentioned that *Das Reich* would launch "at 2030 hours [an] attack on Mortain and [then] thrust onwards to St. Hilaire. [Request *Luftwaffe*] supporting attack by bombs on Notre Dame until 0001 hours and by holding down Allied batteries firing west of line Notre Dame to Bellefontaine."[5]

ULTRA dispatched a warning to Lieutenant General Bradley soon after the second message was decoded. For reasons of security, however, only the vaguest of details could be related to the lower-level American commanders. The Germans, strangely enough, mistakenly believed their opponents knew about the counteroffensive. The *7 Armee* operations journal recorded at 1720 hours on 6 August that "the heavy attacks on *LXXXIV Korps* seem to be due to the fact that the enemy has received information about our plans in regard to Lüttich."[6]

It was not until 0011 hours on 7 August that the Americans possessed an indicator of the actual scope of the counteroffensive. This time a signal from *Jagdkorps 2* was intercepted, stating that "7 Army to attack from one eight through nought hours sixth with strong forces of five panzer divisions from area Sourdeval-Mortain toward the west."[7] Four hours later, a message from *XLVII Panzer Korps* was intercepted, noting that the objective of the counteroffensive was "to cut off the Allies, who have broken through to the south, from supply base and effect junction with the coast." By 0400 hours on 7 August, 12th Army Group possessed a complete picture of *Unternehmen Lüttich*.[8]

At the tactical level, this information had little or no impact. At 0010 hours on 7 August, First Army warned VII Corps that the Germans were preparing to counterattack, prompting Major General Collins to pass on the message to each of his divisions. The 30th Infantry Division operations journal entry at 0038 hours on 7 August recorded that "an enemy counterattack was expected in the vicinity of Mortain from the east and/or north within the next twelve hours." Collins also directed the 30th Division to suspend movement of the 119th Infantry until 1000 hours, move a rifle battalion to le Teilleul, and reinforce Hill 314.[9] However, only one of the three regimental S-3 journals contains any mention of a German counterattack.[10] For most of the Americans at Mortain, the information came too late to be of any use.

SS-Panzer Division 2 and its attached battlegroup from *SS-Panzergrenadier Division 17* fired the opening shots of the battle. *SS-Panzer Division 2* employed three columns in its initial assault. The northernmost column consisted of *Sturmbannführer* Otto Weidinger's *Der Führer (DF)* panzergrenadier regiment. Weidinger's mission was to secure the high ground north of Mortain while maintaining contact with *Leibstandarte* as it moved toward Avranches. Although he received an assault gun company to reinforce his regiment, Weidinger did not believe he possessed adequate resources to complete his assigned task.

Der Führer consisted of only two panzergrenadier battalions rather than the three that originally had been authorized. *I Abteilung* had been broken up to provide replacements for the other panzergrenadier battalions. Weidinger's strongest unit, *III Abteilung DF,* commanded by *Hauptsturmführer* Heinz Werner, would lead the assault, with *Hauptsturmführer* Herbert Schulze's *II Battalion* operating in support.

The southernmost assault column of *Das Reich* was composed of elements of *Obersturmbannführer* Guenther Wisliceny's *Deutschland (D)* panzergrenadier regiment. Wisliceny's regiment represented the main effort of *Das Reich. I Abteilung* had the mission of securing the town of Mortain itself, while *II Abteilung D* would capture the village of Romagny to the south. Since the east-west roads passing through Mortain offered easy access to mounted troops, the bulk of the twenty-six tanks belonging to *SS-Panzer Regiment 2* would be committed in Wisliceny's regimental sector.

Sturmbannführer Ernst August Krag's *SS-Panzeraufklärungs Abteilung 2* would be operating south of Wisliceny's *Deutschland* panzergrenadier regiment. His unit was tasked to secure the undefended gap that lay between Mortain and Barenton as well as prevent any attempt by the Americans to threaten the southern flank of *Das Reich. SS-Panzeraufklärungs Abteilung 2* would accomplish this by securing blocking positions between the villages of Milly and Fontenay. If attacked by a sizable American force, Krag was assured he would receive reinforcements from the *Deutschland* panzergrenadier regiment as well as *SS-Panzer Regiment 2.*

SS-Panzergrenadier Division 17, attached to *Das Reich,* arrived in its assembly area as planned two thousand yards east of Hill 314. One panzergrenadier battalion, however, had remained in Vire to assist *II Fallschirmjäger Korps.* The remaining units of *SS-Panzergrenadier Division 17* were reorganized into two ad hoc formations: *Kampfgruppe Fick,* which consisted of several understrength infantry battalions, some engineers, and the divisional reconnaissance battalion, and *Kampfgruppe Ernst,* which was composed of divisional antiaircraft and artillery units. Because most of the division's guns had been lost in previous battles, *Kampfgruppe Ernst* boasted a significant number of artillerymen fighting as infantry. *SS-Panzergrenadier Division 17,* reinforced by a company of assault guns provided by *Das Reich,* expected to quickly secure Hill 314.

SS-Panzergrenadier Division 17 was also assigned to provide a third battle group commanded by *Hauptsturmführer* Karl Ullrich of *II Abteilung, SS-Panzergrenadier Regiment 37,* to reinforce the efforts of Weidinger's *Der Führer* regiment. *Kampfgruppe Ullrich* was tasked to secure Hill 285 northwest of Mortain, and eight Pzkfw IVs were detached from *SS-Panzer Regiment 2* to support it.[11]

When *Sturmbannführer* Weidinger's *Der Führer* regiment neared its line of departure at 2200 hours, it found the roads clogged with panzers belonging to *SS-Panzer Division 1.* Since the *Leibstandarte* column had a higher movement priority, Weidinger's troops were forced to hold in place until the route was cleared. By the time this occurred, Weidinger's men had been delayed several hours, so he ordered a mounted attack to make up for lost time.[12] With *Obersturmführer*

Harald Scholz's *9 Kompanie* in the lead, the half-tracks of *III Abteilung* began moving slowly toward the tiny village of L'Abbaye Blanche.

The remainder of *Das Reich* began its assault shortly after midnight on 6 August. The attackers, with the exception of Weidinger's stalled *Der Führer* regiment and Krag's reconnaissance battalion, led with dismounted infantry followed at a distance by supporting half-tracks and panzers. Although this tactic resulted in a fairly slow initial rate of advance, it enabled *Das Reich* to gain a measure of surprise in many cases, since the approach of a group of foot soldiers was considerably more stealthy than that of an armored column. As Wisliceny's *Deutschland* regiment began moving west, it encountered the American troops defending la Croix des Sept Coeurs.

Lieutenant Elmer Miller's TD platoon had completed emplacing their three-inch guns near la Croix des Sept Coeurs before night fell on 6 August. Occasional firing had broken out to the south as the sky began to darken. Sporadic artillery also began landing in the town of Mortain, setting one house on the southern outskirts afire. The gunfire grew in intensity until midnight, when two American infantrymen walked up the road toward Staff Sergeant George Wichterich's gun. The infantrymen told the TD crew to get ready for a German attack. Private First Class Blaine Beebe, manning a .50-caliber machine gun sited to defend Wichterich's three-inch gun, pulled the bolt back to check the ammunition feed once more. Beebe was unsure if the warning was genuine or exaggerated.[13]

The warning proved prophetic. Less than an hour later, the leading elements of *Obersturmbannführer* Wisliceny's *II Abteilung* appeared. Three soldiers from the TD platoon's security squad were manning an outpost across the road from Staff Sergeant Wichterich's gun when a grenade landed nearby. All three Americans threw themselves flat to escape the blast, but shrapnel wounded one of the men. A German machine gun located in a nearby grove of pine trees also opened fire, directing a stream of bullets at Wichterich's three-inch gun.

Private Robert C. Clark was manning a .50-caliber machine gun when the shooting started. He replied immediately, emptying two boxes of ammunition in a few seconds at the muzzle flash of the opposing automatic weapon. He ceased shooting only after the Germans had retreated.[14] Following the firefight, Staff Sergeant Wichterich rendered a report on the encounter to Lieutenant Miller. Much to Wichterich's dismay, Miller appeared to be unconcerned about the incident.

Employing infiltration tactics to bypass la Croix des Sept Coeurs, the dismounted elements of *II Abteilung D* continued toward Romagny, while *I Abteilung* skirted the base of the southwestern slopes of Hill 314 heading for the town of Mortain. Hearing the sounds of small arms fire coming from la Croix des Sept Coeurs, Captain Erichson sent his company executive officer to alert his 3d Platoon, who were manning a nearby roadblock. The executive officer arrived just as *I Abteilung D* overran the position. With the exception of six men, the entire 3d Platoon of F Company, including Lieutenant O'Connor and the executive officer, was either killed or captured.

Kampfgruppe Fick began its attack against the 2/10th Infantry on Hill 314 shortly after midnight. The Germans bumped into an American outpost that opened fire after the leading elements of the *SS* had passed its location. Most of the panzergrenadiers composing the point element of *Kampfgruppe Fick* were shot down from behind before they could react. Rather than incur additional casualties, *Sturmbannführer* Fick sent a dismounted reconnaissance company along the base of the southern slope to assail the defenders from the rear. The remaining elements of the German battlegroup headed for the northern outskirts of Mortain.[15]

Kampfgruppe Fick launched an attack against G Company at 0220 hours. Lieutenant Ronal Woody had no warning that an assault was about to occur until the Germans began firing from a nearby wooded area. After spraying G Company with machine-gun fire, the *SS* advanced, screaming "Heil Hitler" at the top of their voices.[16] The Americans fired back furiously, forcing their attackers to seek cover. Despite the fierce resistance, the *SS* troops continued to work their way forward in short rushes. Several of G Company's outposts were overwhelmed. Having failed to knock out G/120th Infantry with a direct assault, small groups of *SS* began infiltrating around the flanks of the American unit. Although G Company continued to offer stiff resistance, the Germans penetrated the widely separated rifle platoons protecting the center of the 2d Battalion perimeter.[17]

The flanking maneuver by *Kampfgruppe Fick,* consisting of *Untersturmführer* Kuske's *3 Kompanie* of *SS-Panzeraufklärungs Abteilung 17,* was able to launch a surprise foray against H/120th Infantry. The American heavy weapons company was at a disadvantage because it was arrayed to provide support to the rifle companies, not repel a direct assault on its own position. In bitter hand-to-hand fighting, the Germans succeeded in overrunning the H Company mortars and company command post. Captain Byrn led his headquarters personnel west to safety. A counterattack by a rifle platoon of G Company failed to dislodge the Germans from the H Company positions.[18]

Soon after H Company was overrun, Lieutenant Colonel Hardaway reported to the regimental command post that heavy firing had broken out near K Company. Several German tanks were also probing the defenses of Lieutenant Ralph Kerley's E/120th Infantry. Additionally, the 2d Battalion antitank platoon had at least one 57mm gun knocked out. Realizing that the 2/120th's situation was becoming more serious by the minute, Colonel Birks decided to commit his regimental reserve.

At 0235 hours, Birks notified Lieutenant Albert Smith to prepare his company for movement into Mortain. C Company's mission was to repel the counterattack directed against Hill 314 and restore the defensive perimeter of the 2/120th Infantry. At 0250 hours, Lieutenant Colonel Hardaway dispatched an officer to guide C Company to his command post at the Hotel de la Poste. As they waited for a guide to arrive, the regimental operations officer briefed Lieutenant Smith as more reports came in over the radio.

Until C Company arrived to bolster his defenses, Lieutenant Colonel Hardaway intended to employ his own headquarters personnel to defend Mortain. Sergeant Frank Pruitt of the 2d Battalion communications section was ordered to take his men to the battalion command post at the Hotel de la Poste, where he was informed that his new mission was to protect the 2/120th Infantry headquarters. The officer charged with establishing the defense assigned a street to Pruitt's section, which was divided up into three-man teams. The men were instructed to shoot anyone they saw in the street because no Americans were supposed to be moving around in the open before daylight. The officer told Pruitt's men to remain in place until morning, at which time he would be come back with further orders.[19]

As Wisliceny's *I Abteilung* reported it was approaching Mortain, *Das Reich* started shelling the center of the town. Single artillery rounds began striking near la Collegial Saint Evoult. The incoming artillery fire picked up in intensity, with rounds landing in the northern portion of town. The 1st Platoon of F Company, led by Lieutenant Tom Andrew, was forced to shift its positions. The men sprinted across the street to begin digging foxholes near Mortain's town cemetery. As shells began landing near the cemetery, the blasts blew the lids off several crypts and toppled headstones.[20]

Shortly before 0330 hours, C/120th Infantry began moving toward the 2/120th command post in Mortain. The commander of F/120th Infantry, Captain Reynold Erichson, arrived at the Hotel de la Poste soon afterward. Erichson informed Hardaway that his 3d Platoon roadblock south of Mortain had probably been overrun. The loss of the roadblock exposed both the southern flank and rear of the 2/120th to attack. When C Company arrived moments later, Hardaway immediately directed Lieutenant Smith to send his 3d Platoon with Captain Erichson. Lieutenant Smith was also ordered to dispatch his 1st Platoon to reestablish a roadblock on the southern outskirts of Mortain. The remainder of C Company would occupy a position on the western outskirts of town as Hardaway's battalion reserve.[21]

After a quick orientation, Erichson led Lieutenant Peyton Thompson's 3d Platoon up the western slope of Hill 314. Upon reaching the crest, Erichson instructed Thompson's lead scouts to turn left along a trail leading to K Company. The morning was still very dark and misty. The lead scout, Private John D. Haynes, encountered a group of *SS* infantry. The Germans opened fire, hitting Haynes in the thigh. The American platoon took up firing positions along the hedgerow as several men rushed forward to drag Haynes to safety.

After a few minutes of indecisive volleying, the German fire intensified, convincing Captain Erichson that his small group faced superior numbers, so he ordered the platoon from C Company to fall back. Cut off from the trail they had originally taken, Erichson led Lieutenant Thompson's platoon down a one-hundred-foot sandstone cliff. At the bottom of the cliff, the men looked up in amazement to discover that Private Haynes was still with them.[22]

The assault mounted by *Das Reich* was not confined to the town of Mortain and Hill 314. *Kampfgruppe Ullrich* was not affected by the traffic jam that delayed the northern wing of *SS-Panzer Division 2,* and it threaded its way slowly along trails and secondary roads. Guided by two French civilians, inhabitants of the local area, *Kampfgruppe Ullrich* penetrated the 120th Infantry Regiment's defensive line without being detected. A brush on the northern outskirts of Mortain with a platoon of 57mm guns from the 120th Antitank Company resulted in the American position being overrun. By 0400 hours, *Kampfgruppe Ullrich* was nearing Hill 285 located northwest of Mortain.

The first indications of an attack on Hill 285 came when A/120th Infantry reported hearing panzer engines at 0440 hours.[23] Continuing west, the German column encountered a roadblock manned by B Company. When the roadblock challenged two French civilians walking in front of a tank, the column halted. Three Americans walked toward the idling vehicle. The French couple explained that they were guiding a "lost" vehicle back to the American lines, while a German machine-gun crew worked their way into a field behind the tank. Resting their MG-42 on a fence, the Germans opened fire, killing all three of the Americans standing in the road. The soldiers manning the roadblock fired back, hitting both of the French civilians.[24]

The Americans scattered in an attempt to escape the machine gun, which now turned its attention to the roadblock itself. The majority of the men, however, were killed or captured.[25] Private Harold Chocklett was able to make his way to Lieutenant Pulver's command post to report what was happening. After listening to Chocklett, Lieutenant Pulver asked him to return to the roadblock to see what was happening. Hesitating for a moment, Chocklett ran off into the fog, heading toward the attacking Germans. Pulver sent another man to warn the rest of the company just as he was told that the Germans were approaching the B Company command post.

Soon after *Kampfgruppe Ullrich* overran the roadblock, part of the attacking column swung north to assault Lieutenant Milton Smith's A/120th Infantry. The Germans surged among the A Company positions, taking six prisoners and inflicting numerous casualties before being driven back.[26] The bulk of *Kampfgruppe Ullrich,* however, concentrated their assault on Lieutenant Pulver's B Company. A mortar shell disabled his radio soon after he informed Lieutenant Colonel Bradford that B Company was under attack. Direct fire also began to slam into the farmhouse near Pulver's dugout, knocking pieces off the roof.[27]

First Sergeant Reginald Maybee handed a bazooka to his company commander as the sound of approaching tank engines grew louder. The B/120th command group crouched behind a stone wall as a Pzkfw IV loomed out of the fog. Waiting until the panzer was ten yards away, Pulver fired the bazooka. The rocket hit the vehicle's turret, rocking the Pzkfw IV to a sudden stop. Although the panzer's engine continued turning over, the explosion killed or wounded all of its occupants.[28]

A dozen *SS* men following the panzer charged forward, yelling "Amerikaner Kamerad."[29] Lieutenant Pulver was surprised by the sudden appearance of Germans emerging from behind a hedgerow he thought was still defended by his 2d Platoon. Pulver fired his carbine at the advancing *SS*, an act that quickly galvanized the other men accompanying him into action. In seconds, the Germans were sprawled motionless or writhing in pain on the ground. None of the Americans were injured in the brief, one-sided exchange. With his command post threatened by German infantry, Lieutenant Pulver decided to withdraw several hundred yards to a safer location.

While the clash at Pulver's command post succeeded in gaining time for B/120th Infantry to establish a new defensive line, the respite proved to be a short one. During the lull, the TD platoon on Hill 285 peered through the gray mist, hoping that the sound of small arms fire would not mask the noise of approaching tanks. When the fog began clearing around midmorning, the crew of one three-inch gun spotted two Pzkfw IVs moving toward B Company's perimeter. The TD fired two rounds, both of which penetrated the frontal armor of the leading panzer. The second Pzkfw IV was knocked out soon afterward. Having lost three of the eight Pzkfw IVs supporting his unit; *Hauptsturmführer* Ullrich halted the assault against Hill 285.

At 0500 hours, the main body of *Der Führer* began moving west in the wake of *Kampfgruppe Ullrich*. Weidinger hoped to avoid becoming entangled in the street fighting in Mortain by using a route that passed north of the town. The German armored column would have to fight their way through the roadblock manned by Lieutenant Springfield's TD platoon and a 57mm gun commanded by Sergeant Miller Rhyne of the 120th Antitank Company. Fortunately, the small arms fire echoing from Hill 314 had provided the TD platoon and Sergeant Rhyne's crew with ample warning of the impending attack.

Sergeant Rhyne had been listening to armored vehicles moving to the north during the early morning hours. Just before dawn, the sound of vehicles drew closer to Rhyne's position. An armored car burst out of the fog driving toward the American 57mm antitank gun. Three rounds barked out in quick succession, striking the thin armor of the German vehicle with bright white flashes. The armored car veered off the road before crashing into a ditch.[30] A moment later, Springfield's TD platoon began engaging half-tracks belonging to *III Abteilung* of *Der Führer.*

Lieutenant Springfield positioned himself where he could control the pair of three-inch guns constituting his First Section. Although the TD gunners were limited to occasional glimpses of German half-tracks through the swirling fog, the Americans fired each time a target became visible. A loud clang followed by a red glow announced each direct hit. As the occupants of the armored personnel carriers tumbled out of their stricken machines, they were sprayed with machine-gun fire.[31] Tracers ricocheted wildly off the road as well as the armored flanks of immobilized vehicles. The roadside ditches in front of Lieutenant Springfield's

First Section began to fill up with dead or wounded *SS* soldiers. *Der Führer* lost six half-tracks and three other vehicles to Springfield's guns.[32]

The crew of Sergeant Rhyne's 57mm gun detected the approach of additional vehicles as several amphibious jeeps, armored personnel carriers, and trucks appeared out of the fog. All of the German vehicles were knocked out, and the anti-tank gunners sniped at the *SS* men who managed to escape the stricken vehicles. The collection of destroyed vehicles, increasingly visible as the fog dissipated, took the steam out of the German attack. By midmorning, *Der Führer* halted its attack on L'Abbaye Blanche.[33] *Sturmbannführer* Weidinger left a small force behind while slipping his *II Abteilung* to the north where it occupied a crossroads marked on the maps as RJ (Road Junction) 278. *III Abteilung* also left troops behind to contain the American roadblock before bypassing L'Abbaye Blanche to the south.

During the lull, Lieutenant Springfield watched a jeep carrying Colonel Birks approach L'Abbaye Blanche at high speed. Birks walked over to Springfield's command post, where he asked the TD platoon leader if he could send his half-tracks up Hill 314 with supplies for the 2/120th Infantry. Springfield replied that he had barely enough men to hold his own position, let alone assist Lieutenant Colonel Hardaway's battalion. Dismayed, Colonel Birks departed L'Abbaye Blanche for his own headquarters. As he passed through Mortain, however, Birks instructed the 1st and 2d Platoons of F Company, commanded by Lieutenants Tom Andrew and George Stewart respectively, to reinforce Springfield's TD platoon.[34]

When he arrived at L'Abbaye Blanche, Lieutenant Andrew split his rifle platoon into three sections. One rifle squad established security for Sergeant Rhyne's 57mm gun. A second squad, augmented by a machine gun and mortar crew from Company F's weapons platoon, set up a roadblock south of the village. Andrew's remaining rifle squad dug in beside Lieutenant Springfield's First Section. Shortly afterward, *SS* troops from *Der Führer* trying to find a bypass south of L'Abbaye Blanche surprised the F Company headquarters platoon, capturing fifteen Americans. Lieutenant Stewart's 2d Platoon, which initially occupied positions north of the village, addressed this unexpected threat by shifting locations to augment the roadblock's southern defenses.[35]

In contrast to the defeat it suffered at L'Abbaye Blanche, *Das Reich* was gaining the upper hand south of Mortain. At dawn, Wisliceny's *Deutschland* regiment launched another assault on la Croix des Sept Coeurs. Lieutenant Miller inexplicably sent Staff Sergeant George Wichterich, accompanied by Sergeant Nard Jacobsen, to pick up mail when the *SS* troops attacked. The sergeants narrowly survived an ambush as they drove back to A/823d TD command post. Both of Wichterich's leaderless gun crews decided to retreat to the platoon command post. Private Walter Clark arrived just as Miller ordered Corporal Alif Cockerham to warn the TD platoon's Second Section. Clark volunteered to accompany Cockerham. The pair roared off in a half-track, driving past Germans heading toward Mortain. Small arms fire pinged off the armor plate during the entire trip.

The half-track soon reached one of the three-inch guns located on the southern outskirts of the town. However, Corporal Cockerham's warning of a full-scale counterattack was not well received. It took some time to persuade the gun commander, who was reluctant to pull back without having seen any Germans. The bullet holes in the half-track's armor were finally accepted as compelling evidence. Unfortunately for the TD crew, the debate had consumed far too much precious time. As the Americans hooked up their three-inch gun to its prime mover, a panzer was spotted heading in their direction. The TD gunners scattered, abandoning both half-tracks as well as the three-inch gun.

When the Germans continued to press their assault, Lieutenant Miller ordered his men to retreat. Hoping to link up with the 2/120th Infantry on Hill 314, the TD platoon leader gathered up ten other soldiers. Unfortunately, his plan suffered a major setback when one of the men accidentally shot himself in the leg while climbing over a stone wall. The rest of the group took turns carrying him up the hill, where they eventually reached a secluded orchard just outside of the 2d Battalion perimeter.

Having disposed of three of Lieutenant Miller's four guns, the Germans turned to finish off the remaining piece protecting the road between la Croix des Sept Coeurs and Mortain. The gun commander, Sergeant Ulrich Clark, was shot when he climbed an embankment to obtain a better view of the situation. Corporal George Simmons caught the mortally wounded man as he tumbled back into the gun emplacement. Simmons dragged Clark to a nearby garage, where the sergeant died in his arms. Simmons headed over to an adjacent apple orchard to get one of his section's jeeps. As he started up the vehicle, he noticed that his other companions had already left.

Simmons drove the jeep around the house where he spotted a German soldier standing in the driveway. He gunned the jeep at the German, who jumped back while wildly firing his submachine gun. Simmons could see bullets hitting the second story of a house across the lane. A few moments later, he picked up Private Joe Olivia, a wounded member of his own gun crew, before heading toward the center of Mortain.[36]

Corporal Simmons's luck finally ran out when he came upon a Pzkfw IV blocking the main street. He attempted to reverse back up the street, but quickly realized he would not escape. Leaping out of the jeep, Simmons dragged Private Olivia toward the town's post office as firing broke out behind them. Passing through the post office, the pair entered an alley across from a hospital. They entered the hospital lobby, where Simmons put Olivia down for a moment before climbing the stairs leading to the second story. Several SS soldiers were calmly chatting in the upstairs hallway. The Germans saw Corporal Simmons at the same time he spotted them. Bolting down the stairs, he dragged Private Olivia out of the hospital, still hoping to reach the safety of the American lines.

Soon after Lieutenant Miller's TD platoon was overrun, Colonel Birks sent Lieutenant Edwin J. Franklin's I&R platoon to determine the situation on his regiment's southern flank. When the I&R platoon entered Romagny at 0540 hours, the leading jeep encountered the advance guard of *Sturmbannführer* Helmut Schreiber's *II Abteilung Deutschland*. Despite foggy conditions, the Americans and *SS* both reacted quickly to the chance contact. Grenade fragments wounded two men as the I&R platoon took up hasty defensive positions on the western edge of the village.[37] The Germans also suffered several killed and wounded, including three men captured by the Americans.

The I&R platoon continued fighting for an hour until their ammunition ran low. Sensing that the end was near, Lieutenant Franklin ordered several seriously wounded men loaded onto a jeep. Private Ralph W. Estevez volunteered to deliver the wounded to the regimental aid station, and the I&R platoon fired their remaining ammunition to cover his escape. Several grenades exploded near Estevez's vehicle, peppering him with shrapnel. Ignoring the blood flowing down his side, he drove to the aid station where medics unloaded his passengers. The medics treated Private Estevez, but his wounds eventually proved fatal.

During the course of the fighting, the I&R platoon interrogated their prisoners, one of whom admitted that a large motorized force was attacking Mortain.[38] This information was immediately passed on to division headquarters. Lieutenant Franklin and several other men were eventually able to escape, but the remainder of his platoon were killed, wounded, or captured. Having finally disposed of the troublesome American platoon, *II Abteilung Deutschland* resumed its westward advance.

Sturmbannführer Helmut Schreiber's II *Abteilung,* spearheaded by four Pzkfw IVs, was observed soon afterward heading toward the 197th FA Battalion. Two Pzkfw IVs, supported by fifteen to twenty foot soldiers, broke off from the main body of the German force intent on attacking the C Battery of the 197th FA. The *SS* men approached C Battery along a small trail leading to the artillery unit. The noise of tank engines alerted the artillerymen, who quickly organized available truck drivers and mechanics into a defensive line. Firing broke out as the Americans began shooting at the *SS* infantry.

A few of the *SS* troopers were able to penetrate C Battery's motor park. Amid a scattering of rifle fire, the intrepid Germans absconded with a jeep containing a radio, map, and code device. The leading panzer shot up a parked 2-1/2 ton truck, which immediately burst into flames. Additional vehicles were damaged as tank rounds raked the American position. The fog, which had concealed the German advance up to this point, was now working to the advantage of the artillerymen. Unsure of how many defenders they faced, the panzers proceeded cautiously, unwilling to expose themselves to bazooka teams lurking in the hedgerows.

Despite their reluctance to close with the defenders, the panzers were able to inflict a number of casualties on the defending American troops. The 197th FA Battalion's operations officer was seriously wounded almost as soon as he arrived to take over the defensive effort. One man was killed helping a .30-caliber machine-gun crew reposition their weapon, and the C Battery first sergeant also was hit. The engagement sputtered indecisively until an American crept forward to knock out one of the Pzkfw IVs with a bazooka. The destruction of the panzer convinced the Germans to retreat.[39]

The southernmost elements of *Das Reich* advanced against little or no resistance following a brief encounter with the 4th Cavalry at 0200 hours. Just before dawn, *Sturmbannführer* Krag's *SS-Panzeraufklärungs Abteilung 2* reached Milly, a small village located between St.-Hilaire-du-Harcouet and Mortain. A convoy of vehicles belonging to the 298th Engineer Battalion approached the village soon after the Germans had arrived. The engineer unit, which was heading south to join Third Army, did not suspect it would encounter marauding German troops several miles behind the front lines.

Lieutenant Creighton Lawson, accompanying the A Company commander, Captain Thomas W. Silva, noticed a jeep and several men standing alongside the road. At first he thought they were friendly, but as the Americans neared the intersection they could hear shouting in German. Silva ordered his driver to halt their command car, and everyone bailed out to seek cover in a roadside ditch. Silva ordered Lawson to inform the rest of the convoy that they had contacted a German patrol. Lawson was making his way back when a German armored car opened fire. The kitchen truck behind the command car was riddled with bullets, as was the fifth vehicle in line, an air compressor truck. The vehicles between the two stricken trucks were trapped. A second armored car now appeared, and more small arms and cannon fire was poured into the stalled American convoy.

The driver of the kitchen truck made his way to safety, but none of the six cooks in the back were able to escape. American vehicles within earshot of the ambush hurriedly turned around in adjacent fields. While the 1st and 2d Platoons of Company A remained behind as a rear guard, the rest of the 298th Engineers extricated their convoy from the stretch of road dominated by the German roadblock. Captain Silva's Company A retreated to Milly, where they established a line of defense covering the roads leading into town. Two bazooka teams, a machine-gun position, and a hasty minefield were placed to cover each avenue of approach.[40]

Kampfgruppe Fick also gained some success in Mortain, forcing the 1st Platoon of C/120th Infantry to vacate several houses on the southern outskirts of the town. However, the Germans continued to fight for every street. An American machine-gun nest in the cellar of la Collegial Saint Evoult dominated the open square in the center of Mortain. The Germans finally knocked out the opposing automatic weapon after suffering numerous casualties. Hand-to-hand fighting went on for several hours before *Kampfgruppe Fick* could finally secure the interior of the church.[41]

As each block was painstakingly cleared, the *SS* began systematically searching each house for straggling Americans. The 2/120th Infantry aid station remained undetected in a small field behind la Collegial Saint Evoult. A tall fence, surrounding buildings, and leafy trees served to hide the medics. The battalion command post, fronting the town's main street, was considerably more conspicuous. One of the guards posted at the corner of the street breathlessly ran into the command post to report that some *SS* were heading toward them. Lieutenant Colonel Hardaway radioed C Company, ordering Lieutenant Smith to launch an assault against the Germans threatening the 2/120th command post. Hardaway then informed Colonel Birks that he would have to temporarily shut down operations.

Shortly afterward, the Germans spotted earlier by the headquarters guard appeared. A destroyed jeep had attracted their attention, and several *SS* men began picking through the wreckage of the vehicle but found nothing. The Germans then walked back down the street, stopping briefly outside the hotel serving as the battalion command post. After examining the building for a moment, the Germans departed. Lieutenant Colonel Hardaway decided to relocate his headquarters before they returned.[42]

Twenty-seven soldiers crept out of the Hotel de la Poste in single file led by the battalion executive officer. The Americans went around a corner when they bumped into an *SS* trooper. Before the German could react, the executive officer shot him. The German slumped in a heap in a doorway as Lieutenant Colonel Hardaway ordered the group to change direction. The 2d Battalion command group finally decided to conceal themselves in a house on a side street. Rather than hide in the cellar, Hardaway instructed the men to remain on the ground floor where he thought they would have a better chance of escaping if the Germans detected their presence.

Two men were tasked by Lieutenant Colonel Hardaway to stand guard at the front door. Due to the shortage of weapons and ammunition, one of the men was armed with a rifle while the other soldier possessed only an axe. Once radio contact was reestablished, Hardaway reported to Birks that he would not be able to rejoin his companies on the hill. For the time being, Hardaway explained, the 2d Battalion headquarters would just remain put.[43] He kept his voice low, however, since there was a water pump in the backyard being used by the Germans.

Responding to Hardaway's call for assistance, Lieutenant Smith of C/120th Infantry led the two platoons remaining under his control toward the Hotel de la Poste. Arriving at 1030 hours, Smith was surprised to discover that the building was empty. The soldiers of C Company vainly searched for an indication of what happened to the 2d Battalion command group, prompting Smith to radio Birks that "I don't think Cuff [2/120th Infantry radio code name] is anymore."[44] Intent on following his orders to secure the center of town, Smith ordered his men to occupy defensive positions in the vicinity of the Hotel de la Poste.

Lieutenant Smith was unaware that his 3d Platoon was making its way toward L'Abbaye Blanche even as the remainder of C Company prepared to defend the center of Mortain. Returning from their unsuccessful attempt to reach the rifle companies on Hill 314, Captain Erichson and Lieutenant Thompson parted company when they discovered that the 2d Battalion command post was no longer located in the Hotel de la Poste. Wishing the young officer luck, Captain Erichson headed back to F/120th Infantry. Unaware that C Company was preparing to enter Mortain from the west, Lieutenant Thompson decided to head back to the 1/120th Infantry on Hill 285 via L'Abbaye Blanche to avoid the Germans entering the town in increasing numbers.

Thompson's platoon headed north down a narrow side street that paralleled the Grand rue. Just before they reached L'Abbaye Blanche, they discovered the platoon from the regimental antitank company that had been overrun by *Kampfgruppe Ullrich* earlier that morning. Three antitank gunners, one of whom was badly wounded in the jaw and near death, had remained with the abandoned 57mm guns. After making their dying friend as comfortable as possible, the unwounded soldiers accompanied Lieutenant Thompson's men as they headed toward Hill 285 once more.[45]

Soon afterward, Lieutenant Thompson's platoon began receiving what they thought was friendly mortar fire. One man threw a yellow smoke canister into the road, hoping the observer spotting for the mortars would realize that Americans were present in the area. However, the "mortar" shells continued exploding unabated. Someone finally noticed that the platoon was being fired upon by *SS* troops using rifle grenades. Several of the Germans also began yelling for the Americans to surrender. Thompson led his platoon into a nearby house to escape the incoming fire, where he decided to link up with the 2d Battalion on Hill 314 instead of returning to his parent unit.

As Thompson's platoon headed up the northwestern slope, they encountered a German machine gun. The lead scouts shot one of the crew and took two others prisoner. The Americans discovered one final obstacle as they reached the crest of the hill. As the lead scout peered over a leafy hedge, a half-track–mounted flak gun opened fire on the Americans. German engineers equipped with flamethrowers also accompanied the vehicle. The Americans returned the fire, killing one of the Germans carrying a flamethrower. The half-track continued shooting until G/120th Infantry engaged it with 60mm mortars, forcing the vehicle crew to seek cover. However, Lieutenant Thompson's platoon was still faced with crossing forty yards of open ground before it could enter G Company's perimeter.

The first man to try crossing the field was shot before he had made it to safety. No one wanted to be the next man to cross the open area. Sensing an impasse, Thompson's platoon sergeant turned to one of his corporals, exclaiming loudly, "Okay, corporal, you are supposed to lead these guys." The corporal jumped over the hedgerow, drawing an immediate response from the hidden Germans. The bullets, however, passed harmlessly overhead as he wriggled across the ground. Stopping to grab the wounded man, the corporal dragged him over to the far side of the field. Once he was safely behind cover, the corporal began firing while shouting for the rest of Thompson's platoon to make a run for it.

More Americans sprinted across the open space. A Browning automatic rifle (BAR) gunner also took up the task of suppressing the incoming German fire. The remainder of the American platoon was able to cross the field without suffering additional casualties.[46] A short while later, the 3d Platoon of C Company entered the newly relocated perimeter of G/120th Infantry.

What Lieutenant Thompson found when he arrived in the 2d Battalion's defensive perimeter on Hill 314 was not very comforting. The isolated rifle companies were in dire straits, and all of the 2d Battalion antitank guns had been overrun. G Company had been forced to retreat from the positions it originally occupied by the *Das Reich* assault guns supporting *Kampfgruppe Fick*. The successful assault by *Untersturmführer* Kuske had also created a serious threat to the rear of E/120th Infantry. Lieutenant Reaser's K Company incurred significant losses when a surprise lunge by *SS* foot soldiers forced the surrender of several rifle squads. Reaser shifted his company to the south, which resulted in G and K Companies colocating atop the central portion of Hill 314. Lieutenant Kerley's E Company remained isolated from the rest of the battalion, with the two groups of Americans separated by approximately one thousand yards.

Supplies were also running low. During the morning of 7 August, German snipers prevented the defenders from replenishing their dwindling stockpile of ammunition from a small dump located behind E Company. The precarious situation was not helped by the fact that very few obstacles had been emplaced by the 2d Battalion. Traffic jams during the afternoon of 6 August prevented the 30th Infantry Division from obtaining mines and barbed wire to reinforce the defenses inherited from the 1st Division.

Lieutenant Kerley sent a runner for his attached artillery observer, Lieutenant Robert Weiss. After briefly conferring with Kerley, Weiss established an observation post near the E Company command post. As reports started flooding in, Weiss directed artillery fire based on preplotted concentrations. Corrections were made on the basis of sound, since it was still too foggy to observe the shells actually landing.[47] Lieutenant Charles Bartz, an artillery observer from the 230th FA located with G/120th Infantry, also began directing fire against the attacking Germans. Confusion, poor visibility, and lack of reliable communications, however, conspired to prevent the supporting artillery from firing their first mission prior to 0900 hours—nearly nine hours after the initial German probe against K Company.

Company commanders absent from their units during the first critical hours began filtering back into the 2d Battalion perimeter. After leading his headquarters to safety, Captain Delmont Byrn of H/120th Infantry made his way into Lieutenant Kerley's company area. Byrn was appalled at the sight of wounded men lying unattended in the open. Incoming mortar shells burst nearby, showering the litter-bound casualties with rock splinters and shrapnel. The screams of the men as they were hit a second time especially shocked Byrn.[48]

Lieutenant Woody of G Company also returned after being cut off from his men. He was forced to climb a sandstone cliff to rejoin his company. When Captain Erichson of F/120th Infantry discovered that his remaining rifle platoons had been shifted to L'Abbaye Blanche by Colonel Birks, he threaded his way through the Germans in Mortain to rejoin the remainder of the battalion on Hill 314. Since Erichson was the senior officer present, Colonel Birks temporarily appointed him as the 2d Battalion commander until Lieutenant Colonel Hardaway was able to rejoin his troops.[49]

As the 2/120th Infantry hunkered down to weather another attack, Lieutenant Woody began questioning the prisoners brought in by Lieutenant Thompson's platoon from C Company. After admitting he was assigned to *SS-Panzergrenadier Division 17,* one of the prisoners also related that Hill 314 was being attacked by *Kampfgruppen Ernst* and *Fick,* which together numbered a thousand men. The prisoner stated that "they were to counterattack but morale is so low it affected their aggressiveness." He also revealed that *Leibstandarte* was present nearby.[50] Despite the disquieting information, Colonel Birks assured Major General Hobbs that the 120th Infantry Regiment was in no danger of losing Mortain.

Based on his perspective, Sergeant Frank Pruitt might have disagreed with Colonel Birks. Sometime during the morning, a soldier ran up to inform Pruitt that the Germans had captured the 2/120th command post. Pruitt decided to pull out before his section was surrounded. He checked all of the buildings occupied by his men but found that several of them were already empty. Collecting five soldiers, Sergeant Pruitt led his small band toward Hill 314, intending to join up with the rifle companies. That hope was soon dashed when he encountered a German patrol. Following a brief firefight, Pruitt ordered his men to fall back toward la Collegial Saint Evoult.

As Pruitt reentered the center of town, he noticed a group of men from C Company occupying the post office. The C/120th Infantry soldiers waved at him to join them. Sergeant Pruitt led his men into the post office, where they started sniping at the Germans. After an hour or so, the SS were finally able to work their way closer to the post office under the cover of adjacent houses. When the Germans were close enough to lob grenades, the Americans decided to abandon their position. The men split into small groups before heading west.

Pruitt, accompanied by two of his men, decided to return to the Hotel de la Poste. After following a small alley to the edge of town, the trio tried to escape by crossing an open field. As Pruitt emerged from behind a building, he was fired on by two machine guns. The Americans scrambled back up the alley to figure out how they could get out of town using a different route. German voices could also be heard coming from the street behind them. Pruitt decided it would only be a matter of time before the Germans reached their hiding place. Taking a chance, he dashed across the open ground with both of his men behind him. This time the Germans were either too surprised to fire or had decided to wait for a better target. The trio safely reached the road leading to the village of le Neufbourg.[51]

Walking toward le Neufbourg, Pruitt and his men encountered the survivors of C Company's 1st Platoon, led by First Sergeant Alfred Ruback. Corporal

George Simmons, still carrying his wounded comrade, joined the group a short while later. Reinforced by the TD soldiers and signalmen, First Sergeant Ruback decided to establish a defensive position facing Mortain. The wounded were taken to a nearby farmhouse while the able-bodied men dug foxholes. The activity attracted the attention of SS troops in Mortain, who opened fire on the group with mortars. The Germans, however, did not follow up the barrage with an assault against Ruback's group. They turned instead to assault the positions held by Lieutenant Smith's C/120th Infantry in the center of town.

At 1423 hours, *Kampfgruppe Fick* attacked the elements of C Company that remained within Mortain.[52] Lieutenant Smith succeeded in disabling one panzer with a bazooka but was killed by return fire. The Americans consolidated themselves in a single house but were soon forced to split up into smaller groups as the incoming fire grew more intense. The headquarters element lost one officer killed, in addition to Lieutenant Smith, and six soldiers wounded. The SS lost a number of men fighting against C/120th Infantry, which fiercely defended its foothold in the town. The Americans pulled out when their opponents succeeded in setting on fire the house occupied by the C Company headquarters platoon.

After pausing to reorganize, the Germans launched a second attack up the western slopes of Hill 314 against G/120th Infantry. The Americans, faced with almost stationary targets as the SS clambered up the steep wooded hillside, were easily able to stop the assault using 60mm mortars. As the fog burned off, the soldiers of Company G had a ringside seat from which they could watch the last stages of the fighting in Mortain. They would occasionally assist their comrades by firing on Germans moving within the town. Their assistance provoked sufficient return fire to persuade Lieutenant Woody to pull back part of his company from the western edge of Hill 314.

By this time, Lieutenants Woody and Reaser had completed consolidating their combined perimeter. Using a radio provided by his attached Cannon Company observer, Reaser reported to Colonel Birks that Company E was just south of his position, but neither he nor Woody was in contact with Lieutenant Kerley's unit.[53]

Although Lieutenant Kerley could not rely on the support of another rifle company to augment his defenses, he still possessed a radio link to the 230th FA Battalion. Beginning at 0900 hours, Lieutenant Robert Weiss called in fire missions on any SS unit that attempted to approach the hill. In addition to fending off numerous probes, Weiss broke up a large attack against E/120th Infantry at 1230 hours.[54] The German assault guns supporting *Kampfgruppe Fick* were dispersed by several accurate salvos of high explosive. Lieutenant Bartz, the artillery observer supporting G Company, also proved instrumental in breaking up several counterattacks against the American perimeter.

Lieutenant Weiss's observation post was located on a prominent stone outcropping. Hoping to put an end to the deadly rain of shells, the Germans wheeled an 88mm gun into position to open fire over direct sights on Weiss's post. The

Lieutenant Robert Weiss, forward observer for the 230th FA Battalion attached to 2/120th Infantry on Hill 314. (Robert Weiss)

duel between gun and observer quickly became personal as several 88mm rounds zoomed past the rock that Weiss was sheltering behind. Amazingly enough, one 88mm round succeeded in clipping off the tip of his radio antenna. Despite the intense shelling, Lieutenant Weiss continued to direct artillery on the attacking Germans.[55]

At division headquarters, it was obvious that the 120th Infantry Regiment was going to have serious problems containing another attack unless reinforcements were immediately forthcoming. Despite the serious threat posed by the German penetration along the boundary running between the 30th Division and the 39th Infantry, Major General Hobbs decided to send his divisional reserve to reinforce the 120th Infantry. At 0350 hours, Hobbs informed the 117th Infantry that he planned to dispatch Lieutenant Colonel Lockett's 2/117th to assist Colonel Birks. However, Hobbs authorized Johnson to send one of Lockett's rifle companies, G/117th Infantry, to reinforce Lieutenant Colonel MacDowell's 3/117th Infantry located near Juvigny le Tertre.

Soon after receiving the message from division, Lieutenant Colonel Lockett departed for Colonel Birks's headquarters. When Lockett arrived at the country manor housing the 120th Infantry command post at 0530 hours, his initial impression was that it resembled a confused madhouse. Reports of the clash taking place between the regimental I&R platoon and German troops in Romagny were coming in as Lockett waited to speak to Colonel Birks. When Birks finally broke away from his staff, he told Lockett that the Germans were attempting to drive Hardaway's battalion off Hill 314. Reluctant to commit his only reserve, Birks waited several more hours for additional information before settling on a plan of action. The 2/117th Infantry's mission, as Birks explained it to Lockett at 0810 hours, was to clear the Germans from Romagny and relieve the 2/120th on Hill 314.[56] Birks also promised Lockett the support of two platoons of Shermans from A/743d Tank Battalion to accomplish that mission.

While Lieutenant Colonel Lockett was meeting with Colonel Birks, the 2/117th Infantry moved closer to Mortain. Although Lockett's battalion completed shifting positions by 0702 hours, the remainder of the morning was spent waiting for the supporting tanks to appear. Shortly after 1300 hours, Lieutenant Colonel Lockett received permission to move his battalion forward; however, there was one significant change to his original orders. Colonel Birks wanted Lockett to launch a simultaneous assault against Romagny and Mortain. In order to accomplish this, Lockett split his battalion into two elements. Captain George Sibbold's F/117th Infantry, aided by Lieutenant Orlyn Folkestad's 2d Platoon of A/743d Tank Battalion, would conduct the attack against Romagny. Lieutenant William F. Richards's E/117th Infantry, accompanied by five Shermans led by Captain Kenneth R. Cowan, commander of A/743d Tank Battalion, would assault Mortain.

The 2/117th Infantry's advance ran into serious difficulty almost as soon as it began. As F Company neared its objective, several German panzers emerged from Romagny on a collision course with the 120th's command post. Colonel Birks directed the 743d Tank Battalion to detach Lieutenant Folkestad's tank platoon from F/117th Infantry in order to defend his command post.[57] However, when the tankers approached the country manor housing the 120th Infantry Regiment's headquarters, the lead Sherman was knocked out by a panzer. Unable to identify the location of their assailant, the remainder of Lieutenant Folkestad's tank platoon sought cover behind a hedgerow.

Private Oscar Shipley, a member of the regimental communications section, aided by a soldier from C/105th Engineers, went after the hidden German panzers armed only with a bazooka and three rockets. Shipley discovered a Panther and a Pzkfw IV hidden in a small copse of trees only two hundred yards from the command post. He fired one rocket, which missed. A second bazooka round succeeded in damaging the Pzkfw IV, but the backblast of the weapon disclosed Shipley's position. Return fire killed the soldier accompanying him. Ducking a storm of bullets, Private Shipley ran back to Lieutenant Folkestad's platoon to inform him of the panzer's location. Folkestad ordered his four surviving Shermans forward, but the Panther escaped before the American tanks arrived. When Folkestad reached the spot where Shipley had fired on the German vehicles, his platoon finished off the damaged Pzkfw IV.[58]

Although his supporting tanks had been called away to deal with the panzers threatening the 120th Infantry's command post, Captain Sibbold continued advancing on Romagny. When F/117th Infantry approached within three hundred yards of the village, the lead rifle platoon was ambushed. Six men were killed and eight others wounded, including Sibbold's first sergeant.[59] Captain Sibbold ordered his company to pull back so he could bring artillery fire on the village. Colonel Birks, however, had not tasked the 230th FA Battalion to provide support for Sibbold. After taking up hasty defensive positions, F/117th Infantry vainly requested artillery support while awaiting the return of Lieutenant Folkestad's tanks. F Company's drive on Romagny was stalled for the remainder of the day when neither Folkestad's tank platoon nor the requested artillery support arrived to assist them.[60]

The main body of Lockett's battalion also encountered trouble as it approached Mortain. Foot soldiers belonging to *Leibstandarte* attacked the rear of the 2/117th Infantry, capturing three jeeps and several trailers belonging to the headquarters company. Fortunately, Lieutenant Colonel Lockett's staff was able to evade capture. The marauding Germans also seized two ambulances transporting wounded to a casualty clearing station. Unable to contact Colonel Birks, Lockett informed his own regimental headquarters of the incident. Lieutenant Colonel Johnson sent his only uncommitted force, the 117th Infantry I&R platoon, to recover the captured jeeps.[61] Although the I&R platoon succeeded in driving away the SS troops, they failed to retrieve any of the lost vehicles.

Colonel Birks had been too preoccupied with another assault against his regimental command post to respond to Lockett's calls for assistance. Shortly after 1700 hours, a number of Royal Air Force Typhoons appeared over L'Abbaye Blanche and Hill 285. The British planes had extended their attack patterns once it was determined that all visible panzers in the vicinity of St.-Barthelemy were destroyed. A flight of Typhoons buzzed the knocked-out Pzkfw IVs sitting in front of Sergeant Levine's three-inch gun on Hill 285. When the British planes turned to make a second pass, they fired a barrage of aerial rockets at the disabled panzers. One errant rocket landed so close to Lieutenant Pulver's shelter that he felt that his hair had been singed off.[62] A second flight of Typhoons dove straight at Pulver's company command post firing their 20mm wing cannon. Shells ricocheted off the ground on all sides, killing one man.

As the fighter-bombers pulled up, Pulver told his men to toss out a yellow smoke grenade in an attempt to signal the presence of friendly troops. The only immediate effect that the smoke grenade had was to attract German mortar fire, as the RAF Typhoons continued their rocket attacks unabated. Their next run destroyed one of the TD platoon's half-tracks and wounded the driver.[63] After several more strafing passes, the British planes finally stopped assaulting the Americans on Hill 285. Although upset by the losses inflicted, Lieutenant Pulver was able to forgive the RAF pilots because he could hear wounded Germans screaming in pain following the attacks.

The British planes also strafed Colonel Birks's command post. One 20mm shell entered a small window in a stone barn next to the country manor housing the 120th Infantry's headquarters, killing the regimental S-4. Colonel Birks angrily radioed division headquarters to demand a halt to the air attacks.[64] Although the division requested that Allied planes cease the assault on ground targets in the Mortain area, Birks's headquarters experienced additional fire before darkness brought relief. All told, the 120th's command post was strafed and bombed ten times during 7 August.

Although the 120th's command post was also the target of German shelling, the attackers generally did not make good use of their advantage in artillery. The Germans fielded superior numbers of artillery at the onset of the counteroffensive, pitting twelve to fourteen battalions against the 30th Infantry Division's four organic, one attached, and four supporting corps battalions. While American gunners were somewhat restricted by ammunition quotas, the Germans could freely obtain ammunition from *7 Armee* dumps located in the Foret de Mortain. The initial advantage held by the Germans was even more pronounced as a result of communications difficulties preventing VII Corps from providing any type of meaningful artillery support to the 30th Division prior to 1200 hours.[65] The American artillery began to play a more decisive role, however, as visibility improved and the situation stabilized.

When given sufficient time to prepare, the Germans were capable of massing artillery against frontline targets. By 1900 hours, Lieutenant Colonel Lockett's 2/117th Infantry was finally nearing Mortain. Passing beneath a railroad overpass west of the town, Captain Cowan's supporting tanks moved into overwatch positions as E/117th Infantry advanced toward a cemetery on the outskirts. A rifleman with one of the leading platoons, Private John O'Hare, absently noted that several headstones in the cemetery had been uprooted by artillery fire. As Company E approached the first row of houses, the defending *SS* troops opened fire.[66]

With his lead elements pinned down, Lieutenant Richards ordered a trailing platoon to outflank the Germans. It seemed to Private O'Hare as if their movement triggered a veritable storm of fire directed at E Company. Shells began screaming in, sending shards of shrapnel in all directions. Dozens of men dropped to the ground in agony as Private O'Hare scrambled for shelter from the incoming artillery. Diving into a large crater, he hugged the dirt wall and waited for the attack to subside.[67] When the shelling died down a bit, O'Hare ran back to the shelter of the railroad overpass. He could clearly see corpses, discarded equipment, and weapons strewn everywhere. E/117th Infantry had suffered twelve killed and sixty-three wounded in a few brief moments.[68]

Company E pulled back until it reached the position occupied by the heavy weapons crews of H/117th Infantry. Captain Cowan's five Shermans covered the rearward movement of Lieutenant Richards's men. The tanks cruised through the outskirts of Mortain, firing 75mm shells at any likely target. Lacking infantry support, however, Cowan also ordered his Shermans to retreat. Gingerly picking their way around bodies lying in the road, the medium tanks trundled back to join the 2/117th Infantry re-forming on the other side of the railroad underpass.

Cowan's tanks quickly took up a defensive position near the perimeter of the 2/117th Infantry. Unfortunately, the RAF Typhoons chose this moment to put in another appearance. The approaching darkness, however, ensured that the aerial onslaught was mercifully brief. Fighter-bombers strafed E Company, wounding at least one man.[69] The 2/117th was only able to continue reorganizing once the British planes departed. The 120th Infantry, although appreciative of the support provided by the fighter-bombers, laconically noted that "if friendly air was as efficient against enemy as against us, enemy vehicle losses should be heavy."[70]

Fortunately for the defenders, Major General Hobbs had not pinned all of his hopes on Lieutenant Colonel Lockett's 2/117th Infantry. As early as 0535 hours, the division operations officer informed the 119th Infantry Regiment to make the necessary arrangements to send the 1/119th, commanded by Major Robert Herlong, on a mission south of Mortain.[71] Instead of being immediately committed to battle, however, the 1/119th was placed in division reserve. Although Major Herlong lacked Captain Carlton Stewart's B Company, which had been dispatched earlier to le Mesnil Adelee, he was reinforced with Lieutenant David Korrison's D/743d Tank Battalion.

As the situation seesawed back and forth across the 30th Infantry Division's front during the morning of 7 August, several times Major General Hobbs found himself on the verge of committing Herlong's battalion to the fray. When German troops threatened to overrun C/197th FA, he decided to send the 1/119th Infantry to the rescue but demurred when he received word that the FA battery had driven off its attackers without assistance.[72] When he was informed of the loss of Colonel Birks's I&R platoon in Romagny, he realized that the village had to remain in American hands if he hoped to anchor his division's exposed southern flank. At 1048 hours, Major General Hobbs decided to send the 1/119th to seize Romagny if the 120th Infantry proved unable to secure the village.[73]

By 2017 hours, the 30th Division was also aware of Captain Sibbold's failure to capture the village. Major Herlong was summoned to division headquarters where he was told to mount his battalion in trucks and conduct a motor march to Romagny. The column would be led by the light tanks of Korrison's D/743d Tank Battalion. Just outside of the village, the 1/119th halted to dismount from their vehicles. Proceeding on foot, they advanced cross-country toward Romagny as the light tanks continued moving along the road. Resistance was initially confined to a few snipers positioned along a creek west of the village.

When the lead vehicle of D/743d rounded a curve five hundred yards west of Romagny, it was fired upon by a high-velocity gun.[74] The thinly armored American tank quickly reversed behind cover while Herlong dispatched a patrol to locate the offending AT gun. Led by Lieutenant Robert J. Heglein, the patrol did not find any antitank guns, but they did encounter a pair of Pzkfw IVs hidden in a wooded area. The leading tank was able to escape, but the second succumbed when Heglein scored two bazooka hits on its engine compartment. The Pzkfw IV ground to a halt at the entrance to Romagny, blocking the only road leading into the village.

Major Herlong decided to capitalize on Heglein's unexpected success by quickly launching a tank-infantry assault against Romagny. With A/119th and C/119th Infantry deployed on either side of the road, the M5 Stuarts of D/743d Tank Battalion began moving forward. Lieutenant Korrison's light tanks, however, were prevented from advancing by German antitank fire. The maneuver options available to Major Herlong were also significantly restricted by a hill that bordered the left side of the road and a steep eight-foot embankment to the right. After losing fifteen men in a futile exchange, the 1/119th halted its attack for the night.

South of Romagny, Captain Tousey's battlegroup was happy to see the tanks of 2d Armored Division's CCB appear late in the afternoon of 7 August. After clashing with *I Abteilung, Panzer Regiment 24* at le Mesnil Adelee, CCB continued moving south to Barenton. The tankers were surprised to see Captain Tousey's men; no one had informed them that American troops occupied the town.

The commanding general of the 2d Armored Division, Major General Brooks, lost no time in requesting that VII Corps attach both 3/120th Infantry and Tousey's battlegroup to his division. Both requests were quickly granted. After briefly talking with Tousey, Brooks invited him to a conference with his regimental commanders. The 3/120th Infantry's commander also attended the meeting. Brooks announced to his assembled commanders that he had decided to seize the town of Ger, located five miles east of Barenton, before nightfall.

The advance of the 2d Armored would be led by Lieutenant Colonel Marshall Crawley's 3/41st Armored Infantry. Captain Tousey's battlegroup had the mission of securing the high ground north of Barenton to protect against Germans interfering with Crawley's advance from that quarter. Lieutenant Colonel McCollum's 3/120th Infantry would remain behind to protect the town.[75]

Major General Brooks knew he was assuming some risk by conducting a hasty offensive immediately upon his arrival in Barenton. A successful attack against Ger would open the way for a subsequent advance on Domfront. However, if the panzers at Mortain turned south in response to the threat posed by 2d Armored Division, there would not be a great deal of American armor to oppose them. The 2/67th Armor, lacking two platoons of medium tanks left behind to act as a rear guard east of le Mesnil Adelee, would not arrive before 1835 hours. The 3/67th Armor had remained in the vicinity of le Mesnil Gilbert until the Germans were driven from le Mesnil Adelee; it did not begin moving toward Barenton until 1855 hours, where it was not expected to arrive until nightfall. Major General Brooks did not want to commit his division reserve, 1/67th Armor, in support of Lieutenant Colonel Crawley's attack.

The 3/41st AIR's assault encountered resistance from elements of *Panzer Lehr* and *Infanterie Division 275* east of Barenton. A number of antitank guns supported by automatic weapons contested the advance of the armored infantry. Antitank guns fired upon Captain Tousey's battlegroup as it attempted to occupy the high ground north of town. When Lieutenant Colonel Crawley decided to pull back, Captain Tousey was also forced to retreat.[76]

When he made the decision to postpone any serious effort to capture Ger until the following morning, Major General Brooks did not realize that additional German troops were en route to Barenton. Von Kluge had not forgotten *General der Panzertruppen* Eberbach's earlier promise to release one panzer division from *SS-Panzer Korps II* as soon as the local counteroffensive staged by the British had run its course. Consequently, *Brigadeführer* Heinz Harmel's *SS-Panzer Division 10* received orders from *Panzer Gruppe West* at 2140 hours on 7 August to move to Mortain. Harmel was expected to have his lead elements there by the following morning.

This decision, however, could not have come at a worse time for Harmel. *Panzer Gruppe West* had just placed *SS-Panzer Division 10* in reserve to rest and recuperate. The panzer inventory for the entire division numbered but five operational Pzkfw IVs, although seven other tanks were in the process of being repaired. Harmel dutifully informed his regimental commanders of their new orders, adding that *Das Reich* had already been alerted to provide the leadership of *SS-Panzer Division 10* with an orientation of their assigned sector immediately upon arrival.

Less than an hour later, *Brigadeführer* Harmel received orders to occupy a sector to the south of *Das Reich*. The boundary between the two *SS* panzer divisions would be the village of St.-Jean-du-Corail. *SS-Panzeraufklärungs Abteilung 10* led the move to Barenton. The reconnaissance battalion departed early on 8 August, trailed closely by *I Abteilung, SS-Panzergrenadier Regiment 21*. The latter would assist the reconnaissance unit in case American troops were encountered, and the remainder of Harmel's division would move against Barenton by the following evening.[77]

CONCLUSIONS

With little time to prepare for the defense or conduct an attack, both sides suffered from tremendous coordination problems during the opening hours of the counteroffensive. The assault of *SS-Panzergrenadier Division 17* provides an example of the difficulties facing the attacker. The fog that cloaked the Germans from Allied airpower also prevented them from employing their artillery and assault guns effectively. The initial artillery preparation fired against the 2/120th Infantry, which relied on preplanned targets and unobserved fire, met with decidedly mixed results. Given the poor visibility that existed, the attached assault guns from *Das Reich* were hesitant to close with the American infantry on Hill 314, which denied *Kampfgruppe Fick* direct fire support. Lacking artillery and armor support, *SS-Panzergrenadier Division 17* failed to secure the high ground overlooking Mortain. As long as the Americans retained Hill 314, the 30th Infantry Division would be able to use its artillery to paralyze the movement of *SS-Panzer Division 2*.

Although the defenders were not as affected by the limited visibility, communication difficulties resulted in poor decisionmaking on the part of the 120th Infantry. Lacking accurate information on the situation in Mortain, Colonel Birks's decision to delay the commitment of 2/117th Infantry effectively doomed C/120th Infantry. Lieutenant Smith's company successfully held the center of town until midafternoon, when it was finally driven out by a combined arms assault mounted by Wisliceny's *I Abteilung* supported by panzers. If Colonel Birks had employed the 2/117th Infantry while C Company retained a foothold in the town, the Germans would not have been able to generate sufficient combat power to secure Mortain on 7 August. By hesitating to commit the 2/117th until late that evening, Colonel Birks may have unwittingly ensured the failure of Lieutenant Colonel Lockett's efforts as well as the continued isolation of the 2/120th Infantry.

6

Stopping the German Advance on Avranches

Panzer Division 116, unaffected by the late arrival of *Leibstandarte*, began its attack shortly after midnight on 6 August. Within the perimeter of C/39th Infantry, Lieutenant Scheffel dozed off only to be awakened by an unusual sound. He left his command post to ask one of the guards if he had heard anything, and the soldier replied that it sounded like something went roaring down the road. Curious to discover what had passed by without setting off the antitank mines emplaced on the road, Scheffel checked to see if they had been removed, but they were sitting undisturbed atop its surface. He headed toward B Company to see if they had heard the mysterious sounds. After walking several hundred yards, he saw a figure standing in the road. From this soldier, he learned that two German motorcyclists had passed through C Company before encountering an alert sentry armed with a Thompson submachine gun. Emptying the entire clip, the GI killed one motorcyclist and wounded the second. A medic treated the injured German prior to sending him back for interrogation.

Lieutenant Scheffel no sooner returned to his own command post than the Germans launched the first of two assaults against his company. The attackers retreated after their first attempt when they failed to overwhelm a pair of Shermans from C/746th Tank Battalion supporting a roadblock manned by C/39th Infantry. The second assault was also turned back by another roadblock covering the la Gallerie trail junction. Since Scheffel's company had experienced several counterattacks during each of the preceding nights, Lieutenant Colonel Tucker interpreted the fighting as a local assault by the Germans.

His opinion changed an hour later when the 1/39th Infantry command post received a report from an artillery forward observer who spotted numerous German tanks. Between 0100 and 0700 hours, 535 rounds were fired by the 26th FA Battalion at the dimly seen vehicles. The shelling, however, did not deter the attacking panzers. Soon afterward, the 3d Platoon of the 9th Reconnaissance

Troop reported the loss of several armored cars at a roadblock west of Grand Dove. Their assailants were Panthers of *I Abteilung, Panzer Regiment 24,* which had been sent by von Schwerin to assist *Panzer Division 2.*[1]

When the Panthers approached the small village of Grand Dove, the leading panzer spotted a black shadow next to the road. The first shot from the Panther struck an M-8 armored car of the 9th Reconnaissance Troop. Aided by the light from the flaming vehicle, the Germans knocked out a jeep and a second armored car as the surviving Americans sought cover. Disregarding the American outpost, the Panthers continued west toward the village of le Mesnil Tove.

On the outskirts of le Mesnil Tove, the gunners of the 39th Infantry's Cannon Company listened apprehensively to the approaching panzers. They knew that their stubby 105mm howitzers would have little chance against the heavily armored Panthers. At 0422 hours, the cannoneers reported that a group of fifteen to twenty armored vehicles had passed through the town.[2] Small arms fire could be heard on all sides of the village, convincing Lieutenant Colonel Bond that his regiment was in the process of being surrounded. Panzers were passing through the rear of his unit, cutting off his regimental command post, antitank company, and cannon company from the rifle battalions deployed north of the See River.

As more panzers continued to swarm around le Mesnil Tove, Bond directed his cannoneers to retreat to Cherence le Roussel. The artillerymen pulled breechblocks off the 105mm howitzers and removed distributor caps from their vehicles before departing. Soon afterward, the abandoned howitzers were found by a company from *Panzergrenadier Regiment 156* as it swept through the village. The German company commander, *Oberleutnant* Fritz Strackerjahn, was surprised to come across what appeared to be an intact American artillery battery. Strackerjahn was sufficiently impressed with the discovery to allow his men to halt for a few moments to search for useful booty.[3]

After passing through le Mesnil Tove, Strackerjahn's *7 Kompanie* headed toward Cherence le Roussel. Avoiding the stone bridge, which he felt would be heavily defended, Strackerjahn sent a platoon wading across the See River to gain a foothold in the town. As his panzergrenadiers began crossing, he discovered that the Americans already occupied most of the houses facing the river. Lieutenant Colonel Bond, intent on keeping the Germans confined south of the See River, had ordered K Company, supported by a platoon from the 899th TD Battalion, to take up blocking positions in Cherence le Roussel.

Strackerjahn's men found themselves under heavy fire as they tried to wade the river. Soon afterward, however, the balance was somewhat redressed when three panzers arrived to support them. As German artillery fire searched out American positions along the riverbank, the commander of K/39th Infantry pulled his men back into the center of town. Strackerjahn, who had accepted the stalemate that had developed, did not pursue the retreating Americans.

The main body of the attacking Germans bypassed Cherence le Roussel, forcing the 26th FA Battalion to cease fire as the range decreased. At 0500 hours,

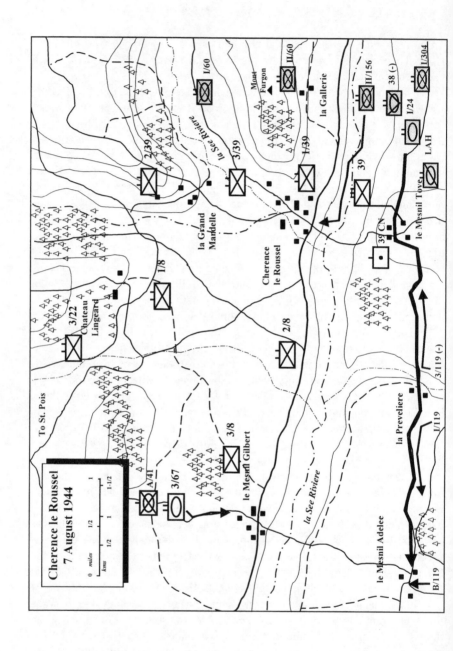

Cherence le Roussel
7 August 1944

0   1/2   1   miles
kms   1/2   1   1-1/2

To St. Pois

3/22
Chateau
Lingeard

1/8

la Grand Mardelle

Cherence
le Roussel

2/8

2/39

3/39

la See Riviere

1/60

Mont
Furgon

1/39

la Gallerie

II/60

II/156

38 (-)

1/24

LAH

1/304

39

le Mesnil Tove

39 CN

A/41

3/67

3/8

le Mesnil Gilbert

la See Riviere

la Preveliere

3/119 (-)

1/119

le Mesnil Adelee

B/119

Lieutenant Colonel Evert Stong informed his officers that they would displace their howitzers to the southwest. One firing battery would stay behind to cover the remainder of the battalion as it pulled back. Reinforced by 40mm and quadruple .50-caliber machine guns of the 376th Antiaircraft Artillery Battalion, Battery A assumed the role of covering force. Cloaked by the fog, the 26th FA was able to reposition itself without interference from the Germans.

The armored vehicles passing through le Mesnil Tove constituted the northern attack column of *Panzer Division 2,* led by *Oberstleutnant* Schake, commander of *Panzergrenadier Regiment 304.* Schake's *Kampfgruppe* was composed of elements of his own *I Abteilung, Panzerjäger Abteilung 38,* and *I Abteilung, Panzer Regiment 24. SS-Panzeraufklärungs Abteilung 1* scouted the roads in advance of the German column. Schake ordered his *Kampfgruppe* to continue moving west after overrunning the 39th Infantry's Cannon Company. Success bred caution as the panzers drove deeper into American-held territory. *Oberstleutnant* Schake halted in le Mesnil Adelee where his *Kampfgruppe* assumed a hasty defense.

Situated to the northwest of le Mesnil Tove, the soldiers of the 4th Division's 8th Infantry had been listening to the gunfire since 0230 hours. At 0415 hours, Major General Raymond Barton telephoned the regimental command post to find out what was happening. Unable to provide him with a coherent explanation of events, the regimental S-3 ordered patrols to be sent south of the river. A five-man patrol from F/8th Infantry unknowingly approached the Germans in le Mesnil Adelee. Just outside of the village, the Americans were ambushed, killing the officer in charge. Three other soldiers were wounded, while the fourth, Private John Cole, escaped injury but not captivity.[4]

Before news of the ambush filtered back to the 8th Infantry, division headquarters telephoned again. Based on reports from VII Corps stating that the situation in le Mesnil Tove was well in hand, Major General Barton directed the 8th Infantry to cease operations south of the See River. Just before daylight, however, a lieutenant and two enlisted soldiers from the 39th Infantry's Cannon Company arrived at the 8th Infantry's command post. The trio reported that thirty German armored vehicles had passed through le Mesnil Tove several hours ago. The sound of artillery and small arms fire seemed to be growing louder, lending credence to their story.

Subsequent calls from division belatedly confirmed that the situation was growing more serious. At 0820 hours, Barton alerted the 8th Infantry to prepare to launch a counterattack to regain Cherence le Roussel. He had been mistakenly informed that the town had been captured. Before the 8th Infantry could carry out his instructions, however, Major General Eddy telephoned Barton to assure him that the 39th Infantry still occupied Cherence le Roussel. The orders to recapture the town were rescinded. Instead, the 8th Infantry was told to establish a defensive position in the village of le Mesnil Gilbert, located just north of le Mesnil Adelee, for the purposes of securing the southern flank of the 4th Infantry Division.

The 2d Armored Division, which started for Domfront by way of Barenton at midnight on 6 August, was approaching le Mesnil Adelee. The 3/67th Armor, acting as the division's advance guard, was unwittingly on a collision course with *Kampfgruppe Schake*. By 0700 hours, patrols from the 82d Reconnaissance Battalion were skirmishing with *SS* troops near the village.[5] After confirming the presence of a sizable force of Germans in le Mesnil Adelee, the 3/67th Armor prepared to remove them from the division's path. Slowed by the fog and rugged terrain, the lead elements of the 3/67th Armor did not reach le Mesnil Gilbert until 0945 hours. The American tanks moved unopposed through the narrow streets of the village before crossing a small bridge just south of it. The leading troops of the 2d Armored Division were now two thousand yards north of le Mesnil Adelee.

To the west of le Mesnil Adelee, the crews of Colonel Boudinot's CCB, 3d Armored Division, were frantically struggling to reassemble their vehicles. The forty-nine-year-old Boudinot, commissioned as a second lieutenant of cavalry by examination in 1917, led the 32d Armored Regiment before moving up to take over CCB after the division landed in France. Most of the units assigned to CCA departed for Mayenne on 5 August. CCB's move south, however, had been delayed for two days to allow maintenance to be performed on its vehicles. Many of the tanks had their guns, sights, engines, or tracks removed. Although Boudinot was told about a possible counterattack at 0115 hours, his mechanics could not begin reassembling vehicles until daylight. Informed that CCB was attached to the 30th Infantry Division as of 0744 hours, he reluctantly admitted that his tanks would not be ready to move before noon.

B/119th Infantry was the first American unit to clash with Schake's *Kampfgruppe*. Major General Hobbs telephoned Colonel Sutherland at 0600 hours, ordering him to establish a roadblock southwest of le Mesnil Adelee. Sutherland told the commander of his 1st Battalion, Major Robert Herlong, to accomplish the mission. Herlong sent Captain Carlton E. Stewart's Company B, reinforced with a pair of 57mm guns from the battalion antitank platoon.

By 0730 hours, Captain Stewart's company was nearing the village. As the Americans approached, they could clearly hear numerous tank motors. Captain Stewart ordered the antitank platoon to send their 57mm guns into le Mesnil Adelee. The antitank platoon cautiously made its way toward the village. A French girl intercepted the Americans on the outskirts, informing them that at least two hundred Germans were occupying le Mesnil Adelee. A rift in the fog revealed glimpses of a mixed force of panzers and infantry.

When three camouflaged Panthers were discovered in a nearby field, the Americans maneuvered one of their 57mm guns into firing position. Aiming carefully, the gun crew fired three rounds before quickly pulling back.[6] The sergeant commanding the gun was sure he had damaged at least one Panther. Return fire, however, wounded the lieutenant commanding the antitank platoon. Judging by the volume of fire directed at the patrol, Captain Stewart was certain that le Mesnil Adelee was held in strength. Retreating a short distance to the south, he established a roadblock on the le Mesnil Adelee–Reffuveille road.

Stewart's report of German tanks in le Mesnil Adelee convinced Major General Hobbs that the village had to be recaptured immediately. He ordered Colonel Sutherland to provide Stewart with sufficient strength to retake le Mesnil Adelee while dispatching a second force to le Mesnil Tove. Colonel Sutherland ordered Lieutenant Colonel Courtney P. Brown's 3d Battalion to undertake both missions. Brown originally planned to send two companies, reinforced by Shermans from the 2d Platoon, C/743d Tank Battalion, to retake le Mesnil Adelee. The remainder of 3/119th Infantry would then attack le Mesnil Tove. After deliberating for a few moments, Brown canceled his original orders. Instead, Captain Earl J. Palmer's I/119th Infantry, reinforced with one platoon from K Company, would proceed to le Mesnil Adelee. The detached platoon from K Company would seize the hamlet of la Preveliere, located halfway between le Mesnil Adelee and le Mesnil Tove, and the rest of 3/119th Infantry would head east to secure le Mesnil Tove.

As the 119th Infantry reacted to the threat from *Kampfgruppe Schake,* confusion caused by changing start times prevented *Panzer Division 2* from carrying out a coordinated assault. A small unit of panzers from the southern attack column mistakenly moved forward while the remainder of von Luettwitz's division waited for *Leibstandarte.* The errant German force encountered a squad from the 3d Platoon of B/117th Infantry commanded by Lieutenant Robert Cushman. Cushman's rifle squad, supported by a 57mm antitank gun as well as a section of heavy machine guns from D Company, was manning a combat outpost northeast of St.-Barthelemy.

At 2300 hours, the American roadblock observed a pair of Kettenkrad motorcycle half-tracks approaching their location, but the Germans retreated when they realized a roadblock barred their path. At approximately 0200 hours, two Panther tanks supported by dismounted infantry attacked Cushman's position. The crew of the 57mm antitank gun opened fire, only to watch helplessly as their shells bounced off the thick frontal armor of the German vehicles. The Panthers retaliated by knocking out the 57mm gun, killing one man, and wounding two others. When the accompanying German infantry began firing *Panzerfaust* antitank rockets at the Americans, Lieutenant Cushman ordered his men to retreat.[7]

Cushman tried to obtain artillery support in an effort to drive off the attacking Panthers. Radio contact with the 118th FA Battalion was intermittent at best, which enabled the Germans to overrun the roadblock. Lieutenant Cushman quietly led a squad to the roadblock to see if he could regain the position. Confirming that the Germans outnumbered his own small group, he pulled back to the hilltop where the rest of his platoon waited. By this time, the attacking panzers realized they were ahead of schedule. Content with their small victory, the German vehicles sat quietly at the roadblock waiting for the remainder of *Panzer Division 2* to catch up.[8]

The southern attack group of *Panzer Division 2,* reinforced by the Panthers from *Leibstandarte,* was unable to begin its advance prior to 0500 hours. This delay was fortunate for the Americans because Lieutenant George I. Greene had been busy overseeing the movement of his TD platoon into St.-Barthelemy until well past midnight. He tried to move his platoon into the village as it became dark, but the TD's were halted by artillery fire. Several rounds struck the village church around 2030 hours, setting it on fire.[9] The burning building lit up the surrounding area, preventing Greene's platoon from moving in unobserved. He asked Lieutenant Colonel Frankland if he could wait until the blaze died down before moving his guns into position, and Frankland okayed the delay.

Upon reaching St.-Barthelemy, Staff Sergeant Robert A. Martin's section, consisting of the No. 1 and No. 2 guns, established firing positions on the southern edge of the village. Staff Sergeant Arthur E. Tucker's section, composed of the No. 3 and No. 4 guns, occupied positions on the southeastern outskirts. The TD gunners frantically raced to prepare their guns for action. Sporadic shelling increased in intensity, with eight to ten rounds landing near the village every fifteen to thirty minutes. What seemed even more ominous were the sounds of moving panzers to the east. The soldiers of the 1/117th Infantry could also hear the Panthers of *SS-Panzer Division 1* as they moved into their assembly areas prior to the counterattack.[10]

The presence of nearby panzers persuaded Frankland that his battalion needed more tank destroyers. When he requested additional TDs, Lieutenant Colonel Johnson instructed B/823d TD Battalion to send a section to reinforce Lieutenant Greene. Captain Wilts dispatched two guns from his 2d platoon to St.-Barthelemy. The lead TD, commanded by Sergeant John W. Vye, entered the village at 0200 hours. Before the three-inch gun could be unlimbered, German shells began falling nearby, and Sergeant Vye's crew scattered as they sought shelter from the artillery fire. Round after round landed in St.-Barthelemy's main street, damaging the newly arrived TD and its prime mover. When the shelling ceased, Lieutenant Greene could locate only Sergeant Vye and his driver. The other seven men had vanished.[11]

Soon afterward, the 117th Infantry began receiving reports of the attack on le Mesnil Tove. As he girded his regiment for imminent action, Lieutenant Colonel Johnson was notified by division headquarters to be prepared to send the 2/117th to Cherence le Roussel or Juvigny le Tertre.[12] Major General Hobbs countermanded the orders just after Johnson telephoned the battalion command post to relay the instructions. Hobbs informed Johnson that the 2/117th minus G Company, was now attached to the 120th Infantry. Hobbs explained that he wanted G Company to remain behind to assist 3/117th Infantry in protecting the division's northern flank.

Immediately after Johnson concluded his telephone conversation with Hobbs, the 1/117th commander called the regimental command post to report that panzers were approaching Company A.[13] Dense fog settled over St.-Barthelemy, reducing visibility to less than twenty yards. The men of Lieutenant Greene's TD platoon could hear the rumbling of numerous tanks drawing closer. The fight for St.-Barthelemy was about to commence.[14]

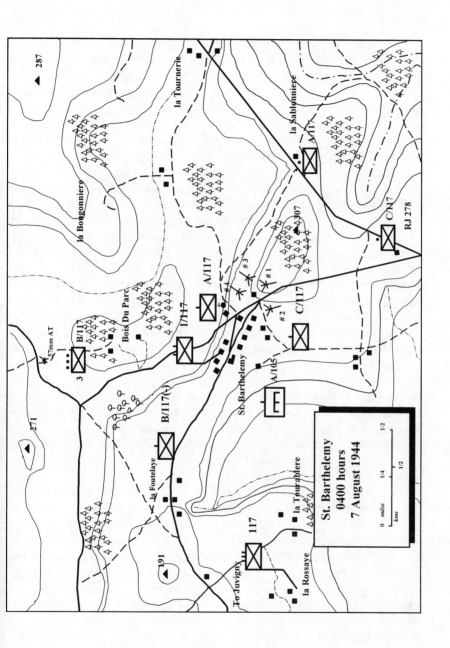

St. Barthelemy
0400 hours
7 August 1944

la Tournerie

la Sablonniere

A/117

C/N7

RJ 278

287

la Bougonniere

Bois Du Parc

B/117

3

57mm AT

271

A/117

1/117

#4

#3

#1

A307

C/117

#2

A/105

St. Barthelemy

E

B/117(-)

la Foutelaye

191

la Tourablere

la Tourablere

117

To Juvigny

la Rossaye

0   miles   1/4   1/2

kms   1/2

The Germans attacked the village from three directions, with Pzkfw IVs of *Panzer Regiment 3* moving in from the north and northeast and the Panthers of *SS-Panzer Regiment 1* closing in from the southeast. The latter quickly overran the weak roadblock at la Sablonniere. In response, Frankland directed the commander of the 117th Infantry's antitank company, Captain William Druckenmiller, to reposition two platoons of 57mm guns to cover the trails leading south from the roadblock.[15] Still plagued by communications difficulties, American artillery observers could not place fire on the attacking panzers.

The attacking *SS* panzers encountered Lieutenant Greene's No. 1 gun. The gunner, Sergeant Chester J. Christensen, carefully aimed at the lead Panther as it approached. The first round from the TD struck the ball mount of the Panther's hull machine gun, knocking out the vehicle. The destroyed tank blocked the path of the remaining Panthers for an hour as the Germans tried to clear it from the road. The TD crew could hear the Germans using a recovery vehicle to drag the knocked-out Panther into a nearby field.[16] Sergeant Christensen fired several high-explosive rounds at the noises in an attempt to delay the Germans, but the TD crew soon decided to withhold their fire until the next Panther came down the road to avoid revealing their position.

Panzer Regiment 3 avoided Lieutenant Greene's TD platoon by attacking from the northeast. The leading Pzkfw IVs unknowingly bypassed A/117th Infantry's weapons platoon to strike the 3d Platoon. The panzers began spraying the American positions with cannon and machine-gun fire, and by 0700 hours, the 3d Platoon ceased to exist. One squad attempted to infiltrate to the northwest to link up with B Company at la Foutelaye, but only five men succeeded in escaping. The remainder were killed, captured, or wounded.[17]

By this time, the Germans had dragged the disabled Panther off the road near Greene's No. 1 gun. The column of Panthers started for St.-Barthelemy once more, with the lead vehicle sweeping the roadside ditches with machine-gun fire. Suddenly a great yellow flash lit the fog as Sergeant Christensen fired at the Panther. The vehicle burst into flames only thirty-five yards in front of Greene's No. 1 gun. The surviving Panthers decided to wait until their accompanying infantry arrived before continuing the attack.

The delay cost *Leibstandarte* additional panzers. South of la Sablonniere, Captain William Druckenmiller had begun supervising the movement of his 2d Platoon into new firing positions when Sergeant Allen Hardy reported that two Panthers were parked nearby. Hardy was leading a patrol near St.-Barthelemy when the shooting broke out. Hearing tank engines, the sergeant peered over a nearby hedgerow to discover the source of the noise: two Panthers sat seventy-five yards away in a small field. Druckenmiller asked Hardy to guide two bazooka teams to the field where the Panthers were located. One bazooka team was led by Captain Druckenmiller, the other by Sergeant Hardy.

The Americans were able to reach their objective without being seen. Peering over the hedgerow, they could see a column of Panthers parked in the road.

Lieutenant George Greene. (George Greene)

Druckenmiller fired first, slamming a rocket into the rear of his intended target. Hardy's bazooka team fired at another vehicle, scoring another direct hit. As both *SS* panzers began burning, Captain Druckenmiller began shooting at the tank crews leaping out of the vehicles. Nearby panzergrenadiers returned the fire, hitting Druckenmiller in the leg. With their wounded captain leading the way, the small group headed back toward Lieutenant Colonel Johnson's command post.[18]

By 0855 hours, German infantry supported by Pzkfw IVs surrounded the weapons platoon of A/117th Infantry. Lieutenant Greene's No. 3 gun tracked one panzer as it moved along the perimeter of the trapped American platoon. When the Pzkfw IV turned right, paralleling the outskirts of the village, the three-inch gun knocked it out with several well-aimed rounds. However, return fire quickly destroyed an ammunition carrier, wounding several men. Private Edmond L. Rachal helped to carry the injured soldiers to a small hotel serving as a makeshift aid station. Once the wounded men were safely deposited in the basement of the hotel, he returned to his gun. The No. 3 gun continued to engage dark shapes in the swirling fog, although the visibility was so poor that the TD's gunner could not tell what type of vehicle he was shooting at.[19]

By 0930 hours, at least one company of Panthers succeeded in bypassing Lieutenant Greene's No. 1 gun. This maneuver also succeeded in cutting off the 2d and 3d Platoons of Company C from the rest of the unit. The defenders hid in their foxholes when the Panthers rolled past, emerging in the midst of the panzer-grenadiers trailing the vehicles. The German foot soldiers, startled by the sudden appearance of Americans, opened fire. Only one squad from each of the C Company platoons managed to escape, and the remaining Americans surrendered after a short fight. The panzergrenadiers, however, had become separated from the Panthers when the shooting broke out. Unaware that they now lacked supporting foot soldiers, the Panthers continued advancing into St.-Barthelemy.

The Germans soon paid for their impetuosity when two privates from Lieutenant Greene's TD platoon knocked out a Panther with a bazooka.[20] Private Peter Preslipski of C Company found a bazooka with two rockets lying on the ground and began stalking the Panthers on the eastern outskirts of the village. He succeeded in knocking out two tanks by firing a rocket into their engine compartments. Out of ammunition, he decided to head for the 1/117th Infantry command post near la Rossaye.[21]

Stung by the loss of three vehicles, the remaining panzers lashed out at their tormentors. Several Panthers swung left to hit C Company's 1st Platoon from the rear. One of the vehicles was knocked out by Lieutenant Greene's No. 2 gun, firing its first shot of the battle. Spotting the Panther approaching from the southeast, the TD crew waited until they had a flank shot at close range. The remaining German tanks continued toward the center of the village.

Lieutenant Colonel Johnson, alarmed by reports of increasing numbers of panzers attacking the 1/117th Infantry, had ordered more tank destroyers into St.-Barthelemy. He instructed Lieutenant Lawson Neel, commanding the 1st Platoon of B/823d TD Battalion, to take a section of guns into the village. Neel decided to send the three-inch guns that were protecting the 117th's command post and rode into the village aboard the lead half-track, trailed by Sergeant Joseph E. Pesak's gun. Neel entered St.-Barthelemy without being fired upon, but at least one panzer began shooting at the half-track, forcing Pesak to retreat to avoid being hit. Rather than return to his original position, Pesak pulled over in a field outside of the village.

Neel ordered the TD crew to unlimber their three-inch gun near the center of St.-Barthelemy, so they pushed it into a position where it could fire down the main street. One soldier had just gone across the street to bring back two rounds of ammunition when several Panthers appeared. The commander of the lead panzer waved to some infantry behind his vehicle before dismounting to talk to them. Private Robert Dunham shot the tank commander as Neel shouted at the gun crew to open fire. The three-inch fired two shots, knocking out the Panther. In return, the German infantry opened fire on the antitank gun crew, wounding two Americans.[22]

A second Panther advanced on Neel's gun. One man volunteered to cross the street to get more ammunition from the parked half-track. He was able to make it to the vehicle, returning with a single three-inch round. Two other men followed to obtain more ammunition but were prevented from returning by small arms fire sweeping the road. The gun was traversed toward the approaching Panther, but a fence obstructed the barrel. Neel ordered his men to retreat just before the panzer knocked it out. The second Panther, anxious not to join its companion burning in the street, also withdrew.[23]

The Panther retreated down the street, parking outside the advance command post of the 1/117th Infantry. The battalion operations officer glanced out the window in time to see the Panther halt in front. He could also see two more panzers behind the first vehicle. Lieutenant Colonel Frankland was distracted by noises coming from the rear of the house and entered the kitchen in time to see two of his radiomen being hustled out the back door. He pulled out his .45-caliber pistol, shooting two German infantrymen who had just taken the Americans prisoner. One of the freed Americans tumbled back inside the house while the other disappeared outside. Frankland yelled for the rest of his command group to follow him to Company A, while his operations officer headed for Company B.

Frankland safely reached Lieutenant MacArthur's command post, only to discover that A Company's radio set was out of commission. Frustrated because he could not raise the regimental command post, he departed for Hendrickson's Company B, where he was able to contact Lieutenant Colonel Johnson. Frankland, realizing the futility of holding on to la Foutelaye, ordered Hendrickson to retreat to Juvigny le Tertre.[24]

As B Company began pulling back, *Panzer Division 2* was in the process of finishing off A Company. MacArthur's rifle platoons were outflanked one by one as foot soldiers of *Panzergrenadier Regiment 2*, supported by Pzkfw IVs, overran the Americans. Several bazooka teams had tried to knock out the panzers but were prevented from doing so by the German infantry. A number of soldiers from A Company, seeing that they were almost surrounded, tried to escape capture by infiltrating to the west and north under cover of the thick fog. Some made it safely to the American lines; others were captured by the Germans. The weapons platoon surrendered after firing off their final rounds of 60mm mortar ammunition.

The surviving remnants of C/117th Infantry were also sorely beset by German panzers by midmorning. The C Company weapons platoon leader, Lieutenant Clinton Robb, tried vainly to persuade Captain Walter Schoener to pull back, but Schoener refused to make such a decision without gaining Frankland's approval.[25] Robb had just returned from a trip to Lieutenant Colonel Frankland's forward command post where he convinced the battalion commander to send reinforcements to plug the gap created by the collapse of C Company's 2d and 3d Platoons. Frankland ordered Captain Hendrickson to send his 1st Platoon to assist Schoener's company.

When Lieutenant Robb learned that Frankland was sending a platoon from Company B to reinforce Company C, he returned to Captain Schoener's command post. Robb volunteered to guide the reinforcements into position, but Schoener informed him that a runner had already been sent back for them. Lieutenant Robb was worried, however, that the reinforcements would arrive too late. He could see Panthers moving along the main street of St.-Barthelemy and counted sixteen tanks rolling past the orchard. Certain that C Company was about to be overrun, Robb pleaded with Schoener to authorize an immediate withdrawal.

By then, German foot troops were approaching the orchard, and one of the Panthers had turned its turret in the direction of the C Company command post. Robb quickly decided that he had stayed long enough. When panzergrenadiers began shooting at the dugout housing the company command post, he bolted toward a nearby hedgerow. Soon after he left, the C Company command group surrendered.[26] Lieutenant Robb made his way along the outskirts of the village until he encountered the platoon of B Company sent to reinforce C/117th Infantry. He placed the men in a defensive line along the southwestern outskirts before returning to lead C Company's 1st Platoon to safety.

Once the American infantry in St.-Barthelemy was neutralized, the Germans turned their attention to finishing off Lieutenant Greene's TD platoon. A high-explosive round that injured several men finally knocked out Greene's No. 1 gun. Staff Sergeant Martin directed the surviving members of his crew to carry the wounded back to a small hotel serving as an aid station.

When news of the loss of No. 1 gun reached Lieutenant Greene, he decided to shift No. 4 gun to cover that sector. Greene gathered up several men from the nearby No. 3 gun to assist in manhandling the three-inch weapon into position. The TD gunners slowly pushed the gun into position, but its field of fire was so poor that Greene decided to move it again. At the second location, the TD crew found that they could not depress the muzzle far enough to engage several vehicles driving up a sunken trail toward them. The men frantically chopped at the hedgerow but could not bring it to bear in time. Rather than risk capture, the gun crew abandoned their weapon after removing the firing pin.

Meanwhile, the volunteers from the No. 3 gun returned to their own piece only to find that it had been knocked out. Several wounded men lay nearby so the uninjured soldiers helped them to a small hotel in the center of the village. The makeshift stretcher detail arrived moments before a Panther pulled up next to the building. One American was killed when he unsuccessfully tried to knock out the vehicle with a rifle grenade. A medic stuck a rifle with a white bandage

Damaged 3-inch towed tank destroyer from Lieutenant Greene's TD platoon at St.-Barthe-lemy, possibly Staff Sergeant Martin's number one gun. (National Archives)

tied to its muzzle out the basement window of the hotel. German infantry cleared the unwounded Americans out of the aid station, herding them toward a nearby apple orchard. The wounded and the medics were allowed to remain in the hotel basement.[27]

Greene's No. 2 gun also could not be depressed low enough to engage the infantry and half-tracks moving along a sunken road. The rattle of tank treads on the pavement of the main road, however, alerted the TD crew to the approach of a Panther moving toward the village. Frantically traversing their three-inch gun, the TD crew hit the tank with one round. Trailing a ribbon of black smoke, the panzer continued on before grinding to a halt against the side of a house.[28] A second dark apparition appeared briefly amid the swirling fog, and the gun crew hesitated for a moment before firing. The indistinct shape turned out to be a Panther that opened fire as soon as it spotted the three-inch gun. After putting the No. 2 gun out of action, the Panther also destroyed the half-track parked behind the disabled weapon before continuing into the village.

Despite the destruction of Greene's last tank destroyer, embers of resistance still flared in St.-Barthelemy. Lieutenant Greene was in his command post when Sergeant John Kronik entered the building. Kronik, a squad leader in A/117th

Infantry, asked Greene to help him cover the escape of some other soldiers. The TD platoon leader agreed, dismounting a .30-caliber machine gun from a nearby half-track heading toward A Company's perimeter.

The pair emplaced the machine gun atop a hedgerow, with Greene handling the weapon while Kronik fed him ammunition. As several soldiers from A/117th Infantry started filtering past the machine-gun position, the Germans opened fire. Greene began peppering the opposing infantry with short bursts, which attracted the attention of a supporting Panther. The tank fired a high-explosive round that blew up the earthen bank directly under the American machine gun. A piece of the projectile's base hit Kronik in the groin, killing him instantly. Greene was knocked backward by the concussion, which jarred all of the fillings loose in his teeth. Groggily righting the weapon, he triggered off a long burst before wearily sitting down next to the hedgerow. A few moments later, he felt the muzzle of a machine pistol shoved against his back and glanced up to see an *SS* soldier motioning him to stand.[29] As he trudged off into captivity, Greene scanned the shocked faces of both victors and vanquished. It was clear to him that both sides had not expected such a fierce battle.[30]

Lieutenant Robb's small force were still holding out near the southwestern corner of St.-Barthelemy. The first group of *SS* infantry making their way toward the American-occupied hedgerow was cut down by small arms fire. When the Germans tried to place several machine guns on the flank of the American position, well-aimed bazooka rockets knocked them out. After suffering several dozen casualties, the Germans finally pulled back. Lieutenant Robb sent a runner back to regimental headquarters for instructions, but the soldier never returned. After vainly waiting for an hour, he decided to lead both of the rifle platoons back to American lines. Splitting the men into four groups, Robb instructed them to head west while avoiding the main roads. After watching the last of his men depart, Robb headed for Lieutenant Colonel Johnson's command post.[31]

By 1100 hours, Lieutenant Colonel Johnson was aware that a large force of German armor had overrun Frankland's battalion. Because the 1/117th Infantry was the only force between his headquarters and the attacking panzers, Johnson ordered the regimental Cannon Company to take up direct-fire positions along the road leading to Juvigny le Tertre.[32] Although he did not intend to relocate immediately, he did send the regimental I&R platoon to scout alternate locations for his command post. Fortunately for the 117th, the Germans were too disorganized following their Pyrrhic victory over the 1st Battalion to exploit their gains. For a period of almost ninety minutes, *Panzer Division 2* did not attempt to resume its advance toward Juvigny le Tertre. The delay would cost the Germans dearly.

Captain Hendrickson's Company B took advantage of the lull to pull back from la Foutelaye. Company B had been whittled down to less than one hundred men after losing part of a platoon manning a roadblock and detaching another platoon to help C Company. Several armored vehicles from *Panzer Regiment 3* took advantage of the latter's departure. Entering the B Company perimeter unopposed, the panzers threatened Hendrickson's command post. A 57mm anti-tank gun supporting it was knocked out almost as soon as it opened fire.

Captain Hendrickson's 2d Platoon leader was also wounded in the exchange of gunfire. Technical Sergeant Grady Workman took command of the 2d Platoon, ordering his men to pull back before the panzers could cut off their escape route to the west. The remainder of B Company, accompanied by A/105th Engineers, began moving back. Captain Hendrickson hoped to break contact with the Germans long enough to establish a blocking position astride the road running between St-Barthelemy and Juvigny le Tertre.[33]

Lieutenant Lawson Neel was also moving back to Juvigny le Tertre, accompanied by the crew of the three-inch gun knocked out in St.-Barthelemy. One of Neel's men, Private Milton Daly, was bothered by his conscience. He asked Neel, "This ain't running away, is it, lieutenant? This ain't running away, is it?" Neel assured Daly that he intended to retreat only as far as Sergeant Pesak's three-inch gun positioned outside of town. Neel soon located the other gun, which was still hooked up behind its prime mover, and told Pesak to site his gun so it could engage any vehicle heading to Juvigny le Tertre from St.-Barthelemy. Neel positioned the TD behind a large hedgerow that would serve to conceal its location until it opened fire.

Just before noon, the first group of Panthers began cautiously nosing out of St.-Barthelemy. Neel gave the order to fire when the lead Panther was a mere fifty yards from the hidden TD. An armor-piercing round penetrated the side of the tank, bringing it to an abrupt halt. When the *SS* crew bailed out to seek shelter on the far side of the stricken panzer, Neel instructed his men to fire a high-explosive round at the crew because he did not want them to point out his location. The second round persuaded the Germans to seek cover instead amid a nearby copse of trees. Two more Panthers rounded a bend in the road moments later, but they quickly pulled into cover once they spotted their knocked-out compatriot.[34]

There was a lengthy pause as the two panzer commanders decided on a strategy to deal with the unseen antitank gun. One Panther finally began moving forward, while the second remained behind to provide covering fire. Neel ordered the TD crew to depart, leaving just himself and three volunteers to operate the gun. The Panther halted for several minutes in a field just to the right of the tank destroyer. The Americans crouched low, watching the long barrel of the Panther lurch forward as it began moving once more. Neel opened fire just as the tank exposed its vulnerable flank, knocking off its track. Seconds later, the second Panther fired, destroying Neel's gun.[35]

The Americans abandoned the disabled weapon, carrying their wounded back with them. Neel led his men to Lieutenant Colonel Johnson's command post, where they joined up with a platoon from B Company. The rest of Company B arrived soon afterward. Captain Hendrickson ordered Technical Sergeant Workman's rifle platoon, accompanied by the B Company weapons platoon, to dig in along a sunken trail north of the St.-Barthelemy–Juvigny le Tertre road. Elements of Company D also arrived to reinforce Hendrickson's men. When Lieutenant Robb's group appeared, accompanied by A Company's 2d platoon, Captain Hendrickson placed the men south of the road.

The critical road junction of Juvigny le Tertre, which marked the starting point of the German avenue of advance toward Avranches, now lay under threat of attack from two directions. The Americans had absolutely no defenses against a sortie into Juvigny le Tertre by German troops in le Mesnil Tove to the north. To the east, only the shattered remnants of Frankland's 1/117th Infantry, augmented by a company of engineers and the regimental Cannon Company, prevented the southern attack group of *Panzer Division 2* from seizing Juvigny le Tertre.

Major General Hobbs, recognizing the seriousness of the situation emerging on his northern flank, directed the 117th Infantry to establish a blocking position northeast of Juvigny le Tertre. Lieutenant Colonel Johnson instructed the 3/117th to send a rifle company to carry out Hobbs's orders. Lieutenant Colonel Mac-Dowell sent Company I to establish a defensive position at the head of a steep wooded draw blocking the most likely dismounted approach into Juvigny le Tertre. To defend against a mounted attack, the 823d TD Battalion dispatched Lieutenant Tom Raney's reconnaissance platoon and a TD platoon from C Company to Juvigny le Tertre. As he watched the TD platoon establish firing positions, Raney doubted that one platoon of three-inch guns would suffice to halt a determined assault by the Germans.[36]

Although Hobbs believed that the situation in Juvigny le Tertre was critical, he did not think it was as dangerous as the penetration made by *Kampfgruppe Schake*. With I/119th Infantry approaching from the east, American units were positioned on three sides of le Mesnil Adelee by midmorning. Elements of the 2d Armored, 4th Infantry, and 30th Infantry Divisions were poised to eliminate the Germans in le Mesnil Adelee. By 1000 hours, artillery units from all three divisions were hurling shells into the small village.

Hobbs assumed that the infantry companies sent to contain *Kampfgruppe Schake* would not suffice to eject a force of panzers from the village, forcing him to employ his own supporting armor if he wanted to achieve decisive results when launching a counterattack. Although Brigadier General Doyle Hickey of CCA had offered his assistance to Hobbs after reporting to the 30th Division headquarters with a battalion of medium tanks, Major General Huebner ordered Hickey to move his tanks to Mayenne regardless of the situation in Mortain. Hobbs was forced to turn for help to CCB, 3d Armored Division, which had been attached to his division at 0700 hours that morning by VII Corps.

At 1015 hours, Colonel Truman Boudinot received orders from the 30th Division to retake le Mesnil Adelee and le Mesnil Tove. The CCB commander immediately passed the mission to Colonel Dorrance Roysdon, commanding the 33d Armored Regiment. The 391st Armored Field Artillery was also in position to support CCB. After issuing a brief warning order to his troops, Colonel Roysdon departed for the 119th Infantry at 1100 hours to coordinate with Colonel Sutherland.

By 1100 hours, Lieutenant Colonel Brown's 3/119th Infantry had passed through Juvigny le Tertre heading north toward the hamlet of la Preveliere. The Americans had not encountered any resistance at this point. Captain Palmer's Company I broke off from the rest of the column to head west toward le Mesnil Adelee. The remainder of 3/119th, minus the platoon from K Company, turned east toward le Mesnil Tove.

As the Americans approached the village, Captain Mason L. Poinsett's L/119th Infantry came under fire. Determined to push forward, Lieutenant Colonel Brown ordered a platoon of supporting Shermans from C/743d Tank Battalion to assist Poinsett. When the American tanks moved forward, however, the leading vehicle was hit. The surviving Shermans pulled off the road to seek cover. Meanwhile, L Company also pulled back after suffering twenty-seven casualties.[37] The first attempt by the 30th Infantry Division to retake le Mesnil Tove ended in failure.

While the 3/119th Infantry attacked le Mesnil Tove, Captain Palmer's company linked up with B/119th. As the senior company commander, Captain Stewart directed I Company to establish defensive positions southeast of le Mesnil Adelee. Colonel Sutherland radioed Stewart to inform him that CCB would conduct an attack on the village. Although the Germans in le Mesnil Adelee did not appear particularly aggressive, B Company had countered a number of probes launched by SS reconnaissance troops, knocking out at least one armored car with a bazooka.

Although there was no direct coordination between the 30th Infantry and 2d Armored Divisions, the latter indirectly assisted Major General Hobbs by deploying a company of Shermans, reinforced by a TD platoon, to engage the Panthers in le Mesnil Adelee. For most of the morning, the opposing armored units traded ineffectual long-range fires against barely visible targets. The 78th Armored FA Battalion, however, scored a direct hit on a Panther sited near the church in le Mesnil Adelee. Return fire knocked out a Sherman from G/67th Armor. A shell also landed near the 3/67th Armor command post, killing a company commander and one other soldier. The accurate shelling prompted the 3/67th to move its headquarters north of le Mesnil Gilbert.[38]

While the Germans exchanged fire with 3/67th Armor, the 8th Infantry moved its 3d Battalion into le Mesnil Gilbert. Company L began digging in along the railroad tracks running parallel to the southern outskirts of the village. The presence of 4th Infantry Division units served to persuade Major General Brooks that he could pull the 3/67th Armor out of le Mesnil Gilbert in order to resume his division's march to Domfront. Shortly after L/8th Infantry arrived, the 2d Armored Division's march column turned west, then south again, in order to bypass le Mesnil Adelee. After a five-hour delay, 3/67th Armor was on the move once more.

Although the 2d Armored Division had departed, it contributed significantly to the fight to restore the 30th Infantry Division's northern flank. *Kampfgruppe Schake* suffered a number of casualties from the artillery supporting 3/67th Armor. One of the parting salvos from the 2d Armored guns killed *Oberstleutnant* Schake, so *Major* Kuno von Meyer assumed command of the *Kampfgruppe*. As the fog dissipated, American fighter-bombers appeared overhead. Twelve P-47Ds of the 50th Fighter Group attacked the panzers, claiming six vehicles destroyed. In reality, only one or two Panthers were damaged, but the aerial assault reminded the Germans of their steadily worsening situation.

The appearance of Allied airpower would have a decisive influence on the course of the battle along the northern flank of the 30th Infantry Division. Brigadier General William K. Harrison had arrived at 117th Infantry's regimental command post shortly before noon. Lieutenant Colonel Johnson updated Harrison on the situation in St.-Barthelemy, admitting that the only report he could confirm was that a portion of C/117th Infantry had been captured. As information continued to filter in, Harrison came to the conclusion that the situation was significantly more serious than division headquarters had realized. In addition to Company C being overrun, Frankland no longer had contact with A/117th Infantry.

Harrison departed Johnson's command post to ascertain the 1/117th Infantry's remaining defensive capacity. His concern grew as he realized how few soldiers from the 1st Battalion had escaped from St.-Barthelemy; he knew there were no reinforcements available. Despite his misgiving, Brigadier General Harrison shouted encouragement to the soldiers digging in along the road, telling them that "the 117th Infantry is here to fight. Let the tanks come through and hit them in the rear."[39] His efforts to raise morale had a significant impact on the exhausted men. One soldier remembered that "everywhere there was a problem. Brigadier General Harrison appeared and got it straightened out."[40]

As the panzers regrouped, *Generalleutnant* von Luettwitz ordered his artillery to begin a preparatory barrage against the American defenders barring the way to Juvigny le Tertre. At half past noon, Germans began preparing for another assault. With the *Leibstandarte* Panthers badly shot up, the Pzkfw IVs of *II Abteilung, Panzer Regiment 3* assumed the role of lead element for the southern attack group. Two Pzkfw IVs, accompanied by a half-track, were seen moving west soon afterward by A/105th Engineers. These vehicles were followed at a distance by six more panzers.

A bazooka team from D/117th Infantry ambushed the leading vehicles before they reached Juvigny le Tertre. Private Frank D. Joseph Jr., a forward observer for the 1/117th's mortar platoon, watched the panzers approach. When the lead vehicle stopped beside the Panther disabled by Lieutenant Neel's TD, Private Joseph's companion, Private Willie Pierce, whispered "shoot him." The two Americans were only five feet from the panzer, which would not provide time for the rocket warhead to arm. Joseph and Pierce crawled seventy-five yards to an embankment where they could see the halted panzers. Private Joseph knocked a track off the lead panzer with his first rocket. When the second tank tried to bypass the disabled vehicles, the bazooka team knocked it out as well. The crippled panzers completely blocked the road leading to Juvigny le Tertre, which prevented the remainder of *II Abteilung* from advancing.[41]

As the 117th Infantry repulsed this latest German probe, the 12th Army Group was coordinating the employment of British and American fighter-bombers in support of the 30th Division. With the congested road network limiting the movement of ground reinforcements, Lieutenant General Bradley intended to blunt the German counteroffensive by employing massed fighter-bombers. First Army had contacted Ninth Air Force to arrange for air support over the battlefield as soon as the fog cleared. American aerial planners were aware that Ninth Air Force did not possess many rocket-armed fighter-bomber groups. Most American fighter-bombers were only capable of dropping bombs, which was not highly effective against moving armored vehicles. The Americans asked the British Second Tactical Air Force to send as many of their rocket-armed Typhoon fighter-bomber squadrons as possible to St.-Barthelemy.

The airmen quickly agreed on a simple plan of action: Ninth Air Force assumed responsibility for warding off *Luftwaffe* attempts to intervene in the battle, and the British Typhoons, accompanied by the American rocket-armed 406th Fighter Group, would attack the panzers. The first Allied warplanes appeared at 1230 hours, when six Typhoons attacked the panzers clustered around St.-Barthelemy. Over the next forty-five minutes, another two dozen British planes struck von Luettwitz's southern attack column, effectively ending any effort by the Germans to seize Juvigny le Tertre.[42]

Leibstandarte lost five Panthers destroyed by the Typhoons, while a number of other panzer crews simply abandoned their vehicles rather than face the diving planes. Allied inspection teams later counted ten intact Panther tanks in the area after the fighting ended, which indicated that the Germans made no effort to reoccupy their vehicles.

A brief lull in the wake of the initial air strikes allowed von Luettwitz to reposition additional antiaircraft guns and conceal the surviving tanks. The second wave of Typhoon attacks met with greater resistance. Two British fighter-bombers were shot down and several damaged in return for moderate to light casualties inflicted on the Germans. As the number of targets diminished, the British planes began widening their search pattern to encompass Mortain, le Mesnil Adelee, and le Mesnil Tove. Although the fighter-bombers were able to inflict additional damage on German units in other portions of the battlefield, they inadvertently struck a number of American positions as well.

During the course of that afternoon, four RAF Typhoon wings flew 271 sorties against the attacking Germans. The British pilots claimed seventy-six tanks as "flamers," twenty-seven as "smokers," and twenty damaged. RAF planes also reported destroying or damaging eighty-six unarmored vehicles as well as nineteen unidentified armored fighting vehicles.[43] The American 406th Fighter Group, equipped with rocket-armed P-47D Thunderbolts, dispatched twelve planes to Mortain on 7 August. The American fighters launched forty-eight rockets, claiming seven tanks, one staff car, five half-tracks, and two trucks as destroyed. Although the claims of actual damage inflicted on the panzers were exaggerated, there was no disputing the fact that the appearance of Allied airpower had driven all thoughts of continuing the counteroffensive from the minds of German commanders.

The Germans enjoyed far less effective support from the *Luftwaffe* during those crucial hours. The initial appearance of the *Luftwaffe* did not take place until nearly three hours after the Allied fighter-bombers arrived. This delay occurred because of the lengthy amount of time required to assemble large formations of fighters after the fog lifted at Mortain. Because most of the *Luftwaffe* fighters were configured for ground attack, they were ill equipped to fend off the Allied planes that were attacking German ground units, which illustrates the lack of understanding between German ground commanders and their *Luftwaffe* counterparts. The former wanted fighters overhead to ward off Allied planes, while the latter defined effective support as sending bomb-armed aircraft to attack American ground units.

The initial bouts of air-to-air combat took place at 1515 hours, when the 396th Fighter Squadron intercepted thirty to thirty-five Me-109s carrying bombs in the vicinity of Lessay, claiming two Messerschmitt fighters destroyed. At 1520 hours, Mustangs from the 354th Fighter Squadron intercepted a second group of Me-109s in the vicinity of Mayenne, claiming seven destroyed and two damaged. In return, two P-51B and two P-51D aircraft failed to return to base. At 1555 hours, a third engagement occurred when the 379th Fighter Squadron tangled with FW-190s near Le Mans, shooting down three German planes.

Although the disappearance of the fog allowed Allied aviators to participate in the fighting, it also revealed American defensive positions to the Germans. Several American units were forced to displace when they came under accurate artillery fire. At le Mesnil Adelee, Captain Stewart was forced to pull back his combined command away from the village. As the tanks supporting him moved to a new location, red smoke shells landed nearby. The red smoke shells, which were employed by Allied units to designate a target for aerial attack, drew the attention of circling fighter-bombers.

I Company, 119th Infantry, was strafed by P-47D Thunderbolts, while British Typhoons launched rockets at the supporting American tanks. Two Shermans were damaged when their external stowage was set afire. Fortunately, the mistaken attack produced few casualties. Most accounts credit the Germans with firing red smoke to deceive the Allied pilots. Because this was an isolated incident on a battlefield that had offered ample opportunity for such a ruse, it is unlikely that the Germans were responsible. Captain Palmer's company was probably mistaken for Germans by an artillery observer from the 2d Armored Division or 4th Infantry Division.

Tanks carrying armored infantry move out of 1/33d Armored Regiment's assembly area near Reffuveille en route to le Mesnil Adelee on 7 August 1944. (National Archives)

The Germans in le Mesnil Adelee chose this moment to counterattack the disorganized Americans. Three Panthers, supported by panzergrenadiers, launched an assault against I/119th. Disrupted by the fighter-bomber attack, Company I scattered at the sight of approaching panzers. Supporting American medium tanks, which had moved out of sight to avoid another friendly air attack, were caught out of position. In the confusion, most of I Company was able to escape capture. When Captain Palmer checked on his rifle platoons, he discovered that six men, including one platoon leader, were missing. Private Daniel Noyes volunteered to search for the missing officer but returned empty-handed after being fired on by a German armored car.[44]

As the Panthers returned to their defensive positions, the 1/33d Armor, commanded by Lieutenant Colonel Rosewell King, departed CCB's assembly area near Reffuveille bound for le Mesnil Adelee. Lieutenant Don L. West's F/33d Armor spearheaded King's column, trailed by Lieutenant Jessie Carter's I/33d Armor.[45] The 1/33d also included a light tank company, an armored infantry company, and supporting TDs, reconnaissance, and engineers. King ordered F/33d Armor to conduct the attack on le Mesnil Adelee. Lieutenant West employed two tank platoons in a frontal attack while a third tank platoon enveloped the village from the north.

Following a thirty-minute preparatory bombardment using high-explosive, the artillery supporting 1/33d Armor switched to smoke to provide cover for Lieutenant West's attack. Smoke and dust limited visibility to several hundred yards, but the Panther crews finally began to discern the shapes of the approaching Shermans. A tracer round impacted against the hull of an American tank, causing a puff of smoke and a loud metallic ring. A flurry of red shell tracers arced toward le Mesnil Adelee as the Shermans halted to return fire. The frontal attack, however, served its primary purpose of distracting the defenders.

The Germans were unaware that the 1/33d Armor was attacking from the north until the lead Sherman lurched onto a trail leading into the village. The commander of von Meyer's *I Schwadron, Rittmeister* Christoph von Helldorf, tried to pivot his vehicle to face this unexpected threat, but the Americans reacted faster. His Panther was knocked out before it could fire a shot. American artillery fire wounded *Major* von Meyer and his adjutant, *Leutnant* Albrecht von Stein, as they were tried to counter the unexpected assault.[46] Assailed from two directions, the defenses of *Kampfgruppe Schake* began to unravel.

After his 3d Platoon reported knocking out several Panthers, Lieutenant West led the remainder of F Company against the southern outskirts of le Mesnil Adelee. The Americans got the worst of this exchange as six Shermans were destroyed or disabled. Despite these losses, F/33d Armor continued on until it reached the outskirts of le Mesnil Adelee. As Lieutenant West's tanks entered the village, supporting elements of the 1/36th AIR moved forward to clear the houses. *Major* von Meyer, recognizing that his position would soon be overrun, ordered *Kampfgruppe Schake* to retreat.

By 1800 hours, von Meyer was leading the survivors of *Kampfgruppe Schake* out of le Mesnil Adelee. The village was burning from end to end, concealing the German exit from 1/33d Armor. As the column wound its way slowly to the east, however, an artillery observation plane from the 4th Infantry Division spotted the retreating Germans. The 155mm howitzers of the 20th FA Battalion began targeting *Kampfgruppe Schake*. Shells plummeted down on the column, killing men and destroying unarmored vehicles. The retreat was turning out to be a very costly one.[47]

Although *Kampfgruppe Schake* had been driven from le Mesnil Adelee, it still packed a potent punch in the form of von Meyer's sixteen surviving Panthers. The artillery fire placed on the column by the 4th Infantry Division devastated the soft-skinned vehicles accompanying the *Kampfgruppe* but had little effect on the heavily armored Panthers. The sight of numerous Panthers moving east persuaded Captain Palmer's I/119th Infantry to shift its position once more to avoid drawing unwelcome attention. Palmer also warned Lieutenant Colonel Brown via radio, prompting the commander of the 3/119th to order his other rifle companies to avoid contact with the tanks.[48]

After the Germans departed, 1/33d Armor took stock of its victory. The 3d Armored Division soldiers counted the hulks of six Panther tanks, two assault guns, a number of half-tracks, and several towed 75mm guns in le Mesnil Adelee. Forty Germans were taken prisoner as the American armored infantry carefully searched each building. Lieutenant Colonel King, however, was frustrated by the refusal of the 119th Infantry to assist with clearing the village. He had hoped to deny the retreating Germans any opportunity to reorganize, but

Members of the 33d Armored Regiment pose behind a knocked-out
Panther tank. (Emmett Tripp)

with only his armored infantry available to secure the village, it would take
longer to complete that task. Regardless of the delay, King ordered 1/33d Armor
to prepare for a night attack on le Mesnil Tove.

Despite these setbacks, *Generalleutnant* von Luettwitz hoped to maintain
sufficient pressure on the Americans to facilitate a successful assault by *Leibstandarte* the following day. After the last of the Allied fighter-bombers departed
at 2030 hours, German infiltrators penetrated the thinly held American line west
of St.-Barthelemy, opening fire on the 117th Cannon Company with rifles and
machine guns. Lieutenant Colonel MacDowell sent a platoon from his Company
K, augmented by a squad from L Company, four cooks from the 3/117th's Head-

quarters Company, and two men from G Company, to eradicate this threat. The assorted group, led by the G Company commander, killed six Germans, wounded one, and took another prisoner. With the threat to their howitzers erased, the 117th's Cannon Company resumed firing on the Germans in St.-Barthelemy.[49]

Von Luettwitz also directed his supporting artillery to fire on the Americans to disrupt their defensive preparations. Lieutenant Colonel Johnson's command post attracted so much artillery fire that his men dubbed it "Chateau de la Nebelwerfer." Although it appeared as if every square yard around the building housing the command post had been hit, the structure itself remained untouched. Despite incoming shells, Lieutenant Colonel Johnson refused to relocate his headquarters, fearing that any movement to the rear might adversely impact the morale of his men.

Sporadic fighting continued to flare up as darkness fell. A German prisoner brought to 117th Infantry's command post admitted that "the planes had disrupted our plans for attacking today but my comrades would be ready to renew the attack either tonight or tomorrow."[50] Just before midnight, Johnson was ordered to send guides to Juvigny le Tertre to meet a company of self-propelled TDs and a battalion of infantry promised to him by Major General Hobbs. The news was heartening, but if the reinforcements did not arrive soon, Johnson knew he would not be able to hold Juvigny le Tertre against a strong attack, especially if the fog shielded the Germans from Allied airpower.

CONCLUSIONS

The German panzers at Mortain exhibited an uncharacteristic lack of tactical flexibility that contributed significantly to the failure of the opening stages of *Unternehmen Lüttich*. *Panzer Division 2*, which represented the main effort of *XLVII Panzer Korps*, never attempted to bypass St.-Barthelemy. Von Luettwitz refused to alter his plans as unforeseen events occurred. He also erred in committing the late-arriving *SS* Panthers against the 1/117th Infantry. The Panthers attacked into the teeth of the American defenses without time to study the terrain they were fighting on. Von Luettwitz also failed to coordinate effective artillery, reconnaissance, and infantry support for the attacking panzers. With the poor visibility cloaking Lieutenant Greene's TDs, the Americans were able to hold their fire until they could be sure of penetrating the heavy armor of Panthers.

Kampfgruppe Schake represents a perfect example of a balanced German combined arms formation that understood its mission. Consisting of an understrength battalion each of Panthers, armored infantry, and reconnaissance supported by assault guns and self-propelled antitank guns, the northern attack column of *Panzer Division 2* rapidly achieved a clean breakthrough. The lack of flexibility and central coordination exhibited by *Panzer Division 2*, however, resulted in a missed opportunity to employ *Kampfgruppe Schake* in a flanking move against Juvigny le Tertre. The northern assault column remained immobile while their comrades fought and died at St.-Barthelemy. Schake's rationale for stopping was not due to the potential appearance of Allied planes, which would not materialize for six hours, but simply because no one was following him.

Generalleutnant von Luettwitz's lack of aggressiveness ensured that the Americans defending the northern shoulder were not confronted with a concentrated divisional attack, but battalion and regimental assaults spread over a wide front. The difficulties that plagued *Panzer Division 2* stemmed in large part from the passive manner in which *LXVII Panzer Korps* coordinated the counteroffensive. Rather than take a position on the line of departure, where he could make critical decisions quickly, *General der Panzertruppen* von Funck contented himself with repeatedly telephoning Hausser to complain about *Generalleutnant* Graf von Schwerin.

Preoccupied with emotional matters, von Funck neglected to coordinate a corpswide reconnaissance effort in advance of the counteroffensive that would have detected many of the American defensive positions as well as the gaps between these positions. If *XLVII Panzer Korps* had conducted preparatory reconnaissance, the counteroffensive might have gained enough momentum to permit the Germans to recuperate from the poorly coordinated opening phase. This course of action, however, presupposes central direction by *XLVII Panzer Korps*.

With effective command and control by the Germans sorely lacking at division and corps level during the critical opening hours, it is no wonder that elements of five panzer and panzergrenadier divisions failed to overwhelm an understrength American infantry division. Although the panzers physically occupied the same battlefield, operationally they were unable to provide mutual support for each other. The *XLVII Panzer Korps* plan did not provide for corpswide artillery coordination, the shifting of forces to exploit success, complementary reconnaissance operations, or maneuver options that permitted one panzer division to enter the sector of another for the purposes of outflanking stubborn defenders. Bound by a rigid concept of operation, the Germans did not exhibit the tactical or operational flexibility required to overcome the 30th Infantry Division on the morning of 7 August.

7

The Lost Battalion

As night fell on 7 August, Americans in Mortain found themselves in an extremely precarious situation. C/120th Infantry had been driven from the town, with only a tattered band of survivors maintaining a toehold on the western outskirts. The counterattack by Lockett's 2/117th Infantry also failed to win back Mortain. Lieutenant Colonel Hardaway's command group was still in hiding, hoping to escape capture. With the town completely in German hands, the 2d Battalion on Hill 314 was cut off from the rest of the 120th Infantry.

When Hardaway was unable to rejoin his men, Colonel Birks appointed Captain Erichson of F Company via radio as temporary battalion commander. Erichson assumed command of a battalion that existed in name only; battalion headquarters, H Company, and the antitank platoon were scattered by the German assault. Although attempts by *Kampfgruppe Fick* to overrun Hill 314 failed, the attackers succeeded in splitting the 2/120th Infantry into several isolated segments. K Company, a platoon from C Company, and elements of G Company were located north of the Bel Air road. E Company, survivors of H Company, a squad from Company F, and the remnants of Lieutenant Miller's TD platoon occupied a wooded area on the southeastern slope. Company E also established a roadblock interdicting the Bel Air road. The American positions were separated by a thousand yards of partially wooded ground.

Captain Erichson, located with the northern group, ordered a survey of the remaining ammunition and supplies. Each of the isolated companies reported severe shortages. Stockpiled ammunition reserves were located in a shallow ravine behind Company E, but snipers prevented the Americans from replenishing their cartridge belts. K Company had suffered about a dozen killed and wounded as well as two squads captured during the initial assault. E and G Companies each lost approximately thirty to forty men killed, captured, or wounded. Company H suffered thirty-six casualties, including eight killed. The Germans had also captured or destroyed most of the 2d Battalion's heavy machine guns, nineteen out of twenty jeeps, and three of six 81mm mortars.

Lacking the radios normally available to a battalion commander, Captain Erichson was limited to passing messages back to regimental headquarters through his fellow company commanders. The radios organic to the infantry companies, however, were not designed to communicate directly with regimental headquarters. Only the artillery radio sets proved powerful enough to consistently contact Colonel Birks. The primary means of communication for the 2/120th Infantry rested with the 120th Cannon Company observer supporting K Company and 230th FA Battalion observers located with E and G Companies.

The American observers on Hill 314 were preoccupied with calling artillery for most of 7 August. As the tempo of the German assault decreased, the forward observers began passing situation reports from Lieutenant Ralph Kerley, commander of E Company, to Colonel Birks, who relayed them to division headquarters. The initial request from the 2d Battalion for additional ammunition and medical supplies arrived at regimental headquarters at 1800 hours on 7 August. This message, sent by Lieutenant Weiss on his own initiative, simply stated: "Enemy N, S, E, W. Request supply and support immediately." When no help was forthcoming, Lieutenant Kerley asked Weiss to send a second message at 2350 hours, noting that E Company was running critically low on ammunition.[1]

These reports created great concern at the division command post. The southern flank of the 30th Division would quickly collapse if the Germans succeeded in capturing Hill 314. Fortunately, artillery support prevented *Das Reich* from expanding upon its initial success in Mortain. As long as the 2/120th Infantry held the commanding heights, the 30th Division could continue to employ artillery effectively against any target visible to the observers on Hill 314. Consequently, the 30th Division gave high priority to fulfilling any request for fire originating from the 2/120th Infantry. As long as the forward observers on Hill 314 maintained radio contact, artillery support would not become a problem for the isolated battalion.

Resupplying the 2/120th Infantry, however, was proving to be a significantly more difficult challenge. Major General Hobbs did not have enough troops to force open a corridor to the 2/120th, and the radio messages sent by Lieutenant Kerley alerted him to the possibility that he might lose Hill 314. When Colonel Birks relayed the messages to division headquarters, he was asked to recommend a course of action for delivering supplies to the 2/120th Infantry. With Mortain in German hands, Birks did not believe that the supplies would get through using ground transportation. He recommended using aerial resupply to deliver food, ammunition, and medical supplies to the surrounded battalion.

The 30th Division did not possess the organic means to airdrop supplies. Permission was required from First Army before an aerial resupply mission would occur, and as the intermediate headquarters between the 30th Division and First Army, VII Corps would be responsible for validating the request. At 0100 hours on 8 August, the 30th Division contacted VII Corps to request an airdrop. The division operations officer told VII Corps that "we have to get supplies to that unit cut off up at Mortain—water, ammunition, 60mm and 81mm mortar, as much as we can get . . . they will mark the place with a big 'X' on the ground . . . we must get supplies to them and we can't reach them."[2]

Unfortunately, prior to the request being made, the 30th Division also passed a report to VII Corps that friendly troops were within eight hundred yards of the isolated battalion. The mistaken impression at VII Corps was that the 30th Division would relieve the 2/120th Infantry before the airdrop request could be processed. This belief also threatened to delay the approval process for the request. Although the 30th Division's operations officer personally explained that the situation had changed significantly since the report was made, VII Corps failed to act with urgency. The VII Corps G-4 responded by quoting a First Army letter of instruction stating that the airdrop would not occur until he received a formal written request listing the specific supplies needed by the 2/120th Infantry.

The lack of urgency exhibited by VII Corps drove the 30th Division to seek other means. Contacting divisional artillery to arrange for a supply drop using light observation airplanes, the division operations officer explained that "we have a battalion cut off on that hill, you know, and one unit in Sicily used Cubs to drop supplies and I was wondering what the chances would be for us to use one to drop some to our people." The division artillery headquarters replied: "We can try it as long as the visibility is poor. If we can try to get over there while the visibility is poor they [the Germans] won't shoot us up."[3]

While the 30th Division continued coordinating an airdrop on Hill 314, *Kampfgruppe Fick* was preparing to launch a nighttime assault against the 2/120th Infantry. The Germans hoped that the darkness would hide the attacking force from American artillery observers. However, the forward observers supporting the isolated battalion had already preregistered potential assembly areas and all of the routes leading to Hill 314. Between 0210 and 0645 hours on 8 August, Lieutenant Weiss directed artillery by sound against three attempts by *Kampfgruppe Fick* to mount an assault against the 2/120th Infantry.[4] Only a single panzer was able to force its way into E Company's defensive perimeter. The Americans lay silent as the panzer drove around for a short while before departing.

Artillery support for the attacking Germans was conspicuous by its absence. *Kampfgruppe Fick* failed to effectively utilize its own indirect fire assets to cover the assembly of the attacking troops or to suppress the defenders. As dawn approached on 8 August, the Germans belatedly attempted to bring their supporting artillery into play. At 0830 hours, a pair of *Kubelwagens* (German jeeps) carrying an artillery reconnaissance party approached the E/120th Infantry roadblock. The Americans killed the driver of the lead vehicle and captured his passenger, an *SS* artillery lieutenant. The wounded *SS* officer was carried up the hill for interrogation, where he admitted that he was a forward observer attached to a heavy artillery battery located at Ger.[5]

As the interrogation was concluded, Kerley asked Lieutenant Weiss to send an updated situation report to Colonel Birks. Weiss willingly obliged, transmitting a terse message that quoted the E Company commander as saying: "Elements of H Company still with me. Point marked with white cross. Need batteries [for] 300 and 610 [radio]. Still in contact with G and K. [Need] medical supplies & food, [plus] basic load for rifle company & 60mm and 81mm mortars. Captured enemy jeep [at] 0830. English speak[ing] German officer captured wounded—his [artillery] battery is at Ger."[6]

By midmorning, the batteries powering Lieutenant Bartz's radio gave out. By default, Lieutenant Weiss was now the sole radio link to the artillery units supporting the 2/120th Infantry. Anticipating just such an emergency, he directed one of his men to retrieve a spare set of radio batteries from their jeep. By continually rotating both sets of batteries, Lieutenant Weiss was able to maintain communications after the other artillery observer's radio ceased transmitting.

Kampfgruppe Fick began shelling Hill 314 in preparation for another attack. The German gunners paid particular attention to neutralizing the opposing forward observers. At 1305 hours on 8 August, white phosphorous (WP) shells began landing near Lieutenant Weiss's observation post. Although the Americans often employed WP, their opponents did not possess many of these shells due to the shortage of raw materials in Germany. WP shells were capable of creating a dense smoke screen, and the phosphorous flakes clung to clothing or skin, proving tremendously difficult to extinguish. The fact that *Kampfgruppe Fick* employed this rarely used ammunition indicates the priority assigned to neutralizing the American observers. Ammunition shortages did not permit the German gunners to blanket the hill with phosphorous, and Lieutenant Weiss and his party were able to find cover to avoid the burning particles, when the shelling stopped as suddenly as it began.

Following the barrage of phosphorous shells, a battery of German howitzers began shelling the 2/120th Infantry. Locating the position of the field pieces, Lieutenant Weiss quickly silenced them. *Kampfgruppe Fick* responded with six self-propelled assault guns borrowed from *Das Reich*. The assault guns fired only a few rounds apiece before American artillery fire also drove them off. That afternoon, the Germans made two more attempts to bring their supporting artillery to bear against the isolated American troops. In both instances, Lieutenant Weiss was able to neutralize the German batteries.[7]

Although the Germans failed to effectively employ their artillery against the 2/120th Infantry, they met with greater success in preventing supplies from reaching the isolated defenders. During the previous night, *SS-Panzer Division 2* ringed Hill 314 with antiaircraft guns. When the 30th Division tried dropping ammunition using a pair of light observation planes on the morning of 8 August, they were greeted by a storm of ground fire. Under normal operating conditions, the light planes avoided antiaircraft fire by remaining at higher altitudes; however, they were required to fly at low levels to accurately deliver supplies. Both planes were heavily damaged, and one pilot was wounded. Concluding that additional attempts would result in prohibitive losses, the 30th Division canceled its plans to use light aircraft to airdrop supplies.

The morale of the 2d Battalion was beginning to waver by the evening of 8 August. The failed airdrop and lack of reinforcements created an acute sense of abandonment. Later that evening, Lieutenant Weiss relayed a report stating: "We have captured several prisoners. We are bothered by snipers. There are several tanks and armored vehicles to the east . . . We need supplies for the 300 and 600 series radios. We need food and medical supplies. We are not worried about the situation as long as the artillery fire [support] continues."[8]

An unknown radio operator at the receiving end added the concluding sentence to the message. The soldiers on Hill 314 were in fact very worried about their situation. The altered report was forwarded through the 120th Infantry to the 30th Division. Like many of the men on Hill 314, Lieutenant Weiss was sure that higher headquarters had no idea of the magnitude of the isolation felt by the soldiers of the 2/120th Infantry.[9]

As *Kampfgruppe Fick* grappled unsuccessfully for control of Hill 314, the remainder of *SS-Panzer Division 2* consolidated its positions. *Standartenführer* Baum ordered *Der Führer* to reduce the troublesome American roadblock at L'Abbaye Blanche while *Kampfgruppe Ullrich* secured the rest of Hill 285. Once both of these objectives were firmly under German control, Baum could divert additional forces against the Americans on Hill 314. Additionally, he hoped that casualties inflicted on the defenders by *Das Reich* would significantly degrade the ability of the 30th Division to retain a firm grip on the commanding terrain anchoring its southern flank.

At midnight on 7 August, *Kampfgruppe Ullrich* prepared to attack the 1/120th Infantry. The casualties suffered by his supporting panzers on 7 August persuaded *Hauptsturmführer* Ullrich that a more deliberate approach was needed. At 0020 hours, a preparatory barrage began striking the 1/120th Infantry. One shell landed near the command post of Company A, destroying the radio of the supporting artillery observer.[10] Once the preparatory barrage ended, a German assault troop consisting of engineers armed with flamethrowers headed out to destroy the American TDs defending Hill 285.

Before they could locate their intended targets, the German assault engineers happened upon an outpost belonging to B Company. A skirmish ensued after one of the Americans tossed a grenade at rustling sounds in nearby bushes. The Germans replied by throwing grenades at the outpost. The *SS* tried to employ their flamethrowers against the defenders, but they failed to ignite. Deprived of the use of their flamethrowers, the *SS* engineers decided to retreat. In their haste to depart, they left behind a wounded man and one inoperative flamethrower.

Lieutenant Colonel Bradford was convinced that another attack was going to occur soon. In the belief that the main effort of the impending German assault would be directed against B Company, Bradford dispatched an additional forward observer team from 230th FA to assist Lieutenant Pulver. The party arrived in the B Company perimeter just after 0600 hours on 8 August.

As the forward observers were settling in, the sounds of approaching panzers were heard in the predawn darkness. Despite a promising attempt to conduct a combined arms assault by dispatching engineers to destroy the TDs, *Kampfgruppe Ullrich* once again sent unsupported armor against the 1/120th Infantry. The Germans did not resume their preparatory barrage as the panzers neared the American positions, and *SS* foot soldiers failed to move forward to support the armored vehicles. When the leading panzer advanced within fifty yards of the perimeter, a well-camouflaged three-inch TD knocked it out. The muzzle blast of the TD, however, obscured the immediate area long enough to permit the other panzers to escape.[11]

The newly arrived forward observers called for artillery on the German troops assembling for an assault against B Company. As the shells began impacting near the destroyed Pzkfw IV, several rounds landed perilously close to American lines, driving the TD gunners into cover. With the TD crews away from their weapons, *Kampfgruppe Ullrich* managed to penetrate the American defensive perimeter using a captured Sherman tank. However, a continuing rain of artillery fire prevented *SS* foot soldiers from following up this success. The captured Sherman reentered German lines a few minutes later, signaling an end to the assault on B Company.

Kampfgruppe Ullrich launched a second attack a short while later, this time against A/120th Infantry. *SS* flamethrower teams set fire to the hedgerow occupied by Lieutenant Smith's center platoon, and the burning foliage threatened to ignite the ammunition stowed beside nearby TDs. The pressure exerted by the Germans also resulted in American infantrymen and tank destroyer gunners alike slowly filtering to the rear. Lieutenant Connors, platoon leader of the supporting TDs, was able to rally a squad of soldiers from A Company. The group knocked out one of the flamethrower teams, which persuaded the Germans to pull back temporarily.

Despite successful efforts by Lieutenant Connors to restore the A Company defensive line, Lieutenant Smith ordered his men to fall back to the crest of Hill 285.[12] This move placed the TDs protecting A/120th Infantry in a precarious position: with the infantry falling back, the three-inch guns were too far forward to be safely extricated. The TD crews returned to their weapons rather than allow them to be captured. By refusing to pull back, Lieutenant Connors found himself in possession of a shallow salient protruding from the American lines.

Efforts by *Der Führer* to overcome the roadblock at L'Abbaye Blanche also met with scant success on 8 August. The Germans initially sent two half-tracks armed with 75mm howitzers toward L'Abbaye Blanche at dawn. Moving slowly through dense fog, the vehicles approached within several hundred yards of the roadblock before they were seen. The TD gunners, despite their surprise at the sudden appearance of the half-tracks, got in the first shots, knocking out both

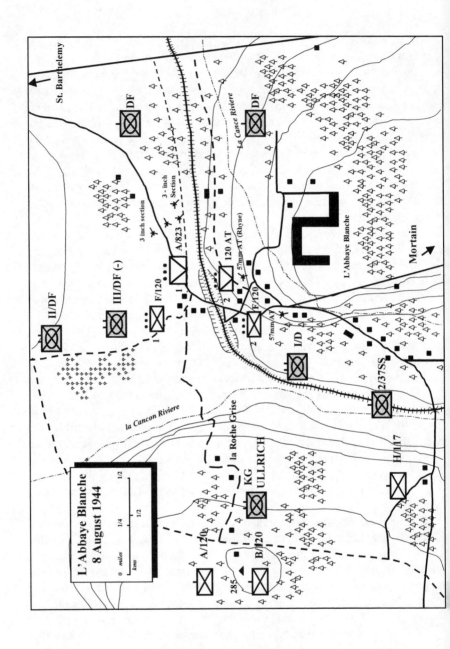

L'Abbaye Blanche
8 August 1944

0   1/4   1/2
miles

1/2
kms

St. Barthelemy

DF

DF

3 - inch
Section

3 inch section

A/823

120 AT

57mm-AT (Rhyne)

II/DF

III/DF (-)

F/120

1

1

2

F/120

57mm-AT

2

I/D

L'Abbaye Blanche

La Cance Riviere

Mortain

la Cancon Riviere

2/37SS

la Roche Grise

H/1/17

KG
ULLRICH

A/120

285

B/120

vehicles before the *SS* could reply. An ammunition carrier following the self-propelled howitzers was also destroyed.[13]

Frustrated in his efforts to capture L'Abbaye Blanche by direct assault, *Sturmbannführer* Weidinger tasked his supporting artillery to neutralize the American TD platoon. An intense barrage pummeled the roadblock for several hours. Several shells exploded near the three-inch guns but did not cause major damage. Other rounds landed near Lieutenant Tom F. H. Andrew's rifle platoon, killing one man. Shell fragments also damaged both of the 1-1/2 ton prime movers belonging to the antitank platoon from the 120th Infantry.[14] However, the artillery fire eventually tapered off when *Der Führer* turned its attention to the 12th Infantry. For the next several days, German probes against L'Abbaye Blanche were limited to small patrols as more troops were diverted to the defense of RJ 278.

With the American defenders of Hill 285 and L'Abbaye Blanche fully occupied, the only hope of opening up an overland route to Hill 314 lay with Major Herlong's 1/119th Infantry. Held up by rough terrain and stubborn resistance, Herlong was in no position to achieve a rapid decision and began lobbying division headquarters for reinforcements. His first order of business was obtaining the release of B Company, which had been attached to the 3/119th Infantry. With the bulk of the 30th Division's artillery employed in support of the isolated battalion on Hill 314, Major Herlong also possessed little in the way of fire support. The 1/119th was forced to rely on its own heavy weapons company and the M5 light tanks of D/743d Tank Battalion, augmented with two medium tanks.

Faced with an obstinate German defense and few resources, Major Herlong focused on employing his forces where they would gain the greatest advantage. By midafternoon on 8 August, C Company worked itself into a position north of Romagny, while A Company was poised to the southwest. Unfortunately, Herlong could not count on significant assistance from Captain Sibbold's F/117th Infantry. Although patrols from F Company had contacted the 1/119th, Sibbold informed Major Herlong that his men were not in a good position to conduct a direct assault on the village.

The 1/119th Infantry's initial assault on 8 August began at 1500 hours, gaining about four hundred yards before incoming fire inflicted approximately ten to fifteen casualties. C Company was badly scattered as it tried to advance while maintaining contact with F Company. Major Herlong was forced to retreat to reorganize his battalion; he also directed his supporting armor to pull back one hedgerow. As the medium tank attached to C Company reversed out of position, a Pzkfw IV hidden near the village church knocked it out. Two of the Sherman's crew escaped, but the others were killed.[15]

Realizing he would not be able to seize Romagny until he received more troops, Major Herlong continued to ask for reinforcements. His persistence finally paid off that afternoon: B Company boarded trucks bound for Romagny, and the 743d Tank Battalion was directed to send an entire company of medium

tanks to assist him. Lieutenant Frederick Fleming's B/743d Tank Battalion subsequently departed Barenton for Romagny. The newly arrived 629th TD Battalion was ordered to send two M-10 platoons to reinforce Major Herlong.[16] One
platoon arrived at Romagny, but the second became misoriented, linking up by
mistake with Lieutenant Colonel Lockett's 2/117th Infantry.

Bolstered by reinforcements, Major Herlong prepared for another attack at
1900 hours. A and C Companies would advance along the road leading into
Romagny, with B Company trailing.[17] Lacking artillery, Herlong tasked Lieutenant Fleming's tankers to provide suppressive fire against the village. When
this task was completed, the medium tanks would follow A/119th Infantry. The
assault began with B/743d Tank Battalion firing high-explosive and white phosphorous shells into Romagny. The shelling wounded the commander of the
defending Germans, *Sturmbannführer* Schrieber. *Obersturmführer* Heinz
Macher, heading the engineer company supporting Schrieber's battalion,
assumed command of the defense.

One of 743d Tank Battalion's dozer tanks also gained a small measure of
revenge when it knocked out a Pzkfw IV next to the village church. By 2100
hours, however, both of the lead infantry companies reported that they were
unable to continue advancing. Conceding defeat, Herlong ordered his troops to
pull back for the night. However, the supporting tanks lost another Sherman
while moving back. The dozer tank was also hit as it shifted position, losing its
right track.[18] Although its entire crew escaped unharmed, the vehicle was abandoned. Having failed twice, Major Herlong sat down to devise another means of
overcoming the unfavorable terrain and stubborn defenders of Romagny.

With the majority of First Army units committed to exploiting the capture of
Vire, which fell on 7 August, Lieutenant General Bradley decided to employ
troops from Third Army to fill the gap in the VII Corps lines between Mortain
and Barenton. Fearing the worst, Bradley initially had halted Major General Walton Walker's entire XX Corps in place to protect Avranches. As more information arrived at 12th Army Group headquarters, Bradley became convinced that
VII Corps could hold Mortain without significant reinforcements. Accordingly,
he released XX Corps back to Third Army on 8 August with the exception of one
infantry division, the 35th, which would assume the mission of plugging the gap
in the VII Corps sector.[19]

The 35th Infantry Division possessed professional credentials similar to the
30th Division. Nicknamed the Santa Fe division, it originally consisted of
National Guard units primarily from Missouri, Kansas, and Nebraska. The 35th
landed in Normandy on 6 July, entering combat two days later. Like many other
inexperienced American units, it suffered heavily during its baptism of fire but
learned quickly from its errors. After a month of combat under First Army, the
35th was transferred to Third Army on 1 August.

The commanding general of the 35th Infantry Division, Major General Paul
W. Baade, was a long-serving regular officer. The fifty-five-year-old Baade,

German vehicles destroyed by Lieutenant Thomas Springfield's tank destroyer platoon at L'Abbaye Blanche. The Mortain–le Neufbourg train station is in the background. (National Archives)

commissioned as an infantry second lieutenant following his graduation from West Point in 1911, was no stranger to overseas service or combat. He previously served a tour in the Philippines and as a rifle company commander in the 332d Infantry of the 81st Division during World War I. A series of interwar assignments culminated with Baade's appointment as commander of the Puerto Rican General Depot and Mobile Force in 1942. He departed Puerto Rico for California where he assumed the duties of assistant division commander of the 35th Division in July 1943. Six months later, he was appointed as the division commander. An able tactician and trainer, Major General Baade was not reluctant to leave his command post to determine the situation at the front.

Lieutenant General Patton cautioned XX Corps not to allow the 35th Division to become so deeply involved that it would be unable to disengage quickly. Adhering to the Third Army commander's guidance, Major General Walker retained control of the 35th rather than attaching it to Collins's VII Corps. XX Corps instructed Major General Baade to employ no more than two regimental combat teams.[20] The remainder of Baade's division, Walker explained, would hold itself in readiness for future operations.[21]

The 35th Infantry Division sat for most of the morning of 7 August in its assembly area southwest of St.-Hilaire-du-Harcouet. Baade, aware of the fighting taking place in Mortain, took the initiative by ordering the 35th Reconnaissance Troop to scout the area between St.-Hilaire and Mortain.[22] In anticipation of an active role, he also ordered Colonel Butler B. Miltonberger's 134th Infantry to move to a new assembly area southeast of St.-Hilaire-du-Harcouet. Miltonberger was a career national guardsman, having served in the 134th in virtually all ranks from private to regimental commander. Baade also directed Colonel Harold R. Emery's 137th Infantry to occupy a new assembly area south of Miltonberger. The forty-eight-year-old Emery was a graduate of the West Point class of 1919. Colonel Bernard A. Byrne's 320th Infantry, designated as the division's mobile reserve, was tasked to guard against an attack from north of the Selune River.[23] Byrne, a forty-six-year-old native of Ohio, was a West Point classmate of Emery's.

By 1745 hours on 7 August, the 134th and 137th Regiments had moved several miles closer to the fighting. At 2000 hours, Major General Walker authorized Baade to push east until he reached the Mortain-Barenton road. The 134th, which occupied the northern half of the sector allotted to the 35th Division, was tasked to establish contact with the 30th Division. The 137th, operating to the south of Colonel Miltonberger, was instructed to link up with the 2d Armored Division.

The 134th Infantry, reinforced with a company each of tanks and TDs, began advancing to the east at 2030 hours. Colonel Miltonberger hoped to let his men travel as far east as possible while remaining mounted but quickly changed his mind when the regimental I&R platoon was fired upon by German machine guns a mile east of Milly. Captain Frederick Roecker, commanding the 2/134th, anticipated the order to dismount. He ordered his men out of their trucks as soon as he saw tracers ricocheting skyward in the evening twilight.

Soon afterward, Captain Roecker's leading company overran a German outpost near la Cross de Berre. After a brief clash, the 2/134th Infantry reached its designated objective at 2230 hours. The 3/134th also reached its limit of advance when it secured the village of Notre Dame du Touchet without opposition. In fact, the only difficulty encountered by Colonel Miltonberger's regiment was an American minefield blocking the road he hoped to use for a supply route. Trucks were unable to move east of that point until the engineers cleared a lane through the mines.[24]

The 137th Infantry also jumped off on schedule, only to collide with vehicles from the 2d Armored Division. However, Colonel Emery's leading battalions were able to work their way through the traffic after a thirty-minute delay. The 137th halted after coming on line with the 134th Infantry. Although Colonel Emery's regiment met with no resistance, his troops were spectators to a duel between assault guns from E Troop, 4th Cavalry, and a German antitank gun.

By nightfall, the 35th Division covered half the distance to the Mortain-Barenton road. After spending a relatively quiet night, Major General Baade's division renewed its advance beginning at 0600 hours on 8 August. The 137th Infantry moved steadily east without encountering any Germans, aside from a lone straggler killed by a 1st Battalion patrol.[25] In the southern half of the regimental sector, the 3/134th failed to meet any resistance. In the northern portion, the 2d Battalion ran into a machine-gun nest that pinned down E/134th Infantry. After a lengthy delay, E Company outflanked the position, forcing the Germans to pull back.

Resuming its advance, the 2/134th Infantry gained a few hundred yards before German machine gunners halted G Company. After another delay, the Americans were able to outflank the SS troops. The 2/134th continued pressing forward until Captain Roecker was wounded at 0850 hours.[26] Lieutenant Colonel Fielder Greer arrived to take charge but departed within a few hours. Responsibility for leading the 2d Battalion subsequently fell on Captain Carlyle F. McDannell.[27]

With the issue of battalion command settled, the 2/134th resumed its advance. When a German machine gun opened fire on the leading Americans, the light tanks of F Company, 4th Cavalry Squadron, began pouring suppressive fire into the hedgerows.[28] TDs supporting the 2d Battalion noticed the muzzle blast of an automatic weapon in the upper windows of a nearby farmhouse. A section of M-10s from the 654th TD Battalion slammed shell after shell into the building until it caught on fire.[29]

With the machine-gun nest neutralized, the Germans began dropping mortars on the 2/134th. Every movement brought an accurate rain of shells. Captain McDannell ordered his men to seek cover until the mortars could be knocked out. In an attempt to prevent a stalemate, Colonel Miltonberger directed the 3/134th to prepare to send a tank-infantry team north to cut off the Germans holding up the 2d Battalion.

The remainder of the 134th Infantry succeeded in advancing to a point southeast of Romagny by midafternoon. The progress achieved by Colonel Miltonberger's regiment, however, created a gap between the 35th Division and 30th Division to the north. VII Corps originally confined the 35th to an area bounded by the Mortain–St- Hilaire-du-Harcouet highway in the north and the towns of Buais–le Teilleul–Barenton in the south.

Although the 2d Armored Division held Barenton, providing a solid southern anchor for the 35th Division, the Germans were in possession of Mortain, which meant they were poised on the northeastern edge of the zone allotted to the 35th Division. As the 134th Infantry continued moving east, its northern flank was increasingly exposed to counterattack. The Germans did not overlook this widening gap as the 35th Division continued moving east. In response, *XLVII Panzer Korps* assembled reconnaissance units from *Panzer Lehr, Das Reich*, and *Panzer Division 116*. Augmented by infantry from Wisliceny's *Deutschland* as well as two platoons of panzers, the Germans prepared to strike the exposed flank of the 134th Infantry.

Three camouflaged armored vehicles were spotted moving southeast from Mortain at 1535 hours on 8 August by aerial observers of the 30th Division artillery. The 30th Infantry Division, however, instructed the observers not to engage them with artillery since the pilots were unable to positively identify the nationality of the vehicles. Moments later, the 30th's command post informed the division artillery headquarters that "the 35th Infantry Division is supposed to have a battalion astride that road. It is a possibility that the tanks are theirs." The artillery operations officer assured division headquarters that "we won't fire on them."[30]

By 1750 hours, a light observation plane from the 35th Division also spotted the trio of heavily camouflaged tanks. When the pilot was finally able to identify them as panzers, the vehicles were too close to the 2/134th Infantry to be safely engaged with artillery. The hedgerows, however, caused the Germans to misjudge the location of the American rifle battalion. Instead of attacking Captain McDannell's lead elements, the panzers headed for support units located to the rear of the 2/134th Infantry.

.The panzers began their assault by ambushing a platoon of medium tanks sent to reinforce the 2/134th Infantry. Four Shermans belonging to the 1st Platoon of A/737th Armor pulled up next to the 2d Battalion command post. Moments later, the throaty roar of panzer engines was heard, and the tank crews dove for cover as a pair of Pzkfw IVs began firing at the stationary Shermans. All of the American vehicles were knocked out before they could fire a shot in return.[31]

A second group of panzers, consisting of three Panthers commanded by *Obersturmführer* Willy Durr, encountered a howitzer platoon of the 134th Infantry's Cannon Company. The American cannoneers, normally positioned well behind the front lines, found themselves unexpectedly thrust into a firefight. The cannoneers slammed shell after shell at the big German tanks, but the 105mm high-explosive rounds burst with little effect. The German tanks returned fire, cutting down seven Americans. The surviving gun crews retreated after disabling their 1-1/2 ton weapons carriers.

Soon afterward, an M-10 from A/654th TD Battalion spotted one of the Panthers approaching from the rear. Hedgerows surrounding the American vehicle prevented it from opening fire. Before the TD could reposition, the Panther slammed an armor-piercing shell into it, putting the sighting mechanism out of action. The American TD pulled back into cover, hoping to hit the Panther at point-blank range without the aid of his sights. The panzer foiled that plan by appearing at the opposite end of the hedgerow, setting the M-10 afire before it could traverse its turret. The same Panther knocked out a second TD several minutes later.[32]

Other panzers overran the 2/134th Infantry's motor park and battalion aid station, and a number of jeeps belonging to the mortar platoon were destroyed. The Germans seized the 2d Battalion aid station, capturing all of the medics and the battalion chaplain, Captain William J. Hayes. The 134th Infantry was trying desperately to reorient itself to counter the unexpected appearance of German panzers. The executive officer of the 1st Battalion formed bazooka teams from signal personnel and headquarters clerks to protect his command post from the marauding German vehicles. He also ordered his attached engineer platoon to provide security for the hastily organized bazooka teams. The headquarters personnel settled down among the hedgerows in the darkening light, anxiously cradling their newly issued bazookas.

By 2100 hours, two Pzkfw IVs were parked astride a crossroads to the rear of the 1st and 2d Battalions, cutting off the only supply road leading to the American units. Captain Alfred B. Stein, a battalion surgeon from the 737th Tank Battalion, was one of the first Americans to encounter the roadblock.[33] Stein was leading a pair of medical jeeps when they rounded a corner, coming face to face with a Pzkfw IV. The Germans motioned for the medics to put up their hands, confiscating medical supplies, jeeps, and cigarettes before releasing them.[34] Given the confused situation, it is no wonder that Miltonberger's staff quipped, "There had been a report that there was a lost battalion of the 30th Infantry Division surrounded near Mortain. Now it looked as if there was a pair of lost battalions here."[35]

The Germans were preparing to commit additional forces to the fight. The lead elements of *SS-Panzer Division 10* departed St.-Clement on the morning of 8 August bound for Barenton. *SS-Panzeraufklärungs Abteilung 10,* spearheading the movement, was directed by *Brigadeführer* Harmel to reconnoiter the new area of operations. Harmel was told that *Infanterie Division 275* held Barenton. However, when he visited *Das Reich,* he was informed that American units occupied the town.[36] Harmel quickly ordered *I Abteilung* of *SS-Panzergrenadier Regiment 21* to reinforce his divisional reconnaissance battalion.

The 2d Armored Division was in the process of expanding its foothold at Barenton. The Americans had committed the 1st and 3d Battalions of the 41st AIR to seizing the high ground to the northeast of the town. The 3/67th Armor, minus Company I, supported the 1/41st AIR, while Company I of the 67th Armored Regiment, less one platoon, was attached to the 3/41st AIR. Captain Tousey's Battlegroup 2 was ordered to seize a crossroads located between the objectives assigned to the 41st AIR.

The news of the American advance electrified the command group of *SS-Panzer Division 10.* The main body of Harmel's division occupied assembly areas near Ger in anticipation of a renewed counteroffensive against Avranches. The advance of the 2d Armored Division on 8 August served to threaten these assembly areas as well as the southern flank of *XLVII Panzer Korps.* When Harmel requested permission to reposition his forces, he was directed to protect the Mortain-Domfront highway. *SS-Panzer Division 10* was also ordered to prevent an American advance in the direction of St.-Georges-du-Rouelle.

In addition to securing commanding terrain around Barenton, Major General Brooks directed the 82d Reconnaissance Battalion to reconnoiter the area between Mortain and Ger in support of his original mission to seize Domfront.[37]

A Company sent out patrols to examine crossings over the Varenne River, while C Company headed north to locate the 35th Infantry Division. Company B of the 82d Recon was dispatched to determine the situation in Mortain.[38]

The 1st Platoon of B/82d Reconnaissance was assigned the mission of reconnoitering Hill 314. Just outside of Mortain, the Americans encountered a heavily defended roadblock. They withdrew after observing two dug-in Pzkfw IVs, an antitank gun, and numerous machine guns. A mortar barrage succeeded in temporarily dispersed the defenders of the roadblock, but heavy return fire made any further advance impossible. As the reconnaissance platoon prepared to depart, artillery fire destroyed four jeeps and killed two men. The survivors returned to report that Mortain was strongly held.

The bid by the 2d Armored Division to seize the high ground northeast of Barenton proved more successful. With *SS-Panzer Division 10* trying to extricate itself from assembly areas near Ger, the Americans were able to secure their initial objectives by 1130 hours.[39] The 3/41st AIR was also able to seize its second objective by 1335 hours. Although the 1/41st AIR did not make as much progress, a platoon of supporting medium tanks engaged a German column, knocking out a pair of towed 88mm guns, two 37mm guns, and two trucks.[40]

By 1530 hours, *SS-Panzer Division 10* succeeded in establishing a cohesive defensive line in the path of the advancing Americans. Reports of increasing numbers of German troops opposite the 41st AIR slowed the advance of the 2d Armored Division to a crawl. The Americans halted when darkness arrived, providing *SS-Panzer Division 10* with a respite used to strengthen its positions in anticipation of renewed fighting on 9 August.

The night of 8 August, however, brought no reprieve to the 2/120th Infantry on Hill 314, who were entering their third day without food, water, or medical supplies. Several of the seriously wounded men at the E Company aid station died from lack of medical supplies. The Germans opposing the 2d Battalion had been reinforced by a platoon of panthers from *Leibstandarte,* and beginning at 0145 hours, *Kampfgruppe Fick* launched several fierce assaults against the isolated American troops prior to the arrival of daylight on 9 August.[41]

The initial attack, aimed at overcoming the E Company roadblock, was repelled by artillery fire. The Germans also apparently overestimated the strength of the opposing Americans. Lieutenant Weiss observed afterward that "if the Germans believed that antitank guns and tanks on the hill were firing directly at them, it might account for their hesitation to punch through the handful of infantry on the Bel Air road and flood across the top of the hill. But one can only speculate why they ultimately failed."[42]

Unable to break through the roadblock, *Kampfgruppe Fick* launched an assault against the western edge of the American perimeter. German infantry silently assembled near la Petit Chapel on the southwestern spur of Hill 314 and at a given signal opened fire on E/120th Infantry with numerous machine guns. The Americans ducked into their foxholes or behind boulders to avoid the streams of tracer bullets playing across their position. Because the Germans were located between E Company and the firing batteries, Lieutenant Weiss was unable to call artillery on the attackers. He could not take a chance on misdirected rounds landing accidentally among the American troops.

Lieutenant Kerley rallied his men, urging them to reply with their rifles against the barrage of machine-gun fire. The Germans retreated, but not before inflicting numerous casualties on the defenders. One infantryman lying next to Lieutenant Weiss was shot through both the head and leg during the attack.[43] *Kampfgruppe Fick* failed to follow up the punishing dismounted assault with another panzer attack along the Bel Air road. Despite the losses sustained by Company E, the 2/120th Infantry remained in possession of Hill 314 as dawn broke.

The coming of daylight brought relief for the 2/120th, although it was not readily apparent. An aerial resupply mission had finally been scheduled, although the drop could not occur before the location of the 2/120th Infantry was determined. In order to accomplish this task, the First Army G-4 section sent Major William K. C. Collonan to conduct an aerial reconnaissance. Collonan traveled to a forward airfield to meet at noon with Major Burl E. Glass Jr. who would lead a flight of six P-38 fighters, one of which was configured as a PB-38J "Droopsnoot," to Mortain. The PB-38J was equipped with a glass nose and bombsight instead of machine guns and cannon. The six planes took off at 1715 hours. Nearing their objective, the escort fighters took up a covering position while the PB-38J dipped down to survey Hill 314, circling as Major Collonan tried to pinpoint the American positions. During its fifth pass, the plane was hit by flak and crashed into a wooded area.[44]

Colonel Birks, growing impatient with the lengthy coordination process, sent one of his own rifle companies into Mortain to deliver supplies. On the evening of 8 August, Birks invited Lieutenant Colonel Bradford and Lieutenant Pulver to regimental headquarters. Colonel Birks told Pulver that "tomorrow morning I want you to pull your company out of line, fight your way through the German line and deliver radio batteries and medicine." When Bradford remarked that the mission was impossible, Birks replied, "We have to make a try. I cannot afford to lose half the regiment."[45]

Armed with new orders from regiment, Lieutenant Colonel Bradford returned to his battalion command post to coordinate the relief operation. He was concerned that the Germans might make another push once they detected the departure of B Company. In order to reduce the chances that the Germans would be aware of what was occurring, A/120th Infantry was ordered to assume responsibility for the entire perimeter before dawn.

During the predawn darkness, Lieutenant Smith's men filtered into positions held by B Company without being detected by the Germans. When the relief was completed, Company B swung south to avoid *Kampfgruppe Ullrich* before heading east. Any hope that Lieutenant Pulver could enter Mortain undetected evaporated when he encountered two German patrols. The *SS* troops, forming up for an attack against the roadblock at L'Abbaye Blanche, were surprised by the appearance of B/120th Infantry. For the loss of only three men, the Americans were able to inflict heavy casualties on the Germans.

B Company reached Mortain by early afternoon, and the Germans reacted to the intrusion by laying a mortar barrage on them. Seeking shelter from the mortar fire, Lieutenant Pulver encountered a reconnaissance platoon from the 629th TD Battalion. The TD men thought his company had been sent to reinforce the 2/117th Infantry. When Pulver informed them of his real mission, the reconnaissance platoon leader replied, "Are you kidding? Come with me."[46]

Lieutenant Pulver accompanied him to an observation post where the other officer gestured toward Hill 314. Pulver raised his binoculars to his eyes to discern signs of teeming German activity along the western slopes of Hill 314. The area designated as a linkup point was a sheer cliff. Lieutenant Pulver was convinced he would never be able to reach the 2/120th Infantry. When he informed Lieutenant Colonel Bradford of the actual situation, Pulver was ordered to return to Hill 285.

The departure of Company B had coincided with a series of probes by *Kampfgruppe Ullrich* against the 1/120th Infantry. The relatively weak reaction to these forays persuaded *Hauptsturmführer* Ullrich to attempt a major assault. Early that afternoon, the Germans sent infantry supported by mortars and artillery against A Company, which succeeded in repulsing the *SS* assault with difficulty. During the fighting, Lieutenant Smith was deafened and shell-shocked by an exploding mortar shell.

When B Company returned late that afternoon, Lieutenant Smith unexpectedly appeared in Lieutenant Pulver's command post. Pulver noticed that Smith's steel helmet sported a jagged hole and that blood was trickling slowly from his mouth and ears. Smith asked Pulver to take over Company A until a replacement officer arrived, explaining that all of his platoon leaders had also been wounded. Before departing, Smith oriented Pulver on the locations of all of A Company's rifle platoons.[47]

When he arrived at A Company, Pulver sensed that the men were on the verge of retreat, and he ordered them to occupy firing positions behind a nearby hedgerow. On his signal, Pulver explained, he wanted everyone to fire two clips from their rifles before throwing all of the hand grenades they possessed. Lieutenant Pulver gave the order to open fire when he saw the Germans emerging from cover to begin their attack. The barrage of fire slammed into the *SS*, forcing them to retreat in disarray. Lieutenant Edwin Franklin, the 120th Infantry's I&R platoon leader, arrived soon afterward to assume command of A Company, freeing Lieutenant Pulver to return to his own unit.[48]

In Mortain, Lieutenant Colonel Hardaway's command group managed to escape detection until the *SS* began systematically searching the town once more. Entering the house where the Americans were hiding on the second floor, the *SS* captured one man guarding the front door. For some reason, the Germans did not search the rest of the building. Taking advantage of the oversight, Hardaway directed his command group to head for Hill 314. The men quietly filed out the back door as they headed up the slope toward the wooded crest.

Lieutenant Colonel Hardaway, flanked by his battalion intelligence officer, Lieutenant Herbert M. Pike, led the group. Halfway up the slope, a burst of machine-gun fire erupted at the head of the column. The Americans surrendered to avoid being cut down on the exposed hillside. In the rear of the column, however, a half dozen men decided to hide in a nearby wheat field rather than capitulate.[49] The Americans spent the day in hiding until an *SS* artillery battery began setting up its guns nearby. The Germans were drinking as they worked, becoming even more intoxicated as evening approached.

When most of the Germans appeared drunk, Lieutenant Guy Hagen suggested that it would be a good time to depart. The six men quietly slipped away into town, making their way to a farmhouse next to the Mortain hospital. They found hiding places in a hayloft after pausing briefly to dip their helmets into a water trough.[50] The Americans had no idea how long it would take to recapture Mortain, but they were determined to avoid capture until help arrived.

When *Sturmbannführer* Fick was informed of Hardaway's capture, he decided to make a surrender offer to the isolated Americans. At 1820 hours, an *SS* sergeant approached the perimeter under a white flag of truce.[51] The Americans sent Lieutenant Elmer C. Rohmiller, accompanied by Private William L. Wingate, to meet the German emissary. Informed that the *SS* wanted to make a surrender offer, Lieutenant Rohmiller sent for his company commander, Lieutenant Kerley. The German emissary told Kerley in fluent English that "I am an officer in the *SS* and am in a position to offer honorable surrender to your command. I personally admire the stand made by your battalion. I must point out, however, that your situation is hopeless."[52]

The German also announced that his unit had captured several American officers from the 2d Battalion, including a lieutenant named Pike and a "one star general" (obviously mistaking the silver oak leaf on Lieutenant Colonel Hardaway's helmet for a star). The *SS* man pointed out that it would be no disgrace to surrender under the circumstances, promising the Americans that they would be well cared for. The emissary's parting remark was a promise to "blow the 2d Battalion to bits" if the offer was not accepted by 2000 hours. Lieutenant Kerley's reply was unprintable and to the point. The *SS* man departed as Lieutenant Weiss relayed the news to Colonel Birks via the 230th FA Battalion at 1850 hours.[53]

Well after the deadline expired, *Kampfgruppe Fick* began preparing for another assault against Hill 314. As German activity increased, Lieutenant Weiss requested an immediate barrage on all registered checkpoints.[54] Despite the shelling, however, he could still hear tracked vehicles moving to the east of the 2d Battalion, as the panzers made several unsuccessful attempts to overcome the E Company roadblock. Only a single tank was able to make its way into the middle of the American perimeter, where one frightened soldier chose to accept the panzer commander's offer of surrender. The panzer withdrew shortly afterward with its captive clinging to the turret, but Hill 314 remained in Americans hands.

Weidinger's *Der Führer* regiment spent most of 9 August unsuccessfully attempting to eradicate the L'Abbaye Blanche roadblock. *Sturmbannführer* Weidinger initially sent engineers with flamethrowers to destroy the American TDs. Corporal Ilfred Leger was sharing a foxhole with T-4 Ralph Sells when a German flamethrower team approached their outpost position just before dawn. Sells pulled the trigger of his .30-caliber machine gun only to hear the bolt slam home on an empty chamber. He then reached down for his submachine gun, firing one round before it jammed. Startled by the shot, the flamethrower operator turned his weapon on the foxhole.[55]

Corporal Leger heard a loud "crack" as a ball of yellow flame shot toward his foxhole. Ducking hastily, he escaped without injury except for some slight facial burns. He could see the flamethrower operator in front of his foxhole with several other shadowy figures behind him.[56] Other members of the TD platoon, including Lieutenant Springfield, opened fire. Two Germans were killed, including the flamethrower operator, and the surviving *SS* retreated out of sight. With pressure increasing against RJ 278, *Sturmbannführer* Weidinger could not afford to mount another assault against L'Abbaye Blanche.

Continuing uncertainty about the situation on his southern flank persuaded Major General Hobbs to bolster his overall position by securing RJ 278 north of Mortain. He intended to commit the 3/33d Armor, augmented by the 2/119th Infantry, to reinforce the 12th Infantry's assault. Hobbs designated Lieutenant Colonel Samuel M. Hogan, commanding 3/33d Armor, to lead the composite infantry-armor force.[57] Hogan's battalion, designated as Task Force (TF) 3 by CCB, had been previously assigned as the reserve for the 30th Infantry Division. After studying the terrain, Lieutenant Colonel Hogan decided to approach from the south, bypassing the swampy ground that prevented the 12th Infantry from employing its own supporting tanks and TDs.

The Americans departed their assembly area at noon on 9 August, with the 2/119th Infantry riding on the decks of Lieutenant Colonel Hogan's tanks. The infantry battalion commander, Lieutenant Colonel Wallis, would not accompany the attacking force to RJ 278. Wallis was responsible for using his own headquarters company and B/83d Reconnaissance Battalion to secure the route between Hill 285 and RJ 278.

Hogan's force halted temporarily at le Neufbourg while he reconnoitered the final segment of the route. Escorted by a platoon of medium tanks, Hogan reached L'Abbaye Blanche without incident. The unexpected appearance of five Shermans surprised Lieutenant Springfield. Dismounting his tank to talk to the TD lieutenant, Hogan questioned Springfield on the dispositions of German troops and the general situation. Springfield passed on what little information he possessed, including a recommendation that Hogan use a nearby secondary route to reach RJ 278.[58]

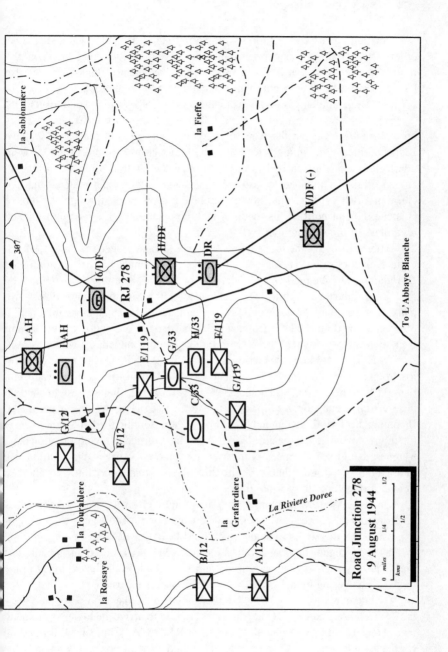

la Sablonnière

▲ 307

la Fieffe

LAH

LAH

16/DF

H/DF

RJ 278

DR

IN/DF (−)

To L'Abbaye Blanche

E/119

G/33

H/33

F/119

C/33

G/119

G/12

F/12

la Tourablere

la Rossaye

la Grafardiere

La Riviere Doree

B/12

A/12

Road Junction 278
9 August 1944

0   miles   1/4   1/2

kms   1/2

Concluding his conversation with Springfield, Lieutenant Colonel Hogan ordered his battalion reconnaissance platoon to examine the route; the recon platoon leader reported that it would support the movement of tanks. He had also located several fields adjacent to the route that were suitable for use as an assembly area. Hogan quickly ordered his tanks to move into position south of RJ 278.

Hogan's advance caught *SS-Panzer Division 2* by surprise. Artillery fire was brought to bear against the American column only after it reached L'Abbaye Blanche, forcing the infantry to dismount. Although the armored vehicles were unaffected, the riflemen had to crawl through the shelling to avoid being hit. Hogan originally planned to lead the attack with infantry but realized that the German artillery had significantly delayed movement through L'Abbaye Blanche. Hogan notified his medium tank companies to be prepared to attack regardless of infantry support.

After waiting for the foot soldiers to appear, Hogan issued the order to attack to his tank companies. He did not realize that the Germans had earlier reinforced *II Abteilung DF,* charged with the defense of RJ 278, as a result of attempts by the 12th Infantry to capture the crossroads. As the Shermans moved forward, panzers and antitank guns opened fire on them, and in less than thirty minutes TF 3 lost nine medium tanks. Lieutenant Colonel Hogan ordered his tanks to pull back to await the arrival of the 2/119th Infantry before launching another assault.

As Hogan withdrew, the Germans counterattacked. Increasing signs of activity around RJ 278 prompted Lieutenant Colonel Hogan to send his assault gun platoon leader, Lieutenant Thomas Magness, forward. Magness established an observation point atop a hillock on the left flank of the American perimeter. Incoming artillery fire wounded his radio operator, forcing the lieutenant to carry the injured man back to the aid station. When he returned to the observation post, Magness could see Germans within several hundred yards of his position. He radioed the assault gun platoon to fire three to five rounds of white phosphorous in an effort to force the SS into the open.

Once the SS were standing upright in a frantic effort to scrape off the flakes of burning phosphorous, Magness ordered his three assault guns to fire highexplosive. As the shells exploded, he could hear Germans screaming in pain. When the SS began shooting at him, Lieutenant Magness shifted his assault guns onto a nearby orchard. The rifle fire stopped as howitzer shells exploded in the orchard, showering branches, leaves, and shrapnel everywhere.

By late evening, the 2/119th Infantry had reached the TF 3 perimeter. Captain Warren Fox, leading E Company, was the first to arrive at Hogan's command tank. Hogan told Fox to immediately attack RJ 278. As Company E formed up for the assault, a barrage of mortar rounds killed Captain Fox and wounded thirteen other soldiers, forcing the unit to pull back to reorganize.[59] When F/119th Infantry noticed Company E pulling back, it also withdrew. TF 3 drew into a defensive perimeter for the night, awaiting the coming of daylight to resume its assault.

A Sherman tank equipped with a bulldozer blade opens a gap in a Norman hedgerow. (National Archives)

South of Mortain, Major Herlong's 1/119th Infantry was also rewarded with scant success on 9 August. Romagny was bordered by a hedgerow-terraced ridge to the north and hedgerow-enclosed fields sloping down a stream to the south. The *SS* had spent most of the previous night improving their positions. The defenders took special care to block the only road leading into Romagny by surrounding the Pzkfw IV knocked out on 7 August with mines.

Lieutenant Frederick Fleming decided to walk into Romagny that morning on his own initiative in an attempt to persuade the Germans to surrender. Accompanied by an enlisted man carrying a white flag, Lieutenant Fleming almost made his way into the village before the *SS* opened fire. Dropping the flag of truce, both Americans ran back to friendly lines chased by bullets. Although the pair received slight cuts, it was obvious that the Germans had not tried to kill them.

Lieutenant Fleming was able to pinpoint the location of two machine-gun nests and an antitank gun emplacement.[60] He radioed the information back to the 743d Tank Battalion's mortar platoon, which began shelling the German positions. American artillery fire also began hitting Romagny, knocking off the top of the village church's steeple. As the Germans replied, the American tanks began shooting up every multistory building in Romagny in an attempt to knock out the opposing forward observers. The Germans reacted by launching a counterattack with several light armored cars and a company of infantry, but C/119th Infantry repulsed them.[61]

At 1830 hours, Major Herlong attacked with A Company deployed to the right of the road leading into the village and C Company on the left. A pair of medium tanks moving along the road supported the assaulting infantry, but the Americans bogged down when the Shermans came under fire from panzers and antitank guns. With the tankers unable to locate the opposing weapons, they pulled back to avoid being hit.

Major Herlong radioed division headquarters to report that "we are getting cross fire from every direction. The tanks can't do a lot of maneuvering on account of the fields, one [of which] is about 8 feet below the other and they can't get over the hedgerow without tipping over."[62] Major General Hobbs promised to assist the 1/119th Infantry with the entire divisional artillery in an effort to break the stalemate.

Even with additional support, the effort to capture Romagny failed. By 2029 hours, Herlong reported that "I have every man in line and every weapon firing, but I can't advance."[63] Ordering his troops to pull back, Major Herlong vowed to find a way to overcome the difficult terrain channeling his battalion's advance.

The 35th Division was unable to provide him with any assistance. The 134th Infantry focused on girding itself to fend off another German counterattack as dawn approached on 9 August. During the previous night, small parties of men crept from hedgerow to hedgerow in the darkness, carrying supplies up to the isolated battalions. On the return trip, medics hauled back the wounded on stretchers. The resupply parties were especially careful when they passed by the intersection occupied by the Pzkfw IVs.

The Americans planned to deal with the threat posed to the northern flank of the 35th Division on two levels. Colonel Miltonberger wanted to employ a platoon of M-10 TDs to destroy the panzers blocking his main supply route. Prohibited from using his reserve regiment without permission from VII Corps, Major General Baade ordered the 137th Infantry to send its 3d Battalion to assist Miltonberger. The 3/137th was instructed to occupy positions north of the 1/134th Infantry with the mission of preventing the Germans from launching another counterattack. Major General Baade compensated the 137th Infantry by placing Colonel Miltonberger's southernmost battalion, the 3/134th, under Colonel Emery's control.[64]

VII Corps provided additional relief to Baade by authorizing him to employ the 320th Infantry. The decision to release the 35th Division's reserve regiment resulted from a telephone conversation between Major General Collins and Major General Walker. After much discussion, the XX Corps commander agreed with Collins that immediate tactical needs took precedence over future operations planned for the 35th Division.

The 320th was tasked to send a battalion to link up with the 30th Reconnaissance Troop near Romagny at first light on 9 August. Once the linkup was complete, the newly committed battalion would be responsible for defending the road connecting Mortain with St.-Hilaire-du-Harcouet. Collins also informed

Baade that two truck companies would shuttle the remaining battalions of the 320th Infantry to the east at first light.[65]

As the 320th moved into position, Major General Baade ordered the 134th Infantry to resume its advance at 0900 hours.[66] At 0650 hours, the regimental operations officer reported to division headquarters that considerable mechanized activity could be heard north and west of the 1/134th. He requested use of an artillery liaison aircraft to find out if the Germans were retreating or preparing to launch another assault.[67] A plane from the 161st FA Battalion arrived at 0830 hours, but it was driven off moments later by a storm of antiaircraft fire.

Colonel Miltonberger was not keen on the prospect of resuming offensive operations that morning. He possessed very little information about the Germans, who were reported to have anywhere from five to fifty panzers, and his resupply parties had been unable to deliver additional bazooka ammunition during the night.[68] Miltonberger telephoned Major General Baade to request permission to delay the scheduled attack, which was denied.[69] Hoping to buy some time, he directed his attached TD company commander to ferret out the opposing panzers. The officer, appalled at the notion of venturing unsupported into the hedgerows, telephoned division headquarters to protest the order. The division chief of staff told Miltonberger to cancel the ill-advised search-and-destroy mission.[70]

Colonel Miltonberger was left with no choice but to order his regiment to attack. Fortunately, the shortage of bazooka ammunition had been alleviated by the arrival of a jeep filled with rockets. When the attack began, the rifle companies of the 134th Infantry quickly encountered machine guns sited in almost every hedgerow in their path. The Americans found the situation bewildering, fighting against SS troops supported by panzers that seemed to appear and disappear with confusing frequency. The German force actually consisted of six to ten panzers supported by several companies of reconnaissance troops. What the SS lacked in numbers, however, they more than made up for in mobility and firepower.

Shortly after noon, four Pzkfw IVs appeared behind the 1/134th Infantry. One panzer headed straight for the battalion motor park, pushing its long barreled 75mm gun through the brush before opening fire on the parked vehicles. Five jeeps and five trucks were turned into flaming ruins in a matter of minutes. The panzers also overran a platoon of C Company, forcing twenty-three Americans to surrender.[71]

Baade had not been able to reposition the 320th Infantry to protect the northern flank of the 134th before the panzers counterattacked. Lieutenant Colonel Clarence Docka's 3d Battalion progressed only three kilometers before being taken under fire by several machine-gun nests. Docka reported to Colonel Byrne that the Germans were using American small arms and jeeps.[72] Fierce resistance prevented him from linking up with the 30th Reconnaissance Troop until 1420 hours.

Lieutenant Colonel Vincent Keator's 2/320th Infantry also began moving east and was met with even greater resistance. G Company was harassed by Germans infiltrating around their left flank, who succeeded in pinning down the Americans for three hours. Company E, 320th, Infantry, advancing abreast of G

Company, reported *SS* troops working their way behind its lead platoons.[73] Colonel Byrne, however, ordered both battalion commanders to continue moving east regardless of the obstacles they encountered.

Although the 320th Infantry was still struggling to get into position, the 134th resumed its advance following the counterattack by German panzers. Colonel Miltonberger informed Baade that he "believed the enemy in this vicinity has been underestimated . . . enemy tanks running around in rear areas and the unwillingness of some people to go in and clean them out, had caused us considerable difficulty."[74] Miltonberger replaced the battered 1/134th Infantry with the 3/137th; the 1st Battalion would assume the mission of regimental reserve.

The 2/134th Infantry came under intense fire as soon as the assault kicked off at 1600 hours. Companies E and F were pinned down until mortar fire finally silenced the German machine guns. When the divisional artillery sent a spotter plane to pinpoint *SS* machine guns on the outskirts of St.-Jean-du-Corail, German fighters forced it down.[75] The unexpected resistance forced Colonel Miltonberger to commit his regimental reserve sooner than he had anticipated, and the 1/134th was ordered to secure St.-Jean-du-Corail.

Miltonberger also dispatched a platoon of M-10s from the 654th TD Battalion to clear the roadblock in the rear of his regiment. Rounding a bend in the road, the leading M-10 came face to face with a Pzkfw IV sheltering behind a barricade of captured American vehicles. The panzer opened fire at point-blank range, knocking out the tank destroyer. Another M-10 pulled around the burning TD to engage the Pzkfw IV and was able to put several armor-piercing rounds into the flank of the panzer, which burst into flames. The tankers spotted a second panzer, but the German vehicle retreated before they could engage it.[76] The road was finally clear.

The 320th Infantry drew increasing attention from the Germans when it continued advancing after the 134th Infantry halted at St.-Jean-du-Corail. Confronted by several minefields hastily laid in its path, the 320th also halted at 1900 hours. *SS-Panzer Division 2* immediately launched a counterattack against Colonel Byrne's regiment. A preparatory barrage was directed against the command post of the 2d Battalion while mortar fire peppered the 3d Battalion area. At 2150 hours, a platoon of *SS* panzergrenadiers supported by several panzers struck the northern flank of 3/320th Infantry.

The German force collided with Lieutenant Charles Pitcher's L/320th Infantry near the railroad line southwest of Mortain.[77] A scout with the leading platoon, Private First Class Al Navarette, shouted a warning to his comrades.[78] Fortunately for L Company, the attacking tanks were funneled into a narrow lane bordered by tall hedgerows, passing completely through Pitcher's unit without halting. Company L retaliated by knocking out the last vehicle in the column.[79] The M Company mortars were firing in support of Lieutenant Pitcher, but their effectiveness was hampered by the confused situation. No one at the 3d Battalion command post knew precisely where L Company was located.

At 2312 hours, Lieutenant Colonel Docka reported to Colonel Byrne that

L Company was cut off, and *SS* troops on the opposite side of a hedgerow were demanding their surrender. Twenty minutes later, a combat patrol from I Company was sent to aid Lieutenant Pitcher. By midnight, several men from Company L had infiltrated back to friendly lines, with the remainder of Pitcher's unit reaching safety several hours later.[80]

As night approached, VII Corps instructed the 35th Division to prepare to launch an attack the following day to relieve the isolated 2/120th Infantry. The 35th had been attached to VII Corps effective at 0001 hours on 9 August, and Major General Collins was now authorized to employ the division without obtaining permission from XX Corps. In addition to securing Hill 314, the 35th Division would continue its effort to cut the road linking Mortain with Barenton.

In order to comply with the orders from VII Corps, Major General Baade was forced to commit his divisional reserve, Major William Gillis's 1/320th Infantry, to the attack on Hill 314. Baade also placed the 737th Tank Battalion under Gillis's command. Each of the infantry regiments was instructed to return their attached tank company to the control of the 737th Tank Battalion. Major General Baade also requested additional tanks, prompting VII Corps to instruct the 2d Armored Division to send a tank company to the 35th Infantry Division. The 2d Armored dispatched D/32d Armor, which was supporting Battlegroup 2, to reinforce the 737th Tank Battalion.

Tasked to simultaneously undertake two major attacks, the 35th Infantry Division was forced to divide the responsibilities of coordinating operations between the division operations officer and the chief of staff. The former would direct the division's advance to the east, while the latter would supervise the attack against Hill 314. Although this option offered a reasonable compromise to meet a resource-intensive requirement, the chief of staff possessed only a fraction of the operations officer's experience.[81]

On the extreme southern flank, *Brigadeführer* Harmel prepared to launch an attack on Barenton. Before his *SS-Panzer Division 10* could act, however, Major General Brooks beat him to the punch. The 82d Reconnaissance Battalion identified Harmel's troops as they shifted positions during the night of 8 August.[82] Early on 9 August, the 2d Armored Division preempted German plans for an advance by sending both of its armored infantry battalions to secure le Gue-Rochoux, a small village located four miles northeast of Barenton. Possession of this village placed the 2d Armored in a position to interdict both the Ger-Barenton road and the Mortain-Ger road.

At 0700 hours, A Company of the 82d Reconnaissance Battalion began searching for Germans near the objective area. By 0800 hours, the recon unit advanced beyond le Gue-Rochoux but encountered resistance before it reached the Ger-Mortain road. A series of small skirmishes quickly broke out, and a barrage of mortar fire finally forced the Americans to pull back. As it retreated, Company A belatedly discovered that the Germans had established a reverse slope defensive position near le Gue-Rochoux.[83]

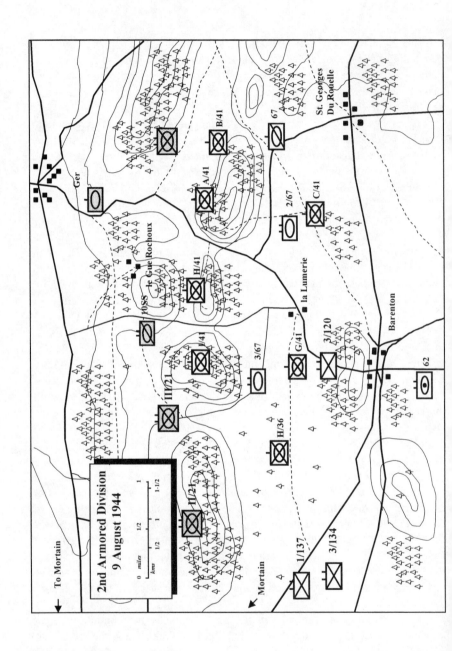

2nd Armored Division
9 August 1944

0 miles 1/2 1
kms 1/2 1 1-1/2

To Mortain

Mortain

Ger

le Grue Rochoux

1/SS

B/41

A/41

H/41

I/41

III/21

II/21

67

St. Georges
Du Rouelle

2/67

C/41

la Lumerie

Barenton

G/41

3/67

3/120

62

H/36

1/137

3/134

After a short artillery preparation, the 2d Armored Division began its attack against le Gue-Rochoux at 1310 hours. A patrol from 3/41st AIR encountered some German troops when it reached a hill overlooking the village. As the Americans approached the outbuildings of a nearby farm, they ran into a German patrol. The armored infantry opened fire, driving the *SS* troops back. Hard on the heels of the American patrol came the main body of 3/41st AIR, accompanied by elements of 1/41st AIR. Both armored infantry battalions established defensive positions on the newly occupied terrain.

The American soon found themselves under increasingly heavy artillery fire. Major General Brooks, sensing that the Germans were gearing up to retake the lost hill, canceled orders for a further advance and directed Colonel Stanley Hinds, the 41st AIR commander, to prepare for a counterattack. At 1850 hours, eight panzers moved down the Ger-Barenton road toward 3/41st AIR.[84] The 3d Platoon of G/67th Armor, aided by a section of M-10s from the 702d TD Battalion, opened fire on the attackers. The medium tanks of E/67th Armor and a platoon of assault guns also joined in. Five German armored vehicles were knocked out, prompting the surviving panzers to retreat.[85]

Following the failed counterattack, *SS-Panzer Division 10* dispatched a platoon of panzergrenadiers to secure a crossroads in the rear of the 41st AIR. Informed of the presence of the *SS* troops, Major General Brooks directed the 3/120th Infantry to retake the crossroads. Lieutenant Colonel McCollum employed L Company, supported by five medium tanks, for the assault. Once his scouts determined the exact location of the German roadblock, L Company pushed forward, covered by fire from the supporting Shermans. The *SS* troops suffered considerable losses, including three half-tracks, while L/120th Infantry only lost one man killed in action.[86] The incident marked the end of the fighting near Barenton that day.

CONCLUSIONS

Continuous attacks by the Americans along the southern shoulder of the battlefield had prevented the Germans from expanding on the gains made on 7 August. By leveraging the superior capabilities of the American artillery, the isolated 2/120th Infantry was able to significantly restrict the movement of German supplies and reserves. Artillery support was largely responsible for the 30th Division's ability to concentrate the bulk of its maneuver assets in the north while relying on massed indirect fires to contain the Germans threatening its vulnerable southern flank. The 30th Division's situation in this sector also improved dramatically on 8 August as the Germans responded to the introduction of the 35th Division south of Mortain.

Although prodding from Berlin would soon have von Kluge examining the possibility of reorienting the main effort of *Unternehmen Lüttich* to the south, he was prevented from doing so by the pressure exerted by the 21st Army Group as well as constant attacks by First Army in the vicinity of Vire. Beset on all sides, the Germans could ill afford to divert additional troops to wrest control of any newly designated line of departure from the American forces holding Barenton and Mayenne. *Das Reich* was prevented from consolidating its gains in Mortain or from extending to the south by the appearance of the 35th Infantry Division. Likewise, the 2d Armored Division successfully fended off attempts by *SS-Panzer Division 10* to seize Barenton. With *Panzer Division 9* contained at Mayenne by the 1st Infantry Division, a renewed German effort from south of Mortain rested on an even shakier foundation than the original counteroffensive plan.

8

Opportunity and Counterattack

A clear picture of defeat emerged as reports from Mortain arrived at *OB West*. In the wake of the 20 July attempt against Hitler's life, *Generalfeldmarschall* von Kluge was aware of the consequences of failure. A shameful travesty began to unfold as the search began for a scapegoat. In response to the anticipated backlash from Berlin, *Generalleutnant* von Schwerin was offered up as the sacrifice to appease Hitler's wrath; his tendency to utter disparaging remarks about National Socialism made him an appealing choice. *General der Panzertruppen* von Funck initiated the process when he telephoned *7 Armee* on the evening of 7 August to inaccurately report that *Panzer Division 116* had failed to participate in the counteroffensive. The *XLVII Panzer Korps* commander claimed that von Schwerin had refused to order his division to attack because he did not believe *Unternehmen Lüttich* would succeed.

When informed of von Funck's report, *Oberstgruppenführer und General der Waffen SS* Paul Hausser's patience snapped, and he telephoned von Funck at 2050 hours to announce that he agreed with the recommendation to relieve von Schwerin. When Hausser's stance softened, von Funck stated that he was prepared to send his own chief of staff, *Oberst* Walter Reinhard, to assume command of *Panzer Division 116*. Von Schwerin would be transferred to the Officers Reserve before being sent back to Germany on leave. Hausser approved the proposal but reminded von Funck that *Oberst* Reinhard would command the division only until a suitable replacement was found.

When von Funck telephoned *Panzer Division 116* to inform von Schwerin of Hausser's decision, he was told that von Schwerin was visiting frontline units. Von Funck testily instructed the division chief of staff to pass along the message. When von Schwerin learned that he was relieved, he telephoned *XLVII Panzer Korps,* demanding to speak with von Funck. Both generals participated in a heated telephonic shouting match, but it was of no avail. Von Schwerin departed with the coming of darkness, the first of several German generals whose professional fortunes would be affected by their participation in *Unternehmen Lüttich*.[1]

Von Schwerin's removal did not suffice to quell Hitler's discontent. From the onset, he had had serious reservations concerning *Generalfeldmarschall* von Kluge's plan and felt that von Kluge had failed to employ the number of panzer divisions needed to achieve a truly dramatic victory. Hitler had not been convinced that *XLVII Panzer Korps* possessed the resources necessary to plan and execute a complicated offensive operation involving five divisions. He also blamed von Kluge for failing to assemble enough artillery to support the attacking panzers.

Unlike von Kluge, Hitler was willing to assume significant risk in other sectors to assemble what he defined as a decisive counterattack force. By promising he could recapture Avranches using a reinforced panzer corps, von Kluge fended off early suggestions by Berlin to alter *Unternehmen Lüttich*. As reports of Anglo-American successes continued to pour in, however, Hitler grew increasingly disenchanted with von Kluge's ability to procure the type of victory he sought in Normandy.

Consequently, even as von Kluge carried out his own preparations, Hitler directed the *OKW* staff to draw up an alternate proposal. He instructed his planners to produce an operation that employed a minimum of eight panzer divisions organized into two panzer corps, under the overall command of a panzer group. This approach would ensure that the attackers possessed adequate command and control, artillery, and logistical support.[2]

Early on the morning of 7 August, Hitler dispatched his own plan via courier to von Kluge. *General der Infanterie* Walter Buhle, chief of the army staff, carried the new instructions. Hitler intended the *OKW* plan to arrive before the attack took place, but Buhle did not reach von Kluge's headquarters until 8 August. Since *Unternehmen Lüttich* was already under way, this meant that the plan he carried was immediately rendered moot.[3] Buhle's late arrival, however, was based on the mistaken impression in Berlin that the counteroffensive against Avranches would not begin for several more days.

Aware that he had fallen into disfavor by seemingly failing to heed Hitler's suggestions about timing the blow against Avranches, von Kluge began revising the existing plan to ensure it conformed with the concept delivered by Buhle. Von Kluge telephoned *7 Armee* headquarters to inform Hausser that "despite the reverses, the attack would be continued at all costs. There must be no doubt about this."[4] He also directed Hausser to make preparations to renew the attack no later than 9 August.[5]

Buhle, who was present when von Kluge spoke with Hausser, dutifully informed Hitler that *OB West* fully supported the *OKW* plan. He also attempted to reduce the considerable tension that existed by explaining that *Unternehmen Lüttich* had been launched early due to concerns that Allied aircraft would discover the assembly areas. Furthermore, Buhle reported that von Kluge planned on expanding

ing the scope of the counteroffensive, but the British offensive south of Caen temporarily delayed the transfer of additional panzers. Only *SS-Panzer Division 10* and a *Nebelwerfer* brigade were available to reinforce *XLVII Panzer Korps*.

The changing situation at Mortain, however, forced von Kluge to begin revising the plan delivered by Buhle. Obviously, *XLVII Panzer Korps* could not expect to launch another assault aimed directly at Avranches. Sure that the Americans were reinforcing the northern flank of the 30th Infantry Division in anticipation of such a course of action, von Kluge would have to request Hitler's permission to designate Domfront as the new springboard for *Unternehmen Lüttich*. Rather than conduct an advance due west, the new axis would angle northwest through St.-Hilaire-du-Harcouet toward Avranches. By continuing to apply pressure at Mortain, von Kluge hoped to prevent the Americans from shifting troops to block the new axis of advance.

The plan developed by *OKW* called for the employment of eight panzer divisions for the counteroffensive against Avranches. A single corps headquarters would prove insufficient to control such a large force, so a new *Panzer Gruppe* was created. *General der Panzertruppen* Heinrich Eberbach of *Panzer Gruppe West* found himself unexpectedly nominated to assume command of the divisions participating in *Unternehmen Lüttich*. Eberbach was originally sent to France in July to replace *General der Panzertruppen* Leo Geyr von Schweppenberg. A skilled panzer tactician, he successfully held the British at bay despite several attempts by Montgomery to break out of the Normandy lodgment.[6] The panzer divisions under his command were designated as *Panzer Gruppe Eberbach*. In keeping with Hitler's aim to ensure that politically reliable *SS* officers were placed in senior command positions, Berlin also directed that Sepp Dietrich, commanding general of *SS-Panzer Korps I,* would replace Eberbach.

General der Panzertruppen Eberbach was indignant upon learning that he had been named to command the formation tasked to recapture Avranches. Sure that the attempt on Hitler's life on 20 July was responsible for his "dismissal" as commander of *Panzer Gruppe West* (which was renamed *Panzerarmee 5* upon his departure), his belief was strengthened when orders arrived naming Sepp Dietrich as his successor. Eberbach did not think that an *SS* officer like Dietrich was qualified to take command of an army-level formation. He also could not help but notice that *Panzer Gruppe Eberbach* would fall under another *SS* general, Paul Hausser.[7]

In addition to creating a new *Panzer Gruppe,* von Kluge allocated an additional intermediate headquarters to satisfy the command and control requirements necessary to direct the operations of subordinate units. *General der Panzertruppen* Walter Krueger's *LVIII Panzer Korps* was assigned to *Panzer Gruppe Eberbach* to fill this void. *LVIII Panzer Korps* would assume command of *SS-Ponzer Division 2* and *SS-Panzer Division 10,* while *XLVII Panzer Korps* would retain control of the remaining divisions. By employing Krueger's corps headquarters, von Kluge hoped to avoid creating additional turmoil within *Panzer Armee 5*. The command structure of the German forces facing the British already experienced several significant disruptions with the transfer of Eberbach and Dietrich. By assigning *LVIII Panzer Korps* to *Panzer Gruppe Eberbach*, von Kluge ensured that the command elements, corps artillery, and heavy tanks of *SS-Panzer Korps I* and *II* remained with *Panzerarmee 5*.

Although von Kluge was able to quickly assemble a command and control element for *Panzergruppe Eberbach* in deference to Hitler's wishes, he encountered significant difficulties trying to align other portions of the *OKW* plan with the situation in Normandy. Hitler had seriously miscalculated the impact that a British offensive would have on German plans to retake Avranches. As early as 4 August, General Bernard Montgomery ordered the First Canadian Army to launch an offensive against the crossroads town of Falaise. The goal of this operation, slated to begin no later than 8 August, was to destroy the German divisions opposing the British and Canadian forces. The offensive, code-named Operation TOTALIZE, would begin with a night attack by the 2d Canadian and 51st British Infantry Divisions. The second echelon, consisting of the 4th Canadian Armored and 3d Canadian Infantry Divisions, was tasked to enlarge the initial breakthrough after daybreak. During the third phase of TOTALIZE, the 1st Polish Armored Division would join the 4th Canadian Armored in a drive to secure the dominating ridges northeast of Falaise.

The task facing the Canadians was made easier by von Kluge's decision to transfer panzers from the Caen front to support *Unternehmen Lüttich*. When the commander of the First Canadian Army was informed that *Infanterie Division 89* had replaced *SS-Panzer Division 1*, he thought the news significant enough to make major modifications to Operation TOTALIZE. Unfortunately, he was under the mistaken impression that *SS-Panzer Division 1* had been placed in reserve. In order to sustain the momentum of the Canadian offensive in the face of substantial German armored reserves, the second and third phases of TOTALIZE were combined. Rather than wait until the breakthrough was enlarged, both of the Polish and Canadian armored divisions would be committed earlier to deny the Germans an opportunity to employ their mobile reserve.

The Canadian offensive began at 2330 hours on 7 August with two armored and two mechanized infantry brigades using specifically designated corridors to penetrate the German defensive line to a depth of six thousand yards. A total of 1,020 four-engined bombers and 720 artillery pieces supported the initial phase of the advance. Although a number of Canadian units were quickly embroiled in bitter fighting as isolated German strongholds were reduced, First Canadian Army declared that the initial phase of TOTALIZE had been successfully completed by 0800 hours on 8 August.

In addition to local counterattacks launched by small groups of panzers, the forward movement of the Polish and Canadian armored divisions encountered traffic jams that severely impeded progress. Ongoing mopping up by the first assault echelon had constricted the use of available roads as well as cross-country maneuver space. A penetration of six kilometers, it would seem, did not provide sufficient maneuver room for two follow-on armored divisions to conduct exploitation. As if these difficulties were not enough, a second bombing raid designed to soften up German positions in depth went astray. Errant bombs hit elements of the 1st Polish and 4th Canadian Armored Divisions. Some 355 Polish and Canadian soldiers were killed or wounded by the mistaken bombing, which also destroyed fifty-five vehicles and four artillery pieces.

The second phase of Operation TOTALIZE had clearly fallen well short of the objectives designated by First Canadian Army. In addition to being struck by friendly bombers, the Polish and Canadian armored divisions were forced to ward off counterattacks by *SS-Panzer Division 12* and *SS-Schwere Panzer Abteilung 101*. As darkness fell on 8 August, the operation settled down to a bloody slugging match.

The Canadian offensive served to divert significant resources from *Unternehmen Lüttich*. *OB West* postponed the transfer of *General der Panzertruppen* Eberbach for twenty-four hours as *Panzer Gruppe West* fought desperately to prevent a complete breakthrough by Canadian troops. More important, von Kluge decided that the situation was serious enough for him to temporarily ignore Hitler's directive to transfer additional panzer divisions to *Panzer Gruppe Eberbach*. Instead he authorized Eberbach to retain control of *SS-Panzer Division 9* and *Panzer Division 21* in anticipation of future attempts by the British and Canadians to capture Falaise.

Rather than transfer additional divisions from *Panzer Gruppe West,* von Kluge considered shifting *Panzer Division 9* from *LXXXI Armee Korps* to *Panzer Gruppe Eberbach*. By exercising this option, he could place seven divisions at Eberbach's disposal, which was only one short of the eight specified by Hitler. Hausser was horrified to learn of his proposal. The *7 Armee* commander informed von Kluge that the commander of *LXXXI Armee Korps* had bluntly stated he would not be able to contain the Americans in Mayenne without *Panzer Division 9*.[8] Von Kluge decided to drop the issue for the time being, pinning his hopes on *General der Panzertruppen* Eberbach's ability to recapture Avranches using only the troops currently at his disposal.

When Hitler awoke on 9 August, he was informed of the abortive Canadian offensive south of Caen. Invigorated by the welcome news, Hitler ordered his staff to find out why the Avranches counteroffensive had not been renewed. *OKW* telephoned von Kluge at 1520 hours to reiterate Hitler's demands for a decisive westward push by eight panzer divisions. *Generalfeldmarschall* von Kluge responded with a request to shift the starting point of the counteroffensive from Mortain to Domfront. He explained that *Unternehmen Lüttich* would angle from Domfront through Barenton before shifting northwest toward St.-Hilaire-du-Harcouet and Avranches. *OKW* approved his request as well as granted permission to shorten the *7 Armee* defensive line to free up additional infantry and artillery units for *Unternehmen Lüttich*.[9]

Following the phone call from *OKW*, von Kluge telephoned *7 Armee* to relay the information to Hausser's chief of staff, *Oberst* von Gersdorff. The *Generalfeldmarschall* explained: "I have just had a decisive conversation with the Supreme Command. Insomuch as the situation south of Caen has been stabilized again and apparently has not brought about the bad results that were expected, I have suggested that we stick to the idea of the attack. The attack must be prepared and carried out, however, according to plan and should not be done too hastily. *General der Panzertruppen* Eberbach will be attached to command the armored forces. The attack forces must be rearranged further to the south. Eberbach will arrive at your command post tonight."[10] Before departing, Eberbach formally relinquished command to Sepp Dietrich. With this appointment, *SS* generals commanded both of the German armies engaged in combat against the Allies in Normandy.

General der Panzertruppen Eberbach and his small entourage arrived at Mortain late on 9 August. With only three radio trucks and a few liaison officers, Eberbach began sorting out the situation at hand. He was forced to borrow resources from Hausser's headquarters to provide his newly formed staff with the bare minimum it needed to function.[11] He also sensed that the commander of *7 Armee* was not happy to see him. It appeared that Hausser believed that the creation of a *Panzer Gruppe* headquarters within the *7 Armee* area of operations would only serve to complicate the command and control process.[12]

Focused on preparing for a renewed counteroffensive, the Germans underestimated the American reaction to their initial attack. Confusing reports from Mortain on 7 August obscured the true extent of the German effort, and the attack was initially described as consisting of "two reasonably fresh infantry divisions of good quality. These could be reinforced by elements of panzer troops of undetermined strength but perhaps equivalent to a full division . . . this force could possibly be reinforced by 2d Parachute Division which is unlocated in the battle area." Security restrictions on ULTRA intelligence contributed to a mistaken impression at corps level and below that "from limited sources of information available it would appear that this is a limited counterattack delivered to aid in the extrication of the German forces in the pocket north of Mortain."[13]

Lieutenant General Omar Bradley, however, was in the process of learning a great deal about the true nature of the German counteroffensive from ULTRA decrypts. Although claiming that he was not overly concerned, Bradley was sufficiently cautious to convene a meeting at 12th Army Group headquarters to discuss "new developments arising from the German counterattack in Mortain." Following the meeting, the 12th Army Group G-3 spent the rest of the day devising a counterattack plan against the German panzers.[14]

Bradley visited the Third Army command post soon afterward, where he personally briefed Patton on the details of the German counteroffensive. In order to forestall any possibility of a German success, Bradley ordered Patton to move the 2d French Armored Division, 35th Infantry Division, and XX Corps artillery into assembly areas between the See and Selune Rivers. Additionally, the 80th Infantry Division would halt its movement south to occupy defensive positions near St.-Hilaire-du-Harcouet.

The divisions named by Bradley belonged to Major General Walton Walker's XX Corps, which was just beginning to transit the Avranches corridor. Walker was present at Patton's headquarters when Bradley arrived to discuss the German counteroffensive. He was in the process of carrying out Patton's instructions to cover the gap between VIII Corps and XV Corps when Bradley issued him a new set of orders. In addition to establishing a defense in depth, Bradley told Walker that he would be responsible for coordinating the actions of XX Corps with the First Army response to the German counteroffensive.[15] He was also informed that he could anticipate sending some troops to reinforce VII Corps.

Once Walker departed Third Army headquarters, Lieutenant General Bradley took the opportunity to brief Patton on a plan designed to envelope Paris using six armored divisions. Bradley was surprised by Patton's reaction to the proposal, noting that "Patton appeared to agree with it—he would lead the wide sweep – but he proposed a lesser 'pivot' role for Hodges' First Army and questioned the use of the airborne corps."[16]

Patton's reaction was governed by his belief that events were moving too rapidly for Bradley's grand plan. Rather than produce a great victory, in Patton's opinion the 12th Army Group proposal would only result in the loss of a priceless opportunity. The Germans had played directly into American hands by concentrating their panzers at Mortain. Patton realized that Haislip's XV Corps, by merely changing its axis of advance to the north, was in a position to threaten 7 *Armee* with encirclement.

Patton had good reason to be optimistic. On the evening of 7 August, Major General Wade Haislip's XV Corps was preparing to seize Le Mans. Immediately upon being relieved by the 1st Infantry Division at Mayenne on the evening of 6 August, the 90th Infantry Division began making preparations to resume its advance. In order to seize Le Mans, XV Corps had to move fifty miles to the east through ideal defensive terrain, force a river crossing, and seize a city that the Germans had ample time to organize for defense. Additionally, Haislip understood that neither XX Corps nor VIII Corps was in a position to assist him if the Germans reacted vigorously to his advance. Lacking protection on either flank, he would be vulnerable to German units counterattacking at right angles to his corps axis of advance.

Early on the morning of 7 August, the 90th Infantry Division dispatched two regimental combat teams toward Le Mans. Both columns fought their way forward against steadily increasing resistance during the course of the day. Working in tandem, the Americans rapidly covered ground using a simple tactic: the unengaged column would outflank and destroy the opposition holding up its neighbor. To the south, the 79th Infantry Division was also advancing on Le

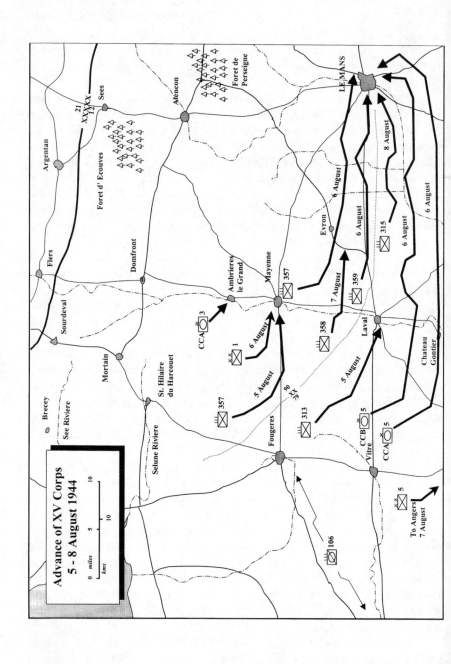

Advance of XV Corps
5 - 8 August 1944

0 miles   5   10

kms   10

Breey

See Riviere

Selune Riviere

Mortain

Sourdeval

Domfront

Flers

Argentan

Foret d' Eouves

Sees

XXXXX
21
12

Alencon

Foret de
Perseigne

LE MANS

8 August

6 August

6 August

8 August

6 August

6 August

Evron

315

359

7 August

357

Ambrieres
le Grand

CCA 3

1

6 August

Mayenne

358

Laval

5 August

5 August

Chateau
Gontier

St. Hilaire
du Harcouet

357

5 August

90
79

313

Fougeres

CCB 5

Vitre

CCA 5

106

5

To Angers
7 August

Mans. Although the *LXXXI Armee Korps* had been able to impede the movement of the 90th Division, albeit at great cost to the defenders, there were very few German troops in a position to block the southern approaches to Le Mans. As a result, the leading elements of the 79th Division entered Le Mans at 2100 hours that evening.[17]

When the news of the 79th Division's entry into the city reached Major General Haislip, he issued instructions for a corps-level assault to secure Le Mans on 8 August. To hasten the fall of the city, he planned to attack simultaneously from the southeast, west, and northwest. At dawn the Americans began their assault. The 5th Armored Division encircled the city while the two infantry divisions battled the Germans for its possession. After considerable street fighting, by the end of the day the 79th Division occupied the southern portion of the city, and the 90th held the northern half.[18]

The loss of Le Mans had a significant impact on *7 Armee*. Numerous fuel depots, maintenance facilities, and ammunition dumps were sacrificed when XV Corps captured the city. Lieutenant General Patton, however, had originally cast a covetous eye on Le Mans for other reasons. The Rouen-Bordeaux and Rennes-Paris highways met at Alencon, located thirty miles north of Le Mans, providing an extensive road network to the north that led directly into the rear of *7 Armee*. The seizure of Alencon would not only sever the *7 Armee* supply lines, but it also would reduce any potential German avenue of retreat to a single east-west highway passing through Argentan.

The seizure of Le Mans also opened Lieutenant General Bradley's eyes to a lucrative opportunity. During the course of 7 August, it became clear that the 30th Infantry Division had halted the German drive toward Avranches. As more information became available, Bradley realized that the quarry he had been seeking to trap by swinging east of Paris was much closer. Von Kluge's decision to launch *Unternehmen Lüttich* placed a number of German panzer divisions deeper within a pocket being slowly formed by Patton's Third Army and Montgomery's 21st Army Group. Bradley felt that "if the Canadians could push into Falaise and beyond to Argentan, and if . . . Haislip [was turned] due north from Le Mans toward Argentan, there was a good chance we could encircle and trap the whole German force in Normandy in a few days."[19]

Lieutenant General Bradley visited Third Army on 8 August to sound out Patton's thoughts on turning XV Corps north from Le Mans toward Alencon.[20] He recorded that the Third Army commander seemed indifferent to the new plan, noting that Patton "leaned toward my idea of the day before—the deeper and wider envelopment along the Seine—perhaps because it was more dramatic, perhaps because the success of my proposed shorter envelopment was heavily dependent on the Canadian Army closing the gap from the north."[21] Regardless of his personal feelings, Patton began preparing Third Army for a change in mission.

As Patton understood his new task, Third Army was to secure a line running from Angers to Le Mans, with an infantry division positioned on either flank. Once this was accomplished, Third Army would launch an attack with all available troops on the axis Le Mans–Alencon–Sees, using the River Loire to cover its eastern flank. XV Corps, which would conduct the attack, would consist of the French 2d Armored Division, the 5th Armored Division, and the 79th or 90th Infantry Division, whichever was available. As soon as the 35th or 80th Infantry Division arrived from Avranches, it would relieve the division holding Le Mans, which would then move north to reinforce XV Corps.[22]

Following his talk with Patton, Bradley arranged a "chance" meeting with General Eisenhower to discuss his new proposal. Bradley found Eisenhower touring the COBRA battlefield near Coutances and over a K-ration lunch explained the main points of his concept. Eisenhower proved so enthusiastic that he returned with Bradley to the 12th Army Group headquarters to discuss the operation in greater detail with maps. Eisenhower, who could find no flaws in the plan, personally telephoned Montgomery to inform him of the new mission for Third Army.

Although Montgomery expressed some reservation regarding the capability of VII Corps to fend off renewed attacks at Mortain, he accepted Eisenhower's pronouncement without protest. Montgomery could not help but agree that "the prospective prize was great." Later that evening, however, Eisenhower visited the 21st Army Group headquarters to "make certain that Monty would continue to press on the British-Canadian front."[23]

Armed with Montgomery's approval, Bradley authorized Patton to conduct a strong attack by XV Corps against the left flank and rear of *7 Armee*. The tentative axis of advance included Le Mans–Alencon–Sees, although XV Corps was not authorized to move north of Sees without Bradley's express approval. The 12th Army Group commander was worried about the possible collision between the Canadians and Haislip's XV Corps. What he did not realize, however, was that Operation TOTALIZE was grinding to a halt far short of its intended objective.

Letter of Instruction Number 4, issued that evening by 12th Army Group, stated that the German commander made a serious error by "concentrating his armored forces for the counterattack . . . he has incurred the risk of encirclement from the south and north." Like Patton, Bradley recognized the opportunity arising from the German decision to launch a counteroffensive against Avranches. He also included a statement that "12th Army Group will attack with least practicable delay in the direction of Argentan to isolate and destroy the German forces to our front."[24] First Army was directed to support Third Army by reducing "the enemy salient in zone, pivoting on Mortain, advance to the line Domfront-Barenton . . . [be] prepared for further action against the enemy flank and rear in the direction of Flers."[25]

Success also depended heavily on the ability of VII Corps to contain the Germans at Mortain. Although *XLVII Panzer Korps* sustained significant losses on 7 August, it remained a potent force. In addition, ULTRA decrypts and tactical intelligence sources disclosed that German reinforcements were heading toward Mortain. Although this information was somewhat disquieting, Bradley authorized the French 2d Armored Division, 80th Infantry Division, and XX Corps artillery to continue moving south on 8 August. Major General Collins had successfully lobbied to retain the 35th Infantry Division, which he intended to employ to fill the gap between Mortain and Barenton. First Army also attached the 2d Armored Division to VII Corps for the duration of the operation.

The defensive line held by VII Corps, extending over twenty miles from St.-Sever to Mayenne, was now manned by five infantry and two armored divisions. Collins quickly began repositioning his units to repel a renewed advance by *XLVII Panzer Korps.* The 9th Infantry Division began preparing to shift to the south to assume responsibility for the 4th Division's sector. The 4th Infantry Division, situation permitting, would then move south to reinforce the 30th Division. Although Collins did not immediately reposition the entire 4th Division, he sent Barton's reserve regiment to reinforce Major General Hobbs during the afternoon of 7 August. The 30th Division, which had become the linchpin of the VII Corps defensive line, was ordered to hold its present position and prevent further penetration west of the line Cherence le Roussel–St.-Barthelemy–Mortain.[26]

Major General Hobbs's battered division needed all of the assistance it could get. Collins had instructed Hobbs that his first priority was to firm up the shoulders to the German penetration. By constricting the panzers to the narrow corridor, it would prove easier to counter future moves by the Germans. Hobbs was also instructed to gain control of all critical road junctions to impede German attempts to reposition forces or exploit a weak point in the American lines. Additionally, Collins expected the 30th Infantry Division to gain control of dominating terrain that enhanced the employment of the defending artillery.

Hobbs initially focused his efforts to the north, where German panzers had severed contact between the 119th Infantry and the 39th Infantry. Opposing the 30th Division was the newly appointed commanding general of *Panzer Division 116, Oberst* Walter Reinhard. Reinhard ordered *Panzergrenadier Regiment 156* to conduct a series of attacks against the Americans during the night of 7 August. Problems began to crop up, however, when the panzergrenadiers launched their assault, and most of the patrols sent to probe the American defenses were dispersed by machine-gun fire. Despite that setback, *Panzergrenadier Regiment 156* moved forward as scheduled just before midnight on 7 August.

The initial bout of patrol activity had earlier prompted Lieutenant Charlie Scheffel to pay a visit on the commander of B/39th Infantry. In order to discourage the Germans from infiltrating the 1st Battalion perimeter, Scheffel convinced Lieutenant Dunlap to set fire to several buildings using tracers from a .50-caliber machine gun, hoping that the flames would illuminate anyone approaching C Company. A short burst of tracers sufficed to set the thatch roofs on fire, and as the flames took hold, the Germans launched an assault against Lieutenant Scheffel's company.

The attackers quickly pushed back C Company's left flank platoon. Retreating soldiers began drifting back past Lieutenant Scheffel's command post, and he yelled at them to stop. The men returned to their foxholes after their company commander informed them that C/39th Infantry would be staying put. As soon as Scheffel rallied his men, he contacted Lieutenant Colonel Tucker to report that C Company was in dire straits. He requested tank support, adding that the Germans were on the verge of running him out of his command post, and warned Tucker that he might have to pull back. In that eventuality, Scheffel proposed falling back on Company B, but Lieutenant Colonel Tucker's response was to hold on at all costs.

Tucker sent his battalion operations officer forward to help Lieutenant Scheffel reorganize his company as Scheffel reinforced the left flank of the perimeter with his weapons platoon. As dawn approached, C/39th Infantry launched a counterattack to eject the Germans from the toehold they had gained within the 1st Battalion defensive perimeter. After a brief clash, the Germans were forced to relinquish the ground they had earlier won. The cost for both sides was considerable: the Germans lost a number of men, while C Company suffered one killed and twenty-four wounded.[27]

As *Panzer Division 116* grappled with the 39th Infantry for control of Cherence le Roussel, the 119th Infantry prepared to launch another assault against le Mesnil Tove. This renewed effort by the Americans took place during the late evening of 7 August when Lieutenant Colonel King's Task Force (TF) 1 executed a mounted attack at 2330 hours. The fighting began on an inauspicious note, when the commander of I/33d Armor was killed when his tank was knocked out on the eastern outskirts of the village. A point-blank duel took place, whereupon the Americans withdrew after claiming the destruction of a Pzkfw IV and 75mm antitank gun.

Following the failure of TF 1's initial attempt to seize le Mesnil Tove, Colonel Sutherland planned to undertake a more deliberate effort employing the remainder of CCB. The forces brought into play by the commitment of CCB included two additional tank battalions and a pair of armored infantry battalions divided between the 33d Armored and 36th Armored Infantry headquarters. Each of the battalions was organized to produce a combined arms group consisting of tanks, armored infantry, reconnaissance, TD's, and engineers. Each regimental headquarters normally controlled three task-organized teams; however, the 36th AIR had already sent a battlegroup to Barenton while a second accompanied CCA to Mayenne. In order to balance out the forces assigned to each regiment, the 2/33d Armor was transferred to the 36th AIR. The 33d Armored Regiment had already lost Lieutenant Colonel Hogan's 3d Battalion, which was designated as the reserve for the 30th Infantry Division, leaving Colonel Roysdon with only Lieutenant Colonel King's TF 1.

The 36th AIR, which was commanded by Colonel William Cornog, chose to reorganize the armored infantry and tank battalion that had been allocated to it by CCB into three teams, each consisting of a tank company, armored infantry company, reconnaissance platoon, and TD platoon. Cornog, a 1924 graduate of West Point, had been in command of the 36th AIR since 18 July. Lieutenant Colonel Vincent Cockefair of 2/36th AIR commanded Team 1, while Lieutenant Colonel William Lovelady of 2/33d Armor led Team 2. Colonel Cornog led Team 3 himself.[28]

Colonel Sutherland ordered the 33d Armor to assault le Mesnil Tove from the west, while Colonel Cornog maneuvered cross-country to attack from the south. Since CCB maintenance personnel spent all morning reassembling the armored vehicles belonging to TF 1, Colonel Cornog's column was not able to get under way until late evening on 7 August. His column departed from Reffuveille bound for Juvigny le Tertre, where it turned north to follow a narrow cross-country trail leading toward Grand Dove.

As Lieutenant Colonel Cockefair's team neared its initial objective, the lead American vehicles were fired upon, and he reported that the Germans held Grand Dove in strength. The rough terrain also prevented Team 2 from deploying, prompting a request for bulldozers to cut holes in the hedgerows. Rather than compound an already poor situation, Colonel Cornog decided to wait until the morning of 8 August before resuming his assault.

American reinforcements began arriving during the early morning hours of 8 August. One of the first units to show up was the M-10–equipped 629th TD Battalion. When the commander of the TD Battalion reported to the 30th Infantry Division headquarters at 0100 hours, he was instructed by Major General Hobbs to send one company to support the 117th Infantry. Aware of the pending arrival of the reserve regiment from the 4th Division, Hobbs had accepted some risk by dispatching a single TD company to reinforce Lieutenant Colonel Johnson's embattled regiment. The remaining TD companies would be attached to Colonel Birks. Within a few hours, the M-10s of A/629th TD were pulling into position outside St.-Barthelemy, while B and C Companies occupied defensive positions west of Mortain.[29]

The 4th Division's reserve, which consisted of Colonel James S. Luckett's 12th Infantry, had been occupying a rest area when it was alerted to be ready to move south. The time of departure, however, was not specified. Preparations to move did not begin in earnest until the division G-3 delivered new orders to the 12th Infantry's command post at 1700 hours on 7 August. Luckett reacted quickly to the new orders, and Major Kenneth R. Lindner's 3d Battalion departed the regimental assembly area at 1932 hours.[30] His convoy was fortunate to have departed early, as the remaining elements of the 12th Infantry encountered XX Corps units when they tried to move south.

Unimpeded by traffic, the 3/12th Infantry arrived outside of Juvigny le Tertre at 0100 hours on 8 August. When Major Lindner contacted the 30th Division for instructions, he was told to link up with the 117th Infantry.[31] The trucks carrying the 3d Battalion were met by guides who led them to positions southwest of St.-Barthelemy. As his men settled down in the unfamiliar terrain, Lind-

Major Kenneth Lindner, commander of the 3/12th Infantry at St.-Barthelemy. (Kenneth Lindner)

ner was taken to the 117th Infantry command post. In a brief meeting with Lieutenant Colonel Johnson, he was told to recapture St.-Barthelemy by 0700 hours.[32] The 117th's intelligence officer tried to soothe Lindner's obvious concern by reassuring him that there were only a few Germans defending the town. Lindner trudged back to his jeep wondering what his battalion would actually encounter later that morning.[33]

As the 3d Battalion dug in, Lindner received a report from Captain John S. Harvey, commanding L Company, that his outposts could hear panzer engines starting up. Harvey passed the word to his men to pull back two hedgerows to await support as he sought aid from a nearby platoon of TDs. Two M-10s followed him back to L Company when they spotted a Panther lumbering down the road from St.-Barthelemy. The M-10s slammed several rounds into the advancing panzer, which slewed to a halt in a small field. With that threat averted, the 3/12th continued preparing for the attack that had been scheduled for 0700 hours.

At dawn, Major Lindner was finally able to make out the terrain that lay between him and his objective. The 3/12th Infantry was perched precariously at the foot of a ridge where St.-Barthelemy was located, enabling the Germans to see every move that Lindner's men made as they prepared to advance. Major Lindner could also clearly see Germans moving around in front of the village. As the visibility improved, both attacker and defender began showering each other with artillery. A combination of the spoiling attack launched earlier against L Company, coupled with the tremendous amount of incoming artillery, brought the 3/12th's assault to a standstill before it even began.[34]

As it prepared to move forward on the left flank of the 3/12th Infantry, the 1/117th Infantry collided with a German assault force. *Brigadeführer* Wisch had sent two battalions from *SS-Panzergrenadier Regiment 2,* supported by tanks, to seize Juvigny le Tertre during the early morning hours of 8 August. Just after 0400 hours, panzer engines could be heard south of the 117th's regimental motor park. The fog rolled in again, prompting the Americans to dispatch patrols to find out what the Germans were doing. One of the patrols spotted *SS* infantry advancing toward the 1/117th's defensive perimeter, and a firefight broke as both sides reacted to the unexpected encounter.

Bolstered by the reinforcements, the American patrol was able to force the *SS* advance guard to retreat. Moments later, the main body of the Germans struck B/117th Infantry. Some of the attackers clambered over the hedgerows, charging into the middle of the American position. Hand-to-hand fighting broke out, with the American troops getting the better of the contest. Faced with an unyielding defense and increasing artillery fire, the *SS* troops finally withdrew back to St.-Barthelemy.

Despite the disruption created by the unexpected German assault, the 1/117th Infantry launched its own attack precisely on schedule. The advance had barely begun, however, when Captain Hendrickson of Company B was wounded as he led a bazooka team against a panzer holding up his progress. By 1043 hours, Lieutenant Colonel Frankland's men had succeeded in capturing just a single hedgerow following an intensive bout of fighting. The 1/117th struggled on to seize two more hedgerows before being halted by the interlocking fire of four German machine-gun nests. Concerned about being caught in an exposed position by a counterattack, Frankland ordered his men to pull back for the night.[35] He also informed regimental headquarters that unless reinforcements were sent forward, St.-Barthelemy would remain in German hands.

Reinforcements were in the process of arriving as the fighting around St. Barthelemy subsided. The 12th Infantry supply vehicles, accompanied by Lieutenant Colonel Charles Jackson's 1st Battalion, reached their new assembly areas at 0520 hours on 8 August. Lieutenant Colonel Gerden Johnson's 2/12th Infantry and B/70th Tank Battalion followed shortly afterward.[36] The 42d FA Battalion, which provided direct support for Colonel Luckett's regiment, began registering on suspected targets within German lines. By midmorning, both of the newly arrived rifle battalions began the long trek from their dismount point to the regiment's final objective at Road Junction (RJ) 278. The 2/12th Infantry led, with 1st Battalion following closely behind.[37]

Resistance during the initial phase of the advance was limited to a few snipers and sporadic artillery fire. The most significant obstacle encountered by Colonel Luckett's men was la Riviere Doree, a marshy creekbed at the foot of the ridgeline where RJ 278 was located. With the ground too soft to safely traverse, the Shermans of B/70th Tank Battalion were forced to wait impotently on the near side of the creek. Colonel Luckett ordered an attached platoon from B Company, 4th Engineers, to construct a crossing point for the stalled tanks as the infantry continued advancing.

By 1700 hours, the 12th Infantry began nearing RJ 278. Despite the lack of contact, the American advance was brought to a halt several times as the lead companies reoriented themselves in the unfamiliar terrain. Forced to rely solely on a compass bearing for direction, the leading elements of the 1st Battalion collided with the flank of the 2/12th Infantry. As Lieutenant Colonel Jackson reorganized his battalion, he was also informed that the commander of C Company had asked to be relieved. The company executive officer took charge as the 1st Battalion moved forward once more. Meanwhile, Colonel Luckett had passed on new instructions to Jackson: after the 1st Battalion secured the southern half of RJ 278, it would head into Mortain to link up with the 2/120th on Hill 314.[38]

The Germans reacted when the 12th Infantry approached RJ 278. The first indications of German activity appeared when a pair of panzers, accompanied by infantry, were seen digging in along a trail north of le Neufbourg. Although the Germans were in a position to threaten the 1st Battalion's right flank, Colonel Luckett ordered the advance to continue. The 2/12th encountered several machine guns when it attempted to cross the road linking L'Abbaye Blanche with St.-Barthelemy. The Germans were able to delay the 2d Battalion for several minutes until several veteran sergeants knocked out the opposing machine guns with grenades. One prisoner, a *Leibstandarte* forward observer, was captured.

The brief delay permitted the Germans to position several tanks in the path of the 2/12th Infantry. One panzer was located squarely on the battalion's designated objective, with another sited just to the south.[39] Three light armored cars accompanied by two motorcyclists were also seen heading north toward RJ 278. As shells began falling in ever increasing numbers, the Germans opposing the 2/12th were reinforced by two more panzers and additional infantry. The advance of the 2d Battalion had inadvertently straddled the boundary separating *SS-Panzer Divisionen 1* and 2 and consequently had attracted the unwanted attention of both.

The 1st Battalion was having troubles of its own. Lieutenant Colonel Jackson's unit once again found itself tangled up when Company C inadvertently broke contact with Company B. The other rifle companies were holding in place awaiting the return of Company C when heavy fire struck the 1/12th Infantry. Several panzers opened fire from hilltop positions overlooking la Riviere Doree. Although the 1st Battalion immediately replied with 81mm mortars, the barrage did not suppress the defending panzers.

As the fighting seesawed back and forth, *Leibstandarte* infiltrated several small groups of infantry into an orchard to the left rear of 2/12th Infantry. German tanks also opened fire on Lieutenant Colonel Gerden Johnson's command post. The first shell hit a house next to Johnson's headquarters, and a second wounded the Company E commander. Johnson, realizing that his supporting tanks and TDs could not move forward, requested permission to withdraw. Colonel Luckett granted the request but stipulated that the 2d Battalion would only pull back far enough to link up with the 1st Battalion on the west bank of la Riviere Doree.

The 2/12th Infantry now faced the difficult proposition of pulling back elements of Companies F and G that had already advanced beyond the Mortain–St.-Barthelemy road. Two panzers were parked out of bazooka range in the middle of the road, periodically spraying the Americans with machine-gun and cannon fire. Chased by bursts of tracer, individual squads from F and G Companies sprinted across the exposed road to safety. F Company suffered only a couple of minor casualties during the retreat, while Captain Fred Sullivan's Company G was able to pull back without losing any men.[40]

The 2d Battalion continued pulling back in small groups to avoid attracting the attention of the German panzers. By 0200 hours, only a few Americans remained east of la Riviere Doree. Captain Francis L. Ware, the 2d Battalion surgeon, had evacuated all but two seriously wounded men. Determining that he would not be able to evacuate the men until morning, Ware decided to leave them behind. A medic volunteered to stay with the wounded until an ambulance could be brought forward. Collecting extra morphine and bandages, the aidman slowly waved to the last riflemen of the 2/12th Infantry as they disappeared into the darkness.

Screened by the growing darkness and rough terrain, the 1st Battalion was also able to pull back without much interference from the Germans. However, the newly appointed commander of C Company had been wounded during the day, along with one of his rifle platoon leaders. The sole remaining officer, Lieutenant Edgar T. Miller, assumed command. Realizing the potential difficulties that could arise, Lieutenant Colonel Jackson shifted C/12th Infantry behind his other rifle companies.[41] The 12th Infantry, however, faced far greater problems than inexperienced company commanders. By retreating west of la Riviere Doree, Colonel Luckett abandoned his foothold atop the commanding terrain to his front. Follow-on attacks by the 12th Infantry would be conducted uphill, lacking tank support until the creek was bridged, against dug-in defenders.

Conforming to Major General Collins's desire to keep the Germans continually off balance, the 30th Division launched another assault against le Mesnil Tove on 8 August. Despite the difficulties encountered by CCB during the evening of 7 August, the division operations officer telephoned Colonel Sutherland with orders to maintain the pressure on the defending panzers. Sutherland was authorized to employ TF 1 as well as 3/119th Infantry to conduct a renewed assault against the village.

Sutherland, accompanied by his regimental operations officer, Major Hal D. McCown, departed soon afterward for the 3/119th's command post. When he asked for feedback on his proposed plan of attack, the assembled officers commented that the objective of the assault should be limited to seizing le Mesnil Tove and establishing a roadblock astride the east-west road running toward Sourdeval. Sutherland agreed with the recommendations and at the conclusion of the meeting telephoned Colonel Cornog to inform him of the plan. Cornog agreed to assist the 119th Infantry by launching another assault against Grand Dove at 1330 hours.[42]

Cornog would have some difficulty living up to that promise. TF 2 had been inching forward slowly all morning, but the coming of daylight revealed that mines and antitank guns interdicted all of the trails traversing the rugged terrain south of the village. Cornog, realizing that he could not advance without suffering prohibitive vehicle losses, ordered bulldozers brought forward to construct additional routes. He also directed Lieutenant Colonel Cockefair to take command of all of the armored infantry in TF 2. Cockefair spent most of the morning securing a line of departure for the mounted elements. The assault could not begin, but a pair of bulldozers could open additional trails.

With German panzers identified in le Mesnil Tove, Colonel Cornog declined to conduct a dismounted assault against the village until his own tanks were in place; he would not be able to assist Colonel Sutherland as promised. When the 3/119th Infantry launched its own attack at 1330 hours, it quickly became the focus of intense German artillery fire. The unrelenting rain of shells, accurately directed by German observers on le Mont Furgon, effectively pinned down the Americans. Counterbattery fire and fighter-bombers were called in to silence the opposing guns but brought only temporary relief.

Lieutenant Colonel King's TF 1 also launched an assault against the village at 1330 hours. Preceded by reconnaissance elements, two armored infantry companies supported by tanks moved along the road connecting le Mesnil Adelee with le Mesnil Tove. The American advance went smoothly at first, encountering little resistance as it moved forward two miles. In sharp contrast to the reception that greeted the 3/119th Infantry, TF 1 did not draw any fire until the leading Shermans reached a road junction half a mile west of le Mesnil Tove.

The leading tank of I/33d Armor, commanded by Sergeant Juan Haines, prepared to turn left at the road junction when he was directed into a nearby field. As additional Shermans moved off the road, machine-gun and antitank fire erupted from a wooded area to the east. The Americans returned the fire, singling out a dug-in panzer for special attention. Sergeant Haines instructed his gunner to knock out the German vehicle. After scoring several hits on the panzer, he then directed his gunner to open fire on the accompanying foot soldiers. Although he was not sure if he had disabled the panzer, Haines could clearly see the German infantry falling as his tracers swept through their position.[43] In return, three Shermans, several armored cars, and a number of jeeps were knocked out.

Lieutenant Colonel King directed his reserve company to bypass the leading elements of TF 1, which had been completely stalled by fierce resistance. Moving cross-country, F/33d Armor entered le Mesnil Tove at 1606 hours with eight medium tanks and a platoon of armored infantry. Two German self-propelled guns succeeded in confining the Shermans for a short period to the western edge of the village. When the armored infantry began stalking the assault guns, both of the German vehicles disappeared to the east. The Germans, who were eventually forced to retreat, had suffered a number of casualties. The commander of *Panzer Regiment 3, Major* Hans Schneider-Kostalsky, was killed by artillery, and all of the platoon leaders of *1 Kompanie, Panzerjäger Abteilung 38*, were wounded trying to coordinate a defense against TF 1.[44]

As the Americans consolidated their positions, the Germans hurriedly shifted their artillery fire to prevent TF 1 from advancing further to the east. Although the Germans halted further movement by TF 1, the 3/119th Infantry was able to resume its advance when the artillery was lifted. By 1700 hours, Lieutenant Colonel Brown's men had begun clearing la Besnardais, a small village southeast of le Mesnil Tove. As soon as la Besnardais was secured, the 3d Battalion began moving to the northwest with the intent of surrounding the Germans holding up TF 1's advance. L Company encountered a slight delay when it ran into a dug-in German tank, but bazooka teams finally forced the panzer to pull out. Once that obstacle was removed, the 3/119th continued toward le Mesnil Tove.

TF 2 was finally in a position by late afternoon to support the assault on the village. After bulldozers opened a path sufficient for a platoon of tanks to move forward, Lieutenant Colonel Cockefair's Team 1 began advancing. He succeeded in cutting the road between le Mesnil Tove and Grand Dove at 1655 hours, and the Germans reacted by inundating Team 1 with artillery. When scouts reported that German panzers were preparing for a counterattack against his team, Cockefair ordered his men to pull back to a less exposed position.[45]

Panzer Division 2 launched a counterattack against Team 1 late that afternoon. Seventeen armored fighting vehicles, supported by infantry, were seen heading toward the village at 1740 hours. L-4 observation planes from the 30th Division and CCB began directing artillery against the panzers. Eight P-47Ds from the 514th Fighter Squadron also strafed the German column; one was shot down by German flak.[46] The combination of air strikes and artillery fire repulsed the German column before it neared le Mesnil Tove.

With the counterattack repeled and the Americans approaching le Mesnil Tove from three directions, the Germans conceded the village to the 119th Infantry. TF 1 was able to complete its occupation without a fight, and by 2040 hours the 3/119th Infantry succeeded in establishing roadblocks astride the Grand Dove–le Mesnil Tove road. Lieutenant Colonel Brown ordered his rifle companies to extend their defensive line until the 3d Battalion physically linked up with TF 1. By 2150 hours, the 3/119th could report to regiment that it was in contact with both TF 1 and TF 2.[47]

Although the 30th Division had succeeded in eliminating the German penetration along its northern flank, Lieutenant Colonel Bond's 39th Infantry remained on the defensive during 8 August as *Panzer Division 116* persisted in its efforts to capture Cherence le Roussel. Abandoning the direct approach favored by von Schwerin, *Oberst* Reinhard ordered his panzergrenadiers to infiltrate on foot to establish blocking positions behind the American defensive line.

The change in tactics quickly paid off. The attacking Germans managed to successfully infiltrate a combat patrol through a gap between the 1st and 3d Battalions at 0741 hours. M Company, however, wiped out a group of ten Germans in that same area an hour later. Shortly after 1200 hours, a patrol from 2/39th Infantry ambushed yet another group of Germans. The Americans, however, did not prevent elements of two companies belonging to *Panzergrenadier Regiment 60* from occupying the village of la Grand Mardelle. Lacking the resources necessary to launch a counterattack against the Germans, who were in a position to threaten the main supply route for the 39th Infantry, Lieutenant Colonel Bond sought help from the 4th Division.

The 4th Division assigned the 8th Infantry to assist in clearing out the Germans from la Grand Mardelle. The 8th chose to send B Company from the 1st Battalion to accomplish the mission, and Lieutenant Colonel Bond promised to provide tank support. Lieutenant Joseph Chapman, a platoon leader with C/746th Tank Battalion, was directed to rendezvous with B Company outside the village. Splitting his platoon into two sections, Chapman left behind a pair of Shermans to support the 39th Infantry while he led the rest of his tanks to la Grand Mardelle.

Unwilling to wait for tank support, B Company advanced toward the village, capturing two unwary German machine-gun crews on the outskirts. As the Americans continued on, they lost one man killed and four wounded when German troops opened fire. Company M, 39th Infantry, alerted by the shooting, began mortaring the village. Convinced that an unsupported assault would result in too many casualties, the commander of B/8th Infantry found himself at an impasse. The dilemma was solved when Lieutenant Chapman's tanks arrived.

Conferring briefly with the infantry company commander, Chapman led his tanks into the village. When the Shermans began pumping high-explosive rounds into each house, the Germans emerged with their hands aloft. B Company rounded up eighty-one enlisted men and five officers belonging to *1* and *3 Kom-*

panie of *Panzergrenadier Regiment 60.* Lieutenant Chapman was wounded by mortar fire after the Shermans returned to their original positions.[48]

The loss of two panzergrenadier companies persuaded *Panzer Division 116* to abandon its attempts to infiltrate behind American lines. Reverting to the familiar tactic of night assault, *Oberst* Reinhard instructed his engineers to clear a path through the minefields protecting the 1/39th Infantry preparatory to conducting another attack. The Germans employed a herd of sheep to open up an initial gap before dispatching teams to defuse the remaining explosives. By midnight, a lane had been cleared through the American mines, enabling *Panzer Division 116* to push forward several Pzkfw IVs. Lieutenant Scheffel called for artillery on the panzers, persuading the Germans to retreat.[49]

Just before 0300 hours, tanks and infantry launched a second assault against C/39th Infantry. Although American machine guns were able to drive off some of the attackers, small groups of German infantry succeeded in outflanking C Company. Lieutenant Scheffel called for final protective fires to be placed around his perimeter. The 26th FA Battalion responded to the request by pumping round after round of high-explosive on preregistered points surrounding C Company. The German assault began to lose momentum just as an incoming shell knocked out the radio belonging to Scheffel's supporting artillery observer. Lieutenant Scheffel frantically requested a replacement, but when it failed to arrive, he was forced to relay corrections through his field telephone connection to the 1st Battalion command post.

By this time, the 39th Infantry had reinforced the fires of the 26th FA Battalion with three other artillery battalions.[50] Punished by the intense shelling, the Germans retreated, but after reorganizing, *Panzer Division 116* attacked the 1/39th Infantry once more. By this time, a replacement radio had arrived for Lieutenant Scheffel's artillery observer. Thirty minutes of constant pounding by American artillery fire persuaded most of the attacking Germans to retreat. However, some of the panzergrenadiers remained behind to occupy positions on both flanks of C Company.[51]

The noise of panzer engines at 0645 hours heralded yet another assault. The 1st Battalion responded by sending a TD platoon and a rifle platoon from B Company to reinforce Lieutenant Scheffel. C Company's supporting forward observer also began shelling the area where the engine noises were coming from, which prevented the German tanks from closing with the Americans. Deprived of armored support, the German panzergrenadiers began pulling back shortly after daylight.

Lieutenant Colonel Bond did not wish to give *Panzer Division 116* a chance to recuperate, so he requested air strikes against known and suspected German positions to his front.[52] Bond also planned to move the 2d Battalion forward in the wake of the bombing attacks. Twelve P-47Ds of the 492d Fighter Squadron arrived at 1127 hours to find their targets precisely marked with red smoke. Four P-47s remained overhead as top cover while the other eight planes conducted dive-bombing attacks. Although Bond was satisfied with the results, the pilots reported that heavily wooded terrain prevented them from assessing bombing results.[53]

As the air strike was taking place, Lieutenant Colonel Bond received word that his regiment would revert to 9th Division control. The same set of orders directed the 39th Infantry to move eastward until it severed the road connecting Sourdeval with St.-Pois. Lieutenant Colonel Bond assigned the mission to Lieutenant Colonel Frank Gunn's 2d Battalion. The 2/39th advanced steadily past the northern slope of le Mont Furgon until it encountered several panzers, which were well sited to block the battalion's advance. The panzers simultaneously opened fire on the right flank platoon of G Company and the left flank platoon of E Company.[54] Attempts to outflank the panzers proved unsuccessful, so Bond ordered the 2d Battalion to hold in place.

As the Americans began digging in, *Panzergrenadier Regiment 60* launched a counterattack against the 2/39th Infantry. Company G, which bore the brunt of the assault, called for artillery on the attacking Germans. Bond initially refused to approve the fire mission because the target grids were too close to friendly positions, and it took the battalion artillery liaison officer several frantic minutes to convince him to change his mind. After being shelled for a solid hour, the Germans slowly retreated.

To the south of Cherence le Roussel, the 12th Infantry began preparing for another assault as daylight appeared on 9 August. At 0800 hours, Colonel Luckett ordered his battalion commanders to begin the attack. Although the 1st Battalion began moving forward at the appointed hour, the 2d Battalion was delayed when it ran headlong into an assault launched by *SS-Panzergrenadier Regiment 1.*[55] In an effort to maintain contact with *Das Reich, Brigadeführer* Wisch ordered his men to secure the area between St.-Barthelemy and L'Abbaye Blanche. The Germans, however, were no more successful than their opponents had been the previous day. Although the appearance of German troops initially disrupted the American assault, the *SS* were soon driven off.

In the wake of the brief clash, the 2/12th Infantry was able to push G Company across the Mortain–St.-Barthelemy road. Before the rest of the 2d Battalion could exploit this success, the *SS* opened fire on Company G from three directions. The incoming fire died down only after American forward observers were able to knock out a dug-in panzer and an infantry gun. Lieutenant Colonel Gerden Johnson ordered G Company to withdraw, which was accomplished successfully under cover of smoke.[56]

When G Company retreated, several panzers moved forward to occupy a copse of trees situated on the flank of the 2d Battalion. The German tanks, emerging singly from the woods, drove slowly down a sunken road pouring machine-gun and cannon fire at the Americans, then reversed back out of sight. Moments later another panzer would repeat the process. Pinned down by continuous fire from the tanks, the 2d Battalion's advance ground to a halt. *SS-Panzer*

Division 2 succeeded in frustrating the advance of the neighboring 1/12th Infantry using similar tactics.[57]

At this point, Colonel Luckett was convinced that his regiment would not be able to secure RJ 278 until heavy weapons could be brought forward.[58] Several American tanks and TDs had already tried to force their way across la Riviere Doree but were uniformly unsuccessful. Luckett was aware of the fact that his attached engineer platoon did not possess sufficient resources to construct an adequate crossing. After reporting that his assault had failed due to the lack of supporting armor, he requested that the 30th Infantry Division furnish his regiment with additional engineer support.

As Colonel Luckett prepared for another assault against RJ 278 at 1600 hours, Lieutenant Colonel Walter Johnson's 117th Infantry launched an attack against St.-Barthelemy. The American assault was delayed, however, when supporting artillery fired a preparatory barrage that landed almost on top of them. Bursting shells prevented the Americans from pushing forward until the friendly artillery was lifted. Alerted by the poorly aimed barrage, the Germans opened fire on the 1/117th Infantry, and incoming artillery quickly knocked out one of Lieutenant Colonel Frankland's supporting TDs. When Major Lindner's 3/12th Infantry began advancing, it was also targeted by indirect fire.

Disorganized by both friendly and German shelling, the 1/117th and 3/12th were unable to advance. By 1700 hours, the opposing artillery fire tapered off sufficiently to permit both rifle battalions to renew their assault. Panzers and infantry emerged from St.-Barthelemy to confront the Americans, and the 1/117th only succeeded in moving forward a single hedgerow during the ensuing fight.[59] As darkness fell on 9 August, both of the American battalions fell back to their original positions.

The 12th Infantry had also assaulted RJ 278 for a second time while the fighting still raged at St.-Barthelemy. The 2d Battalion waded through intense German artillery fire that forced the Americans to halt after securing a single hedgerow. Although Lieutenant Colonel Gerden Johnson committed his reserve company in an attempt to gain additional ground, the newcomers wilted under the unceasing rain of artillery. As the 1st Battalion moved forward, Company B began receiving fire from the front and rear. Caught between German units firing from the eastern slope of Hill 285 and RJ 278, Lieutenant Colonel Jackson's attack soon came to a halt. Colonel Luckett ordered both rifle battalions to pull back and dig in for the night. The 1/12th Infantry suffered thirty-seven casualties during the course of the day, including twelve killed, while the 2d Battalion lost forty-eight men.[60] The majority of these casualties were inflicted by German indirect fire.

Although *XLVII Panzer Korps* was unable to position sufficient artillery to assist the assault on 7 August, within forty-eight hours it was clear that the Germans had moved enough artillery into position to have a significant impact on offensive operations mounted by the 30th Infantry Division. In the midst of the afternoon assault against RJ 278, observation planes spotted forty-two German batteries firing simultaneously. The 30th Division subsequently reported to VII Corps that incoming artillery was "unusually heavy in both caliber and quantity. Many battalion concentrations [were] reported, [including] concentrations of 35, 56, and 60 rounds."[61] In addition to inflicting casualties on the attacking American infantry, the Germans forced the 30th Division to divert its supporting artillery to silencing the opposing batteries, a task it was unable to accomplish.

When the 3d Armored Division elements attached to the 119th Infantry renewed their advance on 9 August, a significant share of the German artillery pieces positioned north of St.-Barthelemy confronted them. Colonel Cornog launched the initial assault at 0645 hours. Pushing forward slowly, the medium tanks of Team 1 succeeded in cutting the road between le Mesnil Tove and Grand Dove by 1000 hours.[62] As TF 2 continued to advance, however, German observers on le Mont Furgon began deluging the column of American vehicles with indirect fire. When E/36th AIR started moving forward, Germans entrenched in the nearby village of la Besnardais also opened fire. TF 2 sought cover as Colonel Cornog called for artillery support to suppress the defenders of la Besnardais.[63]

When TF 1 in le Mesnil Tove prepared to assist Colonel Cornog's advance, it also attracted the attention of German artillery observers. Incoming shells began falling in a field occupied by the 33d Armored command post, the TF 1 command post, and 1/33d Armor mortar platoon. Lieutenant Colonel Rosewell King's command half-track exploded after suffering a direct hit, and shortly afterward, one of the mortar half-tracks also blew up. When Colonel Roysdon's command half-track attempted to shift positions to a less dangerous area, a 150mm round burst next to it, holing the armored sides of the vehicle, knocking out several radios, and wounding one man.

The 33d Armored staff were sheltering under Colonel Roysdon's command tank when they were showered with branches and shrapnel by a tree burst. Moments later, another shell landed beside the front sprocket of the Sherman, lifting it several inches off the ground. Although the explosion did not result in any casualties, the officers decided to seek cover elsewhere. TF 1 remained pinned down until the shelling finally tapered off at 1600 hours. Colonel Sutherland, realizing that TF 1 would not be able to move any vehicles without attracting artillery fire, authorized Colonel Roysdon to pull his tanks out of le Mesnil Tove. TF 1 would have to hold the village using dismounted armored infantry.

Colonel Cornog forbade additional attacks by TF 2 until the German artillery fire could be suppressed. However, he could only count on the support of two armored FA battalions, which he had to share with Colonel Roysdon. Because the armored FA units did not possess sufficient smoke shells to obscure the advance of TF 2 for an extended period of time, Cornog visited Colonel Sutherland at 1400 hours to request assistance in laying a smoke screen to blind the German observers on le Mont Furgon. Since le Mont Furgon now lay in the

9th Division's sector, the 119th Infantry was required to ask division headquarters to coordinate the request. With the 9th Division's artillery fully committed to supporting the defense of the 39th Infantry, the request for assistance in laying the smoke screen was refused.[64]

Colonel Sutherland instructed TF 2 to seize Grand Dove, regardless of the incoming artillery, promising to support Cornog with a simultaneous attack by the 3/119th Infantry. At 1700 hours, Colonel Cornog telephoned Sutherland to reassure him that TF 2 was doing everything it could to get moving again. He also requested air support while asking once more for a smoke screen on le Mont Furgon, but Sutherland was unable to provide the support that Cornog sought.[65]

Major General Hobbs personally telephoned the 36th AIR command post twenty minutes later, promising to support TF 2 with his entire divisional artillery. He also asked Colonel Cornog to provide him with the proposed time of TF 2's assault, explaining that VII Corps was pressing him for the information. After a slight delay, Cornog replied that he would begin the assault at 1800 hours.[66]

Trapped by a promise that would prove difficult to keep, Colonel Cornog called his officers together for a hurried briefing at Lieutenant Colonel Cockefair's command post. The officers assembled in a small clearing near the farmhouse serving as Cockefair's headquarters. As Colonel Cornog began the briefing, several rounds of artillery exploded nearby, which had the effect of hurrying the meeting along. When it concluded, Colonel Cornog walked fifty feet from the building, then hurriedly turned around to ask everyone to step into the Team 2 command post while he added a few details to his earlier order.

Seconds later, a shell made a direct hit on Cockefair's headquarters, and most of the officers present at the briefing were injured. Lieutenant Colonel Cockefair died instantly and Colonel Cornog was mortally wounded. The surviving officers scrambled to restore the shattered TF 2 chain of command; until that could occur, TF 2 was unable to launch an attack. Executive officers eventually took command of the four armored infantry companies that lost their commanders. Lieutenant Colonel Lovelady of 2/33d Armor replaced Colonel Cornog, while the battalion executive officer of the 2/36th AIR took over for Lieutenant Colonel Cockefair.

When informed of the incident, Colonel Sutherland was convinced that the continued presence of armored vehicles would only result in increased German artillery fire. He telephoned Lieutenant Colonel Lovelady, who was in the midst of reorganizing TF 2, directing him to pull back all of his tanks back once it got dark. Sutherland explained that he wanted the tanks ready for immediate use, but until they were called forward again, the vehicles would be hidden in a defilade position. As soon as night fell, most of the Sherman tanks belonging to TF 2 began pulling back under cover of artillery. A single platoon of medium tanks from D/33d Armor remained forward to support the infantry.

With CCB immobilized by German artillery fire, Colonel Sutherland relied on the 3/119th Infantry to gain his regiment's assigned objectives. The 3d Battalion initially began advancing at 0645 hours, but a dug-in panzer positioned in front of L Company held it up. Rough terrain prevented the Shermans of C/743d Tank Battalion from destroying the German tank, and when elements of TF 2 were finally diverted to deal with it, the German vehicle withdrew. As the 3d Battalion slowly worked its way toward Grand Dove, L/119th Infantry became the target of incoming artillery. The shelling was intense enough to prompt the L Company commander to request that he be replaced by another officer. Lieutenant Colonel Brown put one of the company's rifle platoon leaders in command.[67] After a short delay, the 3/119th began moving forward once more as the incoming artillery slowly tapered off.

Lieutenant Colonel Brown soon found himself wedged between TF 1, pinned down by artillery in le Mesnil Tove, and TF 2, sitting astride the road leading to Grand Dove. Altering direction, K/119th Infantry pushed beyond the le Mesnil Tove–Grand Dove road to secure the high ground to the northeast. Brown, concerned that K Company had moved too far forward, decided to hold in place to consolidate his position against a possible counterattack. Colonel Sutherland informed Brown soon afterward that 3d Battalion was scheduled to begin a coordinated attack with TF 2 at 1800 hours. Moments later, Brown was told that Colonel Cornog had been killed and that the assault would continue regardless of TF 2's absence.

Advancing rapidly, L/119th Infantry found itself north of the road leading to Grand Dove, with K Company echeloned to the left and rear. Company I trailed to the rear of the leading elements. When Company K ran into some tough resistance, L Company was forced to wait until its sister company could fight its way forward. At 2015 hours, the attack resumed again with L/119th Infantry in the lead, followed by K and I Companies. As the Americans neared Grand Dove, they began to encounter increasing opposition.

Soon afterward, Colonel Sutherland received a call from division headquarters asking him to consider halting the 3/119th Infantry for the night. Sutherland replied that he would prefer to continue moving until his troops encountered a prepared defensive position. By 2140 hours, however, Lieutenant Colonel Brown decided to call his advance to a halt. When Sutherland learned that 3d Battalion was digging in for the night, he instructed Brown to prepare for an attack against Grand Dove early the next morning.

CONCLUSIONS

The 30th Infantry Division failed to achieve its objectives along its northern boundary during the period 8–9 August, and VII Corps had not helped matters by attaching the 39th Infantry to the 4th Division. As a result of Major General Collins's decision, the situation north of the See River was beyond the influence of the 30th Division. Additionally, instead of orchestrating the battle at division level, Major General Hobbs allowed his regimental commanders to conduct their own fight. Consequently, numerous American assaults employed no more than two maneuver battalions supported by one or two artillery battalions. With a four-hour interval between assaults, the Germans were afforded sufficient time to reorganize their defenses and reposition reserves.

The defenders were also able to turn the full weight of their artillery against each American thrust, which ultimately proved to be a decisive factor during the two-day period. Although Major General Hobbs may have been distracted by events unfolding on his southern flank, continued failure to coordinate operations would lead to increased casualties among the American units fighting to restore the northern boundary of the 30th Infantry Division.

9

Holding the High Ground

Kampfgruppe Fick conducted its most ambitious attempt to secure Hill 314 during the early morning hours of 10 August. Strong formations of infantry and panzers were heard approaching the 2/120th Infantry, but despite massive preparatory fires, the *SS* forces were unable to penetrate the ring of artillery protecting the surrounded Americans. The 30th Infantry Division had allocated five battalions of field artillery to continually interdict all avenues of approach to Hill 314.[1] After several hours, the Germans finally called an end to their assault, although Lieutenant Weiss continued to hear vehicles moving to the east.

By midmorning *Kampfgruppe Fick* grew increasingly active. Despite the fact that seven tanks had been lost to bazooka teams from E Company, German panzers began probing the roadblock astride the Bel Air road once more.[2] The appearance of *SS* infantry at 1010 hours spurred Lieutenant Weiss to request artillery support. As he waited for an acknowledgment from the 230th FA fire direction center, he discovered that his radio batteries were rapidly failing. Fortunately, Lieutenant Weiss was able to complete his request for artillery on all registered defensive concentrations before going off the air.

As the incoming shells pummeled the attackers, he replaced the batteries in his radio with a spare set that his section sergeant retrieved from atop a nearby rock. He had discovered several days before that he could extend the life of his batteries by frequently rotating them and placing the spare set in bright sun in an effort to recharge them. Replacing the failing batteries with a "new" set, however, did not produce instant results, and it took several hours of fruitless attempts to contact the 230th FA fire direction center before radio contact was regained.

Lieutenant Weiss did not realize that considerable efforts were being made to provide him with new batteries. Early that afternoon, division headquarters notified Colonel Birks that supplies would soon be air-dropped to the 2/120th Infantry.[3] Birks alerted the 230th FA Battalion, who relayed a message to Lieutenant Weiss directing E Company to display air-ground panels.[4] Relief was en route in the form of twelve C-47s belonging to the 98th Troop Carrier (TC) Squadron. The cargo planes had departed Ramsbury, England, that morning. Their route took them to Greenham Commons, then across the channel to airstrip A-22, where the transports linked up with sixteen P-47 fighters of the 494th Fighter Squadron.[5] As the C-47s neared Mortain, they descended to three hundred feet in preparation for dropping supplies.

At 1625 hours, the transport pilots sighted Mortain. The flight leader, Lieutenant Colonel Bascomb Neal, altered course toward the crest of Hill 314. When the spire of la Collegial Saint Evoult passed beneath the formation, he gave the signal to drop the supplies. A few feet beneath Neal's plane, a parapack filled with ammunition exploded after being hit, violently rocking the low-flying transport. His plane flew on undamaged, and none of the other aircraft were hit. The rest of the formation dropped seventy-one bundles of supplies to the isolated battalion.[6]

An easterly breeze sprang up as the parachutes were released, and only a small portion of the supplies landed within the American perimeter.[7] E Company was the fortunate recipient of the most supplies landing within easy reach. The 1/120th Infantry on Hill 285 could clearly observe soldiers from the 2d Battalion picking up bundles in the wake of the airdrop, and Lieutenant Kerley radioed Colonel Birks that his troops had collected a fair amount of food and ammunition. Lieutenant Reaser's K Company to the north, however, was much less fortunate, as the nearest parachutes landed fifteen hundred yards to the east of his positions.

Captain Delmont Byrn led a group of volunteers to recover supplies that landed outside the perimeter. As the Americans crawled toward the parachutes, the Germans opened fire with mortars, artillery, and 20mm antiaircraft guns. Since the group had only one chance to retrieve supplies, Byrn directed the men to recover only ammunition, rations, radio batteries, and medical supplies. At times, the incoming fire was so intense that bundles had to be dragged into nearby ditches before their contents could be examined. Despite attempts to recover all of the parachute bundles, the Americans were only able to retrieve food and ammunition. None of the medical supplies and radio batteries could be found. Upon his return, Captain Byrn supervised the distribution of all the items.[8]

Shortly after the aerial resupply took place, Major General Hobbs asked Colonel Birks for his "personal statement as to whether or not it was a successful supply drop."[9] He replied that the "big group" (G and K Companies) reported that most supplies dropped fifteen hundred yards away from their positions, but a fair amount of the airdrop had landed near E/120th Infantry. Colonel Birks's assessment was only partially accurate. Each company received some ammunition and two K ration meals per man, but the defenders still lacked radio batteries and medical equipment.[10] When the 30th Infantry Division initiated coordination for a second airdrop, the VII Corps G-4 cautioned that it would take a full day to arrange for another resupply mission.

Colonel Birks was approached by the 230th FA battalion commander, Lieutenant Colonel Lewis D. Vieman, with a proposal for an alternative means of supplying critical items to the isolated troops on Hill 314. Vieman suggested firing radio batteries and medical supplies packed in hollow smoke shells into the 2d Battalion's perimeter. Although Birks was skeptical about the prospects of success, at this point he was willing to try anything.

Having obtained Birks's approval, Lieutenant Colonel Vieman notified Lieutenant Weiss of the plan. The first step in the process consisted of firing inert smoke rounds into an area where they could be safely retrieved. Communications problems, compounded by the difficulty in adjusting the strike of the inert rounds, resulted in a considerable delay. When the initial batch of six rounds filled with medical supplies were fired at 2145 hours that evening, the fading light prevented them from being recovered.[11] The next attempt was postponed until first light on 11 August.

With Weidinger's *Der Führer* regiment preoccupied with defending RJ 278 against TF 3, the Americans at L'Abbaye Blanche spent a quiet night on 9 August. The Germans did not send patrols to probe their positions, nor was any artillery fire directed at the roadblock. The relatively peaceful night, however, lulled the defenders into a false sense of security, and at least one German vehicle successfully made its way into Lieutenant Springfield's defensive perimeter: a misoriented German ambulance driver with a load of wounded *SS* men negotiated his way through a daisy chain of antitank mines strung across the eastern approaches to L'Abbaye Blanche.[12]

The ambulance crossed over the railroad bridge heading into the northern outskirts of Mortain. When it approached Lieutenant Springfield's command post, he sleepily leaned out of a second story window to see a German half-track, prominently marked with red cross flags, halted by the sentries in front of the building. Directing his men to ensure that none of the Germans were armed, Springfield informed the injured *SS* troops that they were now prisoners of war. The captured half-track was sent to the rear under escort.

Major Herlong's 1/119th Infantry also spent a quiet night preparing for its next assault on Romagny. At dawn on 10 August, the 1st Battalion began probing the German defenses. After waiting several hours for his supporting armor to arrive, Herlong launched his assault at 1040 hours. He deployed two rifle companies, supported by two medium tanks, astride the road leading into Romagny. His remaining rifle company, accompanied by B/743d Armor and a platoon of TDs, trailed behind the leading elements. The participation of F/117th Infantry was limited to supporting the attack by fire.

The 1/119th Infantry, hampered by the fact that its supporting tanks were confined to a single road, was easily repulsed. When the leading companies were pinned down by machine-gun and mortar fire, Major Herlong ordered his trailing rifle company to swing south. As this maneuver unfolded, the Germans launched a counterattack against the 1st Battalion. C Company began retreating in the face of this onslaught, but a platoon leader, Lieutenant Earl C. Bowers,

German halftrack knocked out by the defenders of the L'Abbaye Blanche roadblock. (National Archives)

finally rallied his men long enough to halt the counterattacking *SS*. Major Herlong instructed his company commanders to pull back to positions where they could reorganize without interference from the Germans.[13]

A combination of factors had prevented the 30th Infantry Division from launching a coordinated series of attacks along its southern flank on the morning of 10 August. *Kampfgruppe Ullrich* launched an early morning assault against A/120th Infantry that disrupted attempts by the 1st Battalion to regain Hill 285.[14] *Kampfgruppe Fick* had also succeeded in severing the supply lines that ran between L'Abbaye Blanche and TF 3. Rather than maintain pressure on the Germans in Mortain, the 120th Infantry refocused its efforts toward destroying the *SS* roadblock.

The German roadblock was discovered when a medical half-track traveling between the 2/119th Infantry aid station and TF 3 was destroyed by mines. The two medics in the rear of the vehicle escaped to report what happened. An infantry patrol accompanied by several light tanks was dispatched to rescue the wounded driver. The patrol retreated after being fired upon, however, without accomplishing its mission. With fuel and ammunition running low, TF 3 would be unable to conduct an attack until it could be resupplied.

One of Lieutenant Springfield's half-tracks also fell victim to the German roadblock. The vehicle was transporting wounded to the A/823d TD command post when it ran over a mine.[15] The Germans captured the driver, but two other men were able to make their way back to report the incident to Lieutenant Springfield. A short while later, the Americans obtained a small measure of revenge when a *Das Reich* half-track halted in front of a minefield near the L'Abbaye Blanche.[16] The Americans were surprised by the appearance of the vehicle since it had approached the rear of the roadblock. A BAR gunner shot one *SS* man who dismounted to inspect the minefield while a bazooka team scored a direct hit on the German half-track.[17]

The havoc being created by the Germans between le Neufbourg and L'Abbaye Blanche was primarily the work of 2 *Kompanie, SS-Panzergrenadier Regiment 37.* Reinforced by an engineer platoon, the *SS* panzergrenadiers had been ordered to establish a roadblock behind American lines for at least twenty-four hours. Most of the Germans felt that their assignment would turn out to be a suicide mission. Infiltrating to his objective that evening, the *SS* company commander recorded that "the night march was a catastrophe. The troops were tired and made tremendous amount of noise . . . we must have alerted every American outpost, but they left without a fight. Surprise was lost." Despite his misgivings, 2 *Kompanie* was able to successfully emplace the minefield directed by Fick.[18]

Later that morning, an M8 armored car from the 2d Reconnaissance Platoon of the 629th TD Battalion also ran afoul of the German roadblock. After being immobilized by a mine, the American armored car was knocked out by an *SS* tank-hunting team that scored a direct hit on the disabled vehicle, killing one man and wounding three others. A jeep trailing behind the armored car was also knocked out.[19]

Colonel Birks ordered his attached engineer company to clear out the German mines. The panzergrenadiers opened fire on the Americans as they began lifting the mines, pinning them down until a Sherman tank was called forward. The engineers also radioed for artillery on the German position, and several volleys of high-explosive shells persuaded 2 *Kompanie* to retreat.[20] As soon as the *SS* pulled out, C/105th Engineers finished removing the mines from TF 3's supply route.

With the flow of supplies restored, Lieutenant Colonel Hogan began preparing for another attack against RJ 278. He planned to advance with both of his medium tank companies moving abreast, each supported by an infantry company. Captain Carl Cramer's G/33d Armor, accompanied by G/119th Infantry, would advance on the left, while Lieutenant Edmund Wray's H/33d Armor, supported by F/119th Infantry, moved up the opposite side. Since H/33d Armor was attacking through hedgerows that had not been breached during the initial assault, Sergeant Emmett Tripp's tankdozer would accompany Wray.

Late that afternoon, G/33d Armor moved forward with G/119th Infantry in support. As the Shermans neared RJ 278, an antitank gun knocked out two American tanks. No one was able to spot the muzzle flash of the German gun. Rather than lose additional vehicles, Captain Cramer ordered his tank company to pull back. G/119th Infantry, after losing two men killed and two more wounded, withdrew when the tanks retreated.[21]

Sergeant Tripp's tankdozer led the advance of H/33d Armor. The eight surviving tanks of H Company were lined up behind him when he punched a hole through the first hedgerow. His tankdozer moved through, followed closely by Lieutenant Wray. While Tripp backed into position to provide covering fire, Wray continued moving forward. Halfway across the field, Wray's tank was struck by a *Panzerfaust,* and the remaining H Company Shermans broke off the assault when it burst into flames. Sergeant Tripp ordered his driver to reverse through the gap in the hedgerow before they were also knocked out, and the tankdozer returned to the 3/33d Armor perimeter without further incident.[22]

Lieutenant Edward C. Arn's 3d platoon of F/119th Infantry watched as Wray's Sherman was hit. He saw Wray fall "to his hands and knees beside the tank. Then he pulled himself to his feet and started back toward the hedgerow he had just busted through. It seemed as if he remembered something because he went back to the tank and tried to pull somebody else out. He helped get another man out and they both started to run, but the Jerries cut them down with a burst of machinegun fire."[23]

Quiet descended over the field where Lieutenant Wray's tank lay smoking. Lieutenant Arn saw several SS men emerge from behind a hedgerow to examine the destroyed Sherman. The Germans began searching the knocked-out vehicle for souvenirs. Lieutenant Arn ordered his platoon to wait until more SS entered the clearing. Satisfied that all of the Germans who intended to search for souvenirs were already in the open, Arn ordered his men to commence firing. The SS men walking around Wray's tank died in a hail of bullets.

The Germans responded to Hogan's latest attempt to seize RJ 278 by launching a counterattack against TF 3. *SS-Panzer Division 1* sent three panzers supported by infantry against Hogan's left flank, forcing E/119th Infantry to pull back. As the Germans pressed the retreating Americans, a light machine-gun squad began raking the attackers with lengthy bursts of fire.[24] Their accurate shooting forced the SS to seek cover. When American artillery began landing on the stalled Germans, the attackers retreated.[25]

South of Mortain, the 35th Infantry Division hoped to gain greater success on 10 August by employing a coordinated assault by two regiments. An unexpected visitor, however, entered the lines of the 3/320th Infantry before the assault began. Chaplain William G. Hayes of the 1/134th Infantry had been released from captivity to deliver a note from the Germans. The contents of the message discussed the possibility of a limited prisoner exchange. *SS-Panzer Division 2* offered to return thirty-five Americans, both wounded and medical personnel, for five German doctors taken prisoner at Cherbourg.[26] Chaplain Hayes was quickly transported back to division headquarters.

Major General Baade chose to turn down the German offer. Informed of his commander's decision, Chaplain Hayes insisted that he deliver Baade's response to his former captors, patiently explaining to puzzled onlookers that he had given his word to return. The division staff realized that Chaplain Hayes's conscience would remain clear only if he could be physically prevented from returning so they placed him in protective custody until Mortain was recaptured.[27]

Soon afterward, Major General Baade received instructions from VII Corps to relieve the 2/120th Infantry on Hill 314. He intended to execute his latest set of instructions without altering the existing plan of operations and decided to commit his division reserve, consisting of the 1/320th Infantry reinforced by the 737th Tank Battalion, to the relief effort. The 1st Battalion, commanded by Major William G. Gillis, would be committed in its parent regiment's sector, which allowed the 320th Infantry to attack as previously ordered. Major General Baade contacted VII Corps to ask for additional tank support. In response, Major General Collins directed the 2d Armored Division to provide him with a company of medium tanks. Captain Tousey's Battlegroup 2 was instructed to send its attached tank company, D/32d Armor, north to reinforce the 737th Tank Battalion. The tank company departed Barenton early that morning, reaching the 35th Infantry Division command post at 0930 hours on 10 August.[28]

At 1115 hours, Colonel Byrne reported to Baade for his initial briefing on the proposed relief operation. He was appalled by the amateurish concept that had apparently been devised by the division chief of staff. In Colonel Byrne's opinion, the "plan had no control element, no real fire plan other than air support, and time was tragically short."[29] He asked his regimental operations officer and the commander of the 216th FA battalion to meet him at the division command post. Using the division plan as a framework, Byrne tried to create a realistic concept at regimental level that would aid Major Gillis in successfully carrying out his assigned mission.

Lieutenant Colonel James M. Hamilton of the 737th Tank Battalion arrived at division headquarters a few minutes later. The division chief of staff told Hamilton that "the 1/320th Infantry, supported by the 737th Tank Battalion will attack . . . north along road toward Mortain. Objective—relief of the 30th Division troops who are cut off on Hill 317 [sic]. Method of attack—all medium tanks of the battalion will be used. They will cross the line of departure at 1500 hours. The tanks will travel north in column. All tanks will carry five infantrymen each except for the first five. If a tank is knocked out, the remaining tanks will bypass it and carry out the mission. Remainder of the infantry from 1st Battalion will follow on foot and reinforce those who arrive on tanks."[30]

Lieutenant Colonel Hamilton was informed that he would be reinforced by D/32d Armor. The welcome news of additional tanks was eclipsed by the uncompromising language of the attack orders. Hamilton was appalled that his tanks were being ordered to attack along a road, ignoring harsh lessons learned over the past several months. He was convinced that his men would suffer heavy casualties.

The commander of the 1/320th Infantry, however, did not learn of the intended operation until 1200 hours. Somewhat belatedly, Major Gillis was summoned to the division command post to be informed that his battalion would attack to relieve the 2/120th. Task Force Gillis, as the tank and infantry team was now designated, would advance along a secondary road running northeast to Mortain until it reached the southwestern slopes of Hill 314. Gillis would then await the arrival of the rest of the 320th Infantry.

At 1330 hours, Colonel Byrne gathered his battalion commanders at the regimental command post for a briefing. He explained that the 1st Battalion had been chosen to relieve the 2/120th Infantry. The 3/320th would provide direct support to Gillis by severing the Mortain-Barenton road, while the 2d Battalion would trail behind to provide whatever assistance was required by the leading elements. The regimental assault, which was slated to begin at 1500 hours, would be preceded by an air strike and artillery preparation.

At 1420 hours, Major Gillis briefed his company commanders on the attack that would take place in forty minutes. Lieutenant Frank Gardner's B/320th Infantry would ride into battle atop the attacking tanks, accompanied by one platoon from Lieutenant Carlton Thornblom's C/320th Infantry. The remaining platoons of C Company, joined by Captain Malcolm Kullmar's A Company, would advance cross-country to provide flank security to the tank column. Major Gillis, along with the battalion mortar platoon and his command group, would trail behind A Company.

Lieutenant Colonel Hamilton returned to his battalion headquarters to brief the tank company commanders. Captain George D. Zurman's C/737th Tank Battalion was slated to lead the attacking column, and Captain Martin V. Conde's Company A would follow Zurman's tanks. Captain Harry J. Vaughn's Company B, under the temporary command of its executive officer, would bring up the rear, and Lieutenant Frank Vinal's D/32d Armor would remain in reserve. When the questions were raised, Hamilton silenced them with the comment, "we know it's not how tanks fight, but those are our orders from division."[31]

Moments after the briefing was concluded, C/737th Tank Battalion departed for the rendezvous point with the 1/320th Infantry. When the Shermans arrived, there was some confusion regarding which platoon was to mount the leading tanks. Since this was the first time that any of the riflemen had ridden on a tank, many men had difficulty locating someplace to sit.[32] Lieutenant Hank Morgan, commanding the 1st Platoon of B/320th, had arranged for his men to ride the leading tank platoon. The Shermans designated to carry his men, however, halted in front of Lieutenant Sam Belk's 2d Platoon, who scrambled aboard. The tanks moved out before the question could be settled.

The leading Sherman of C/737th Tank Battalion, commanded by Sergeant Junior K. Lambert, crossed the line of departure precisely at 1500 hours. Lambert advanced barely a hundred yards before his vehicle was struck in rapid succession by three rounds from a 50mm antitank gun. The first two rounds ricocheted off the front slope, but the impact of the third caused some metal to flake off the interior, setting the driver's instrument panel afire. The assistant driver, shaken by the experience, did not respond to Lambert's instructions to release the hatch in the floor. Lambert finally had to drop the escape hatch himself as the crew crawled out the belly of the damaged Sherman into a nearby ditch.[33]

A second Sherman, commanded by Sergeant Vernon Hoff, engaged the gun after pulling around Lambert's disabled vehicle. Hoff succeeded in scoring a direct hit that killed the entire crew of the AT gun. In retaliation, the defenders raked the length of the stationary tank column with long-range machine-gun fire, forcing B/320th Infantry to dismount. The riflemen, huddling in ditches along the road, were unable to communicate with the tank commanders who refused to open their turret hatches.

Prodded by radio calls from Lieutenant Colonel Hamilton, the Shermans began edging forward without waiting for their passengers to remount. When the tanks started moving, the infantry was forced to run after them, hauling themselves onto any available vehicle. The unit integrity of Lieutenant Gardner's B Company was badly mixed up by the uncoordinated departure of the tanks. Many of the infantrymen who succeeded in climbing aboard a vehicle found themselves atop a different tank looking at a mixture of strangers and familiar faces.

The remainder of the 320th Infantry had also began advancing at 1500 hours. By 1525 hours the 3d Battalion reported that it was receiving heavy mortar, 88mm, and small arms fire. Despite reinforcing its leading company with rifle platoons from each of the other two rifle companies, the 3/320th was unable to make any headway. Twenty-five minutes later, the 2d Battalion radioed Colonel Byrne to report that G Company was receiving fire from three directions. A platoon from F/320th Infantry sent to assist G Company found itself cut off from the rest of the battalion.[34]

As Task Force Gillis pushed further east, Sergeant Vernon Hoff's tank fell victim to another hidden 50mm antitank gun. Two Shermans immediately to the rear of Hoff's stricken vehicle knocked out the opposing gun.[35] Unlike the initial engagement, most of the infantry remained aboard the Shermans rather than dismount. The few soldiers who sought cover when Hoff's tank was hit were again forced to run after the departing tanks.

By 1600 hours, the 1/320th Infantry successfully penetrated the defenses of the *Das Reich* reconnaissance battalion. German troops were beginning to retreat from the threatened sector in some disarray, and the exodus was clearly visible to Lieutenant Weiss atop Hill 314. He radioed the 230th FA command post at 1613 hours to report that "the enemy is withdrawing . . . to their front and vehicles are streaming east."[36] Moments later, Weiss also reported seeing friendly troops south of his position as the 2/120th Infantry assisted the advancing American troops by directing artillery fire on German troops assembling for a counterattack against the 1/320th Infantry.[37]

As Task Force Gillis pressed onward, the supporting rifle companies discovered that they could not maintain pace with the tank column. In a desperate attempt to keep up, the Americans began bypassing all resistance except for Germans trying to block the road. The Shermans also noticed that their supporting infantry on either flank had fallen behind. In an effort to discourage SS tank-hunting teams, the lead tank platoon began to machine-gun the hedgerows alongside their intended route. The tanks littered the road with brass cartridges and empty ammunition boxes as they expended thousands of rounds of small arms ammunition.

The *Das Reich* reconnaissance battalion commander, *Sturmbannführer* Krag, exerted tremendous efforts to restore his collapsing defenses. With the American artillery observers on Hill 314 preventing reinforcements from reaching him, he had to make do with forces already on hand and began organizing a blocking force to halt the American tank column. Under Krag's direction, the SS reconnaissance troops wheeled three 75mm antitank guns into a nearby wooded area, although six Shermans trundled past the ambush position before the guns could be readied. When the seventh vehicle appeared, all three AT guns fired simultaneously, knocking out two American tanks.

The tanks halted to deal with this new threat. Most of the infantry dismounted hurriedly to avoid begin caught up in a duel between the Shermans and the AT guns. Wounded tank crewmen, their faces blackened and clothing smoldering, ran past Lieutenant Hank Morgan's rifle platoon, shouting for medical assistance. The appearance of the injured tankers triggered a retreat by B/320th Infantry, but the exodus was halted when Morgan stood in the middle of the road swearing at the retreating men. With great effort, he was able to place them into hasty defensive positions on either side of the road.[38]

As order was restored within B Company, Lieutenant Thornblom's C/320th was struck by a counterattack. As the SS opened fire with machine guns at point-blank range, the C Company 60mm mortars replied by pumping out round after round of high-explosive at the Germans. The mortar fire halted the counterattack but proved insufficient to force the SS to pull back. Lieutenant Thornblom ran along the tank column to seek assistance and returned with a pair of Shermans in trail. As soon as the tanks opened fire, the SS hurriedly retreated.

By this time, C/737th Tank Battalion had succeeded in knocking out one of the German antitank guns, and machine-gun fire forced the other gun crews to temporarily abandon their weapons. As the six leading tanks continued on by themselves toward la Croix des Sept Coeurs, the remainder of the column began to untangle itself. Steel prongs welded onto the front of the vehicles, originally meant to aid them in passing through a hedgerow, now served only to impede movement. The C Company commander's tank turned onto its side in a ditch, injuring Captain Zurman. Having lost four tanks as well as its company commander, C/737th Tank Battalion was temporarily rendered combat ineffective. B Company had also been badly disorganized by this latest ambush. With Major Gillis's command group falling behind, control of the attacking force passed to Captain Kullmar of A Company.

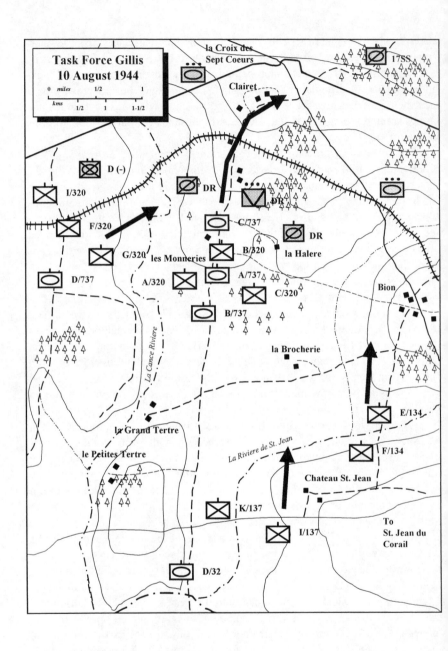

**Task Force Gillis
10 August 1944**

0   miles   1/2   1

kms   1/2   1   1-1/2

la Croix des
Sept Coeurs

17SS

Clairet

D (-)

DR

DR

I/320

F/320

C/737

DR

G/320   les Monneries

B/320

la Halere

A/320

A/737

D/737

B/737

C/320

Bion

La Cance Riviere

la Brocherie

la Grand Tertre

E/134

le Petites Tertre

La Riviere de St. Jean

F/134

Chateau St. Jean

K/137

I/137

To
St. Jean du
Corail

D/32

While Task Force Gillis was reorganized under Captain Kullmar's supervision, the leading Shermans reached la Croix des Sept Coeurs. Of the soldiers from B Company, only Lieutenant Sam Belk and four riflemen remained with the tanks. The Shermans were crossing an open field when an antitank gun sited to protect the command post of *SS-Panzeraufklärungs Abteilung 17* opened fire. Two of the American tanks burst into flames, while the third was immobilized. The crew of the damaged Sherman bailed out, leaving the vehicle sitting in the middle of the road with its engine running. The remaining Shermans safely ran the gauntlet of German fire.[39]

By this time, A Company, 737th Tank Battalion, assumed the lead from Captain Zurman's company as the remaining vehicles of C Company prepared to return to the rear to reorganize. After loading the remnants of B/320th Infantry and a platoon from Lieutenant Thornblom's company onto the Shermans, the American column resumed its advance. The Shermans had traveled only a short distance when they encountered a Pzkfw IV, which pulled off the road in an attempt to ambush the American column. The German vehicle opened fire first but missed its intended target.[40] Several American tanks returned fire, knocking out the panzer before it could fire a second round.

Moments later, a hidden antitank gun opened fire, knocking out two A Company tanks. Before the Americans could retaliate, however, the German gunners abandoned their weapon.[41] Recognizing that the AT gun no longer posed a threat, the American tanks resumed their advance. As the Shermans neared les Monneries, a mile south of la Croix des Sept Coeurs, machine-gun fire peppered the column, forcing the infantry to dismount.

While the column was halted, Captain Kullmar radioed Major Gillis to report that A Company was still finding it difficult to keep up. Gillis ordered Kullmar to mount one of his rifle platoons on the Shermans and directed Lieutenant Thornblom to place the rest of C Company aboard as well. Lieutenant Gardner's B Company would dismount to join the remaining rifle platoons of A/320th Infantry in providing flank security for the tank column.

Major Gillis's instructions were quickly proven impractical. Each time the Americans attempted to remount, German machine guns would open fire. The Shermans tried to silence the offending weapons, but the *SS* positions were exceedingly difficult to locate. Captain Kullmar, who was convinced that Gillis could not control the assault from the rear, requested permission to assume command of the forward elements. To his credit, Major Gillis assented. Calling together his fellow company commanders, Kullmar instructed them to prepare for a renewed advance. This time, however, all of the rifle companies would conduct the assault on foot.

After a short delay, the 1/320th Infantry moved out with the remaining tanks in tow. The hedgerows lining the road screened the dismounted troops from the machine guns that had been harassing the tank column.[42] The tanks continued to trail the dismounted infantry until Task Force Gillis reached the Mortain-Bion railroad station. As the lead Sherman approached the station, the tanks began pulling off into adjacent fields. Captain Kullmar, accompanied by Lieutenants Gardner and Thornblom, walked over to Captain Conde to find out why his Shermans halted. The infantry company commanders were shocked to hear that the tankers did not intend to continue advancing toward Hill 314. When questioned about his decision, Conde explained that he had to move his Shermans back to refuel and rearm. Kullmar countered by stating that the tanks could not retreat without Major Gillis's permission. When Kullmar tried to contact Gillis, however, he was unable to reach him.

Conde tried to contact his own battalion for guidance but could not reach Lieutenant Colonel Hamilton. He stated, however, that he was sure Hamilton would agree with his decision to pull back for refueling and rearming. Despite the protests of the infantry officers, Conde instructed his tanks to move out. Kullmar tried unsuccessfully to convince him to leave one or two tanks behind, but moments later, all of the Shermans began heading to the rear.[43]

Despite the lack of armored support, the 1/320th Infantry continued advancing toward its objective. Giving the knocked out Shermans near la Croix des Sept Coeurs a wide berth, A Company occupied a hasty defensive position just beyond the crossroads.[44] Captain Kullmar also directed the other rifle companies to do likewise. Meeting with the company commanders, he explained that he wanted to establish an all-around defensive position before nightfall since there was little doubt in his mind that the Germans would soon counterattack.

Prior to the arrival of the remainder of the 1/320th Infantry, Lieutenant Sam Belk had spent most of the afternoon at the base of Hill 314 crouched near a parked Sherman tank commanded by Lieutenant Keith Winger. The Sherman was one of three surviving vehicles from the leading elements of C Company, 737th Tank Battalion. The trio of vehicles reached their objective several hours before the remainder of the 1st Battalion had approached the Mortain-Bion railroad station. Lieutenant Belk had been listening intently to the progress of Task Force Gillis over the radio. Staff Sergeant Ben Hackman and Lieutenant Winger's Shermans were parked nearby. As the day wore on, all three of the tank commanders grew increasingly concerned about the prospect of spending the night alone.

The small band of Americans had also been watching Germans flock to a nearby farmhouse. They did not realize that the building served as the headquarters for *SS-Panzeraufklärungs Abteilung 17*. More *SS* arrived carrying *Panzerfaust* antitank rocket launchers. It was obvious that they were planning to ambush the tank column when it approached the crossroads so Lieutenant Belk persuaded Lieutenant Winger to open fire in order to prevent that from occurring. When Winger protested that nearby trees prevented him from obtaining a clear shot, Lieutenant Belk's runner, Private Ben Guskin, volunteered to correct the fall of the shot.

The Shermans opened fire with their 75mm cannon, sending high-explosive rounds through the trees toward the farmhouse, and Private Guskin shouted back corrections after each shell exploded. Dead and wounded piled up in the farm-yard before the shelling forced the surviving SS to retreat.[45] When the Shermans ceased fire, the American lieutenants began reexamining their options. Belk pre-ferred to wait for the rest of the tank column to arrive, but Winger disagreed, arguing that his Shermans were critically low on ammunition and gasoline. After deciding that they had already revealed their location by firing at the farmhouse, both lieutenants decided to head back down the road to safety.

Lieutenant Winger told Belk that he would lead, followed by the other two Shermans. Lieutenant Belk placed a pair of his men inside the lead tank, two more in the second vehicle, and himself in the trailing Sherman. The trio arrived at la Croix des Sept Coeurs without encountering any Germans. As they moved through the crossroads, the Germans opened fire when the three Shermans slowed down to thread their way past the burning tanks that sat there. Winger's vehicle accelerated down the road with antitank shells zipping behind him. Staff Sergeant Ben Hackman, commanding the second tank in the small column, was also able to follow Winger down the road without being hit. The pair headed south until they met guides from C Company, 737th Tank Battalion, who inter-cepted them near the railroad station.

The driver of the Sherman carrying Lieutenant Belk became agitated when he saw the Germans firing at the lead vehicles. Disregarding his tank comman-der's orders, the driver turned left onto a secondary trail. Peering out of the tur-ret, Belk saw a camouflaged panzer parked nearby, and just around a bend, he could also see the barrel of an antitank gun. The Sherman sped past, providing Belk with a glimpse of two Germans standing in the open hatches of the panzer, their mouths wide open in surprise. The German antitank gunners, however, had plenty of time to line up their shot. Belk felt a round strike the Sherman, which veered off the road before turning onto its side.

The Sherman burst into flames as it lay in the ditch. Luckily, Belk had been thrown out of the hatch, landing in a ditch on the opposite side of the road. One of his legs, however, had been seriously burned. Realizing his injuries would pre-vent him from moving quickly, Belk buried his map in a hole he scooped into the side of the hedgerow. Moments later, an SS man cautiously peered around the corner of the hedgerow. The German approached warily, relaxing only when he saw that Lieutenant Belk was injured and unarmed. Through sign language, the SS man reassured Belk that he would return with a medic.

Lieutenant Belk was determined not to be captured. He attempted to get away by crawling over the hedgerow, only to painfully fall back down. A second try car-ried him over in a searing wave of pain as he tumbled into the field on the oppo-site side. Belk crawled until he finally reached a small farmhouse. As the American lieutenant neared the front door, two SS men emerged to take him prisoner.[46]

A few hundred yards south of Lieutenant Belk's location, Captain Kullmar dispatched a patrol to find a suitable location for an overnight defensive position. After checking out several sites, the patrol returned to report that they had dis-

Lieutenant Sam Belk of B Company, 320th Infantry Regiment. (Samuel E. Belk III)

covered a series of hedgerow-enclosed fields that would accommodate the entire battalion. After giving orders for his own company to relocate, Captain Kullmar instructed B and C Companies to shift their position to the new site.

The 1/320th Infantry reestablished itself just to the northeast of la Croix des Sept Coeurs. B and C Companies manned the northern half of the circular perimeter, with A Company responsible for the southern portion. No one was allowed to dig lest the noise of entrenching tools striking the ground give away their presence. After the 1/320th had completed the move, Captain Kullmar sent a patrol back to report their new location to Major Gillis.[47]

The men returned several hours later with a message from their battalion commander. Major Gillis informed Kullmar that it would be impossible for him to join up with the rifle companies until morning, so he would remain in charge until Gillis could make his way forward. When Captain Kullmar sent a second patrol to provide an update, they returned with the unwelcome news that the Germans had reestablished a strong defensive line along the railroad south of la Croix des Sept Coeurs.

The 1/320th Infantry would remain totally isolated from the rest of the regiment until daybreak on 11 August. Given the overall lack of progress made by the 320th Infantry, Colonel Byrne halted the attack when darkness fell. At 2230 hours, he ordered the 2/320th to withdraw while leaving a small covering force behind. As soon as this move was accomplished, the 2d Battalion would shift to the south until it reached the road used by Task Force Gillis, following it into Mortain. The 3d Battalion would remain in place until dawn to prevent the Germans from interfering with the movement of the 2/320th Infantry.[48]

The effort by the 35th Infantry Division to relieve the isolated battalion on Hill 314 had a greater impact than Colonel Byrne imagined. For several hours, the entire southern flank of *SS-Panzer Division 2* was in danger of collapse, and Lieutenant Weiss watched as the German troops began retreating from la Croix des Sept Coeurs. He sent back several reports stating that "they have the German Army on the run on the main east-west road; [including] guns, mortars, infantry." Moments later, American P-51 Mustangs began strafing the exposed Germans, whose strength was estimated by Weiss at battalion size or greater.[49]

The American assault also disheartened the *LVIII Panzer Korps* commander, *General der Panzertruppen* Krueger. He received several reports, although inaccurate, which stated that American tanks had simultaneously broken through the defensive lines of *SS-Panzer Division 2* at RJ 278 and Mortain. From Krueger's perspective, it appeared that the Americans were well on their way to regaining contact with their surrounded rifle battalion on Hill 314. He was convinced that the shifting fortunes of battle would soon force *LVIII Panzer Korps* to cease its attempts to capture the hill.[50]

The actions of the 2d Armored Division at Barenton also contributed to the growing pessimism exhibited by Krueger. Just before midnight, French resistance fighters informed the Americans of an imminent counterattack by *SS-*

Panzer Division 10. Several hours later, the Germans struck the 41st AIR positions near le Gue Rochoux. Infantry from *SS-Panzergrenadier Regiment 21* infiltrated among the defenders, tossing grenades at their foxholes. The Americans returned the compliment in kind, with one private throwing so many grenades that he had to report to his battalion aid station with a sore arm. Despite the fierce fighting, the 41st AIR succeeded in repulsing all of Harmel's counterattacks.[51]

SS-Panzer Division 10 dispatched a mixed force consisting of *III Abteilung, SS-Panzergrenadier Regiment 21,* reinforced by *SS-Panzeraufklärungs Abteilung 10,* to Barenton during the early morning hours of 10 August. The Germans marched boldly in column along a secondary road, convinced that the Americans were sheltering in the town for the night. The *SS* soon made contact with outposts from Battlegroup 2. When Captain Tousey received a report that H/36th AIR could hear German voices and clanking equipment, he ordered a tank platoon from F/67th Armor to go to the aid of the armored infantry. When firing broke out, Tousey left his command post to find out what was happening.

Captain Stewart Meyer, commanding Tousey's supporting FA battery, asked for assistance from the 2d Armored Division; soon after he made his initial request, four FA battalions began shelling the surprised Germans.[52] When Captain Tousey arrived, he could see two Shermans from F/67th Armor shooting up a nearby line of trees. When the return fire died down, Tousey ordered the artillery fire lifted long enough to permit a patrol to scout out the area.

The American patrol found many dead and wounded lying in front of the positions held by H/36th AIR. Eleven unwounded *SS* men, including one officer, were taken prisoner.[53] The commander of H/36th AIR remarked that the *SS* had come "marching down here in column, no skirmishers, no nothing." Captain Tousey personally counted at least sixty-five Germans lying killed or wounded in front of H Company.[54]

Although *LVIII Panzer Korps* had suffered significant losses, the 2/120th Infantry remained isolated on Hill 314 as the morning of 11 August approached. During the night, the 113th FA Battalion laid a continuous barrage of 155mm high-explosive rounds on road junctions and trails leading to the isolated troops. The big guns, with their correspondingly greater lethality, stood a better chance of destroying a panzer than the lighter 105mm howitzers. Every twelve minutes, the howitzers switched to a new target, working their way in a complete circle around Hill 314 before beginning the process again. It was not until daylight that the gun crews of the 113th FA stood down.

German tanks began probing the E/120th Infantry roadblock astride the Bel Air road at 0851 hours. A pair of Panthers approached but was driven off by artillery. An hour later, *Kampfgruppe Fick* sent a company of infantry supported by panzers against Lieutenant Kerley's men. Again, Weiss lashed the attackers with an accurate barrage of high-explosive. The Germans responded by shelling E Company with mortars emplaced on the westernmost spur of Hill 314. Although Lieutenant Weiss's observation post bore the brunt of the barrage, none of the men assigned to his section were hit. The attackers were personally driven off by Lieutenant Kerley, who supervised his sole 60mm mortar as it accurately landed its last high-explosive round next to an opposing German mortar crew.[55]

The German mortar crews, however, were able to capture a number of men from Lieutenant Elmer Miller's TD platoon. Private George Poulson and several other men had been hiding in an orchard tucked behind some trees on the southwestern slope of Hill 314 since 7 August. For four days, the GIs evaded capture while fighting raged all around them. Since the TD men possessed only a few rounds of ammunition, the question of resistance was quickly dismissed. When the German mortar crews approached their secluded orchard, Poulson and his companions stood up with their hands in the air. Expecting to be roughly handled, Private Poulson was amazed at how well the SS treated them. After a cursory interrogation, the TD gunners started walking east. The Germans, it seemed, no longer had trucks to spare for transporting prisoners.[56]

Elsewhere within the 120th Infantry's sector, the Americans were taking the offensive. Several thousand yards to the west of the 2d Battalion, the survivors of E/117th Infantry girded themselves for an attack against the Germans holding Mortain. Following their catastrophic assault on 7 August, E Company numbered only forty-four unwounded soldiers but had launched an attack every morning against the Germans defending the town. On 11 August, Lieutenant Richards's rifle company once again crept along hedges on the southeastern slope of Hill 285 before descending into the valley between le Neufbourg and Mortain. The "lost" platoon from 629th TD Battalion provided support for the attackers.

As the Americans neared the western outskirts of the town, the Germans opened fire with machine guns. The TDs responded by hurling high-explosive rounds at the defenders. Although the American assault consisted of little more than a noisy demonstration, Lieutenant Richards hoped to prevent the Germans from sending their troops to reinforce other sectors. After skirmishing for several hours, E Company pulled back to their original positions. As they retreated, the survivors of E Company rescued a soldier from H/120th Infantry found hiding in le Neufbourg.[57]

By the fourth day of battle, Lieutenant Colonel Bradford's 1/120th Infantry had begun to gain the upper hand in the struggle for control of Hill 285. During the previous night, patrols from B Company captured several SS panzergrenadiers, one of whom bluntly stated that he was tired of the fighting.[58] Bradford was sure the Germans would retreat if he could apply enough pressure against them. The 1st Battalion launched an attack that morning with the intent of pushing *Kampfgruppe Ullrich* off Hill 285. By 1133 hours, Lieutenant Franklin's A Company reoccupied the cluster of houses that originally served as B Company's command post. The 1st Battalion, which paused shortly afterward to permit an artillery barrage to be placed on the suspected German positions, resumed its assault at 1700 hours. Moving forward in alternating bounds, the 1/120th secured the eastern half of Hill 285 against little resistance.

By 2027 hours, the 1/120th began sending patrols to the northeast in an attempt to make contact with the 12th Infantry. Bradford was concerned about la Roche Grise, a small village immediately east of Hill 285. Prisoners claimed that the German force facing the 1st Battalion had withdrawn there for a last-ditch stand. Based on this information, Lieutenant Colonel Bradford ordered his companies to prepare for a counterattack. He also moved up a platoon of towed three-inch guns from A/823d TD to prevent the Germans from employing panzers against his battalion.

The 120th Infantry experienced additional successes along its extreme southern flank. Two companies of the 1/119th conducted a sham attack on Romagny shortly after dawn, accompanied by a ten-minute preparatory artillery barrage. Major Herlong wanted to convince the Germans that he was making another push from the west. In reality, he secretly positioned A Company, supported by B/743d Tank Battalion, south of the village. Herlong hoped that the diversion by B and C Companies would distract the Germans while A/119th launched a surprise attack from a different direction.[59]

The ploy devised by Herlong worked. Caught off balance by the assault from the south, *II/Deutschland* was unable to prevent A/119th Infantry from seizing a foothold in Romagny. Return fire slowly tapered away as the *Das Reich* troops retreated from the village. When Herlong reported his success to division headquarters, Major General Hobbs told him to "keep pushing and you can go into Mortain from the west. To get in there is all we ask. I will get in touch with Major General Baade and tell him about the situation. I will try to get someone on the flank."[60]

When A/119th Infantry finished clearing Romagny, Major Herlong ordered the remainder of his battalion to continue advancing to the east. The Americans initially encountered little resistance. By late afternoon, Herlong's leading elements were nearing the railroad west of Mortain. The further he advanced, however, the more he began to worry about his flanks. Telephoning the division operations officer, Herlong reported that he was ordering his men to halt until the 35th Infantry Division came on line. He also asked division headquarters to "tell the unit on the right not to throw so much in there, we are up to the railroad now." Moments later, Herlong called headquarters once again to report that "we are still getting shelling from that unit on the right, it is falling behind our front lines and our rear elements are catching it now."[61]

Anxious to exploit the gains made by Herlong, Major General Hobbs met with Major General Baade soon afterward. Although both divisions had been fighting alongside each other for the past three days, this was the first attempt by their respective commanding generals to synchronize operations. Hobbs explained that the 1/119th Infantry was making a concentrated push to reach the outskirts of Mortain, but it was not getting any support from the 3/320th to the south. Baade promised Hobbs that the 320th Infantry would do anything it could to support the 1/119th. He also agreed to prohibit firing across the Mortain–

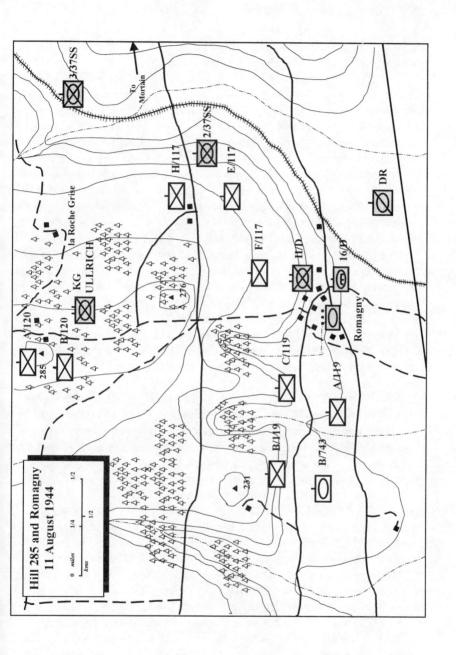

Hill 285 and Romagny
11 August 1944

0 miles   1/4   1/2

kms   1/2

St.-Hilaire-du-Harcouet road. At the conclusion of the meeting, Major General Baade departed for Colonel Byrne's command post.[62]

The 1/119th remained stationary as the meeting between the division commanders took place. While he was waiting, Major Herlong made radio contact with Lieutenant Kerley on Hill 314. Kerley tried to send a patrol to the west to link up with the 1st Battalion, but it was turned back by German resistance. By 1850 hours, the 3/320th slowly came on line with Major Herlong's battalion. Supported by a platoon of medium tanks, A/119th Infantry resumed its advance toward Mortain, but the Shermans quickly ran into a minefield that halted their advance. The 3d platoon of A Company deployed to cover the tankers as they dismounted to begin clearing the mines from the road. When a tankdozer arrived to construct a bypass through the hedgerows, a German antitank gun opened fire. The tankdozer burst into flames as several high-velocity shells hit it.

The remaining tanks retreated once all of the dismounted crew members returned to their vehicles. Two of the Shermans, bogged down in marshy ground, were unable to move. Fearful that the hidden antitank gun would destroy them, both crews abandoned their vehicles.[63] As the tanks pulled out, the soldiers of A Company also began heading back to Romagny. The rearward movement of the Americans was hastened by a German counterattack. One rifle platoon sergeant tried to rally his soldiers to cover the withdrawal but succeeded in gathering up only four men. When the five infantrymen opened fire, the *SS* troops broke off their assault.

When Major Herlong reported this latest turn of events to division headquarters, Major General Hobbs told the commander of the 1/119th Infantry that "you have done a good job. I know you want to continue on, but when you get a good position you had better dig in for the night." Herlong replied, "When I start in the morning, I am not stopping until I reach that hill." He then directed his company commanders to set up defensive positions in Romagny for the night.

When TF 3 prepared for another assault against RJ 278 on 11 August, Lieutenant Colonel Sam Hogan tried to approach his objective from an unexpected direction. Summoning Lieutenant Robert T. Resterer of C/33d Armor to his command post, Hogan explained that his mission was to locate a gap in the German defenses. Resterer's light tanks, reinforced by a platoon of infantry, would attack RJ 278 from the rear while the remainder of TF 3 launched a frontal assault. Hogan also instructed Resterer to take Sergeant Tripp's tankdozer with him. The foot soldiers would ride on Lieutenant Resterer's five M5 Stuart light tanks, which in turn would follow the tankdozer as it opened a path through the hedgerows.[64]

After several hours of difficult cross-country movement, Resterer found himself eight hundred yards south of RJ 278, where he discovered an impassable cliff that halted the Americans. By this time, the suspicions of the defending Germans were aroused, and *Sturmbannführer* Weidinger could plainly hear the vehicular activity near L'Abbaye Blanche. As a precautionary measure, he ordered a spoiling attack launched against the Americans.

Lieutenant Springfield at L'Abbaye Blanche was the first to spot dismounted *SS* infantry heading toward the perimeter held by the 3/33d Armor. When artillery fire began landing near his command tank a short while later, Lieutenant Colonel Hogan also realized that he would have to temporarily shelve his plans for a coordinated assault against RJ 278. The Germans had greatly complicated matters by attacking the southeastern corner of Hogan's perimeter, and the steeply sloping ground prevented the tanks from firing on the dismounted *SS* infantry. TF 3 would have to rely on its mortar and assault gun platoons to defeat the counterattack.

The Germans, who had chosen the ground carefully, knew where the opposing mortars and assault guns were located. They began shelling the H Company, 119th Infantry's mortar platoon, forcing the men to seek cover. One mortarman was killed and two others wounded by shrapnel. Lieutenant Clair Askew, the mortar platoon leader, left the shelter of his foxhole to set an example for his men. A shell exploded nearby, killing him before he could convince his men to resume firing.[65]

Staff Sergeant Arnold Schlaich left one of his section sergeants in charge of the TF 3 assault guns before running over to the field where Askew's platoon was located. Despite the incoming fire, he succeeded in rallying the shaken mortar platoon. The 81mm tubes soon began coughing out six rounds per minute, saturating the attackers with high-explosive. Satisfied that everything was under control, Schlaich sprinted back to his assault guns to supervise their part in the ongoing fight. Faced with increasing resistance, *Sturmbannführer* Weidinger ordered his men to retreat.

Lieutenant Resterer, who had taken up a temporary defensive position during the counterattack, began searching for a way to negotiate the cliff. After he and Tripp carefully examined the terrain, they agreed that it was impossible for a tank to negotiate the steep slope. When Resterer reported that he could not find a bypass, Lieutenant Colonel Hogan reluctantly ordered him to return.[66]

The 30th Infantry Division was making progress on its southern flank due to the pressure placed on *SS-Panzer Division 2* by the 35th Division. Determined to erase the lodgment established by the 1/320th Infantry, the Germans shifted their available forces south of Mortain during the night of 10 August. At 0100 hours, two platoons of *SS* launched an assault against the Americans supported by artillery and mortars firing illumination and high-explosive. With indirect fire masking the noise of its tracks, a Pzkfw IV began moving toward C Company. As it neared the perimeter, the panzer started firing streams of tracer bullets at the hedgerows occupied by the American infantry. Heartened by the appearance of tank support, the attacking Germans renewed their advance.

The Pzkfw IV was within seventy-five yards of C Company when a bazooka team destroyed it. The *SS* infantry pulled back soon afterward, leaving behind four dead and one seriously wounded man, as *Das Reich* ceased probing the American perimeter to build up strength for a major assault. By 0400 hours, Captain Kullmar estimated that an infantry battalion reinforced by panzers was preparing for an attack when he heard the *SS* shouting orders and revving vehicle engines for several hours. Lieutenant Hank Morgan was not sure if the Germans were deliberately employing psychological warfare or merely ignorant of the location of the Americans. He thought that even if the noise generated by the German counterattack force was inadvertent, it was still an effective psychological tool.

The American company commanders met to discuss the impending counterattack. Lieutenants Thornblom and Gardner both wanted to relocate away from la Croix des Sept Coeurs, where panzers would have a difficult time reaching them. Captain Kullmar, however, pointed out that it would take several hours to plan and execute an orderly retreat in the presence of German troops. Although he remained adamant that their defensive perimeter must be held, Kullmar did agree to reposition one of his rifle platoons to bolster the line held by C Company.

At 0700 hours, the Germans launched their counterattack against the 1/320th Infantry. Several companies of *SS* infantry, supported by tanks and artillery, assaulted the American perimeter, overrunning B Company's outpost line in their initial rush. Lieutenant Morgan glanced up to see three panzers emerging from behind a ridge. The leftmost vehicle traversed its turret in one smooth motion, opening fire on the abandoned Sherman sitting near the crossroads.[67] The panzers then backed out of sight as quickly as they had appeared.

The *SS* had also sited a pair of MG-42 machine guns atop an elevated roadway located to the left and slightly to the rear of the American perimeter, a position that provided a clear view of C Company. The German machine guns opened fire, raking one of Lieutenant Thornblom's platoons with a sustained burst of bullets. The Americans lost fourteen men killed and six others wounded in a matter of seconds. Thornblom ran over to a machine-gun crew from D Company. Ordering them to return fire, he watched as tracers poured into the hedgerow sheltering the *SS* automatic weapons. The MG-42s ceased firing almost as suddenly as they had begun.

The three panzers chose that moment to put in another appearance. Moving forward under the cover of the noise of small arms fire, the vehicles materialized directly in front of B Company. All three panzers simultaneously opened fire, killing or wounding eight men, including Lieutenant Gardner, who was hit in the leg by shrapnel. The sudden onslaught persuaded Gardner to order his men to retreat. When the rest of the 1/320th saw B Company retreating, they also began to fall back. A steady stream of individual soldiers headed south, followed by squads and entire platoons as all three rifle companies began retreating to avoid the attacking panzers.

Lieutenant Thornblom and Captain Kullmar tried to organize a rear guard to hold off the *SS* for as long as possible. A bazooka team from C Company succeeded in disabling one panzer by knocking off its track, but the remaining panzers continued to press their assault. It quickly became apparent that the American rear guard would have to retreat to avoid being taken prisoner. Most of the men who remained behind to cover the retreat of the 1/320th Infantry were able to escape. Ten soldiers from C Company, however, were forced to surrender.

The 1st Battalion began reorganizing in a field three hundred yards south-west of their original perimeter. The surviving officers of each rifle company sited their troops to repel another German counterattack, but the *SS* continued moving south rather than pursue the retreating Americans. Having won a temporary respite, Captain Kullmar led the men to a heavily vegetated sunken road near the Mortain-Bion railway station, where he planned to await the arrival of the rest of the 320th Infantry. All three of the American rifle companies were in bad shape. The single available medic was kept busy treating twenty wounded men. When Captain Kullmar took stock of the ammunition supply, he was shocked to find that no one had more than a few clips left.[68]

The situation appeared equally grim on the morning of 11 August to the company commanders of the 737th Tank Battalion. Rather than pull back to their battalion assembly area, A and B Companies spent the night parked in a field a mile south of the railroad line. Lieutenant Colonel Hamilton attempted to send supplies forward, but the convoy carrying fuel and ammunition was ambushed. The German force that had counterattacked 1/320th Infantry approached the parked American tanks as the dawn sky grew bright. Lacking infantry support, both of the tank company commanders decided to pull out.

As they continued south from la Croix des Sept Coeurs, the *SS* panzers came to an abrupt halt at the sight of an entire company of American tanks emerging onto the road. Recovering their composure, the *SS* panzers opened fire, knocking out the last Sherman as A Company disappeared around a curve. The tank ground to a halt alongside a C Company tank destroyed the previous day, the hulks of both Shermans blocking the road.

The executive officer of B/737th Tank Battalion, who had waited until Company A departed, spotted the leading company of 2/320th Infantry approaching. Bolstered by the appearance of supporting riflemen, B Company chose to contest the German advance. A brief firefight took place, which resulted in the Germans retreating. The leading company of 2/320th Infantry continued moving along the road until it encountered *SS* infantry between the villages of la Gandonniere and la Halere.[69]

While *SS-Panzer Division 2* regained control of la Croix des Sept Coeurs, *Standartenführer* Baum was forced to surrender terrain further to the south in order to assemble a counterattack force against the 1/320th Infantry. The *Das Reich* reconnaissance elements immediately north of Barenton had pulled out the previous afternoon to avoid being encircled. When the 1/134th Infantry sent out several patrols during the morning of 11 August to locate the German defenses, they only found three panzers acting as mobile strongpoints. Relaying the information to forward observers, the Americans began firing artillery at the German armored vehicles. When the dust cleared, the panzers had departed. Patrols dispatched by the 3/137th Infantry encountered only slight resistance in the form of sporadic machine-gun fire. Other patrols searching the hedgerows east of the 2/134th discovered a complete absence of German troops.

Colonel Miltonberger correctly assumed that the 320th Infantry's attack on 10 August had siphoned off most of the Germans arrayed against the 134th Infantry. Facing what appeared to be only token forces, he also concluded that *Das Reich* was preparing to completely pull out of the area between Mortain and St.-Jean-du-Corail. Based on this latest assessment, Miltonberger planned to launch a coordinated assault using all of his rifle battalions.

By 0830 hours, the 134th Infantry began advancing once more. The 1st Battalion crossed the railroad spur extending south from Mortain to St.-Jean-du-Corail without encountering German troops. By 0912 hours, it bypassed St.-Jean-du-Corail to the north while the 2d Battalion was moving south of the village. The 3/137th Infantry protected the regimental boundary separating the 134th from the 320th Infantry to the north. Meeting little resistance, the 3/137th had almost reached the village of Bion by midmorning. Colonel Miltonberger hoped to have all three rifle battalions astride the Mortain-Barenton road by noon.

Although Miltonberger's 1st Battalion successfully crossed the Mortain-Barenton road shortly before noon, *LVIII Panzer Korps* was not prepared to allow the 35th Infantry Division to seize control of the primary north-south road linking *SS-Panzer Division 2* with *SS-Panzer Division 10*. As the 3/137th approached Bion, it was held up by German machine gunners. Rather than launch a costly assault against defenders sheltering within the village, Colonel Miltonberger ordered the 3d Battalion to pull back while artillery was employed against Bion. Three dozen howitzers of the 216th, 161st, and VII Corps Artillery's 183d FA Battalions began firing on the village. Almost every building was knocked flat by high-explosive rounds as Bion quickly disappeared in the clouds of dust and smoke.

Although the artillery fire was able to quell resistance in Bion, another threat against the 3/137th materialized from the direction of Mortain. At 1450 hours, the 30th Division's operations officer telephoned the command post of the 35th Division to report that E/120th Infantry on Hill 314 had sighted four panzers moving south. He apologized for not engaging them with artillery, explaining that the vehicles were already too close to the last known position of the 1/320th when first observed. The four panzers passed through la Croix des Sept Coeurs heading toward Bion.[70]

The information was not passed down to the 134th Infantry in time to permit the 3/137th to establish a hasty defense. The 3d Battalion had already advanced beyond the rubbled village when the quartet of panzers appeared. A single rifle platoon, which had been left behind to secure Bion, opened fire with small arms. Buttoning down their hatches, the panzer crews lost sight of their tormentors, and the Americans hid as the tanks roamed the ruined streets. Well aware that they could not afford to remain in one place for any length of time, the German vehicles headed back north.[71] Several M-10s from the 654th TD Battalion entered Bion soon afterward, securing it against future counterattacks.[72]

The Germans followed up the abortive thrust with an emissary carrying a flag of truce. An American private named John Dudley had originally proposed to his captors that he could successfully negotiate a prisoner exchange, although several *SS* officers were sure he had suggested the idea only to win his own freedom. Despite their suspicions, Dudley's offer was ultimately approved, and *Rottenführer* Kurt Forster of *III Deutschland* was chosen to accompany him. Forster was assigned to carry a note offering to exchange captured American medical personnel for four German doctors taken prisoner when Cherbourg fell.

Rottenführer Forster and Private Dudley were escorted to no-man's-land, where they cautiously walked into the open waving a white flag. At 1555 hours, the 3d Battalion command post reported their arrival to Colonel Byrne, who directed that the pair be immediately transported to his headquarters.[73] The jeep carrying Forster arrived at the 320th Infantry command post at 1615 hours. He handed Colonel Byrne a note that read: "To American Red Cross—[from] Christian Tychsen, APO 408800. Wounded July 28 during an American armored attack near Trelly. Two American doctors and 20 American medics are offered in exchange for four German doctors and a few medics. Lieutenant Colonel Roschmann, Major Schmidt, Captain Ott, and another doctor whose name is unknown at present. This offer has already been made to an American priest who was sent across the lines on 9 August near Romagny."[74]

When he was informed a short while later by Major General Baade that there would be no prisoner exchange, Colonel Byrne told his regimental intelligence officer to take Forster back to the German lines. The Americans returned him to the front, motioning him to rejoin his comrades. When he was out of sight of the Americans, Forster broke into a run, breathing a sigh of relief only when he entered the defensive positions occupied by his own battalion.

Major General Baade had visited the 320th Infantry that morning for a different reason. Dissatisfied with the fact that the 1st Battalion was still isolated from the rest of the regiment, Baade bluntly told Colonel Byrne that "the 3/320th Infantry was the only battalion in the division not able to move forward" and instructed him to send a company from the 2/320th to outflank the Germans holding up Lieutenant Colonel Docka's battalion.

After departing Byrne's headquarters, Baade decided to visit Docka's command post. He was not happy with what he found, returning to the 320th's headquarters to inform Byrne that he had not heard any firing while visiting the 3d Battalion. Baade telephoned Docka from Colonel Byrne's headquarters. With two officers acting as witnesses, he told Docka over the telephone, "You will advance, you will move forward. Do you understand?" Lieutenant Colonel Docka quietly acknowledged the order.[75] With that task completed, Major General Baade returned to his division command post.

Colonel Byrne sent his regimental executive officer, Lieutenant Colonel

William Northam, to check on the 3/320th Infantry. When Northam returned, he reported that although the company commanders were doing fine, they were receiving little in the way of combat leadership from their battalion commander. Shortly after 1300 hours, Byrne directed the 3d Battalion to move to the vicinity of the village of Clairet. Once there, it would assume the mission of regimental reserve. While moving toward Clairet, the 3d Battalion encountered a German machine-gun nest located in a farmhouse. Supported by several riflemen, the SS troops brought the battalion's advance to a halt.

Soon afterward, Lieutenant Colonel Docka was relieved of command. Major General Baade telephoned Colonel Byrne to direct that "Lieutenant Colonel Docka be relieved and reclassified. Place Northam in command."[76] There was no indication in the G-3 journal of what triggered Baade to make that decision. Accompanied only by a pair of radio operators, Lieutenant Colonel Northam joined his new command that afternoon. In accordance with Byrne's latest instructions to link up with Major Gillis, Northam ordered the 3d Battalion to move toward la Croix des Sept Coeurs, and by 1850 hours it began heading east toward the last known position of the 1/320th Infantry.[77]

The survivors of the 1st Battalion remained unaware of the turn of events within the 3d Battalion sector. Captain Kullmar, anxious to reestablish contact with Major Gillis, sent out three patrols at thirty-minute intervals beginning at 1400 hours. All three successfully reached the Mortain-Bion railroad, but when they tried to cross, they were greeted with machine-gun fire. Alerted by the sounds of battle, Kullmar sent reinforcements to aid the patrols. After prolonged fighting, the Americans succeeded in forcing open a gap in the SS defenses along the railroad tracks where the patrols could infiltrate to continue with their mission.[78]

As darkness approached, Captain Kullmar was becoming concerned that he had not heard from Major Gillis. He did not realize, however, that one of his patrols had already reached the 1st Battalion command post and informed Gillis that the SS had occupied a defensive line along the railroad tracks. The conversation was interrupted by a radio call from Colonel Byrne, who informed Gillis that the 3/320th was heading toward la Croix des Sept Coeurs. Byrne also mentioned that he believed the Germans were preparing to pull out. Heartened by this information, Gillis decided to send supplies forward rather than order Kullmar to pull back south of the railroad.[79]

Unaware of the relief efforts being organized by Gillis, Captain Kullmar began planning to infiltrate back to friendly lines. Trailed by the remainder of the 1st Battalion, Lieutenant Morgan's platoon headed south shortly before nightfall. Before the column had ventured very far, the Americans ran into a small group of German infantry. Lieutenant Morgan's men quickly opened fire, inflicting several casualties on the surprised SS troops, while the surviving Germans scattered to avoid being killed or taken prisoner. Morgan did not realize in the wake of the brief firefight that the rest of the 1/320th was no longer following his rifle platoon. During the skirmish, the relief parties led by Major Gillis had rendezvoused with Captain Kullmar, and in the excitement he forgot to send out a runner to bring back Morgan's men, who had continued moving south.[80]

Gathering his company commanders, Major Gillis informed them of Colonel Byrne's orders to resume the attack, explaining that the 1st Battalion would trail the 3/320th as both battalions advanced on Hill 314. Despite the considerable challenges facing them, the morale of the 1st Battalion remained high. When Gillis asked if anyone had comments or questions, no one spoke out in protest. During the meeting, Gillis had tasked Captain Vignes to meet the 3d Battalion at the railroad tracks. After waiting for several hours, he heard the footsteps of a large number of men moving along the gravel bed of the railroad. A muffled curse in English confirmed that the battalion had arrived, and Vignes whispered a tentative challenge that was answered by the lead scouts of L Company.

Captain Vignes took Lieutenant Colonel Northam to meet with Major Gillis. Northam quickly agreed to move his troops into a field near the 1st Battalion's perimeter. Returning from his visit with Gillis, he gathered up his company commanders to inform them that they were going to move forward to Hill 314 at first light. Northam also directed his battalion intelligence officer, Lieutenant Homer W. Kurtz, to lead a patrol up the hill in advance of the battalion's movement.[81] He told Kurtz to immediately inform him of any indications that the Germans were preparing to counterattack with panzers. Northam was unaware, however, that the cost of the fierce fighting over the past two days meant that the *SS-Panzer Division 2* no longer possessed the resources necessary to launch a determined counterattack against the 320th Infantry.

Fortunately for *LVIII Panzer Korps,* the pressure exerted on *SS-Panzer Division 10* was not as intense as it had been the previous day. Rather than launch a coordinated attack, the 2d Armored Division contented itself with sending out patrols to seek a weak spot in the German defenses. However, *Brigadeführer* Harmel had been surprised that morning by American reconnaissance troops filtering undetected through Lonlay L'Abbaye. Considering that his divisional reserve consisted of one weak engineer company, elements of *SS-Panzeraufklärungs Abteilung 10,* and some assorted odds and ends, Harmel could not afford to allow the Americans to penetrate his forward defenses. Fortunately for the Germans, the 2d Armored did not follow this success with a larger force.[82]

The next American attempt to test the defenses of *SS-Panzer Division 10* came when the 3/67th Armor sent out a platoon from its attached infantry company, B/41st AIR, which made contact with the Germans after advancing only several hundred yards. The *SS* reacted quickly by sending several groups of infantry to flank the Americans, who soon found themselves pinned down by machine-gun and small arms fire coming from three directions.[83]

Major Clifton B. Batchelder, executive officer for 3/67th Armor, began directing artillery and tank fire against the German troops encircling the armored infantry platoon. The shelling forced the *SS* to pull back, opening up a gap for the trapped soldiers to infiltrate back to American lines. In pairs and groups of three or four, the platoon made its way to safety.[84] The 1/41st AIR dispatched a second patrol at 1545 hours, but it also experienced similar troubles when attempting to penetrate the German defensive positions.[85]

The commander of the 67th Armored Regiment, Colonel Paul Disney, had ordered his 2d Battalion to secure a crossroads northeast of Barenton. The 2/67th Armor dispatched a small tank-infantry team, consisting of the 2d platoon of F Company and a platoon of C Company, 41st AIR. The leading Sherman, commanded by Lieutenant Ralph Waffle, was hit when the Americans neared their objective. Although mortally wounded, Waffle directed return fire from his tank platoon against the opposing German troops. The Shermans were able to inflict a number of casualties on the SS, as well as knock out the antitank gun that had hit Waffle's vehicle. The Germans finally withdrew when the remainder of the 2/67th Armor moved forward to occupy positions in the vicinity of the crossroads.[86] The engagement that took Lieutenant Waffle's life marked the end of the fighting on 11 August in the Barenton area.

CONCLUSIONS

The latter phase of the fighting was marred by poor lateral coordination by the Americans. Although Major General Collins ordered Major General Baade to relieve the troops on Hill 314, the VII Corps commander failed to synchronize the efforts of the 30th and 35th Infantry Divisions. The conduct of operations at Barenton provides another example of Collins's inefficient use of available forces. VII Corps permitted the 2d Armored Division to adopt a passive stance instead of launching a coordinated assault against *SS-Panzer Division 10*. Under continuous strain since Operation COBRA began on 25 July, Collins's ability to visualize battlefield events and make decisions appeared to be faltering.

The handling of American artillery during this portion of the fighting at Mortain also lacked decisiveness and flexibility. By focusing on the defense of Hill 314, the 30th Division's artillery failed to provide effective support by reinforcing the FA units of attached elements, such as the 12th Infantry and TF 3, who were tasked with complex offensive missions. Failure to employ massed time on target (TOT) fires, which were designed to simultaneously place a large number of rounds on a single point, had ultimately resulted in a tremendous number of American casualties when the 12th Infantry and TF 3 failed to quickly secure RJ 278.

The lack of clear direction from VII Corps had a negative impact on the employment of supporting fires at Mortain. Although the 12th Infantry and TF 3 might have been reinforced by VII Corps FA assets, primary sources reveal that the brunt of the fight was carried by the divisional guns by a ratio of 5 to 1 or greater. Many VII Corps FA units rarely fired, while divisional artillery battalions were constantly in use. The efficient use of artillery was especially critical given the reluctance of the 30th Infantry Division to employ close air support.

Rescuing the isolated battalion on Hill 314 had become the primary concern of VII Corps and First Army, and by the evening of 11 August, the 30th Division was finally in a position to effect the relief of the 2/120th Infantry. The 35th Division gained a similar foothold. The German defenses were significantly weakened by persistent attacks by the 120th and 320th Infantry, and with losses mounting, *SS-Panzer Division 2* abandoned Romagny and Hill 285. After four days of fierce combat, the Americans were finally gaining the upper hand along the southern shoulder.

10
Impending Defeat

General der Panzertruppen Eberbach spent most of his first day in command of *Panzer Gruppe Eberbach* identifying what troops he had available to carry out his mission of capturing Avranches. In addition to the two panzer corps assigned to him, he also assumed de facto control of *General der Panzertruppen* Adolf Kuntzen's *LXXXI Armee Korps*. Kuntzen's mission was to protect the southern flank of *Panzer Gruppe Eberbach* as it prepared for another attack. When *Unternehmen Lüttich* resumed, *LXXXI Armee Korps* would guard Eberbach's left flank as the panzers advanced to the west. Eberbach was painfully aware that although his ad hoc command represented the main effort of the German Army in Normandy, he could expect little assistance. Sepp Dietrich's *Panzerarmee 5* was fully occupied in halting the Canadian offensive against Falaise, and Hausser's *7 Armee* was tied up protecting Eberbach's northern flank against the threat posed by the American First Army.

General der Panzertruppen Walter Krueger, commanding *LVIII Panzer Korps,* found himself in much the same situation as Eberbach. He had disengaged his makeshift staff from the Caen sector before moving south to assume command of two divisions he had never worked with before. To compound matters, his newly organized corps was scheduled to conduct offensive operations no later than 11 August. Upon its arrival south of Mortain, the headquarters of *LVIII Panzer Korps* quickly set about establishing its forward command post while Krueger met with the commanders of *SS-Panzer Divisionen 2* and *10*. *Standartenführer* Otto Baum and *Brigadeführer* Heinz Harmel both assured Krueger that their units were in relatively good shape considering the circumstances. Both formations possessed 50–60 percent of their overall personnel strength, although the majority of combat losses had been suffered by their panzergrenadiers. *SS-Panzer Division 10,* however, could count on less than a dozen operational panzers.

Standartenführer Baum reported that the American battalion on Hill 314 had proven to be "a thorn in the flesh" that "paralyzed all movements in the Mortain area."[1] *General der Panzertruppen* Krueger instructed his newly assigned subordinates that they would have to defend their present positions until the counteroffensive was resumed. He was favorably impressed with both men, although his first impression was that Baum was the more proficient of the pair when it came to tactics. Although he had directed his division commanders to temporarily revert to the defensive, Krueger privately protested those instructions to his superiors, claiming that the "line reached by the attack on 7 August, was suitable as a jump off for the coming attack, but not for defensive operations, which [his corps] was now compelled to make."[2]

Krueger had no choice in the matter. *Panzer Gruppe Eberbach* had been directed by Hitler to prepare for an immediate resumption of the counteroffensive against Avranches. The plan developed by Eberbach's staff, which was approved by von Kluge, called for a simultaneous attack by both panzer corps. To the north, von Funck's *XLVII Panzer Korps,* consisting of four divisions (2, 116, 2SS, and 1SS), would constitute the main effort. Krueger's *LVIII Panzer Korps,* which would be composed of *SS-Panzer Divisionen 9* and *10* as well as the Panther battalion of *Panzer Division 9,* would support *XLVII Panzer Korps.* The assaulting panzers would enjoy the support of two *Nebelwerfer* brigades. Von Kluge also promised Eberbach that *SS-Panzer Division 12* and *Infanterie Division 85* would be sent to reinforce him;[3] Eberbach tentatively planned to employ both to defend Avranches once it was recaptured.

Eberbach discovered, however, that he would not receive any of the panzer divisions promised to him by 11 August. Although Hitler repeatedly made it clear that he desired a decisive blow struck against Avranches, *Generalfeldmarschall* von Kluge postponed the movement of *SS-Panzer Divisionen 9* and *12* to Mortain because he wanted to make sure that the Canadian offensive against Falaise was halted before he transferred troops from Sepp Dietrich's *Panzerarmee 5.* In addition, at least one of the *Nebelwerfer* brigades as well as the Panther battalion of *Panzer Division 9* were ordered to Falaise.

Eberbach desperately needed the extra panzer divisions to offset significant equipment shortages that existed within the divisions already under his command. When he directed an inventory of the panzers assigned to *XLVII* and *LVIII Panzer Korps,* he learned that *Panzer Gruppe Eberbach* possessed only seventy-seven serviceable Panthers, forty-seven Pzkfw IVs, and an undetermined number of assault guns. Eberbach felt that this number was insufficient for a new attack on Avranches, but given the dire situation confronting *Panzerarmee 5* and *7 Armee,* he did not expect to receive replacement equipment from either of those formations. Instead he would have to wait for panzers to be sent from outside Normandy, a process that would take at least seven to ten days, provided replacement vehicles were readily available in depots east of the Seine River.

At first Eberbach was not overly concerned with the projected delay. He believed that the failure of the initial counteroffensive against Avranches was largely due to hasty planning. This time, he mused, success would be gained through deliberate preparations. Eberbach was particularly concerned with avoiding a repeat of the air attacks that took place on 7 August. Realizing that he had to rely on night and early morning fog to negate Allied air superiority, Eberbach sought permission to delay his counteroffensive until 20 August. German meteorologists had predicted that a weather front would arrive in Normandy that would produce cloud conditions and precipitation severe enough to curtail or halt Allied air operations. His panzers would also be able to make use of the available moonlight to navigate and identify targets.

Accordingly, Eberbach proposed to von Kluge that the counteroffensive be postponed until 20 August to await the arrival of favorable weather and additional equipment.[4] In the meantime, he realized that he would be forced to temporarily assume the defensive. Although Eberbach left some panzer units in forward positions to fend off expected American attacks, he planned to withdraw the bulk of *SS-Panzer Division 1* and *Panzer Division 116* to assembly areas in the rear, where they would have been joined by *SS-Panzer Divisionen 9* and *12*. Von Kluge, however, had a far different concept in mind for the panzer divisions that Eberbach hoped to pull off the front lines. The commander of *OB West* wanted to use them to deliver a blow against the Americans who appeared to be threatening the southern flank of *7 Armee*.

Von Kluge needed permission from Berlin before employing any of the panzer divisions earmarked for the counteroffensive since Hitler had made it clear that he alone possessed the authority to terminate *Unternehmen Lüttich*. Until battlefield events somehow convinced Hitler that the counteroffensive would not succeed, his standing orders to von Kluge were to hold the panzer divisions in place at Mortain. He did concede, however, that the counteroffensive would not be resumed if the Canadians were able to achieve a decisive breakthrough. To counter against this eventuality, Hitler directed that *SS-Panzer Korps I* would be given all of the resources it required to prevent the Canadians from achieving that goal. He concluded his guidance to von Kluge by instructing him to avoid counterattacks against Allied units in order to preserve his combat forces for the upcoming decisive battle.[5]

Although he had been specifically ordered by Hitler to conserve his panzers by avoiding costly counterattacks, von Kluge knew that he could not afford to wait until 20 August without doing something to protect the southern flank of *7 Armee*. He sent the remnants of *Panzer Lehr, Infanterie Division 352,* and a *Kampfgruppe* of *Fallschirmjäger Division 6* to reinforce *LXXXI Armee Korps*. When he was informed of the heavy fighting taking place between *Panzer Division 9* and the 5th Armored Division, von Kluge telephoned Berlin at 2115 hours to report that American forces advancing from Le Mans were heading directly toward Alencon.

The American armored spearheads, von Kluge noted, were receiving direct air support from strong formations of fighters and bombers. He explained that the loss of Alencon would create a logistical crisis of such magnitude that it would rule out any possibility of renewing the advance toward Avranches. He asked Berlin for permission to temporarily employ two of the panzer divisions committed to the Avranches counteroffensive to make a violent, but brief, counterattack against the Americans threatening Alencon. The request was approved.[6]

Generalfeldmarschall von Kluge telephoned Hausser to pass on the guidance he had received from Berlin. Since Hausser was not immediately available, he spoke with the *7 Armee* chief of staff, *Oberst* Rudolf von Gersdorff, informing him that "the enemy must be prevented from advancing from Le Mans to Alencon."[7] *Panzer Division 116, Panzer Division 2,* and *SS-Panzer Division 1* would be employed against the American units heading north toward Alencon. Von Kluge instructed von Gersdorff that the counterattack would take place no earlier than 13 August. He also noted that the operation would take no more than three days, which would allow these divisions to rejoin *Panzer Gruppe Eberbach* before the counteroffensive was renewed on 20 August.

Von Gersdorff was not sure that the counterattack would achieve the aims desired by von Kluge. He had just finished speaking to *General der Panzertruppen* Kuntzen, commanding general of *LXXXI Armee Korps,* who reported that his troops were incapable of obstructing the American advance. Kuntzen predicted that Alencon would fall within twenty-four hours.

Kuntzen's pessimism was well founded. During the night of 9 August, XV Corps surprised the Germans by constructing two bridges over the Sarthe River, permitting the French 2d Armored Division to move into position along the Orne River. At 0800 hours on 10 August, the American 5th Armored and the French 2d Armored began surging northward. The XV Corps commander noted that the fighting was characterized by a number of "sharp tank actions" as his armored divisions encountered determined German resistance while securing several towns and forcing a crossing over the Orne River. Although congested roads initially hampered the movement of the French 2d Armored, by 1930 hours it was advancing rapidly. When reports of the successful advance of his armored divisions reached XV Corps headquarters, Major General Haislip gave orders for the partially motorized 79th Infantry Division to follow in their wake. By nightfall, the Americans justified von Kluge's growing concern by covering half of the distance to Alencon.[8]

As XV Corps moved north, Bradley studied the situation maps in his command post. The symbols marking the lead elements of Third Army were moving rapidly. Hourly intelligence reports indicated that the Germans were determined to maintain their precarious foothold at Mortain, despite the threat posed by XV Corps moving north from Le Mans. However, information provided by ULTRA convinced Bradley that Mortain could be held.[9] The actions of 12th Army Group during the period 10–11 August had created an operational dilemma for the Germans: they could risk certain destruction by continuing to prepare for a renewed counteroffensive or they could retreat to the Seine River, which meant they would have to abandon their plans to recapture Avranches.

Lieutenant General Courtney Hodges was of a like mind. The previous evening he discussed the situation with his staff, noting that "it is still uncertain tonight whether the Boche is going to have another 'go' at a breakthrough or not. Stopped at Mortain, he has been pushed into a new effort to strike further to the south, near Barenton . . . if he fails to break through, there is a strong possibility that the Third, still making its great end sweep past Le Mans toward Alencon, may yet succeed in drawing tight the string around his neck. This would be inevitable disaster for his forces."[10] Hodges planned to spend the morning of 10 August at Collins's VII Corps command post in an effort to gain an accurate impression of future German intentions. Meanwhile, First Army would continue launching frontal attacks against *7 Armee*.

During the afternoon of 10 August, Bradley asked Patton to visit the 12th Army Group command post to discuss plans for the next major attack. He wanted to extend the northern boundary of XV Corps beyond the Alencon-Sees line to Argentan-Carrouges. The previous day, Bradley had boasted to visiting Secretary of the Treasury Henry Morgenthau that "this is an opportunity that comes to a commander not more than once in a century. We're about to destroy an entire hostile army. If the other fellow will only press his attack here at Mortain for another forty-eight hours, he'll give us time to close at Argentan and there completely destroy him." Privately, however, Bradley expressed doubts to Patton about the capabilities of Haislip's XV Corps. Both of Haislip's armored divisions were relatively inexperienced, and Bradley also had misgivings about the senior leadership of the 79th Infantry.[11] Patton reassured him that XV Corps was capable of driving north to seize Argentan.

Although Patton did not fully share Bradley's concern about XV Corps, he was worried about the apparent weakness of the First Army line between St.-Hilaire-du-Harcouet and Mayenne, as well as the open flank of Haislip's corps southwest of Alencon. Patton's concern stemmed from a briefing from his intelligence officer noting that "the situation on the axis of our northward advance Le Mans–Alencon–Sees is very obscure. The enemy has the capability of reinforcing in this sector for blows against the shoulders of our striking column or our exposed E (eastern) flank." The Third Army G-2 also felt that "the enemy is capable of attempting a breakthrough to the SW in the St. Hilaire–Laval–Le Mans area . . . the far reaching consequences possible to the enemy by disordering our lines of communications are so clearly apparent that he can be expected to exert every effort, even to suicidal operations, to accomplish this end."[12]

Uncharacteristically sensitive about the dangers posed to his eastern flank, Patton tried to draw Bradley's attention to these threatened areas. Although Major General Walker's XX Corps was released to Third Army several days earlier, Hodges's First Army had not repositioned any units to protect St.-Hilaire-du-Harcouet against a German breakthrough south of Mortain. However, the 12th Army Group commander merely replied that his staff did not believe there was any serious danger of a German riposte at this stage in the battle. As soon as he returned to his command post, Patton decided to issue orders on his own initiative instructing the 7th Armored Division to concentrate at Fougeres, with the mission of responding to a German counterattack against Mayenne or Alencon.[13]

As the two generals discussed the northward drive of XV Corps as well as potential future operations, Montgomery telephoned Bradley for an update on the situation in the American zone of operations.[14] Although the Canadian drive against Falaise had clearly ground to a halt, Montgomery intended to renew his southward push within the next several days. It was clear to the 21st Army Group commander that the Germans would not be able to resist an attack on Falaise by the Canadians and British, as well as the northward thrust by Third Army, while continuing to hold at bay the American First Army. Montgomery wanted to coordinate British and Canadian operations against Falaise with the XV Corps attack on Alencon. Additionally, he sought the 12th Army Group commander's assurance that Mortain could be held. Concluding his conversation with Bradley, General Montgomery instructed his staff to prepare an order calling for a coordinated assault by the American 12th Army Group, Second British Army, and First Canadian Army with the objective of destroying the Germans between the Seine and Loire Rivers.[15]

Hodges's First Army bore the immediate responsibility of containing the panzers at Mortain. If the Germans succeeded in launching another counteroffensive against Avranches before Montgomery could implement his own plan, they stood a chance of disrupting Allied operations by threatening the lines of communication supplying Third Army. While Patton was voicing his concerns to Bradley regarding this exact scenario, First Army already began implementing measures to preempt the Germans from exploiting just such an opportunity. VII Corps directed the 4th Infantry Division to move south of Barenton, occupying positions between it and Passais.[16] The 4th Division, however, would leave behind the 8th Infantry Regiment to protect the northern flank of the 30th Infantry Division.

Despite continued counterattacks by Hodges's First Army throughout 10 August, the Germans succeeded in retaining most of the ground they had won as a result of *Unternehmen Lüttich*. By the next day, however, the situation to the south worsened to the point where it began to significantly influence German intentions to retain their foothold at Mortain. As reports of an American advance north from Le Mans reached *LVIII Panzer Korps* headquarters, *General der Panzertruppen* Krueger was convinced that *LXXXI Armee Korps* was too weak to halt a determined assault. He duly reported his concerns to Eberbach, who telephoned von Kluge to discuss this latest turn of events. Both commanders agreed that a renewed counteroffensive against Avranches was out of the question until the entire Normandy front was stabilized. In addition to the growing threat in the south, *Panzer Gruppe Eberbach* still faced strong opposition at Mortain.

Eberbach was particularly concerned with the threat posed by the American Third Army against the road network and supply depots located at Alencon.[17]

The Canadian offensive against Falaise and the American advance north of Le Mans also appeared to be converging on Alencon. If the Canadians and Americans were permitted to meet there, *Panzer Gruppe Eberbach* would find itself encircled. With the Canadians temporarily held in check by *Panzerarmee 5,* von Kluge instructed Eberbach to prepare for an immediate counterattack to the south. He also told Eberbach to expect orders to carry out the counterattack as soon as Hitler gave permission to conduct the operation.[18]

Hausser agreed with Eberbach's pessimistic assessment. In a memorandum dispatched to *Generalfeldmarschall* von Kluge, he explained that *7 Armee* had only two choices: his panzer divisions could continue following Hitler's orders to capture Avranches, or they could fall back to a defensive line running from Alencon to Domfront. Although Hausser stated that he would carry out whatever decision the Supreme Command made, he intimated that *Unternehmen Lüttich* would eventually fail unless the shoulders of the attack could be secured. He also warned von Kluge that the counteroffensive would quickly grind to a halt if the *7 Armee* main supply depots located at Alencon were overrun.[19]

Confident that he now had the consensus of both of his senior commanders, von Kluge telephoned Berlin to speak to *Generalfeldmarschall* Alfred Jodl in an attempt to gain permission to launch the counterattack against the Americans north of Le Mans before it was too late. Correctly reading the prevalent mood in Hitler's headquarters, von Kluge did not mention that he wanted to table the notion of conducting another counteroffensive against Avranches. Instead, he explained how Canadian and American operations would impact *Unternehmen Lüttich* if nothing was done to prevent them from converging on Alencon. Von Kluge informed Jodl that Eberbach had agreed that he could not launch another counteroffensive until he received additional troops, equipment, panzers, and supplies. The counterattack against the Americans would only require two panzer divisions, which von Kluge hoped to transfer from Mortain to Alencon during the night of 11 August. He also reassured Jodl that the counterattack would be completed within three days.

Jodl did not dismiss von Kluge's request out of hand. Hitler had already ordered von Kluge to shift his avenue of attack farther south to avoid the American forces defending Mortain. As envisioned by Hitler, the second phase of *Unternehmen Lüttich* would originate from the Barenton-Domfront area, and the attacking panzer divisions would advance northwest through St.-Hilaire-du-Harcouet to their final objective at Avranches. However, Hitler had let it be known that he wanted the counteroffensive to begin on or about 11 August, and he also had reserved choosing the exact hour that the assaulting troops crossed the line of departure. Since von Kluge's request did not violate the overall aim of Hitler's plans, however, Jodl promised to provide him with an answer once Hitler was briefed on the situation later that morning.[20]

Generalfeldmarschall von Kluge telephoned Berlin once more at 1215 hours on 11 August to report that all commanders "regarded the attack against

Avranches as no longer possible. The breakthrough to the sea could only be achieved by a tough, long drawn-out battle for which the panzer units lacked the necessary striking power." He then added his strong endorsement to Hausser's assessment, noting that "the situation had become more critical during a very brief period of time though the enemy's rigid pivoting to the north and the strong commitment of his air force."[21] Von Kluge doubted that Kuntzen's *LXXXI Armee Korps* would stop the Americans moving north of Le Mans; the only forces that he possessed with the combat power to stop them were the panzer divisions committed to *Unternehmen Lüttich*. Von Kluge strongly urged *OKW* to release the panzers at Mortain so he could "annihilate the enemy at Alencon with all available panzer forces."[22]

Von Kluge attempted to persuade Berlin that the panzer divisions chosen to conduct the counterattack against the Americans would be well positioned to secure future *Unternehmen Lüttich* assembly areas in the Domfront sector. The situation facing *LXXXI Armee Korps* was deteriorating so rapidly, however, that an immediate decision was necessary. Von Kluge warned Berlin that additional delay would undoubtedly necessitate employment of a larger counterattack force to secure the southern flank of *7 Armee,* which would further increase the delay before another counteroffensive could be launched against Avranches. The *OKW* staff at Berlin, however, was not in a position to approve von Kluge's request; they were still awaiting a decision from Hitler on the matter. Exasperated with the delay, von Kluge issued his own warning order to his commanders directing them to prepare for a counterattack against the Americans at Alencon.

Von Kluge was also worried about his northern flank. He wholeheartedly agreed with Sepp Dietrich's sober pronouncement that *Panzerarmee 5* no longer had sufficient fighting strength to halt another full-scale British offensive against Falaise. Given Hitler's unwillingness to surrender terrain, von Kluge's only viable course of action was to defeat the Americans south of Alencon before shifting troops to reinforce *Panzerarmee 5*. In effect, he was gambling that he could stabilize the southern flank *of 7 Armee* before the British could mount another offensive. All thoughts of resuming the drive on Avranches were gone.

By assuming that Canadian and American operations were centrally coordinated, however, von Kluge unwittingly anticipated Montgomery's 21st Army Group directive of 11 August. In the directive, Montgomery pointed out that the seizure of Alencon by the Americans, followed closely by the capture of Falaise by the Canadians, would cut two of the three main east-west roads available to the Germans. Narrowing the corridor that the Germans used to transport supplies and reinforcements to a single road would have the effecting of placing "the enemy in a most awkward situation."[23]

Montgomery believed that the Germans could react to the threat of encirclement in one of two ways. They would attempt to employ forces from outside of Normandy to stabilize the situation, or they would pull out the panzer divisions fighting at Mortain for use in a counterattack against the converging Allied

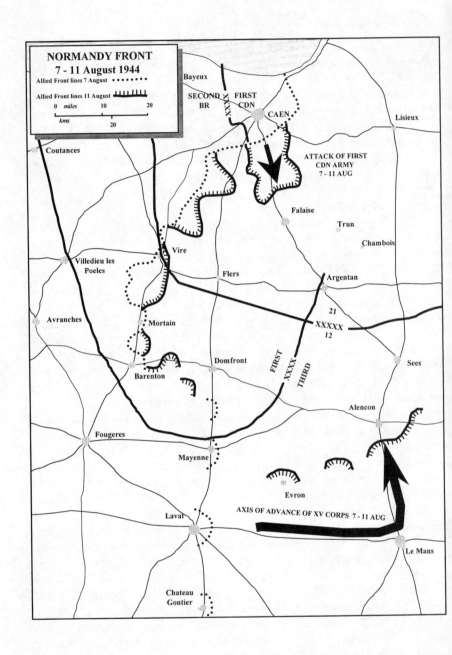

NORMANDY FRONT
7 - 11 August 1944

Allied Front lines 7 August ••••••••

Allied Front lines 11 August

0   miles   10   20

kms   20

Coutances

Bayeux

SECOND
BR

FIRST
CDN

CAEN

Lisieux

ATTACK OF FIRST
CDN ARMY
7 - 11 AUG

Falaise

Trun

Chambois

Villedieu les
Poeles

Vire

Flers

Argentan

Avranches

Mortain

21

XXXXX

12

Sees

Barenton

Domfront

FIRST

XXXX

THIRD

Alencon

Fougeres

Mayenne

Evron

AXIS OF ADVANCE OF XV CORPS 7 - 11 AUG

Laval

Le Mans

Chateau
Gontier

forces. Montgomery was sure that the Germans would transfer their panzers from Mortain to Domfront instead of waiting for additional troops from outside Normandy to arrive. This course of action, in addition to bringing the panzers closer to the fuel and ammunition dumps in Alencon, would place the Germans in a position where they could seriously threaten Patton's eastern flank.

Expecting the Germans to mass their panzers against Patton, General Montgomery surmised that his own troops would meet weaker resistance as they advanced. He directed the First Canadian Army to continue its efforts to seize Falaise, while the British Second Army would also advance, paralleling the right flank of the Canadians. Patton's Third Army was authorized to move northward to a point just below Argentan. The final phase of Montgomery's plan called for a linkup between the Canadians and Americans south of Argentan, followed by a mopping up operation by the British Second Army to destroy those German units trapped by the Canadian and American linkup. The American First Army, in turn, would squeeze the pocket shut by attacking from the west.

The commander of the 12th Army Group, Lieutenant General Bradley, was also sure that the only viable course of action left to the Germans was to pull their panzers out of Mortain. What puzzled him was the fact that they had not done so already. His aide recorded that "our lead elements on the flankward sweep are now well beyond Le Mans, approximately 80 miles from Paris. General is amazed at the failure of the Germans to grasp seriousness of the situation and feels they are either dumb or thoroughly oblivious to our intentions."[24]

Following his habit of personally reconnoitering what he considered the most critical point on the battlefield each day, Patton visited XV Corps on 11 August. He was very interested in learning anything that indicated the Germans were preparing for a counterattack. Patton was informed that Haislip's American and French tankers had experienced severe fighting on 10 August, losing forty tanks between the two divisions. However, reports indicated that XV Corps had inflicted equal or greater casualties on the Germans while taking several thousand prisoners. The remnants of *LXXXI Armee Korps* were no longer capable of halting Haislip's advance.

In preparation for launching the proposed counterattack, Eberbach departed his command post on the afternoon of 11 August to conduct a personal reconnaissance of the terrain between Le Mans and Alencon. He found troops without officers, panzers wandering aimlessly, and units awaiting orders that never arrived. Burning vehicles, some destroyed by Allied planes and others bearing the unmistakable marks of having been hit by tank fire, littered the roadways. The *LXXXI Armee Korps* command post was preparing to displace in an effort to avoid being overrun by American tanks. Eberbach took steps to reorganize *Panzer Division 9,* which he recognized had suffered serious losses. He also ordered the fixed antiaircraft guns defending Argentan to prepare to repel an Allied ground attack. Satisfied that he had accomplished all he could during the course of the day, Eberbach departed for his own command post to accelerate preparations to shift two panzer divisions south for a counterattack against the American spearheads nearing Alencon.[25]

Patton had already began implementing measures to forestall any German attempt to halt XV Corps by positioning the other corps of Third Army on either flank of Haislip. In this manner, he hoped to halt any German threat against XV Corps before counterattacking panzers could slow Haislip's momentum by forcing the Americans to temporarily assume the defensive. Patton initially ordered the 7th Armored Division to move north to Alencon. The 80th Infantry Division would also travel north along the Laval–Le Mans road until it joined with the 7th Armored. As soon as First Army released the 35th Infantry Division, Patton intended to have it rendezvous with the 7th Armored and 80th Infantry to form XX Corps, whose mission it was to protect the left flank of XV Corps.[26]

Patton planned to use the XII Corps under Major General Gilbert Cook to shield the right flank of XV Corps. The 5th Infantry Division, less one regiment at Angers, would assemble at Le Mans, where the 4th Armored Division would join it. VIII Corps had already been ordered to release the 4th Armored within forty-eight hours. Once both divisions were assembled, XII Corps would advance northeast echeloned to the right rear of XV Corps.[27]

Even before Third Army began shifting additional combat power to the north, First Army had directed VII Corps to maintain pressure on the panzer units remaining in Mortain. As dawn broke on 10 August, Major General Eddy's 9th Infantry Division prepared to conduct offensive operations designed to fix in place both *Infanterie Division 84* and *Panzer Division 116*. In order to keep the Germans off balance, Eddy ordered all three of his regiments to launch a coordinated attack on the morning of 10 August. At 0046 hours, Lieutenant Colonel Bond notified his 2d and 3d Battalions that they would spearhead the regiment's assault beginning at 0930 hours. The 39th Infantry's initial objective was to sever the road connecting Cherence le Roussel with St.-Pois. Rather than join in the opening phase of the assault, Lieutenant Colonel Tucker's 1st Battalion would guard against a counterattack by *Panzer Division 116*.

All three of Lieutenant Colonel Bond's battalions conducted vigorous patrolling during the night of 9 August to prevent the Germans from disrupting preparations for the assault by infiltrating into the American defensive positions. The Germans were also active in the northern portion of the regiment's sector during the predawn darkness. Patrols from the 3/39th heard panzers and wheeled vehicles moving to the east as well as troops digging in. The 1st and 2d Battalions, however, reported little or no activity. Although it may have seemed that the Germans were not taking special precautions against an American assault, Bond planned to liberally employ close air support against his opponents.

The planes were scheduled to arrive over the target area at 0900 hours, thirty minutes before the regiment attacked. At 0830 hours, however, Lieutenant Colonel Bond received notice that unfavorable visibility would postpone the aerial attack for at least one hour, so he passed the word to his assault battalions that the advance would not begin until the air strikes took place.[28] He then moved forward to joint Lieutenant Colonel Tucker at the latter's battalion observation post to watch the bombing.[29] At 0940 hours, eight P-47Ds of the 81st Fighter Squadron were the first planes to arrive overhead.

The big Thunderbolts peeled off one by one to dive-bomb German artillery located to the northeast of the 39th Infantry, dropping sixteen 500-pound bombs before strafing the surrounding woods. German flak filled the sky with tracers and puffs of black smoke from exploding shells. Despite the warm reception, however, none of the P-47s were lost.[30] The 26th FA Battalion began firing a preparatory barrage as soon as the planes cleared the area. One volley of high-explosive shells prompted a camouflaged panzer to shift positions. Observers from G Company called for more artillery on the vehicle, and succeeding volleys brought it to a halt. As if galvanized by that success, the 39th Infantry began advancing westward.[31]

By 1030 hours, the 39th Infantry had almost reached its initial objectives. As his assault battalions prepared for a final rush against the Germans, Lieutenant Colonel Bond asked for another air strike. Twelve P-47D aircraft from the 365th Fighter Group launched a second attack against the opposing German artillery. Although the planes were able to accurately place most of their bombs, some residual haze made target identification difficult. One 500-pound bomb landed within fifty yards of L Company, but no friendly casualties resulted.[32] German flak gunners were able to shoot down one P-47.[33]

Lieutenant Colonel Gunn's 2d Battalion continued moving forward, reaching its initial objective by 1225 hours. He ordered E and G Companies to establish a hasty defense centered on the village of le Temple. As the 3/39th Infantry began consolidating on its initial objective, Bond requested another air strike to prevent the Germans from launching a counterattack against his assault battalions. In response, a third flight of American fighters swooped down on *Panzer Division 116* at 1230 hours. Twelve planes of the 50th Fighter Group attacked targets northeast of Cherence le Roussel, claiming one panzer destroyed and one damaged, three other vehicles knocked out, as well as two trucks and two gun emplacements destroyed. The 39th Infantry reported towering clouds of black smoke rising from the target area in the wake of the air strike.[34] This success, however, cost the Americans two additional fighters downed by antiaircraft fire.

Satisfied with the day's progress, Lieutenant Colonel Bond ordered a halt to his regiment's advance soon afterward. Aided by the skillful use of artillery and air support, the 39th Infantry had succeeded in securing the initial set of objectives chosen by Major General Eddy with a minimum of casualties. Accordingly, Lieutenant Colonel Bond spent the remainder of the day establishing defensive positions against a counterattack by *Panzer Division 116*. The 8th Infantry assisted by dispatching two platoons from its antitank company to defend the southern and eastern approaches to Cherence le Roussel. By nightfall, Bond's troops were able to tie in with the 47th Infantry to the north and the 119th Infantry near le Mesnil Tove.

60mm mortar section from 2/39th Infantry engages German troops. Note the distinctive "AAA-O" insignia painted on their helmets. (National Archives)

Immediately to the south, Colonel Sutherland's 119th Infantry had also been ordered to launch an attack that morning. In an effort to synchronize his division's efforts that day, Major General Hobbs personally directed his regimental commanders to be prepared to begin operations at 0630 hours. Sutherland, however, was instructed to wait until the 117th Infantry and Colonel Luckett's 12th Infantry began their attack before he launched his own assault. Hobbs hoped that the Germans would not be able to fend off near simultaneous attacks all along the northern portion of their front. He neglected, however, to coordinate his division's assault with the 9th Infantry to the north.

Colonel Sutherland planned on conducting an attack employing both of the infantry battalions under his control. He informed Lieutenant Colonel Brown that the 3/119th Infantry would continue pursuing its mission of seizing Grand Dove and directed Lieutenant Colonel Lovelady to deploy the armored infantry companies of TF 2 to the north in order to close the gap between the 39th Infantry Regiment and the 119th. The tanks belonging to Lovelady's TF 2 and Colonel Roysdon's TF 1 would occupy reserve positions near Juvigny le Tertre.[35]

The 3/119th kicked off its advance at 0630 hours, only to run into heavy machine-gun fire after moving forward several hundred yards. The American infantrymen went to ground and called for artillery fire on the German positions. After several volleys of 105mm high-explosive rounds, the German machine-gun crews were persuaded to retreat. By 1000 hours, L Company occupied an orchard just west of Grand Dove, while K Company advanced to take up positions on its right flank. One German panzer, which had been loitering in the vicinity, retreated as both American companies converged on the village.[36]

When the armored infantry companies under Lieutenant Colonel Lovelady tried to extend their lines to the north, they drew an immediate reaction from the German artillery. The advance quickly ground to a halt as the German guns shifted targets to begin pummeling 3/119th Infantry. With his assault elements pinned down by German indirect fire, Colonel Sutherland requested assistance from the 30th Division Artillery, and an aerial observer was quickly dispatched to pinpoint the location of the offending guns.

The promised aerial observer arrived too late; however, to prevent the German guns from inflicting a number of casualties on TF 2. An artillery round wounded Major Albert L. Robinett, commanding Lovelady's Team 2, at 1200 hours. The headquarters company commander and the operations officer of 2/36th AIR were also wounded, and wire communications connecting Lovelady with Colonel Sutherland's headquarters were cut. The Americans were finally able to retaliate effectively once artillery observation planes arrived and spotted the muzzle flash of a German 150mm howitzer that had been tormenting TF 2. The 30th Division fired three counterbattery missions against the German gun, which silenced it for the remainder of the day.[37]

By 1919 hours, a patrol from TF 2 made its way north to contact the 1/39th Infantry. Upon arrival, the armored infantry asked Lieutenant Colonel Tucker for help in knocking out a mortar position that had been shelling their company all afternoon. The patrol had pinpointed the German mortars but could not contact their own artillery for fire support. Tucker obliged by calling in a fire mission by the 26th FA battalion, and the mortars were silenced after a few volleys of high-explosive shells. Two more patrols from TF 2 succeeded in linking up with the 1st Battalion before dark, exchanging information on radio call signs, frequencies, and unit dispositions.[38]

Colonel Sutherland's 119th Infantry achieved all of the objectives assigned to it by Major General Hobbs. Not only had TF 2 gained contact with the 39th Infantry, but Grand Dove was in the hands of Lieutenant Colonel Brown's 3d Battalion. German artillery, however, continued to interfere with attempts by the 30th Division to move west of le Mesnil Tove. Sutherland had hoped that the absence of his supporting armor would lead to a decrease in German shelling, but that was not the case. Despite the heavy volume of incoming artillery fire, he would have been gratified to know his efforts had led to *XLVII Panzer Korps* reporting that the Americans maintained constant pressure along the entire corps front, with their main effort west of le Mesnil Tove.[39]

Lieutenant Colonel Johnson's 117th Infantry suffered from coordination difficulties that resulted in a thirty-minute delay. Major Lindner's 3/12th Infantry launched its assault at 0700 hours, only to run into heavy opposition from alerted German defenders. A dug-in Panther and two machine-gun nests took Company

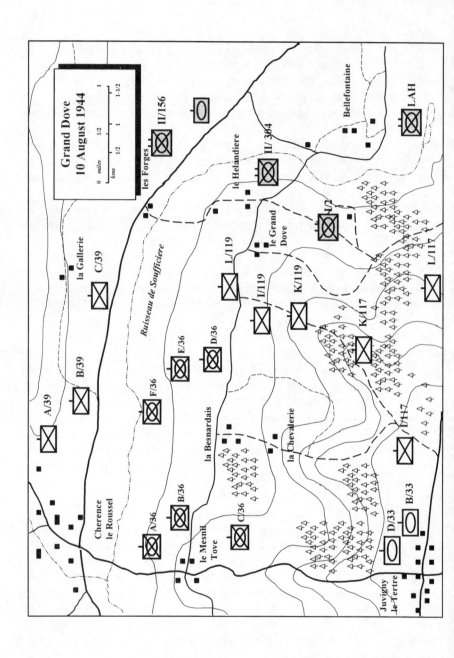

Grand Dove
10 August 1944

0 miles 1/2 1
kms 1/2 1 1-1/2

les Forges

II/156

II/ 304

le Helandiere

Bellefontaine

LAH

la Gallerie

C/39

Ruisseau de Soufficiere

le Grand
Dove

N/2

L/119

L/1/7

A/39

B/39

E/36

D/36

I/119

K/119

K/1/7

F/36

la Chevalerie

Cherence
le Roussel

B/36

la Besnardais

I/1/7

A/36

le Mesnil
Tove

C/36

D/33

B/33

Juvigny
le Tertre

L under fire as it tried to advance, and five men were wounded before the remainder could find cover. K Company lost a platoon leader and another man killed, as well as six wounded. Major Lindner sent Captain Alvin Wilcox's I Company around the left flank of B/117th Infantry, but its advance was halted when the Americans encountered a number of dug-in Panther tanks.[40] The lead platoon of Wilcox's company was able to extricate itself with the loss of only two men wounded.[41]

Lieutenant Colonel Frankland's 1/117th Infantry had also run into stiff resistance. A pair of Pzkfw IV tanks positioned two hedgerows in front of B Company held up all attempts by the battalion to advance. The 3/12th Infantry found itself in much the same predicament after it launched a second assault. When Major Lindner visited his companies to determine why they were no longer moving, he discovered that the heavy shelling had resulted in his men refusing to advance. Although the veteran soldiers were willing to try once more, most of the new replacements could not see the sense in attacking an objective in the face of artillery fire that controlled every approach into St.-Barthelemy.

Nothing Major Lindner said could persuade his men to change their minds. As he went from company to company trying to coax them forward, German forward observers noticed him moving about, and artillery fire soon began landing nearby. Lindner had hoped the Germans would not bother with firing at a single man, but the shelling continued unabated. Although his commanders understood why he was visiting their companies, they asked Lindner to discontinue his efforts because of the artillery fire that his presence drew. Following his unsuccessful attempts to persuade his men to attack again, Lindner reported to Lieutenant Colonel Johnson that "neither he nor any of his O's [officers] can get the men moving again. [My] troops absolutely will not budge. The battalion is composed largely of replacements which accounts for the predicament."[42]

Major Lindner's radio message convinced the 117th Infantry that he did not have enough men to retake St.-Barthelemy without some assistance. The 1st Battalion had not received any replacements since 7 August, which meant all three of its companies possessed fewer men than a single full-strength rifle company. Given the pressing needs in the rest of the 30th Division sector, it did not seem as if Lieutenant Colonel Walter Johnson could count on receiving reinforcements in the near future. Faced with the reality of the situation, he asked his regimental executive officer to relay that bleak assessment to the division operations officer. In turn, the division operations officer persuaded Hobbs that it was time to shift to the defensive along the divisional front. Major General Hobbs relented, ordering the 117th to dig in rather than continue attacking.[43]

The attack of the 12th Infantry also got off to a late start. Intense German shelling had ranged throughout Colonel Luckett's entire regiment's area during the night of 9 August. Direct hits were scored on the regimental command post, severing the telephone lines connecting Luckett with his subordinate units. Although the 42d FA Battalion worked hard to place counterbattery fire on the opposing German guns, it could not expect to quell the artillery arrayed against the 12th Infantry without assistance from the 30th Division. Assistance was not forthcoming, however, as the requirement to surround Hill 314 with artillery fire each night prevented the 30th Division from providing substantive aid. Colonel Luckett's riflemen could not help but notice that the volume of incoming artillery greatly exceeded the outgoing fire.

The Germans did not content themselves with disrupting the operations of the 12th Infantry using only artillery fire. Several times during the night of 9 August, it seemed as if SS combat patrols had surrounded the leading companies of both rifle battalions. The 2/12th Infantry repeatedly reported bursts of machine-gun fire criss-crossing from three directions. As each artillery concentration landed among the 2d Battalion's positions, the SS machine guns would rake the hedgerows in an attempt to catch Americans trying to escape the shelling.

Despite the German patrols and intense shelling, Colonel Luckett notified both of his battalion commanders to be prepared to attack as directed at 0630 hours. Frantic activity began in preparation for the planned assault. Engineers worked on opening up a road to the rifle companies, signal teams strove to repair the breaks in critical telephone lines, and battalion ammunition and pioneer platoons struggled forward with desperately needed ammunition, all of which took place without interruption despite the constant whine and crash of nearby falling shells.

Lieutenant Colonel Gerden Johnson, concerned that the Germans would use the cover of darkness to move troops into a ravine behind his rifle companies, asked for assistance from regimental command, justifying his request by noting that the 2d Battalion was seriously understrength after suffering numerous casualties. Colonel Luckett sent a platoon from the regimental antitank company to protect Johnson's right flank. Luckett also could not disregard the threat posed by *Kampfgruppe Ullrich* on the eastern slope of Hill 285. If left unchecked, he was sure the Germans would infiltrate machine-gun teams behind American lines to halt Lieutenant Colonel Jackson's advance in the morning. To counter this threat, he ordered the 1st Battalion to regularly send patrols to maintain contact with the 1/120th Infantry.

Despite German attempts to prevent another assault by Luckett's 12th Infantry, the Americans launched their attack at 0615 hours. Lieutenant Colonel Jackson's 1st Battalion was able to move forward three hundred yards without hitting any resistance. Lieutenant Colonel Hogan's assault the previous afternoon had apparently drawn off most of the Germans facing Jackson's men. The 2d Battalion, however, received intense small arms fire as it began moving forward, but Lieutenant Colonel Johnson directed his company commanders to continue advancing rather than allow themselves to become bogged down in a firefight.

By 0745 hours, the 12th Infantry had progressed far enough to provoke the Germans into launching a counterattack against Lieutenant Colonel Johnson's battalion. Three panzers attacked the 2d Battalion, pinning down the Americans with cannon and machine-gun fire. Colonel Luckett, realizing that his attack would slow down again unless his own armor was brought forward, called the 30th Division to report that "we have a growl [complaint] on this company of the 294th Engineers. They are not up here working on our bridge where they should be. We have no supply route in our sector at all and we want them up here to work on our bridge." The division operations officer replied, "I think they were drawn in close last night." Colonel Luckett, exasperated because his advance was being held up by the lack of armored support, shouted back, "We didn't know anything about that. Get them back over here." The division staff officer promised that he would get the matter resolved.[44]

Within ten minutes, Colonel Luckett received a call that the engineer company was on its way to the crossing site. Somewhat mollified, he greeted the news with, "All right, that's better." An hour later, however, the engineers were still not working on the crossing site spanning la Riviere Doree. The 12th Infantry's operations officer telephoned his counterpart at the 30th Division to report that "I cannot locate C Company of the 294th Engineers this morning. They were up here working on the roads and last night they wandered off and we [still] cannot locate them. There is a liaison officer here but he doesn't know a thing about them. Will you try and find them for me or let me know where they are, we need them up here to move some of our heavy stuff up."[45] Realizing that the 12th Infantry might fail through lack of engineer support, Major General Hobbs personally got involved in the matter. Prodded by German shelling as well as an irate division commander known for temperamental outbursts, the engineers tackled their road building mission with a will, completing the task by 1000 hours.[46]

Things began looking a little brighter for the 12th Infantry once the crossing site was completed. The 42d FA Battalion finally forced the counterattacking panzers to withdraw as the first American vehicles crossed la Riviere Doree. Colonel Luckett chose to test the route by sending ambulance jeeps forward to evacuate the wounded; both of his assault battalions had suffered approximately thirty to forty casualties during the morning's fighting.[47]

As soon as he received reports that the ambulances had successfully negotiated the crossing site, Colonel Luckett decided to commit his supporting armor, informing his battalion commanders that he expected B/70th Tank Battalion to begin crossing the creek no later than 1245 hours. Once the tanks linked up with 2/12th Infantry, he explained, Lieutenant Colonel Johnson's battalion would immediately begin swinging north to seize RJ 278. A second tank platoon would support Lieutenant Colonel Jackson's 1st Battalion, which would continue advancing in support of 2d Battalion's effort.

Colonel Luckett was feeling optimistic about seizing RJ 278 that afternoon. Not only was his supporting armor preparing to move forward, but he also had received information indicating that a linkup between his regiment and Lieutenant Colonel Hogan's TF 3 would occur shortly. Elements of 2/119th attached to TF 3 were reported in the vicinity of the 1st Battalion, which contributed to this impression by erroneously reporting that it had actually linked up with 3/33d

Armor at 1225 hours.[48] Thirty minutes later, Jackson's unit retracted that claim, stating that they had not made physical contact with Lieutenant Colonel Hogan's battalion.[49]

The damage had already been done, however, since the 12th Infantry's executive officer reported to 30th Division that "our 1st Battalion just now made contact with CCB."[50] Once the error became known, Colonel Luckett's executive officer, rather than admit the 1st Battalion had not linked up with TF Hogan, informed the 30th Division that "the contact that was made was not a very firm one because they are still fighting in there. Some of those Germans are holding out to the last man."[51]

The first Shermans from B/70th Tank Battalion attempted to cross over la Riviere Doree at 1246 hours, only to have the lead tank bog down. When a second Sherman tried to bypass the stuck vehicle, it also became mired in the marshy terrain. Until engineers could extricate them, the immobilized tanks prevented the remaining armor from advancing, so Colonel Luckett decided to postpone his attack until the tanks could make their way forward. It took the engineers and tankers an hour to free the mired Shermans, but extricating them did not entirely solve the problem. The effort to retrieve the immobilized vehicles had severely damaged the temporary bridging, and both wheeled and tracked vehicles were unable to cross until it was fixed. The engineers pronounced that it would take several hours before repairs could be made to the bridge site.

The Germans had been shelling the 12th Infantry as it waited for its supporting armor to arrive. However, the artillery fire hitting Colonel Luckett's regiment slackened somewhat after a battery of *Nebelwerfers* was shelled by the 42d FA Battalion at 1530 hours. After five minutes of concentrated fire, an L-4 observer plane circling above the target reported that the *Nebelwerfers* had been destroyed.[52] Despite the fact that his own tanks had not arrived, Colonel Luckett ordered both of his battalions to attack when he was informed that Hogan's TF 3 would launch another assault against RJ 278 at 1600 hours. At the appointed hour, Lieutenant Colonel Johnson's 2d Battalion moved forward in a column of companies with F/12th Infantry in the lead, while Lieutenant Colonel Jackson's 1st Battalion advanced just south of them. In sharp contrast to earlier experiences, the leading company of 2/12th Infantry was not fired on as it began moving forward. In fact, both battalions were able to gain several hundred yards before they encountered resistance.

Johnson's lead company had reached the orchard where the wounded soldiers had been left behind following the regiment's initial attack. One of the casualties had died, but the other wounded man and the medic who had cared for them were still alive. Both men were quickly evacuated to the rear. By 1702 hours, however, F Company reported that a machine-gun nest was holding up its advance. Several minutes later, Lieutenant Colonel Jackson's battalion reported that it was pinned down by heavy machine-gun and mortar fire; a German self-propelled gun added to the carnage by firing on its leading company.[53]

The Germans launched a counterattack against the 2d Battalion soon afterward as a panzer headed down the road toward F Company. A bazooka team hit the panzer with a rocket but failed to knock it out. Rather than take unnecessary chances, the panzer hurriedly reversed out of sight. After it finally grew dark, a patrol armed with bazookas was sent out by F Company to finish off the damaged vehicle. The Americans were ambushed, however, before they could reach the panzer, and only one of the five soldiers was able to return to friendly lines.[54]

While the German assault gun was still engaging the 1st Battalion, Colonel Luckett informed Lieutenant Colonel Jackson that TF 3 would be sending a platoon of medium tanks down the main trail at 1745 hours to aid his battalion. At 1830 hours, the regimental executive officer also informed Jackson that Lieutenant Colonel Hogan's task force was advancing. Moments later, regimental headquarters radioed 1/12th Infantry again to report that TF 3, supported by a platoon of infantry, was pushing north toward RJ 278. Colonel Boudinot, commanding CCB, was convinced that the linkup between TF 3 and the 12th Infantry would occur soon, so he ordered his command post vehicles to move forward to colocate with Colonel Luckett. The move proved premature, however, as TF 3 suffered heavy losses in an unsuccessful attack against RJ 278. The 3d Armored Division tankers, who had pulled back to their original perimeter at the conclusion of the failed assault, were no closer to the 12th Infantry than they had been that morning.

After repelling German counterattacks launched against the flanks of both the 1st and 2d Battalions, Colonel Luckett gave orders to his regiment to dig in for the night. Fortunately for the 12th Infantry, the crossing site had been repaired sufficiently to support the movement of tanks across la Riviere Doree, and by 1907 hours, the first pair of Shermans successfully negotiated the crossing. Colonel Luckett planned on renewing his regiment's advance the following morning after his supporting tanks and TD's were finally in a position to provide assistance to the attacking rifle companies.

Throughout 10 August, Major General Hobbs had been closely monitoring the progress of the three infantry regiments attacking in the northern portion of his division's zone. All of the units were seriously understrength: when combined, the regiments totaled barely five battalions of infantry instead of the nine battalions they would have normally had. The difficult terrain as well as the liberal use of artillery by the Germans prevented the 30th Infantry Division from effectively employing the equivalent of three medium tank battalions. With the bulk of his guns dedicated to defending Hill 314, Hobbs was also denied the opportunity to employ the full weight of his divisional artillery to break the deadlock developing in the north. Lacking the resources necessary to gain ground without suffering excessive losses, he issued an order at 2200 hours directing all units of the 30th Division to "dig in and actively defend the best defensive positions in present locations. Vigorous patrolling will be conducted to determine the strength of the enemy opposing each unit and to determine any indications of withdrawal by the enemy."[55]

Although all of the combatants at Mortain were exhausted at the conclusion of four days of continuous fighting, several American commanders had begun to view the situation much more optimistically during the night of 10 August. When reports of the rapid progress of Third Army were distributed to subordinate elements of VII Corps, they sparked a growing feeling that the Germans would soon be forced to retreat. In the 39th Infantry's sector, Lieutenant Colonel Bond ordered patrols sent out to determine if panzers heard earlier that evening were moving south or merely repositioning themselves. The 3d Battalion sent out a reconnaissance patrol from each rifle company at 0400 hours on 11 August. After establishing listening posts, the Americans waited for German mechanized activity to begin. At 0610 hours, the listening posts overheard panzers passing to the east of their location. Lieutenant Ralph Edgar's A Company also reported the sounds of moving panzers, which appeared to be heading east, not south.[56] It seemed to Lieutenant Colonel Bond that his hunch about the Germans pulling back just might prove correct, so he decided to postpone a major assault until he could ascertain whether the Germans intended to retreat.

In the 1st Battalion sector, Lieutenant Colonel Tucker told A and B Companies to send out patrols with the mission of determining German intentions. The patrols discovered that *Panzer Division 116* had pulled out of a small village to the northeast of the perimeter held by 1/39th Infantry. Tucker called his company commanders together for a quick conference; he intended to occupy the northeastern slope of le Mont Furgon before the Germans returned.[57] Company A would send out one platoon to occupy the village immediately. If the platoon did not meet with serious resistance, the remainder of the company would follow soon afterward.

The platoon reached its objective by 1324 hours without encountering any Germans. As soon as the news was relayed to Lieutenant Colonel Tucker, he ordered artillery observers and communications personnel to link up with the platoon from A Company. When Tucker passed on a situation report to the regimental command post, Lieutenant Colonel Bond directed the 3d Battalion to shift K Company south to tie in with A Company.

Tucker directed Lieutenant Scheffel to send out a patrol to see if the Germans positioned along the northern bank of the See River had also pulled back, but Scheffel's men were chased back to their foxholes by machine-gun fire as soon as they attempted to move forward. *Panzer Division 116,* it seemed, was not ready to relinquish its hold on Sourdeval.[58]

The 1/39th Infantry finally stirred up a reaction from the Germans late that afternoon as a battery of *Nebelwerfers* began shelling Lieutenant Colonel Tucker's command post at 1630 hours. The barrage provoked a response from the 26th FA Battalion, which lobbed back seventy-six rounds of 105mm high-explosive.[59] By this time, Lieutenant Colonel Tucker had also decided to push B Company forward to tie in with Company A. He coordinated with A/899th TD Battalion to move up their M-10s to support Company A once it became dark. Brushing aside a German patrol encountered en route, B Company joined up with A Company at 1955 hours.

Lieutenant Scheffel's C Company was directed by Tucker to send out another patrol later that evening. Spotting a battery of German mortars, the patrol called for support from the 26th FA Battalion. The 105mm howitzers began shelling the Germans, inflicting several casualties and forcing them to move the mortars out of sight. The Germans then began shelling the western edge of Cherence le Roussel with two batteries of 150mm howitzers in retaliation. A second battery of *Nebelwerfer* rockets opened up on Lieutenant Colonel Tucker's command post, setting fire to the camouflage nets stretched over two 2-1/2 ton trucks. One truck was loaded with mines and the other held the battalion records. Both vehicles were consumed by the flames, which eventually reached the ammunition in the first truck. The mines began exploding, forcing both the 1/39th Infantry's command post and battalion aid station to evacuate.[60]

Reviewing the situation map in his regimental command post, Lieutenant Colonel Bond noticed that the 1/39th's advance had completely pushed the Germans off le Mont Furgon. In anticipation of a renewed push on Sourdeval the next day, he ordered Lieutenant Colonel Frank Gunn's 2d Battalion to take over the sector currently held by Tucker's 1st Battalion, which he intended to pull back to prepare for the attack on Sourdeval. Bond planned to have the 1st Battalion, augmented by additional antitank guns as well as a platoon from F Company and a company from the 3d Battalion, spearhead the advance on 12 August.[61]

South of Cherence le Roussel, Colonel Sutherland's 119th Infantry found itself defending the gains it had made over the past few days. German artillery observers, who occupied the high ground to the south and east, were able to identify all of the positions held by the Americans. When the morning mist lifted at 0930 hours on 11 August, Lovelady's TF 2 found itself targeted by German guns. The 36th AIR reported that 105mm, 150mm, and 170mm rounds were causing serious casualties despite the fact that all of the armored infantry companies were sheltering in foxholes.[62] Pinned down by the shelling, TF 2 suffered twenty-three casualties during the course of the day. Losses would undoubtedly have been significantly higher if the armored infantry companies had been ordered to attack. The Americans were desperate enough to ask the local civilians for volunteers willing to go aloft to pinpoint the hidden German batteries. A carpenter from St.-Barthelemy, Victor Guerinel, answered the call.

Guerinel, who had secretly wanted to be a pilot for most of his adult life, was overjoyed by the fact that he was finally going to do battle from the air. He was transported by jeep to le Mesnil Rainfray, where he boarded an L-4 artillery observation plane. Flying over the ridges overlooking the beleaguered troops of TF 2, Guerinel spotted eight hidden artillery positions by identifying irregularities in the terrain. As the location of each German battery was confirmed, American artillery began engaging them.

Flying over the Chateau du Houx, Guerinel noticed camouflaged guns surrounding the stately building. The information was passed on to American batteries that began showering the chateau with high-explosive shells and white phosphorous. German artillery fire directed against the 119th Infantry dropped off markedly after Guerinel's flight. Thanks to the courage of the intrepid thirty-nine-year-old Frenchman, the Americans at le Mesnil Tove lost significantly fewer men to incoming shells than during the previous two days.[63]

In sharp contrast to Colonel Sutherland's situation, Lieutenant Colonel Walter Johnson's 117th Infantry enjoyed a quiet morning in the wake of severe shelling that knocked out several tank destroyers from A/629th TD Battalion the previous night. Two patrols from the 3/12th Infantry probed the German positions but discovered nothing out of the ordinary. It was not until 1205 hours that Major General Hobbs telephoned Johnson's command post for a situation update. Although he was not present at the time, his regimental executive officer informed Hobbs that the 118th Field Artillery was firing on the crossroads at la Foutelaye, where eight panzers had been spotted earlier.

Hobbs responded by telling Johnson's executive officer to inform the division operations officer when the 117th Infantry was ready to assault la Foutelaye. The 30th Division's commanding general made it clear that he expected the 117th to seize the crossroads by nightfall. When he was informed of his commanding general's latest orders, Lieutenant Colonel Johnson called together Lieutenant Colonel Frankland and Major Lindner to begin planning the attack on la Foutelaye.[64]

Vividly aware that his regiment was dramatically understrength, Lieutenant Colonel Johnson ordered the 1st Battalion to send out patrols to see if they could find a gap in the German lines. Traffic to and from Johnson's headquarters, however, eventually attracted the attention of *Leibstandarte* artillery observers. At 1710 hours, the first German shells began landing near the 117th's command post, disrupting preparations for the attack against la Foutelaye. Lieutenant Robb from C Company reported a few minutes later that his patrols were unable to find any weak spots in the German defenses. Johnson had no sooner finished talking to Robb than another German barrage landed nearby. No one was injured or killed by the shelling, but by this time, everyone at the regimental command post had dug themselves very deep foxholes.[65]

German artillery also began landing among the 3/12th Infantry, killing two soldiers from M Company and wounding four others. Fortunately for the 3d Battalion, the casualties suffered by M Company proved to be its heaviest loss on 11 August. Major Lindner had ordered his men to stay low until it was time to launch the attack against la Foutelaye. In return, the Americans scored a direct hit on one of the *Leibstandarte* panzers that was shifting its position in full view of the 3/12th Infantry.[66]

In the midst of the shelling, the 3/117th Infantry reported six C-47's dropping green, orange, and red parachutes to the northeast of their positions. As the information was passed to division headquarters, it surprised everyone. An investigation later disclosed that VII Corps had coordinated an airdrop to the 2/120th Infantry but had neglected to inform the 30th Division. The well-intentioned C-47 crews mistook Cherence le Roussel at the foot of le Mont Furgon for the town of Mortain, a navigation error probably due to the low-lying haze affecting visibility that afternoon. There was little or no chance that the planes could have rectified their mistake since the 2/120th had never been informed of the impending supply drop, which meant that their marker panels were not displayed to identify the correct drop zone.

Lieutenant Scheffel watched the planes as they headed toward his company. Wary of mistaken air attack, he ordered his men to lay out orange marker panels to identify their location to the pilots. From a distance of several miles, however, the parapacks beneath the C-47s took on the appearance of fixed undercarriages. Since German dive-bombers were the only aircraft Scheffel knew that possessed fixed landing gear, he ordered the marker panels hidden. After a few moments, however, he realized that the approaching planes were friendly. When he told his men to put out the marker panels once more, one of his soldiers asked, "Lieutenant, would you please make up your mind?" The orange panels were displayed as the C-47s flew directly overhead. The planes released their loads over American lines, but all of the parachutes were blown by the wind to the east. The 39th Infantry recovered none of the supplies. When Scheffel's company moved farther east the next day, they discovered handwritten notes attached to tree branches. Written by English-speaking members of *Panzer Division 116,* the notes read, "Thank you for the cigarettes and chocolate."[67]

A reprieve for the 117th Infantry also arrived soon afterward. Perhaps the division operations officer had reminded Major General Hobbs of the orders published the previous evening directing the 30th Division to assume a defensive stance. Regardless of the reason, Hobbs telephoned Lieutenant Colonel Johnson at 1950 hours with instructions to cancel the attack against la Foutelaye. Relieved, Johnson relayed the news to his battalion commanders.[68]

The 12th Infantry, however, would not get a reprieve from attacking RJ 278 again on 11 August. Major General Hobbs informed Colonel Luckett that his regiment would continue its assault until the crucial road junction was secured. During the night of 10/11 August, the remainder of B Company, 70th Tank Battalion, crossed la Riviere Doree to join up with the infantry at the foot of the ridge leading to RJ 278. A pair of M-10s from C/634th TD Battalion as well as two platoons of half-tracks towing 57mm guns from the regimental antitank company also linked up with the rifle battalions. By daybreak, the 12th would finally be able to count on the support of tanks, TDs, and antitank guns as it made yet another assault on RJ 278.

Preparations for the attack took up most of the morning. By 1205 hours, the executive officer of the 12th Infantry telephoned the 30th Division to report that "we are planning to jump off at 1330 hours with 1st and 2d Battalions . . . we are having an artillery preparation starting at 1330 hours and we will follow right behind it. [We] have our tks [tanks] and TDs over, [but] the road isn't so good, that company [294th Engineers] is working on it." The 30th Division also promised to have the 1/120th Infantry keep *Kampfgruppe Ullrich* busy that afternoon. Although the Germans had failed to take Hill 285, they proved able to pin down the 1/12th Infantry with flanking fire whenever it tried to advance.[69]

The 12th Infantry began its attack as soon as the preparatory barrage by the 42d FA Battalion concluded. The 2d Battalion moved out as scheduled, inching forward despite heavy resistance. Casualties quickly began to mount up, and by 1430 hours, the 2/12th was able to advance only one hedgerow to the east while suffering seven killed and forty-seven men wounded.[70]

Private Gerald Harrington, a member of F Company's 1st Platoon, was sure that he was going to be wounded that day. Artillery fragments had struck a good friend two hours earlier, triggering a sense of premonition in the young soldier. He was abruptly shaken out of his reverie, however, by what appeared to be Germans dressed in American uniforms probing his platoon perimeter. When he caught another glimpse of the intruders, Harrington asked his squad leader if there were any Americans in that area; his squad leader replied that there were not. The next time he saw movement, he fired several rounds. A short while later, a German waving a Red Cross flag stepped from behind an adjacent hedgerow. The *SS* medic slowly walked out into the open, followed by four other Germans carrying a stretcher. Harrington's squad leader allowed them to pick up a casualty lying nearby before waving them back toward their own lines.

Private Harrington's squad leader gave him a bazooka to carry during the assault that afternoon. When it came time to move forward, he jumped over a hedgerow followed by another soldier who carried the rockets for his bazooka. The pair ran up to another hedgerow chased by bullets from two German machine guns shooting from different directions. As they lay there, several more men from their platoon ran past. and Harrington and his assistant followed them through a gap between two hedgerows. As he emerged on the far side, Harrington noticed the rest of his platoon making their way along a nearby hedge. Just then, a machine gun opened fire, hitting him in the back of the head.

Private Harrington staggered back through the gap in the hedgerow, fumbling for the first aid pouch on his webbing belt. He lay down heavily, looking up a moment later to see the silver eagle of a full colonel on the helmet of a nearby officer. A lieutenant trailed behind the colonel. The officer, undoubtedly Colonel Luckett, told his aide to take care of Harrington while he continued forward. The lieutenant protested that his job was to take care of Colonel Luckett, not a wounded man. Luckett looked sharply at the lieutenant before telling him that Harrington was in much worse shape. With that remark, Colonel Luckett continued on alone, trailing the movements of F Company.[71]

Lieutenant Colonel Jackson's 1/12th Infantry attacked as scheduled at 1338 hours, only to run into machine-gun and mortar fire that quickly pinned down the advancing Americans. The 1st Battalion lost three men killed and nine wounded in the first few moments of the assault and was only able to advance one hedgerow by 1455 hours.[72] There the Americans were halted by a dug-in panzer that opened fire on C Company. A Sherman from B Company, 70th Tank Battalion, finally forced the German vehicle to pull back.

Major Kenneth Lay was sent by Colonel Luckett that afternoon to assist the 2d Battalion. Lieutenant Colonel Gerden Johnson had been running his battalion with little or no assistance ever since his executive officer had been wounded several days previously. When Major Lay arrived, he noticed that Johnson seemed exhausted so he decided to stick close to him during the attack to help as much as he could. When the assault began, the 2/12th command group moved up a trail behind the leading rifle companies. Lay could tell that the 2d Battalion had been through that area before by the casualties scattered about. It was obvious that the majority of the dead men had been there several days.

Lieutenant Colonel Johnson's party followed the trail until it crossed the road connecting RJ 278 and St.-Barthelemy. Major Lay could see a platoon from E Company preparing to clear out a nearby wheat field. As the infantrymen emerged cautiously into the open, a German machine gun on the far side of the field sprayed them with bullets. The platoon, accompanied by Johnson's command group, quickly sought shelter behind a nearby hedgerow, and Lay watched as the E Company platoon sergeant pulled several late-arriving soldiers over the top of the hedgerow into cover.

As the Americans lay there trying to figure out what to do next, a Sherman tank appeared. When Lieutenant Colonel Johnson stood up to point out the machine-gun nest to the American tank, he noticed a German armored vehicle situated by a house across the road and motioned for the Sherman to open fire on it. He also instructed the rifle platoon from E Company to resume their advance once the Sherman began firing. The riflemen nodded their understanding while clutching their weapons tightly in anticipation of facing the German machine gun again. Johnson could see the grim expressions on the faces of his soldiers, who were hoping that the Sherman would also be able to knock out the machine gun before it caused too many casualties. Despite their obvious concern, the riflemen from E Company appeared ready to move.

At Lieutenant Colonel Johnson's signal, the Sherman trundled forward, prompting the German vehicle to hurriedly retreat. As the Sherman rounded the hedgerow, it opened fire on the building. The appearance of the American tank drew a quick response from the defenders as three Panthers moved forward with the mission of stopping the 2d Battalion. The trio opened their assault by firing on Lieutenant Colonel Johnson's command group. Major Lay was sitting next to Johnson when a round exploded nearby. Lay was peppered with shrapnel, and Johnson was severely injured. Several other members of the group were also hit. Colonel Luckett, when informed of the incident, dispatched Lieutenant Colonel Franklin Sibert to take command. Johnson, wounded in one arm, both legs, and the face, continued to direct operations until his replacement arrived.[73]

After shooting up the 2d Battalion command group, the three Panthers turned their attention to two nearby half-tracks from the antitank platoon. The crew of the leading half-track, with the exception of the driver, bailed out of their vehicle as soon as they spotted the tanks. The leading panzer fired three rounds that penetrated the thinly armored half-track before exiting to explode in an adjacent hedgerow. The driver of the half-track, trying to reverse his vehicle out of the line of fire, refused to bail out until the third round hit. Satisfied that the lead half-track had been destroyed, the Panthers turned their attention to the one behind it, also knocking it out.[74] However, both of the 57mm guns being towed behind the half-tracks were undamaged. As soon as the Panthers departed, the American gun crews sited their 57mm guns to repel another attack.[75]

Private Michael Burik watched as the three tanks advanced along the road toward E Company. Grabbing his bazooka, he stepped out into the open to engage the lead panzer. On his first attempt to fire, the bazooka would not go off. Burik checked the weapon to discover that he had forgotten to release the safety catch. He tried again, firing a rocket at point-blank range into the tank. The panzer returned the fire with its 75mm cannon, seriously injuring Burik with a near miss. He rose, loaded his bazooka, and fired again. The panzer fired another round at him, knocking him down once more.

Dragging himself toward a nearby ditch, Burik loaded the bazooka for a third time. Resting the weapon on the edge of the ditch, he fired again, and the crew of the Panther decided to pull back rather than risk serious damage. As the tank disappeared from sight, he crawled to another soldier who had been wounded and, fearful that the panzer might return, pushed him into the shelter of an adjacent foxhole. After the Panthers had departed, Burik called out to the other men in his platoon for more bazooka ammunition, then fell unconscious. He died two days later.[76]

The 12th Infantry suffered ninety-six casualties, including Lieutenant Colonel Johnson, during the course of the assault that afternoon. His replacement, Lieutenant Colonel Sibert, began reorganizing the battalion as soon as the counterattacking Panthers disappeared. The 1st Battalion commander, Lieutenant Colonel Jackson, also reported that his unit would have to pull back to avoid heavy shelling by German artillery. The panzer that had held up C Company also successfully thwarted the efforts of his supporting Shermans, who lost two of their own M4s trying to destroy the German vehicle.[77] The first American tank was knocked out when ambushed by the hidden panzer, and the second was hit when it attempted to pick up the crew from the first . The panzer took advantage of the resultant confusion to escape.

Colonel Birks, as promised, dispatched a patrol from Lieutenant Franklin's A/120th Infantry to assist the 1/12th as it struggled toward RJ 278. The patrol from the 30th Division quickly ran into German troops, and an infantry skirmish soon escalated into a full-scale firefight in which the Americans called for support from the 120th Cannon Company. One of the opening volleys of American artillery ignited a German supply dump nearby, sending a towering column of smoke into the sky. As the *SS* retreated, the patrol from A Company continued forward until they could see other American troops but were forced to pull back without making contact when they began receiving heavy mortar fire.[78]

At 2141 hours, Major General Hobbs authorized the 12th Infantry to suspend their assault for the night. He was insistent, however, that the ground gained during the day would be retained. Colonel Luckett attempted to reassure Hobbs, noting that his troops were only two hundred yards from RJ 278, which was sure to fall into American hands the following day. Forty minutes later, the 12th Infantry's executive officer telephoned division headquarters with a request to postpone the regiment's next attack until 0900 hours the following morning. The division operations officer replied that Major General Hobbs had already set the time for the next coordinated attack at 0800 hours. Left with little choice but to comply, the 12th began preparing for an assault on RJ 278 that would begin at 0800 hours on 12 August.[79]

CONCLUSIONS

The assassination attempt on Hitler could not have come at a worse time for the Germans, as his natural mistrust of the professional officer corps within the German army grew alarmingly as the situation in Normandy significantly deteriorated. Despite his initial misgivings, he allowed von Kluge to plan and execute the counteroffensive against Avranches. When it failed, Hitler was determined to personally orchestrate preparations and planning for the second counteroffensive. With the responsibility for operational planning transferred to Berlin, the German forces in Normandy found themselves bound by a rigid decisionmaking process at the precise moment when the situation had grown increasingly fluid. Instead of decentralizing decisionmaking to the lowest level possible, the Germans had virtually ceded battlefield initiative to the Allies by adopting an increasingly unresponsive command and control system dependent on a single man located outside of the theater of operations.

Although von Kluge had no choice but to support Hitler's plans for a renewed counteroffensive, he believed that a retreat to the Seine River constituted the only viable course of action. With Hitler and his field commanders holding diametrically opposed viewpoints regarding future courses of action in Normandy, the Germans discovered that they were postured neither to execute a counteroffensive nor to conduct a fighting retreat. The opposing viewpoints had resulted in a lack of clear operational guidance governing the employment of tactical forces. Given the fact that the Germans already lacked sufficient resources to address the increasing number of operational challenges they were facing, the inefficient employment of the military resources they did possess significantly decreased the probability that they could eventually stabilize the situation in Normandy.

Lack of reliable intelligence had a tremendous impact both on Hitler's decisionmaking and on von Kluge's own perception of the battlefield. The Germans chose to use their ground reconnaissance units for combat missions rather than for gathering information. Compounded by the fact that the *Luftwaffe* did not possess a reliable aerial reconnaissance capability, this choice resulted in *OB West* conducting its planning in a vacuum. The lack of critical information, which resulted in lethargic decisionmaking and inadequate planning by the Germans, conferred upon the Allies a significant operational advantage when their opponents could least afford it.

In essence, the situation in Normandy rested on the uncertain ability of *Panzer Gruppe Eberbach* to extricate itself from Mortain quickly enough to counterattack the Americans north of Le Mans before the Canadians could resume their advance on Falaise.

11

Tightening the Noose

Deeply concerned by continuing reports of American progress in the south, von Kluge and Hausser agreed that *Panzer Gruppe Eberbach* would have to retreat from Mortain or face encirclement. *LXXXI Armee Korps* was unable to assemble sufficient combat power to stop the Americans, and its defeat placed *Panzer Gruppe Eberbach* in danger of being surrounded and destroyed. Von Kluge knew that he would have to shift panzer divisions from Mortain to counterattack the American XV Corps north of Le Mans. However, gaining Hitler's approval for this action would require all of his considerable powers of persuasion.

Von Kluge initially telephoned Berlin at 1215 hours on 11 August to report that Hausser "regarded the attack against Avranches as no longer possible. The breakthrough to the sea could only be achieved by a tough, long drawn-out battle for which the panzer units lacked the necessary striking power." He added his own personal endorsement, noting that "the situation had become more critical during a very brief period of time through the enemy's rigid pivoting to the north and the strong commitment of his air force."[1]

The only forces with the combat power to stop the Americans south of Le Mans, von Kluge pointed out, were the panzer divisions already consigned to *Unternehmen Lüttich*. Sepp Dietrich's *Panzerarmee 5* was still occupied fending off the latest Canadian attempt to seize Falaise, and the panzer and infantry divisions recently transferred to Normandy, with the exception of *Fallschirmjäger Division 6*, had already been committed to battle. Von Kluge urged *OKW* to release the panzer divisions for a counterattack designed to "annihilate the enemy at Alencon."[2] Since Hitler had to be consulted before the proposed counterattack could be approved, no answer was immediately forthcoming.

Although numerous messages were exchanged between *OB West* and *OKW*, *Generalfeldmarschall* von Kluge still lacked a definitive answer from Berlin by late afternoon on 11 August. In anticipation of a positive response, he prepared orders transferring three panzer divisions from Mortain to assembly areas north of Le Mans. He also informed *Oberst* von Gersdorff at 1515 hours that "no decision has been made as to the launching of the attack against the Americans . . . I intend to withdraw the front salient east of Avranches to the line Sourdeval-east of Mortain . . . the previously planned attack [against Avranches] can no longer be carried out. In case of a success, this attack could perhaps still be revived."[3]

In response to von Kluge's guidance, *General der Panzertruppen* Eberbach planned on employing *Panzer Division 2, Panzer Division 116,* and *Leibstandarte* to conduct the counterattack. *Panzer Division 2* and *Leibstandarte* would initially occupy an assembly area southeast of Foret d'Ecouves, and both divisions were slated to be in place no later than the evening of 12 August. *Panzer Division 116* would be sent to occupy a separate assembly area, bounded by the villages of Sees-Mortree-Tanville, just north of Foret d'Ecouves. After the panzer divisions arrived in their new assembly areas, Eberbach allocated each unit a full day to conduct planning and logistical sustainment prior to conducting the counterattack.

Although Eberbach incurred significant risk by delaying the counterattack until 14 August, he had little choice. The Americans were moving north rapidly enough to pose a threat to the panzer divisions while they were still in their assembly areas. However, each division would require two nights to move in order to avoid overwhelming the road network. *XLVII Panzer Korps* would also have to take steps to discourage pursuit by VII Corps, which meant that each panzer division had to leave behind a strong rear guard whose elements would rejoin their parent divisions on the evening of 13 August.

The departure of von Funck's *XLVII Panzer Korps* from Mortain also resulted in a significant change of mission for *LVIII Panzer Korps. General der Panzertruppen* Krueger assumed responsibility for the protection of the southern flank of *Panzer Gruppe Eberbach* and *7 Armee.* In order to execute this mission, *LVIII Panzer Korps* ordered *Das Reich* to move from Mortain to La Ferte Mace during the night of 11 August. *SS-Panzer Division 10* would follow within twenty-four hours, shifting from Barenton to occupy defensive positions west of Domfront.[4]

The decision to retreat resulted in five German panzer divisions, totaling perhaps fifty thousand men and five thousand vehicles, shifting their logistical lifeline from fuel and ammunition stockpiles near Mortain to the uncertain prospect of receiving supplies from *Panzerarmee 5.* With the loss of Le Mans, *Panzer Gruppe Eberbach* could no longer count on receiving supplies from *7 Armee. General der Panzertruppen* Eberbach, realizing that Sepp Dietrich could not support two armies for an indefinite period, hoped to support his counterattack by seizing American supplies and recapturing *7 Armee* depots.

Von Kluge was also prepared to accept significant risk in the early stages of the counterattack. Confident that events would prove his actions correct, he issued new orders to Eberbach without waiting for permission from Berlin. However, von Kluge delayed his decision until the last possible moment. Although he hoped to avoid accusations of defeatism, he succeeded only in truncating the preparation time necessary to conduct the counterattack, with participating units unable to obtain authorization to conduct planning and reconnaissance until literally the last minute. Even though Eberbach had been aware of von Kluge's intentions for some time, very few of his subordinates would have adequate time to prepare for what would turn out to be a very complex operation.[5]

For example, the selection of routes for each panzer division was primarily based on map reconnaissance because most units did not have time to physically reconnoiter the approaches to their new areas of operations. Given the fluid state of the Alencon-Sees sector, the panzer divisions ran the risk of making unexpected contact with the Americans while en route to their new assembly areas. Lack of time for more thorough preparations also resulted in many units departing Mortain lacking full basic loads of fuel and ammunition. *Panzer Division 116* also gained a new commanding officer in the midst of preparing for the counterattack: *Oberst* Gerhard Paul Muller was sent to replace *Oberst* Reinhard, who resumed his duties as chief of staff of *XLVII Panzer Korps.*

Each of the panzer divisions had a lot of work to do in a very short time. Disabled vehicles had to be repaired, destroyed, or prepared for towing. Stockpiles of artillery ammunition had to be fired or loaded for transport. Given the Allied command of the air, many tasks would prove difficult to accomplish during daylight. With very little time, the panzer divisions began preparing to shift their subordinate units to the southeast. In some instances, however, the lack of adequate preparation would prove costly.

All of the panzer division commanders were greatly concerned about their retreat being prematurely discovered. The Germans knew that American artillery fire would inflict serious losses if their units were caught on the roads. Accordingly, each division took precautions to ensure its departure was not discovered. Some chose to depend on stealth to avoid discovery. *Brigadeführer* Wisch, commanding *Leibstandarte,* decided to fire off his excess ammunition rather than slink away without a sound. At the very least, he reasoned, the shelling would keep the Americans from becoming too inquisitive. The *Luftwaffe* also promised to launch strikes against Cherence le Roussel, Mortain, and Barenton to cover the withdrawal of *Panzer Gruppe Eberbach.*

The 39th Infantry was probably the first American unit to suspect that the Germans were preparing for a major withdrawal. The initial clue came when Company C captured a talkative prisoner just before daybreak on 12 August.[6] The prisoner, a medic assigned to *10 Kompanie, Panzergrenadier Regiment 2,* revealed that his unit was planning to retreat to a new line east of St.-Barthelemy. Since limited movement was detected by 39th Infantry patrols earlier that night, there was not much in the way of corroborative information, although the lack of activity by the Germans was not particularly suspicious. Lieutenant Colonel Bond had been focusing his efforts on coordinating a regimental assault slated to begin at 0730 hours and could not afford to adjust his plans based on one report of a potential German withdrawal.

At the appointed hour, Lieutenant Colonel Tucker's 1st Battalion led off the assault, trailed by the 2/39th Infantry. He arrayed his rifle battalion in two echelons: A and B Companies spearheading, with C Company in trail. Although few Germans were encountered, the lead elements of the 1st Battalion found themselves enmeshed in a maze of minefields and booby traps. Fortunately for the struggling Americans, incoming artillery was almost nonexistent. Despite the obstacles strewn liberally in its path, the 39th Infantry succeeded in advancing rapidly enough to narrowly miss trapping the rear guard of *Panzer Division 116.*

The rear guard opposing the 39th Infantry, composed of elements of *Panzeraufklärungs Abteilung 116,* was already under pressure before Lieutenant Colonel Bond's men began their assault. Earlier that morning, the northern flank of *Panzer Division 116* was placed in serious jeopardy when the 28th Infantry Division captured Sourdeval. To avoid being decisively engaged by the 28th, *Panzeraufklärungs Abteilung 116* began moving southeast. However, forward observers from the 26th FA Battalion spotted the retreating Germans.[7]

Pinned down by American shelling, *Panzeraufklärungs Abteilung 116* was alarmed to discover that the 39th Infantry was steadily approaching from the west. Disregarding mounting casualties, the Germans resumed their retreat. Although the 39th Infantry had seized all of its assigned objectives, Lieutenant Colonel Bond was not ordered by division headquarters to pursue the departing Germans.

Few German units, however, found themselves in such a serious predicament on 12 August. The precautions they had taken to prevent premature discovery of their retreat paid off during the night of 11 August. Lieutenant Colonel Walter Johnson's 117th Infantry noted that "all night long there was a lot of harassing fire, burp gunners, no changes in the people opposing us."[8] When the 120th Infantry reported that a patrol had gone out but did not spot any Germans, division headquarters replied, "Check on that and see how far they went."[9] For the most part, the heavy shelling confused the Americans as to the intentions of *Panzer Gruppe Eberbach.* When the 30th Division command post was informed that vehicular traffic could be heard, the G-2 abruptly dismissed it as either resupply activity or reinforcements.

As dawn broke, the 30th Division reported to VII Corps that there were "no indications of enemy withdrawal; heavy traffic heard to our front last night. Interdiction fires placed on all routes."[10] Although *XLVII Panzer Korps* slipped away undetected, the American artillery fire resulted in casualties and delays. The most significant impact was the fact that *SS-Panzer Division 2* had been prevented from departing on time. With *Das Reich* behind schedule, *Kampfgruppe Fick* would be forced to wait until daylight before moving east.

Although the 119th Infantry noticed the activity within German lines, it did not lead Colonel Sutherland to automatically conclude that a retreat was taking place. However, Major General Hobbs instructed him to send out a platoon from L Company on a circuitous route to gain more information on likely German intentions. Hobbs explained that he wanted the platoon to determine the validity of "reports from left and right [that] indicate a general enemy withdrawal. Purpose of your movement by patrol is to penetrate deeper and see how far the enemy has withdrawn."[11]

The patrol quickly ran into strong resistance. *Leibstandarte* artillery observers directed high-explosive at the Americans as soon as they moved out, wounding two men. Lieutenant Colonel Brown ordered L Company to hold up the patrol rather than expose the men to unnecessary casualties. More incoming artillery fire was received, sending shrapnel and earth flying into the air across the entire battalion sector. P-47s from the 366th Fighter Group tried to silence the German guns but were unsuccessful. The American fighters claimed one artillery piece destroyed by dive-bombing but lost one plane to intense light flak.[12] Pinned down by shelling, Lieutenant Colonel Brown's entire battalion was unable to move until 1515 hours, and by that time the Germans facing Colonel Sutherland's 119th Infantry had already departed.

Opposite *Leibstandarte,* the 12th Infantry prepared to resume its assault against RJ 278 at first light. It was quite apparent to Colonel Luckett, however, that something unusual was going on when the 12th Infantry was shelled repeatedly throughout the night of 11 August. One of the regimental staff officers exclaimed that the Germans were "getting rid of all their stocks of artillery and mortar shells by dumping them on us."[13] Observers from E Company also reported that they could see a great number of vehicles moving along the highway from RJ 278 toward the village of la Tournerie. According to the incredulous Americans, the German vehicles were lined up practically nose to tail.[14]

Forward observers with the 3d Battalion spotted movement within St.-Barthelemy as *Leibstandarte* began pulling out. Private Marc Dillard was sleeping next to his 81mm mortar when the telephone rang softly. When he answered, his company commander told the mortar platoon to fire a cloverleaf on the village (a cloverleaf consisted of a pattern of 108 rounds laid systematically across an area target). Dillard could not believe what he heard. Mortars were normally not fired at night because sparks from the propellant charges left a visible trail skyward. Even though the Germans might miss seeing a few shells, they could not fail to identify the source of a sustained mortar barrage. All six 81mm tubes opened fire soon afterward, sending the cloverleaf raining down on St.-Barthelemy.

Soon after the barrage ended, the mortar crews heard a low "poof" in the distance followed by the express train screech of a shell rushing toward them. The Americans dove into their foxholes to escape the blast. A large-caliber shell landed one field away, and the explosion was so violent that Dillard thought the shell came from a railroad gun. Moments later, it seemed as if the Germans simultaneously opened fire with artillery, mortars, and *Nebelwerfers,* all aimed at their tiny field. Several of the new replacements began to crack up under the pressure as they waited for the inevitable direct hit. During a lull in the shelling, the mortar platoon rapidly relocated to a safer spot.[15]

At 0800 hours, the 12th Infantry launched another assault on RJ 278. Colonel Luckett directed the 2d Battalion to hold in place while the 1st Battalion advanced. Pushing westward with all three companies on line, the 1/12th halted temporarily when it encountered rear guard panzers left behind by *Leibstandarte*. When the 2/12th began advancing, a single Panther briefly delayed it, but bazooka teams succeeded in knocking out the German vehicle. With the surviving panzers in retreat, Lieutenant Colonel Jackson's 1st Battalion reached its objective at 1023 hours, followed by the 2d Battalion at 1101 hours. Setting up a defensive perimeter with B Company oriented to the north and A Company defending to the east, the soldiers of the 1/12th prepared to defend their gains. The 2d Battalion established positions on line with the 1st Battalion, pivoting slightly to the southeast to protect the northern flank of their neighboring unit.[16]

As Colonel Luckett's regiment consolidated its positions, patrols from the 1st Battalion headed south to make contact with TF 3. The Germans defending the crossroads had departed before daylight, and sensing that his objective was free for the taking, Lieutenant Colonel Hogan walked to RJ 278, accompanied by Sergeant Emmett Tripp. The pair crossed a field littered with the scorched hulks of tanks belonging to 3/33d Armor.[17] Numerous German bodies lay scattered about, victims of American artillery.

Glancing around, Lieutenant Colonel Hogan was unable to pinpoint the source of the deadly antitank fire that had savaged the ranks of TF 3. His battalion had lost fourteen medium tanks, two M-5 light tanks, one M-10 tank destroyer, three armored cars, one M-8 assault gun, three half-tracks, and six jeeps trying to capture RJ 278. The 2/119th Infantry also had suffered heavily. When the personnel casualties were totaled, TF 3 lost 26 killed, 142 wounded, and 64 missing.[18]

The 117th Infantry completed its preparations for an assault against St.-Barthelemy just prior to RJ 278 being secured. In order to avoid German artillery, Lieutenant Colonel Johnson directed the 3/12th and 1/117th Infantry to infiltrate forward in small groups. When the attack began, the 117th reported to division headquarters that "our units are moving up gradually, they are meeting some mortar and light small arms fire. This opposition seems to constitute a rear guard action."[19]

Despite waning resistance, Major Lindner still found it necessary to personally lead his battalion's advance. When his rifle company commanders reported that their men were unwilling to attack, Lindner took matters into his own hands. Climbing over a hedgerow marking the front lines, the commander of the 3/12th Infantry began slowly walking toward St.-Barthelemy. After he had gone about a hundred yards, he glanced behind to see that his rifle companies were also following him.[20]

The Germans did not leave St.-Barthelemy undefended. Bazooka teams knocked out two panzers barring the 3d Battalion's entry into the village. *Leib-*

standarte engineers had also left behind mines and trip-wired explosives to slow their pursuit. Despite the numerous obstacles, the 1/117th Infantry recaptured the crossroads of la Foutelaye at 1320 hours, and St.-Barthelemy fell to the 3/12th by 1410 hours. As his men took up positions around the shattered village, Lindner instructed his antitank platoon to simulate the movement of tanks by driving a half-track through the streets of St.-Barthelemy. He hoped the ruse would convince the Germans that the village was strongly held, thus discouraging any thoughts of counterattack.

Lieutenant Colonel Walter Johnson visited St.-Barthelemy as soon as Lindner reported that it was secure, counting at least thirty abandoned Panthers and Pzkfw IVs in the vicinity of the village.[21] As he walked through the town, he was greeted by the sight of a disheveled American soldier cautiously emerging from the basement of a ruined hotel. Glancing around, the man shouted down into the basement that help had arrived. Between sixty and eighty wounded, all of whom had been hit during the fighting on 7 August, were sheltering in the hotel. Captured medics from 1/117th Infantry and B/823d TD had cared for them throughout the course of the ensuing battle. After inspecting the makeshift aid station, Lieutenant Colonel Johnson ordered ambulances brought forward to evacuate the wounded as soon as the roads were cleared of mines.

The German troops defending Mortain had less success in breaking contact with the Americans before daylight. As dawn arrived, Lieutenant Robert Weiss watched with unbelieving eyes as heavily camouflaged vehicles emerged from cover in a swirl of diesel smoke and dust. Tanks, accompanied by foot troops and trucks, crowded each other as they headed east along the Bel Air road. Weiss's initial call for fire against this lucrative target was transmitted at 0655 hours, followed by others too numerous to capture individually in the 230th FA Battalion journal.

Based on the information provided by Lieutenant Weiss, Brigadier General James M. Lewis, commander of the 30th Infantry Division's artillery, decided to reinforce the 230th FA with five other field artillery battalions. The resultant deluge of high-explosive forced many Germans to abandon their vehicles as the retreating column stalled, and small groups of *SS* were seen making their way through the fields bordering the road. Despite the incessant shelling, *Kampfgruppe Fick* succeeded in pulling out that morning. The cost to the retreating Germans, however, was considerable. Catching sight of the smoking hulks lining the route later that day, Colonel Birks estimated that artillery fire alone had destroyed fifty to one hundred vehicles during the morning of 12 August.[22]

As *Das Reich* completed disengaging from Mortain, the 320th Infantry readied itself for a final push on Hill 314. Lieutenant Colonel Northam's 3d Battalion, trailed by the battered 1st Battalion, began advancing at 0625 hours. Both battalion commanders found themselves somewhat shorthanded. The 1/320th still lacked the group led by Lieutenant Hank Morgan, who did succeed in leading three officers and thirty-five men to safely, reaching the 3/137th Infantry by

The pair of knocked-out American medium tanks that blocked the relief supplies bound for Hill 314 on 12 August 1944. The nearest vehicle has been pushed out of the center of the road by a bulldozer. (National Archives)

0500 hours that morning. The confused situation during the night of 11 August had eroded Northam's available combat power, and the 3d Battalion could only muster two understrength rifle companies for the assault on Hill 314.

Colonel Byrne had hoped to commit the 2/320th Infantry in support of his leading echelon, but a patrol reported the presence of several armored vehicles moving along a road between the 2d Battalion and the rest of the regiment.[23] However, he did spare his men from carrying supplies to Hill 314. Rather than allocate riflemen to transport food and medicine to the isolated battalion, Byrne asked the 35th Quartermaster Company to provide a truck to bring food, medical supplies, and ammunition forward. When the commander of the quartermaster unit asked for volunteers, almost every man in the company stepped forward. Corporal Verlin Young and T-5 Hans Gehlen were chosen.

Reporting to the 320th Infantry's command post, the truck drivers were personally briefed by Colonel Byrne. In addition to transporting supplies to Hill 314, he instructed Corporal Young to remain on Hill 314 until his vehicle could be loaded with wounded. Once that task was complete, the truck would transport the wounded to the regiment's aid station. Byrne also arranged for three M5 light tanks from F Company, 4th Cavalry Squadron, to escort the truck.

The 320th Infantry began moving toward Hill 314 as the relief convoy was being organized. The 3d Battalion advanced uphill until Company I unexpectedly encountered la Petit Chapel. Puzzled by the stone chapel, which was not marked on his map, Lieutenant Colonel Northam instructed Lieutenant Homer Kurtz to verify their exact location. Kurtz led a patrol forward, dodging fallen trees and dead Germans. As the first man stepped cautiously into a clearing, he heard a voice shout, "Don't shoot, they're Yanks."[24] The 3/320th made contact with G/120th Infantry at 0830 hours on 12 August.

Once Colonel Byrne was informed that Northam had reached the 2/120th Infantry, he ordered the relief column to depart for Hill 314. The four vehicles departed at 0845 hours, traveling along the road used during the attack on 10 August. The convoy was nearing la Croix des Sept Coeurs when further progress was blocked by the hulks of two destroyed Sherman tanks. The truck was delayed for several hours as it waited for a bulldozer to open a path through the hedgerows bordering the wrecked tanks.

Bypassing the panzers that blocked its path to Hill 314, the 2/320th Infantry advanced to the east. By 1025 hours, Colonel Byrne's entire regiment was situated atop the commanding heights, and any lingering concern that the Germans might counterattack dissipated as additional troops arrived. The soldiers who had been surrounded for the past five days were happy to have been relieved, although a perhaps more welcome sight than the 320th Infantry was the first 2-1/2 ton truck loaded with supplies. After waiting for a bulldozer to clear the route, the truck arrived atop Hill 314 at 1105 hours.[25] Medics carried twenty wounded men onto the vehicle after unloading the supplies, while the most seriously wounded awaited the arrival of ambulances. Lieutenant Kerley also turned over eight captive SS men to the 320th.

The 1/119th Infantry began advancing toward Hill 314 at dawn intent on relieving the 2/120th Infantry. During the previous night, however, the 30th Division's chief of staff stated, "I want Mortain demolished . . . hammer that all night, burn it up so nothing can live in there."[26] Up until that point, the town had been spared to avoid inflicting casualties on Americans hiding there. Freed from these restrictions, Mortain was transformed into a wasteland overnight. Major Herlong's leading elements had reached the outskirts of town by 1000 hours, but delayed by rubbled streets the 1st Battalion was unable to link up with the 2/120th until 1159 hours.

The deluge of shells descending on Mortain during the previous night had fortuitously missed the last survivors of 2/120th Infantry hiding in the town. Lieutenants Irby and Hagen, T-4 Forrest Hodges, and two men from Lieutenant Miller's TD platoon remained in hiding in a hayloft throughout the night, climbing down only after they heard voices speaking English.[27] Hodges looked out a hole in the roof to see an infantry squad walk by the barn, and the men clambered down a ladder to emerge into the sunlight where they immediately noticed Colonel Birks. Hagen, Irby, and Hodges, elated to see their regimental commander, unashamedly hugged Birks in the middle of the street.[28]

When VII Corps learned that the 2d Battalion had been relieved, Major General Collins ordered the 35th Division to continue moving east in an effort to regain contact with the retreating Germans. The 320th Infantry was instructed by Major General Baade to turn over responsibility for defending Hill 314 to the 1/119th. Colonel Byrne directed the 3d Battalion to push eastward, trailed by Major Gillis's 1/320th Infantry.[29] Lieutenant Colonel Northam ordered Lieutenant Curtis Alloway's K Company to lead his battalion's advance.

With the 1st Platoon in the lead, the American rifle company made its way down the eastern slope of Hill 314 before unexpectedly encountering some SS troops moving along a sunken road. The ensuing fight came as a surprise to both sides; however, the Germans rapidly recovered from their initial shock. Maneuvering machine-gun teams to either flank of K Company, they succeeded in isolating the 1st Platoon from the rest of Lieutenant Alloway's company. When a quick survey disclosed that the isolated platoon had only a few rounds of ammunition left, the Americans had little choice but to surrender. Thirty-five men marched into captivity.[30] Colonel Byrne ordered Northam to halt rather than suffer additional losses.

The 134th Infantry to the south had jumped off at 0700 hours intent on seizing the high ground east of the Mortain-Barenton road. Colonel Emery's 137th Infantry, operating to the south of Colonel Miltonberger's regiment, also began its advance early that morning. The commander of the 3/134th Infantry, still attached to the 137th Infantry, sent out a rifle platoon prior to dawn to determine if the Germans were preparing to contest his advance. Lieutenant Colonel Robert Moore instructed the platoon to return upon meeting resistance but if no SS were encountered, to continue on to the final objective. After a few tense hours, the platoon reported that they had made it to the objective without meeting any Germans, and the remainder of the 3d Battalion followed at first light.[31]

Colonel Miltonberger's 134th Infantry met little or no resistance as it began moving east and by 0855 hours had reached its initial objectives just west of the Mortain-Barenton road.[32] Pausing to reorganize, the regiment surged across the Mortain-Barenton road at 1230 hours. The 1st Battalion led the assault, trailed by the 2d Battalion. Colonel Miltonberger intended to secure his final objective, a string of hills located two thousand yards to the east, before nightfall.

The 1st Battalion was delayed for thirty minutes while bazooka teams maneuvered to destroy a dug-in German tank blocking its advance. Knocking out the panzer, the 1/134th resumed its advance only to encounter a heavily defended stronghold. When the 2d Battalion attempted to bypass the dug-in Germans to the south, it was embroiled in a firefight. For the remainder of 12 August, the 134th Infantry fruitlessly probed for a weak spot in the German line, and at nightfall Colonel Miltonberger finally called off the attack. New orders had just arrived from division headquarters: the 35th Division was going to rejoin Patton's Third Army.

Colonel Emery's 137th Infantry was also involved in sharp fighting on 12 August. Against light resistance, both the 1st and 2d Battalions as well as 3/134th Infantry were able to gain their initial objectives. At 0825 hours, the 1st Battalion overwhelmed a small German force, and by 1300 hours, Emery's regiment progressed to a point where the forward elements could observe American planes bombing German units retreating from Mortain. However, the 137th Infantry began encountering stiffening resistance in the form of artillery and mortar fire. When orders arrived reattaching the regiment to its parent division, Colonel Emery called off the attack in preparation for a relief in place with the 4th Infantry Division later that evening.

The 35th Division was ordered by VII Corps to turn over its sector to the 30th and 4th Divisions during the night of 12 August. The 320th Infantry, located slightly east of Hill 314, was directed to conduct a relief in place with the 119th Infantry. Colonel Sutherland's regiment would be shifted south of Mortain when the 9th Division extended its lines south of the See River. On the morning of 13 August, the 35th Division would leave to rejoin the Third Army.

Although the Germans continued to contest the Americans in the Barenton sector, *LVIII Panzer Korps* was also preparing to pull back according to plan. *Brigadeführer* Heinz Harmel's *SS-Panzer Division 10* had already begun stepping up activities in an effort to shield the withdrawal of *Panzer Gruppe Eberbach,* launching an attack at 0130 hours on 12 August against the left flank of 3/41st AIR. The Germans also massed a number of machine guns and mortars against 1/41st AIR, prompting Lieutenant Colonel Marty Morin to report that his "entire position [was] under fire."[33] Taking advantage of the prolific covering fire, the Germans infiltrated several small groups into the 1/41st AIR's defensive perimeter where they opened fire at point-blank range on the dug-in Americans, causing considerable anxiety but few casualties. The attacking *SS* faded away before the sun rose.

The initiative was passed to the 2d Armored Division once air support could make its presence felt with the coming of daylight. Major General Brooks ordered CCB to cut the Mortain-Ger road, while Combat Command R (CCR) would assume responsibility for the defense of Barenton. The advance began at 1100 hours, with CCB's armored infantry spearheading the thrust.[34] The 1/41st AIR, supported by the medium tanks of I/67th Armor (-), a platoon of light tanks from C Company, as well as the assault guns and mortars from 3/67th Armor, attacked on the right with 3/41st AIR moving on the left. Since the 3/41st AIR was advancing over much rougher ground, it was accompanied by a single platoon of medium tanks. However, the 3/67th Armor also provided covering fire for the attacking armored infantry from commanding positions along the line of departure.

The American assault bogged down when *SS-Panzer Division 10* launched a series of counterattacks against the left flank and rear of 3/41st AIR. *Brigadeführer* Harmel had committed *I Abteilung, SS-Panzer Artillerie Regiment 10,* and *III/SS-Panzergrenadier Regiment 21*, along with his few remaining panzers, to fend off this latest effort by CCB. In response, Colonel Paul Disney ordered a platoon of G/67th Armor forward to reinforce 3/41st AIR.

The 3d Battalion soon required the support of a second platoon of reinforcing medium tanks, which were attached to I Company. The commander of Company I was instructed to make an assault around the flank of H/41st AIR, accompanied by the platoon of tanks, with the intent of securing the villages of la Conerie and la Boucharie near the Mortain-Ger highway. Company I gained a few hundred yards, but stubborn resistance halted the Americans short of their intended objective.[35]

Realizing that CCB was not going to make any significant progress before nightfall, Major General Brooks ordered it to establish hasty defensive positions. As the American armored infantry began digging in, the 3d Battalion sent out a platoon from H Company, commanded by Lieutenant Roy Green, to locate any Germans in the immediate vicinity of the battalion perimeter. When he failed to discover any SS troops, his orders were amended. Green, reinforced with a section of heavy machine guns and four M-10s from the 702d TD Battalion, was instructed to establish a roadblock protecting the 3/41st AIR from surprise attack.

At 1830 hours, Green detected a German force forming up for a counterattack against the 3d Battalion. He radioed for artillery, breaking up the assault before it could be launched. When the troops from *SS-Panzer Division 10* tried to reorganize, Lieutenant Green called in another artillery barrage, and the SS lost twenty to thirty vehicles, two artillery pieces, and a complete flak battery to the indirect fire. His platoon also took eight prisoners when it swept the area after the SS unit finally retreated.[36]

The abortive counterattack marked the final efforts of *SS-Panzer Division 10* in the Barenton sector, and during the night of 12 August, *Brigadeführer* Harmel supervised his division's retreat. *SS-Panzer Division 10* pulled back until it linked up with *Kampfgruppe Fick*, occupying a line running from east of Hill 314 through the village of la Boisonnieres (eight kilometers east of St.-Georges-de-Rouelle) to a point east of Lonlay L'Abbaye. Although Harmel's panzer division had suffered serious losses over the past few days, it still numbered approximately ten thousand men, and the number of operational panzers in *SS-Panzer Division 10* actually increased from eight to fourteen as vehicles were repaired by the divisional workshops. Available fire support numbered twenty-five artillery pieces and eleven antiaircraft guns.[37]

By the evening of 12 August, the Americans finally realized that *Panzer Gruppe Eberbach* had retreated from Mortain, belatedly recognizing that the Germans had shifted their attention from regaining Avranches to protecting their southern flank against Patton's Third Army. A British intelligence assessment accurately concluded that the panzers withdrawn from Mortain "have hard fights ahead of them. They must first contact the American threat to the left flank . . . then make quite sure of FALAISE, which is vital as an escape route now that axes running SE are denied, and finally protect the infantry while it footslogs back eastward across the tributaries of the Upper Orne [River]."[38]

With the threat to Avranches averted, the Americans redoubled their efforts

American soldiers examine the ruins of Mortain after the town was recaptured. Most of the damage was inflicted by the 30th Infantry Division artillery during the night of 11–12 August 1944. (National Archives)

to defeat Hausser's *7 Armee*. First Army issued orders for XIX Corps to take over the sector between Sourdeval and Mayenne. XIX Corps, composed of the 2d Armored Division and the 28th and 30th Infantry Divisions, was instructed to secure the road junctions of Ger and Domfront. Major General Leonard Gerow's V Corps, consisting of the 2d and the 29th Infantry Divisions, took over the VII Corps sector between Vire and Mortain, freeing it up for a move further south. Gerow also had the mission of securing the crossroads town of Tinchebray.

Major General Collins's VII Corps, consisting of the 3d Armored Division as well as the 1st, 4th, and 9th Infantry Divisions, was ordered to assemble near Mayenne. His primary objective was the road junction of la Ferte Mace, located on high ground northwest of Carrouges. The 3d Armored, accompanied by the 1st Division, would spearhead the assault. Major General Barton's 4th Division, situated on the left flank of VII Corps, would maintain contact with XIX Corps, while the 9th Division trailed in support of the leading elements.[39] Collins scheduled the attack for 0630 hours on 13 August.

While the First Army was maintaining pressure from the west, Third Army continued to support the northward drive by XV Corps. Patton's first priority was the destruction of the German forces north of Alencon. Never one to miss a golden opportunity, he exceeded his orders from 12th Army Group by directing Major General Haislip to push slowly in the direction of Falaise as soon as

Argentan was secured. Patton did not believe that Montgomery would move fast enough to trap the retreating Germans, and the capture of Falaise by Third Army would deny the Germans an opportunity to escape to the east. Upon securing Falaise, XV Corps would continue advancing until it contacted the British and Canadians. Patton directed XX Corps to protect the left flank of XV Corps, while XII Corps secured Haislip's right flank.[40]

As Third Army continued moving north, the Canadian First Army was preparing to unleash yet another offensive against *Panzerarmee 5*. General Montgomery had ordered the Canadians to continue their efforts to capture Falaise and proceed from there to Argentan. He projected a linkup between the Canadians and Americans just south of Argentan, which would complete a literal encirclement of the Germans. The offensive, code-named Operation TRACTABLE, would begin with a massive aerial effort concentrated against *SS-Panzer Korps I*. Once the heavy bombers departed, two Canadian divisions (one armored and one infantry) would advance on Falaise.

While the Canadians completed preparations for their new offensive, von Kluge's plans to prevent the noose from tightening around his troops began to go awry on 12 August. *Panzer Gruppe Eberbach* encountered Major General Haislip's XV Corps as the panzers were heading for their new assembly areas. Eberbach was one of the first German generals to realize that the Americans were moving north much faster than anyone had anticipated. In preparation for the counterattack, he decided to visit *General der Panzertruppen* Kuntzen's *LXXXI Armee Korps* command post that afternoon. Eberbach wanted to personally impress upon Kuntzen that he was depending on *Panzer Division 9* to protect the *Panzer Gruppe Eberbach* assembly areas from an American surprise attack.

Narrowly avoiding Allied fighter-bombers, *General der Panzertruppen* Eberbach arrived at Kuntzen's command post at noon. *General der Panzertruppen* Kuntzen began the meeting on a positive note, remarking that he was fully prepared to provide whatever support Eberbach required. However, he noted that *Panzer Division 9* had been significantly weakened by casualties during the recent fighting, and it still lacked its Panther battalion, which had not yet arrived from southern France. With *Panzer Division 9* facing at least one complete American armored division, Kuntzen doubted that it would be able to hold out for much longer. He also admitted that he did not expect good news from any of the other divisions in *LXXXI Armee Korps*.

Late in the afternoon, *Panzer Division 9* reported that American tanks had broken through its defenses, and its surviving elements were trying to reassemble at the edge of the woods north of Alencon. *General der Panzertruppen* Kuntzen ordered his staff to prepare for an immediate departure, but it was already too late. Tank fire could be heard nearby, and artillery began exploding among the headquarters motor park, where staff cars and radio vans were bursting into flames. Although both of the German generals decided to stay put rather than attract attention trying to escape, Eberbach instructed one of his liaison officers to take new orders to *Panzer Division 116*. Instead of participating in the counterattack, *Oberst* Muller's division would block any threat to the *Panzer Gruppe Eberbach* assembly areas north of Foret d'Ecouves.[41]

At nightfall, Eberbach was finally able to escape from the *LXXXI Armee Korps* command post. Returning to his own headquarters, he telephoned von Kluge to obtain permission to assume command of *Panzer Division 9* and *Infanterie Division 708*. Assisted by *Panzer Division 116*, both of these divisions would be employed to defend assembly areas occupied by *Panzer Division 2* and *Leibstandarte*. Von Kluge also modified the plan to accommodate the changing situation. Instead of advancing along a southerly axis aimed at Le Mans, the counterattack would follow an eastward path headed toward the left flank of XV Corps.

LXXXI Armee Korps was shifted east to protect the deep southern flank of *Heersgruppe B*. Although it had given up two divisions to *Panzer Gruppe Eberbach*, in return Kuntzen received *Infanterie Division 331, SS-Panzergrenadier Division 17, Infanterie Division 352,* and a newly arrived parachute infantry regiment. Kuntzen was now responsible for protecting a 100-mile front stretching between Gace-Dreux-Chartres.[42]

Eberbach's absence for most of 12 August, however, contributed significantly to a growing confusion within the German ranks. *Generalleutnant* von Luettwitz, traveling with a portion of his headquarters, arrived at a small wooded area near Carrouges hoping to coordinate his division's operations with the staff of *Panzer Gruppe Eberbach*. Although he arrived at midnight on 12 August, von Luettwitz was unable to contact Eberbach's headquarters until 0900 the following morning. When the linkup finally took place, the staff of *Panzer Gruppe Eberbach* was unable to provide him with any useful information.

Von Luettwitz did not have any good news to pass on to Eberbach's staff. *Panzer Division 2* was forced to halt its movement after traveling only a relatively short distance, and his subordinate commanders reported significant delays due to traffic jams. Consequently, *Panzer Division 2* would not arrive at Carrouges before the morning of 14 August. A short while later, Allied reconnaissance elements surrounded the division's command post, and several German commanders were killed or captured making their way to headquarters. Fortunately for von Luettwitz, his immediate staff was able to escape undetected with the onset of darkness.

Eberbach gained little from the fact that *Panzer Division 116* was not severely impeded by traffic. Unaware of the progress made by XV Corps, the *Panzergrenadier Regiment 156* command group unexpectedly collided with a column from the 2d French Armored Division. The regimental commander, *Oberst* Otto Fischer, was wounded and taken prisoner.[43] Two panzergrenadier battalions were also caught in an assembly area by Allied armor. In addition to the significant losses suffered by *Panzergrenadier Regiment 156*, the commander of *Panzer Regiment 16* was severely wounded by American tanks near the village of Mortree.[44]

The unit history of the 5th Armored Division recorded "the mass movement of German vehicles grinding along every passable road . . . many of these clanking enemy columns crashed into the Fifth Armored roadblocks and were destroyed or captured." Claims by the 5th Armored on 12 August alone totaled 301 Germans killed and 362 captured. Additionally, seventy panzers and half-tracks, two armored cars, seven artillery pieces, and eighty-eight wheeled vehicles were knocked out.[45]

Both *Panzer Division 2* and *Panzer Division 116* lost a number of key personnel in these unexpected encounters with Allied armored columns. With their chain of command disrupted, both divisions were unable to coordinate an effective response against XV Corps, and the fighting quickly degenerated into a series of uneven clashes involving isolated German companies and battalions. The poor logistical situation also grew worse with panzers constantly on the move as each division headquarters tried to reassemble scattered subordinate units.

There was at least one bright spot in the dismal situation. On the evening of 12 August, the chief of staff of *Panzer Division 116* intercepted a road-bound column of twenty-five to thirty tanks. The Panthers, which belonged to *Panzer Division 9,* had arrived only the previous day after many delays en route. Commandeering the unit, *Panzer Division 116* placed them under the command of *Rittmeister* Fritz Scholz. During the early morning of 13 August, *Panzer Pioniere Abteilung 675* and *Flak Abteilung 98* were dispatched to reinforce the Panthers, and the newly designated *Kampfgruppe Scholz* was tasked with the defense of Argentan.[46]

The main routes connecting Falaise to Le Mans and Vire with Paris converged at Argentan, which meant that the city represented the only viable escape route for *7 Armee* units that were still located west of the Orne River. Acutely aware of the fact that Argentan was only thirteen miles from Falaise, Eberbach was prepared to immediately commit *SS-Panzer Division 1* and *Panzer Division 2* against XV Corps. If the Allies succeeded in rapidly securing Argentan and Falaise, both *Panzerarmee 5* and *7 Armee* would find themselves completely encircled.

Sepp Dietrich also recognized the impending danger of encirclement. On 13 August, he warned von Kluge that "if every effort is not made to move the forces toward the east and out of the threatened encirclement, the army group will have to write off both armies . . . therefore, immediate measures are necessary to move to the east before such movement is definitely too late. It will soon be possible for the enemy to fire into the pocket with artillery from all sides."[47]

Although XV Corps was capable of moving on Falaise, Bradley was reluctant to order Patton to continue moving north. He was not sure that the effort would produce worthwhile results since intelligence reports indicated that most of the German units west of the Orne River had already pulled out.[48] The slight opposition encountered by Hodges's First Army seemingly reinforced this mistaken belief. Along the entire First Army front, the American advance was rapid, characterized by light casualties and few prisoners. In the V Corps sector, the 2d and 29th Infantry Divisions seized Tinchebray by 15 August. Although Major

General Gerow's troops advanced rapidly, only twelve hundred Germans were taken captive. XIX Corps also launched a successful drive toward Domfront, seizing the city on 14 August, but only a few Germans were taken prisoner by the victorious Americans.

VII Corps advanced twenty miles against light resistance until *LVIII Panzer Korps* held it up at Ranes. *General der Panzertruppen* Krueger was carrying out orders from Eberbach to defend the approaches to Argentan and Flers. During the resultant fighting, VII Corps claimed thirty-three hundred prisoners and a considerable amount of destroyed equipment. By 15 August, the British Second Army crossed paths with the American First Army near Flers. The British pivoted to the east, assuming responsibility for a portion of the American sector. First Army and the British Second Army, pressing from the west, had been assigned the mission of herding the Germans westward, where they would encounter the Canadian First Army and Patton's Third Army. If the Germans succeeded in escaping encirclement, General Montgomery planned to send Patton farther east to the Seine River.[49]

Conforming to Montgomery's intent, Patton issued new orders to Third Army on 13 August. Rather than employ Walker's XX Corps to protect the left flank of Haislip's XV Corps, he shifted it to the east. The new mission of XX Corps was to secure the city of Dreux, after which it would be prepared for further advance to the north, northeast, or east. The 80th Infantry Division would remain behind to close the gap between XV Corps and First Army. XII Corps was instructed to concentrate southeast of Le Mans, preparing to advance further to the north, northeast, and east. Patton's previous instructions authorizing an advance to Falaise were countermanded, and XV Corps was directed instead to assemble in the vicinity of Argentan.[50]

Patton visited Haislip's command post soon afterward to provide additional guidance. As a result of this meeting, Major General Haislip directed the 5th Armored Division to "prevent German use of the roads leading east from Argentan without becoming involved in a serious fight for the town, and with cutting roads leading out of Gace to the east." He also ordered the French 2d Armored Division to break contact south of Foret d'Ecouves, moving to the east toward Argentan. After relieving the French, the 90th Infantry Division was to occupy the high ground west of the forest between Alencon and Carrouges, while the 79th Division would remain in corps reserve.[51]

During the morning of 13 August, the 5th Armored probed the defenses of Argentan, and CCA's Task Force Bartel moved into positions southwest of the city at 0700 hours. Cloaked by thick fog, Task Force Bartel reached its line of departure just as the fog suddenly lifted, exposing the Americans. The Panthers of *Kampfgruppe Scholz*, situated on high ground overlooking them, quickly opened fire. Within moments, seven Sherman tanks were destroyed, and Lieutenant Colonel Bartel was wounded when his half-track was knocked out. Return fire had little effect on the panzers.[52] When CCR, 5th Armored, attempted to seize the town of Gace to the east, it was repulsed by *Infanterie Division 331.*

While it may have appeared to von Kluge that the southern flank of *7 Armee* was temporarily stabilized, the Canadians shattered any illusions he may have had about salvaging the situation. Saturation bombing in support of Operation TRACTABLE occurred during the midafternoon of 14 August, and soon afterward the Canadians launched a massive armored assault against *Panzerarmee 5.*

Just prior to the Canadian onslaught, von Kluge received an order from Hitler directing *Panzer Gruppe Eberbach* to launch a counterattack against the American XV Corps in the Carrouges-Alencon area and to employ *SS-Panzer Division 9, SS-Panzer Division 10,* and *Panzer Division 21* for the assault. In order to free up these units, Hitler approved a limited retreat west of Flers. He also proclaimed that "the destruction of the enemy near Alencon was the immediate *OB WEST* mission and that all further directives . . . would depend on the course of the battle there."[53]

Von Kluge telephoned *7 Armee* headquarters to direct Hausser to conduct a phased withdrawal to a new line just beyond Flers. Immediately upon concluding his conversation, he instructed Sepp Dietrich to transfer *SS-Panzer Korps II,* which consisted of *SS-Panzer Division 9* and *Panzer Division 21,* to *Panzer Gruppe Eberbach.* Later that afternoon, von Kluge departed *Heeresgruppe B* headquarters to personally oversee Dietrich's compliance with Hitler's latest orders. As he drove toward the *Panzerarmee 5* command post, he noticed that the roads were clogged with disheveled and dispirited troops.

When von Kluge arrived, Dietrich briefed him on the deteriorating situation. According to the commander of *Panzerarmee 5,* fuel and ammunition were critically short. The latest Canadian offensive already threatened to completely breach the defensive line of *SS-Panzer Korps I,* and he had given orders to send *Panzer Division 21* to seal off the threatened breakthrough. The situation confronting *7 Armee* was scarcely better. When von Kluge telephoned from Dietrich's command post for an update, Hausser informed him that *SS-Panzer Division 10* was fully involved in a rearguard action against American troops west of Domfront, while Harmel's division lacked sufficient fuel to participate in the counterattack directed by Hitler. Of the three panzer divisions, it seemed to von Kluge that only *SS-Panzer Division 9* was immediately available.

When Eberbach was informed that he would not receive the promised panzer divisions; he immediately ordered his troops to "pass to the defensive." He already believed that Allied air superiority, as well as shortages of replacement tanks, gasoline, and ammunition, would prevent the planned counterattack from achieving any sort of lasting success. Upon learning of his decision, von Kluge realized that the situation in Normandy had taken an extremely grim turn. If Dietrich could not hold the Canadians and Eberbach was unable to arrest the progress of Patton's Third Army, the only viable alternative was to move through the Argentan-Falaise gap to escape the threatened encirclement.[54]

Generalfeldmarschall von Kluge departed Dietrich's headquarters on the morning of 15 August with the intent of meeting Hausser and Eberbach. While visiting *Panzer Division 116*, Eberbach received a radio message asking him to meet von Kluge in Necy so he went there and waited in vain for von Kluge to appear. Eberbach finally drove back to his own headquarters. That night, he was summoned to the headquarters message center to answer an urgent radio call from *Heeresgruppe B*. It turned out that von Kluge's staff was trying to find out where the *Generalfeldmarschall* was. He had disappeared soon after leaving Dietrich's command.

Eberbach grew even more concerned when he received a second radio message from *OKW* in Berlin. *General der Panzertruppen* Eberbach was tersely instructed to "ascertain whereabouts KLUGE. Report results hourly."[55] The matter was not made any easier by the fact that von Kluge's son had been assigned as Eberbach's chief of staff. Von Kluge finally appeared at midnight, explaining that fighter-bombers had shot up his command vehicle as well as the two radio trucks accompanying him. Afterward, he had been caught up in the chaotic night-time traffic as he made his way to Eberbach's headquarters. Eberbach notified *Heeresgruppe B* that von Kluge was safe before sending him back to Le Roche Guyon in a borrowed staff car.

Soon after his return, von Kluge convened a meeting with Eberbach, Hausser, and von Funck to discuss the situation on the southern flank. All of the German generals unanimously agreed that a counterattack against the Americans, using panzer divisions that did not possess sufficient fuel or ammunition, was unthinkable and counseled *Generalfeldmarschall* von Kluge to evacuate the pocket before it was too late. He agreed but reminded them that he had to obtain permission to do so from Hitler and was not sure he would obtain approval for a retreat. Discussing the situation with the assembled officers, he remarked that "the people there [Berlin] lived in another world, without any idea of the actual situation here."[56]

Departing the meeting, *General der Panzertruppen* Eberbach could sense impending defeat. For the first time, he noticed, not only the Poles and the Alsatians but also Germans were deserting to the Allies. Eberbach was painfully aware that "a glance at the map was sure to suggest doubt even to the common soldiers whether he was commanded in a reasonable way. He had not time for thinking, but his feeling told him that this war could no longer be won. He felt himself betrayed. He no longer fought with a belief in victory and a reliance on his command but only from a soldier's pride and for fear of defeat. The sinking of the soldier's spirit was even more evident in the 'morale of the arms.' Some tanks were left standing without being blown up, MGs were thrown away, guns were left lying, and stragglers without arms were numerous. 'Catch lines' in the rear of the front had to be inaugurated. Even the SS was no exception to this rule. The 1. SS Pz Division has never before fought so miserably as at that time."[57]

The situation was steadily worsening for the Germans. By 15 August, the Canadians had finally succeeded in forcing an opening in Dietrich's defensive line along the boundary of *SS-Panzer Korps I* and *LXXXVI Armee Korps,* and their leading elements quickly reached the Dives River at Mezidon and St.-Pierre. Knowing that von Kluge would not be able to get Berlin to approve a limited withdrawal by *Panzerarmee 5,* Dietrich ordered his troops to retreat behind the Dives River.

By 16 August, the Allies had nearly surrounded *Panzerarmee 5,* portions of *7 Armee,* and *Panzer Gruppe Eberbach* within a pocket shaped like an elongated U lying on its side. Bounded by the towns of Fourches-Trun-Chambois-Sevigny-Montabard with the open end resting on the River Dives, this area was approximately forty miles in length and eleven to fifteen miles wide. Because the tract was relatively narrow in terms of width, there were very few places safe from incoming artillery fire within it. Von Kluge's planners had estimated that it would require four nights to evacuate all of the units within the sector.[58] Success, however, depended on the ability of the Germans to hold open the shoulders of the pocket while maintaining sufficient crossing points over the Dives River.

At 0200 hours on 16 August, von Kluge telephoned Berlin to inform Jodl that he would not be able to mount the counterattack against Le Mans previously ordered by Hitler because the panzers did not possess enough fuel and ammunition to conduct an offensive operation. Increasing numbers of inoperative armored fighting vehicles were being abandoned as maintenance units failed to locate the spare parts necessary to repair them, and even fully serviceable panzers were being left behind as they ran out of fuel. Additionally, he explained that two of the designated panzer divisions were decisively engaged against Allied troops. Given the rapidly declining effectiveness of the German armored force in Normandy, the most that von Kluge could hope for was a fighting withdrawal.

Generalfeldmarschall Jodl sympathized with von Kluge, agreeing that a withdrawal seemed unavoidable. However, he also remarked that the retreat only seemed possible if the counterattack ordered by Hitler was conducted. Von Kluge replied that "the troops cannot, are not able to, are not strong enough to defeat the enemy. It would be a fateful error to succumb to a hope that cannot be fulfilled, and no power in this world [can accomplish its will simply through] an order it may give. That is the situation."[59] Jodl promised to personally plead his case to Hitler.

Generalfeldmarschall von Kluge, convinced that authorization to retreat east of the Seine River would eventually arrive from Berlin, instructed his staff to prepare a withdrawal order for the following morning. When Hausser was informed of von Kluge's intentions, he immediately began making the necessary preparations. *General der Panzertruppen* Walter Kreuger's *LVIII Panzer Korps* was responsible for controlling the movement across the Orne River, while *LXXXIV Armee Korps,* which would be reinforced by *SS-Panzer Division 10,* was assigned the mission of covering the withdrawal of *7 Armee.* *SS-Panzer Division 2* was attached to *SS-Panzer Korps II* in order to support the withdrawal of *Panzerarmee 5.* The task facing *7 Armee,* however, was not as momentous as Hausser may have presumed. A number of German division commanders had already taken it upon themselves to send their support elements out of the pocket while the commander of *Panzer Lehr* was in the process of relocating his entire division to a new assembly area just west of Paris.

As one German participant noted, "the precipitate retreat of the remnants of *7 Armee* and *Panzerarmee 5* threw all [counterattack] plans in confusion. Before new decisions could be made and set in motion, they were overtaken by dramatic events."[60] In view of the rapidly deteriorating situation, Dietrich instructed *SS-Panzer Korps II* to conduct a daylight road march to an assembly area outside the pocket near Vimoutiers. Once it had arrived, *SS-Panzer Korps II* would begin preparing for a counterattack against the flank of the First Canadian Army. Although *SS-Panzer Divisionen 2* and *9* had to run a gauntlet of air attacks, they were able to safely reach their designated assembly areas.

As the Germans began preparing in earnest to retreat, General Montgomery instructed the First Canadian Army on 17 August to close the gap between the leading elements and Patton's Third Army to the south. He then telephoned General Bradley to suggest a new linkup point between the two armies. Rather than meeting south of Argentan as originally planned, Montgomery recommended a linkup point seven miles to the northeast, between Chambois and Trun. Bradley agreed, ordering General Patton to quickly make contact with the Canadians at Chambois. The Canadian 4th Armored and the Polish 1st Armored Divisions were directed to capture Chambois as soon as possible. Advancing on a line roughly parallel to the Dives River, the two divisions broke through the defenses of *SS-Panzer Korps I* to reach a point approximately two miles north of Trun as night fell.

In addition to linking up with the Canadians at Chambois, Patton was also in the process of extending his line farther to the east in order to snare the Germans attempting to escape. During a visit to the XV Corps command post on 15 August, he directed Haislip to seize the city of Dreux. As long as the Germans controlled the road network passing through it, they would be able to retreat to the east toward Paris. Haislip complied by sending half of XV Corps toward Dreux, taking over the mission assigned previously to Walker's XX Corps. Walker was subsequently ordered by Patton to change direction toward Chartres.

Executing his latest orders from Third Army, Haislip instructed the French 2d Armored Division to relieve the 5th Armored Division at Argentan, while the 90th Infantry Division was brought up from Alencon to protect the eastern flank of the French division. Hoping that the two divisions, reinforced by the 155mm guns of the corps artillery, would be able to halt the flow of German troops still moving east through Argentan, Haislip sent the 5th Armored and the 79th Infantry Divisions toward Dreux.

Early on 15 August, both American divisions began their advance, only to collide with columns from XX Corps. Although it was delayed by the inevitable traffic jams, the 79th Division closed in its assembly area west of Nogent-le-Roi during the morning of 16 August, remaining there for the rest of the day after establishing a bridgehead over the Eure River in the face of considerable resistance. That afternoon, the 5th Armored launched its assault on Dreux, securing the city by 1730 hours. Patton ordered XV Corps to continue advancing the following night. By noon on 18 August, the 79th Division occupied commanding terrain northeast of Langes, while the 5th Armored was concentrated at Breval, with elements holding the nearby high ground overlooking the Seine River.[61]

Since a considerable distance separated both halves of XV Corps, Haislip turned over his troops at Argentan to Major General Hugh Gaffey, Patton's chief of staff. Gaffey's command, designated as a provisional corps, consisted of the 90th Infantry Division, 80th Infantry Division (minus the 319th Infantry Regiment), 2d French Armored Division, 773d Tank Destroyer Battalion, and four battalions of corps artillery. Patton ordered Gaffey to "attack, take, and hold line Argentan-Trun as part of a pincer movement," although he only intended Gaffey to command the provisional corps until a replacement arrived from First Army. Bradley had revised the interarmy boundaries on 17 August, placing Argentan within its area of control.[62]

On 18 August, the German situation continued to deteriorate. The 4th Canadian Armored secured Trun, while advanced spearheads captured the village of St.-Lambert. The assault of the Polish 1st Armored also met with success. The Poles captured the high ground overlooking the main east-west route connecting Falaise with the interior of France, while elements of the divisional reconnaissance regiment approached to within a mile of Chambois. To the west, the British Second Army advancing from Falaise covered half of the distance to Argentan.

At 0900 hours on 18 August, Major General Leonard T. Gerow arrived at the command post of the provisional corps, at which time it was redesignated V Corps. As his first act of command, he postponed the attack on Chambois scheduled for 1000 hours, giving as his reason the fact that most of the supporting corps artillery had not yet arrived. Gerow also redesignated the high ground crowned by the village of le-Bourg–St.-Leonard as his new line of departure.

While waiting for additional artillery to arrive, Gerow revised the existing plan of attack to reflect a simultaneous assault by all three divisions. The French 2d Armored would act as the base unit for a double envelopment aimed at securing both Argentan and Chambois. Major General Horace L. McBride's 80th Infantry Division was directed to secure Argentan while simultaneously cutting the road linking Argentan with Trun, and Major General Raymond McLain's 90th Division was given the mission of seizing the high ground dominating Chambois. After securing his objective, McLain would wait for the Canadian First Army to secure the city.

Major General Gerow's initial attempt to grind down the southern shoulder of the Falaise gap achieved only mixed success. *Kampfgruppe Scholz* repulsed the attack of the 80th Division, and although the 90th Division gained some ground, it was prevented from securing all of its assigned objectives. Advancing cross-country, the Americans were able to sever the le-Bourg–St. Leonard–Chambois road before being halted by a desperate counterattack launched by *Panzer Division 116*. The 90th Division retook the ground it had lost within twenty-four hours.

The Americans were unaware that this counterattack represented virtually the last instance of coordinated offensive maneuver originating from within the pocket. *Panzer Gruppe Eberbach* had not been resupplied with fuel and ammunition for five days, and logistics columns dispatched by Eberbach for the purpose of gathering supplies from *Panzerarmee 5* met with consistent disappointment. Many supply columns arrived only to discover that supply depots had been destroyed by retreating German troops.

While the supply units searched for intact depots, they suffered losses to air attack, became hopelessly snarled in traffic jams, were overrun by American or French tanks, or were simply unable to relocate parent units upon their return. The Germans tried to offset the growing fuel shortage by abandoning damaged panzers and nonessential wheeled vehicles. As the shortages grew worse, fully serviceable wheeled vehicles, artillery pieces, and armored fighting vehicles were left behind, their crews forced to make their way on foot to the east. The combat effectiveness of panzer divisions within the pocket began to rapidly disintegrate as a result of fuel starvation and lack of spare parts.

Changes were also taking place within the German command structure in Normandy. On 18 August, *Generalfeldmarschall* Walter Model appeared at *OB West*, announcing that he had been appointed by Hitler to assume the dual functions of *Heeresgruppe B* commander and commander in chief *West*.[63] He informed the *OB West* staff that von Kluge had been recalled to Berlin for reasons of ill health. Von Kluge had been surprised by Model's appearance but quietly accepted his dismissal. He chose to avoid Hitler's wrath, however, by committing suicide before he returned to Berlin.

During the night of 18 August, the Germans resumed their efforts to escape encirclement by converging Allied forces. *Panzer Division 116* and *SS-Panzer Division 10* even formed a *Kampfgruppe* for the express purpose of spiriting the commander of *7 Armee* to safety.[64] The pocket enclosing the retreating Germans had been compressed to an area seven miles wide and six miles deep. Although many troops were already east of the intended juncture of the Allied pincers, approximately eighty thousand Germans remained within the sector. These included seven German infantry divisions, two parachute divisions, and elements of five panzer divisions.

The Germans faced the challenge of retreating across the Dives River after successfully crossing the Orne River, which would prove to be a much more difficult task. The entire pocket now lay within the effective range of Allied artillery, and American, Canadian, and Polish units occupied commanding terrain overlooking crossing points along the Dives River. Recognizing that command and control problems, exacerbated by an extremely poor supply situation, prevented him from

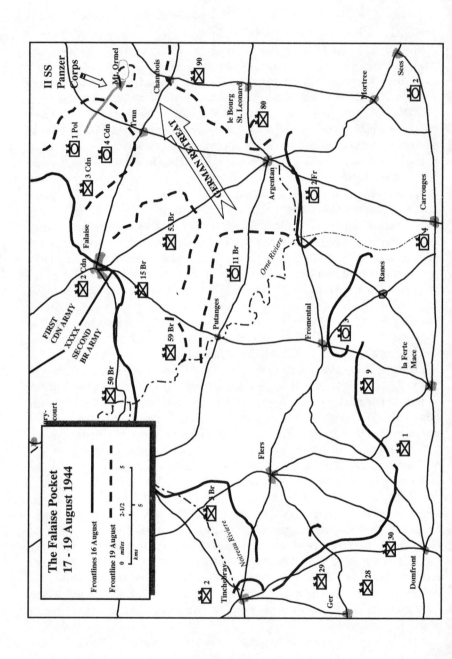

The Falaise Pocket
17 - 19 August 1944

Frontlines 16 August

Frontline 19 August

0   miles   2-1/2   5

0   kms   5

II SS Panzer Corps

Mt. Ormel

1 Pol

4 Cdn

Trun

3 Cdn

Falaise

Chambois

90

le Bourg St. Leonard

80

GERMAN RETREAT

Argentan

2 Fr

53 Br

11 Br

Orme Riviere

Mortree

Sees

2

Carrouges

4

Ranes

3

Fromental

9

la Ferte Mace

1

Flers

Putanges

59 Br

15 Br

2 Cdn

FIRST CDN ARMY

XXXX

SECOND BR ARMY

50 Br

....court

7 Br

Noireau Riviere

Tinchebray

2

Ger

29

28

30

Domfront

taking coordinated action, the commander of *LXXXIV Armee Korps* directed his troops to conduct "independent breakout by individual Kampfgruppen."[65]

Only a few of the remaining east-west roads would support the movement of mechanized units, and these routes converged on Chambois and St.-Lambert-sur-Dives. The latter was occupied on 18 August by a small detachment from the Canadian 29th Armored Reconnaissance Regiment. The Polish 1st Armored and the American 90th Infantry Divisions also succeeded in linking up in Chambois that afternoon.[66] A series of desperate counterattacks succeeded in pressing the Canadians back into a corner of the village, thus opening the way for German units seeking to escape the area. *Panzer Gruppe Eberbach,* however, was too weak to eject the Polish and Americans from Chambois. Eberbach decided to employ his remaining troops against the Canadians at St.-Lambert in an attempt to maintain the corridor being used by German units to escape.

In an attempt to open additional routes, *SS-Panzer Korps II* launched a counterattack from outside the pocket against the Polish 1st Armored Division when the initial assault by *SS-Panzer Division 9* was repulsed by Polish troops defending the high ground between St.-Gervais–Champeux. *SS-Panzer Division 2* enjoyed greater success, isolating a Polish reconnaissance regiment on Mont Ormel. Pushing further west, *Das Reich* established a covering position to aid German units trying to escape through St.-Lambert.

The relief would prove short-lived. The southern flank of *7 Armee* began collapsing when *Kampfgruppe Scholz* abandoned Argentan on the morning of 20 August. Although the Germans reached Foret de Gouffern, they lost a number of Panthers and 20mm flak guns en route. The 90th Division was firmly ensconced on high ground overlooking routes leading out of Foret de Gouffern, and attempts by the Germans to push through Chambois met with a storm of artillery fire. *Kampfgruppe Scholz* was eventually destroyed when it tried to fight its way to Trun, and only a single engineer platoon succeeded in rejoining *Panzer Division 116.*

Fog began to appear each morning within the Falaise pocket. For those who had taken part in *Unternehmen Lüttich* barely two weeks earlier, the gray mists may have reminded them of 7 August. *General der Panzertruppen* Eberbach ordered his remaining troops to move toward St.-Lambert in an effort to escape through the corridor provided by *SS-Panzer Division 2*. By 1000 hours, the main body of *Panzer Division 2,* led by fifteen tanks, approached St.-Lambert after overrunning or bypassing several Canadian and Polish roadblocks. The Allied artillery, strangely silent up to this point, responded by shelling the German unit as it attempted to break out.

Between St.-Lambert and Aubre-en-Exmes, German troops disintegrated in confusion as a hurricane of artillery fire descended upon them. *Generalleutnant* von Luettwitz noted that "without break, new high fire columns from hit tanks of gasoline were rising toward the sky; ammunitions exploded, horses without master were lying on the ground, many severely wounded . . . the crossing of the

Dives bridge was especially difficult: people, horses, vehicles, etc., had fallen from the bridge . . . and there formed an awful heap."[67]

Panzer Division 2 had literally ceased to exist as an organized unit. Most of its wheeled fleet, artillery pieces, and armored fighting vehicles had been abandoned as a result of gasoline shortages or hopelessly clogged roads. Von Luettwitz succeeded in gathering several small groups of soldiers, leading them out of St.-Lambert with the assistance of his personal staff. Although they eventually reached safety, every step of the journey resulted in more casualties, and von Luettwitz himself was wounded in the neck and back by small arms fire.

SS-Panzer Divisionen 1 and *10* nearly suffered a similar fate. A counterattack by a mixed *Kampfgruppe* on the evening of 21 August opened a temporary escape route near St.-Lambert for *Brigadeführer* Harmel's surviving units. He watched as "under protection of guarding panzers, the still driveable Flak, Nachrichten [signals] vehicles, and other vehicles rolled over the Dives bridge. Many men waded across the Dives, which was as deep as a man's height."[68] Fortunately for Harmel, his supply vehicles had already been sent to Beauvais (sixty miles north of Paris) on 17 August. Unencumbered by a lengthy logistics tail, *SS-Panzer Division 10* was able to pass through St.-Lambert and link up with *SS-Panzer Korps II* before daylight.

On 19 August, *Leibstandarte* dispatched its reconnaissance battalion to locate crossings over the Dives River, and a second *Kampfgruppe* was sent to find out if a route through Chambois was available. When it was determined that American and Polish troops firmly held Chambois, *SS-Panzer Division 1* turned north toward St.-Lambert. By this time, however, most of the remaining vehicles belonging to *Leibstandarte* were abandoned due to lack of fuel, forcing many men to escape through the Allied cordon on foot.

The commander of *7 Armee, Oberstgruppenführer und General der Waffen SS* Paul Hausser, also hoped to reach safety through St.-Lambert. He related that "on the road leading from Mont Ormel [Hill 262] . . . heavy artillery fire reached us from a direction we could not determine. We had to wait for nightfall. We managed to form a small panzer assault force and to supply it with fuel from abandoned vehicles . . . during the wait a mortar shell found me and left me wounded. But by dawn on 21 August, we reached the reconnaissance battalion of *SS-Panzer Division 2*."[69]

The remnants of *Panzer Division 116*, led by *Major* Heinz Günther Guderian, underwent a different experience. Preceded by two commandeered assault guns, the Germans moved quietly along country lanes toward St.-Lambert after darkness fell. When Guderian neared the village, he halted his column every hundred yards to listen for Allied activity. As the winding column passed near St.-Lambert, hundreds of German soldiers hiding in nearby cellars and wooded areas took the opportunity to join Guderian's band. At Champosoult, he finally made contact with *SS-Panzer Division 2*.

The remnants of *Panzer Division 116*, minus heavy equipment, were among the last to escape from the Falaise pocket during the early morning hours of 21 August. Only a few stragglers would follow. Hitler's proud panzer divisions, which had marched to Normandy confident in their ability to throw the Anglo-American invaders into the sea, had been reduced to small bands of desperate men intent only on moving silently through the night in a desperate attempt to escape destruction.

CONCLUSIONS

The Germans were presented with a singularly difficult operational dilemma following the initial failure of *Unternehmen Lüttich:* they were being assaulted on both flanks by Allied armies that could operate during daylight without fear of air attack while their own units were forced to move at night. Two complete German armies as well as a specially formed panzer group depended for sustenance on depots designed to provide for the needs of a single army. The resultant lack of fuel proved to be a significant factor in preventing the Germans from maneuvering their panzer divisions to block an impending Allied envelopment. Senior German commanders also were forced to cope with a political leader who disregarded Allied threats to the flanks of his armies in Normandy.

The decision to commit *Panzer Gruppe Eberbach* against XV Corps had enormous ramifications. After the fighting ended, British teams from No. 2 Operational Research Section (ORS) conducted a thorough search of the battlefield, examining the areas around Falaise, Chambois, and roads leading to the Seine River in detail. Some 470 panzers and self-propelled guns were found, 81 percent of which were abandoned intact or destroyed by their crews. The vast majority of these vehicles would not have been left behind if the panzer divisions still had fuel.[70]

By employing *Panzer Gruppe Eberbach* against the American Third Army, the Germans severely curtailed the defensive options available to *Panzerarmee 5*. Sepp Dietrich had no choice but to slowly retreat in the face of the attacking Canadians when Operation TRACTABLE was launched. Lack of fuel prevented *Generalfeldmarschall* von Kluge from sending reinforcements to *Panzerarmee 5,* and despite an unimpressive Allied effort, it was powerless to avert the loss of Falaise, Trun, and Chambois soon after the Canadian offensive began.

Although *SS-Panzer Korps II* succeeded in opening a corridor at St.-Lambert, *Panzer Gruppe Eberbach* was incapable of achieving a similar success. Fuel shortages prevented the panzer divisions from mounting a coherent offensive effort at Chambois and Argentan. Unable even to coordinate an effective defense against V Corps, *Panzer Gruppe Eberbach* was virtually destroyed in the subsequent fighting, and Hausser's *7 Armee* fared little better.

Although the eventual outcome of the Normandy campaign was never in doubt, the defensive success achieved by the Americans at Mortain clearly laid the foundation for the events that took place between 12 and 20 August. If the Germans had gained an initial victory at Mortain, it is doubtful that Bradley would have allowed Third Army operations to continue in both Brittany and southeastern France. The pressure on *LXXXI Armee Korps* in the Mayenne–Le Mans area undoubtedly would have eased, and with the threat to their southern flank reduced, the Germans could have shifted additional combat power against the British and Canadians in the north. The valiant stand of the 30th Infantry Division, however, prevented this alternate version of history from occurring.

12

Unternehmen Lüttich—A Final Assessment

Many of the crucial decisions made in Normandy during August 1944 are directly related to the German attempt to recapture Avranches. The loss of that city, which anchored the southern flank of the German defensive line, forced von Kluge to choose between remaining on the defensive or changing to the offense. He initially hesitated to risk his weakened forces by conducting offensive operations in the wake of Operation COBRA. Instead, he focused on reestablishing a cohesive defense in the *7 Armee* sector. When Patton turned west into Brittany, von Kluge quickly saw that the time for decisive action had arrived. As he studied the changing situation, he became convinced that the benefits of a counteroffensive against Avranches far outweighed the risks involved.

If Patton had initially turned into southeastern France instead of Brittany, it is extremely doubtful the Germans would have launched their counteroffensive. An American advance into southeastern France, however, might have actually placed the Germans in a better position in the long term. Unable to ignore the immediate threat posed by Patton, the Germans would have been forced to employ *XLVII Panzer Korps* against Third Army. Instead of facing a single panzer division as XV Corps outflanked the Germans, the leading echelons of Third Army would have faced two or three panzer divisions shifted to Le Mans from Vire. *XLVII Panzer Korps* would also have benefited from its close proximity to the *7 Armee* supply installations located nearby.

Bradley's decision to redirect the Third Army's main effort from Brittany to southeastern France proved to be the catalyst for a German defeat in Normandy. Lacking accurate intelligence, the Germans were slow to react to Patton's advance on Le Mans, and after 1 August, the Americans benefited significantly from their ability to sustain Third Army operations at a pace and scale greater than the Germans anticipated. When von Kluge ordered *LXXXI Armee Korps* to defend the southern flank of *7 Armee*, it was clear that he had miscalculated the speed at which the Americans could assemble sufficient forces to threaten Le Mans.

Confident that *LXXXI Armee Korps* would prove capable of protecting the southern flank of *7 Armee,* von Kluge committed *XLVII Panzer Korps* to the Avranches counteroffensive. Since *XLVII Panzer Korps* consisted only of three divisions, von Kluge authorized the transfer of panzer divisions from several other points on the Normandy front in an effort to assemble a force large enough to produce a rapid victory. Previous German counterattacks against the Americans consisted only of one or two panzer regiments aimed at obtaining a limited objective. The fact that the elements of six panzer and panzergrenadier divisions were eventually allocated to take part in this counteroffensive illustrates the importance that Hitler placed on recapturing Avranches.

However, the defensive success achieved by the 30th Infantry Division at Mortain deprived the Germans of their best opportunity to restore the situation in Normandy. By shifting the bulk of their panzer divisions to the west, the Germans exposed *XLVII Panzer Korps* to encirclement by American units advancing to the east. Once the German troops at Mortain were stalled, Lieutenant General Bradley redirected Patton's advance north from Le Mans in an attempt to surround the bulk of the German panzer divisions in Normandy, which were now halted east of Avranches.

Events taking place in the British sector to the north were also influenced by the German decision to undertake a counteroffensive against Avranches. Von Kluge's decision to transfer two panzer divisions from *Panzer Gruppe West* to *7 Armee* only succeeded in placing his northern flank at risk. Previous British and Canadian efforts to expand the 21st Army Group lodgment had been defeated by counterattacks launched by German panzer divisions. Throughout June and July, the bulk of the German tanks were committed to defending Caen and Falaise rather than to contesting the American advance on St.-Lô during that same period. This balance began to shift in the wake of Operation COBRA when two panzer divisions were transferred south on 28 July in a vain attempt to halt VII Corps. When von Kluge began assembling troops for *Unternehmen Lüttich,* he shifted two additional panzer divisions to the south.

This decision meant that when the 21st Army Group launched Operation TOTALIZE on 7 August, only three panzer divisions were in a position to oppose the Allies. The defensive power of *Panzer Gruppe West* also suffered from the recent infusion of inexperienced infantry divisions sent to replace newly departed panzer units. Although the Germans temporarily succeeded in halting the Canadian offensive, they did so at considerable cost to the defending panzers. Lacking armored reserves, the Germans were unable to defeat a renewed Canadian advance on 14 August.

The culminating point in the Normandy campaign can arguably be traced to von Kluge's decision to launch a counteroffensive against Avranches. His hopes for victory, however, were dashed when the 30th Infantry Division held

XLVII Panzer Korps long enough for the Allies to employ airpower and send reinforcements. The Americans also kept the Germans from reorganizing for a renewed counteroffensive by applying continuous pressure at Mortain. Fixed in place by indecision at senior command levels, the Germans proved unable to regroup their panzer divisions in time to prevent the bulk of their troops in Normandy from being forced out of position by the Canadian and American threat on either flank.

The success realized by Third Army proved especially detrimental to the German position in Normandy. The fall of Le Mans, with its extensive road network, set the stage for a rapid American advance toward Alencon. *Panzer Gruppe Eberbach* was not authorized to react to the threat posed by the Americans until after the *7 Armee* main supply depots were overrun. Deprived of their logistical support, the panzer divisions subsequently lost hundreds of armored fighting vehicles due to lack of fuel and spare parts. These losses also meant that the Germans were prevented from organizing a breakout when a significant number of their best troops were surrounded east of Falaise. With their panzer divisions decimated, the Germans were also unable to offer significant resistance as the Allies advanced toward Paris and Belgium.

Despite the fact that they ultimately failed, the Germans obviously hoped to gain a victory when they originally launched their counteroffensive against Avranches. Although the Allies posed a significant threat to both flanks, the Germans accepted some risk by committing the bulk of their panzer divisions in Normandy to *Unternehmen Lüttich*. The advance of VII Corps, however, pushed the German line of departure further east, which made it more difficult for the panzer divisions to obtain sufficient momentum to carry them to Avranches in the first rush.

As the distance between their start line and eventual objective increased, the Germans were forced to allocate a greater percentage of the attacking force to protecting their flanks against an American counterattack. However, events in other sectors conspired to force them to divert troops from *Unternehmen Lüttich* at the very time that they were seeking to reinforce the attacking panzers. By pitting four panzer divisions, reinforced by an assault gun brigade and rocket artillery, against a single American division, the Germans hoped to gain a favorable ratio of attacker to defender. By diverting troops to protect the *Unternehmen Lüttich* assembly areas, reinforce *II Fallschirmjäger Korps,* and bolster *LXXXIV Armee Korps*, this ratio decreased significantly. Consequently, the Germans would find it increasingly more difficult to reach Avranches.

The Germans also were unable to make the most efficient use of the troops that were available for the counteroffensive. Lacking accurate battlefield intelligence, they were unable to identify avenues of approach that avoided American strength. Additionally, the planning process itself suffered from lack of intelligence. Planning information is normally gathered through air and ground reconnaissance, signal intercepts, and prisoner interrogation. Signal intercepts could not provide a complete picture of American intentions, while prisoners were difficult to obtain when one's own forces were in retreat. Allied air superiority also negated the *Luftwaffe*'s ability to conduct air reconnaissance.

As for ground reconnaissance, a German participant noted that "reconnaissance operations by Army Group and 7th Army to determine where the enemy was located were poor. Air reconnaissance could not give them the answers they needed. They also neglected to use the available panzer reconnaissance battalions by positioning them closer to Mortain. *Panzer Division 116* had their reconnaissance battalion safeguarding their left flank, but should have moved it down towards the *SS-Panzer Division 2* sector to protect the road between Barenton and Mortain. This would have revealed that southwest of Mortain there were no enemy forces."[1]

Hampered by inadequate reconnaissance, *7 Armee* remained unaware that only a single American cavalry squadron initially screened the gap between Barenton and Mortain. Lacking such information, Hausser subsequently discarded that sector as a viable avenue of approach, deeming it unworthy of reconnaissance effort. Rather than utilize thinly defended secondary roads to bypass the American defenses, *7 Armee* opted for a direct route that placed the panzer divisions on a collision course with the defenders. By emphasizing mass rather than maneuver, the Germans were forced to rely on brute force to produce the victory they sought.

However, brute force was simply not available. The poor planning and coordination between arms as well as the diversion of critical units to other sectors combined to dissipate the opening shock of the German counteroffensive. Although the Americans were significantly outnumbered at the onset of *Unternehmen Lüttich,* they were not simultaneously confronted with an overwhelming number of challenges that would have produced a rapid collapse. The attackers moved along predictable routes into the teeth of the thinly spread American antitank defenses. When confronted by resistance, the panzers failed to bypass the defenders, which resulted in a prolonged delay and heavy casualties for the attackers. This surprising lack of tactical flexibility doomed the initial German effort to failure.

Tensions within their command and control structure prevented the Germans from revising their operational plan when it quickly proved inadequate. When the first attempt failed, Hitler took personal control of *Unternehmen Lüttich,* severely limiting von Kluge's ability to orchestrate the fight. The sheer mechanics associated with controlling a counteroffensive in Normandy from distant Berlin, however, resulted in an unwieldy decisionmaking process that proved unable to cope with the rapidly changing battlefield situation. The discord between von Kluge and Hitler also meant that the Germans were ill prepared for a major operational transition in the wake of the failed Avranches counteroffensive.

The German plan was also heavily influenced by senior commanders who were psychologically overwhelmed by Allied air superiority. Instead of proactively tackling this challenge, the Germans depended completely on passive measures to protect them from Allied planes. The Avranches counteroffensive was timed to ensure that it would initially take place during the hours of darkness and under foggy conditions. When Eberbach took command of the tanks at Mortain, he also depended on weather conditions to counter Allied airpower. Rather than immediately resuming the counteroffensive against Avranches, he recommended waiting until full moon conditions on 20 August.

While the tendency of German senior commanders to rely on passive means was somewhat understandable given the lack of *Luftwaffe* support, German units had already developed tactics to offset Allied air superiority. Selected routes were saturated with antiaircraft guns to deter Allied planes from attacking moving vehicles. If Allied fighter-bombers persisted, the intense volume of antiaircraft fire significantly degraded their ability to deliver an effective strike. By using assets transferred from *III Flak Korps* or those panzer divisions not taking part in *Unternehmen Lüttich*, more mobile antiaircraft protection could have been provided for *XLVII Panzer Korps*. Additionally, German ground commanders would have been better served if they had clearly stated their requirements to the *Luftwaffe* prior to 7 August.

Strangely enough, the farther the Germans advanced on 7 August, the more likely that Allied planes would have been even less effective. Tactical airpower, a crucial player in the Allied combined arms team, could only be applied forcefully if the opposing troops were clearly identified and separated. Failure to do so often resulted in high casualties for American ground units mistaken for German forces. The numerous cases of air-ground fratricide that took place on 7 August, when attacker and defender were intermingled, provide a glimpse of what might have happened on a larger scale if the panzers had advanced farther to the west. This observation also highlights just how decisive the contribution of the 30th Infantry Division was during the opening hours of *Unternehmen Lüttich*.

Although a flawed plan and the diversion of forces certainly decreased the German prospects for success, a narrow chance for victory did exist. Despite planning errors and interrupted preparations, the Germans succeeded in massing a large force of panzers without being detected. The Americans also unwittingly cooperated in providing the Germans with an opportunity to recapture Avranches. With the gap between First Army and Third Army widening, Lieutenant General Hodges ordered VII Corps to send the 1st Infantry Division to Mayenne. The 30th Infantry Division, which replaced the 1st Division, had only had a few hours to improve the defensive positions it inherited, which meant that the German counteroffensive was timed almost perfectly to take advantage of the Americans at their weakest.

Why did the Allies prevail? They succeeded because the Germans were prevented at the start from setting the conditions necessary for achieving victory at Mortain, not because the Americans possessed a solid indication that the Germans planned a counteroffensive aimed at regaining Avranches. Quite the contrary was true, as the operational security measures imposed by the Germans had proven quite effective in masking their preparations. However, during the first week of August, the 12th Army Group maintained pressure against *7 Armee* in an effort to seize Vire and prevent the Germans from threatening Third Army's exposed flank. Operation BLUECOAT, which was launched by the British in late July, also prevented *Panzer Gruppe West* from sending additional divisions to reinforce *7 Armee* prior to 7 August.

By maintaining continuous pressure, Hodges's First Army and Montgomery's 21st Army Group prevented von Kluge from gathering sufficient panzer divisions to assure the success of his plan. Not only was von Kluge repeatedly forced to alter his original plan, but also the American progress east of Avranches pushed the Germans farther away from their intended objective. First Army efforts to seize Vire also succeeded in siphoning off a number of units designated to participate in *Unternehmen Lüttich,* and these diverted units may have proved sufficient to tip the scales from defeat to victory for the Germans.

Good fortune also intervened on behalf of the Americans. When the Germans failed to quickly achieve success, the 30th Infantry Division was able to commit CCB, 3d Armored Division, to counterattack the penetration at le Mesnil Adelee. VII Corps also gained the services of a significant portion of 2d Armored Division, which was diverted from its original mission of seizing Domfront. If the German assault had been properly coordinated, however, it is doubtful that VII Corps would have been able to recover as quickly. CCB faced the grave possibility of being overrun before it could reassemble its combat vehicles, while a larger German force in the Reffuveille–le Mesnil Adelee area could have prevented the 2d Armored from moving south on 7 August.

While the Germans grappled with the difficult transition from von Kluge's original plan to the concept of operations imposed upon *OB West* by Hitler, senior American commanders were free to make a number of crucial decisions that significantly altered the situation south of Avranches. First Army moved rapidly to plug the gap between Mortain and Barenton with the 35th Infantry Division. Bradley reacted decisively by ordering Patton to turn north from Le Mans when ULTRA disclosed that *XLVII Panzer Korps* had been committed at Mortain. Two days later, General Montgomery issued a new operational directive that sought to coordinate British and Canadian operations with Third Army's drive on Argentan. These actions are in sharp contrast to the indecision exhibited by the Germans during the period 7–11 August.

Although First Army had prevented the Germans from adequately preparing for a counteroffensive, Third Army proved to be the defeat mechanism that forced von Kluge to shelve his plan to regain Avranches. By pushing more troops south of Avranches than the Germans anticipated, Patton could conduct a wider range of operations than his opponents thought possible. Not only did Third Army destroy the *7 Armee* sustainment base at Le Mans, but it also presented von Kluge with a threat that he could not afford to ignore. The Germans abandoned their efforts at Mortain as they sought to counterattack XV Corps. However, the Americans had already gained positional advantage that allowed them to defeat *Panzer Gruppe Eberbach* long before it could launch its assault. Deprived of supplies and fuel by the loss of the depots at Le Mans, the armored fighting vehicle inventory of the panzer divisions dwindled away as they sought to escape to the east.

Given the indifference that many German generals exhibited toward logistics, it is not surprising that *Panzer Gruppe Eberbach* ran out of fuel. As one noted historian commented on the German officer corps, "All planning evolved around the maneuver concept; the operations officer would set up first and then call in the logisticians . . . supply officers, like their counterparts in intelligence, were junior in rank and position to the operations officer. Their job was to support the operation however they could."[2] While panzer divisions could operate independently from a supply base for a short period of time, special provisions had to be made in advance to carry extra fuel. Lacking either the means or foresight to do so, von Kluge condemned *Panzer Gruppe Eberbach* to defeat.

At the tactical level, there are many dramatic examples of successful American defensive actions during the Mortain fighting, most notably the struggle for Hill 314. Although suffering heavy casualties and lacking supplies, the 2/120th Infantry endured repeated assaults by determined *SS* troops. The Germans expended considerable resources, both physical and psychological, against the Americans on Hill 314 that might have served them better elsewhere. In an attempt to identify which American unit contributed the most to the victory at Mortain, however, one must examine the German plan rather than battlefield events. It is clear that *XLVII Panzer Korps* designated *Panzer Division 2* as its main effort, upon which the failure or success of the entire operation normally hinges. Even though secondary or supporting efforts might fail without materially hampering an operation, victory is usually unattainable when the main effort is defeated.

By focusing on the dramatic fighting that took place over a five-day period on Hill 314, previous accounts have failed to accurately identify the decisive contribution made by the 1/117th Infantry and its attached TD platoons on the morning of 7 August. A single battalion of American infantry, reinforced by one and a half platoons of towed three-inch guns, succeeded in delaying several reinforced panzer battalions for seven hours. *XLVII Panzer Korps* was prevented from gaining immediate access to the most direct route leading to Avranches. The fierce resistance by the 1st Battalion also convinced von Luettwitz that his troops would not reach Avranches, and after 7 August, the Germans launched only halfhearted attacks against the Americans barring the way to Juvigny le Tertre.

The struggle for Hill 314 assumed truly significant proportions as *XLVII Panzer Korps* reorganized after its initial failed attempt to reach Avranches. The Germans continually diverted troops from their main effort in a vain attempt to seize the commanding heights. There is no doubt that they viewed Hill 314 as

Knocked-out Panthers from SS-Panzer Division 1 in a field bordering the road linking St.-Barthelemy with Juvigny-le-Tertre. (Dwight D. Eisenhower Library)

dominant terrain, or they would not have tried so hard for five days to capture it. Even after all thoughts of offensive action against Avranches evaporated, the Germans continued to send troops and tanks against the 2/120th Infantry. Although the fighting at Hill 314 might be classified as purely tactical in nature, it diverted significant resources at the operational level to play a significant role in preventing the Germans from launching *Panzer Gruppe Eberbach* against Avranches on 11 August as Hitler desired.

Most German participants have chosen to credit their defeat to the introduction of Allied airpower on 7 August. Nothing could be further from the truth. General Dwight D. Eisenhower himself commented that "one shining example [of the proper use of airpower] was when the enemy launched, at Mortain, the counterattack to try to get out of the terrific position we placed him in by the break-out at Avranches." However, Eisenhower went on to clarify his statement by noting that "the effect of the rockets on the tank, while not as great as the enthusiastic pilots reported, was certainly serious and terrifying to the Germans."[3]

An analysis of the Mortain battlefield shortly after the fighting disclosed that the claims of physical damage by Allied pilots were considerably exaggerated. A British Operational Research Survey team found only nine panzers destroyed by air attack, five of which belonged to *SS-Panzer Regiment 1*.[4] However, prisoners revealed that most vehicles hit by rockets and bombs were too badly damaged to repair. Consequently, tanks destroyed by aerial weapons were usually left behind. The psychological impact of the repeated air attacks had a much greater impact on tank crews, and ten Panthers were discovered near St.-Barthelemy, either abandoned intact or destroyed by their own crews.

The effects of Allied airpower, however, were felt long before the first Typhoons launched their rockets at St.-Barthelemy. By permitting Allied ground forces the opportunity to maneuver in daylight while denying that same capability to the Germans, airpower allowed the Americans to theoretically conduct operations around the clock. Confined to maneuvering at night or during bad weather, the Germans, on the other hand, were limited to operating only seven hours a day. Therefore, air superiority permitted the Americans to move farther and faster, enabling them to gain positional advantage more frequently than their opponents. This advantage was most evident when both *LXXXI Armee Korps* and *Panzer Gruppe Eberbach* were defeated in detail by XV Corps south of Argentan.

Airpower also had other indirect effects on ground operations. By protecting American supply convoys traveling through Avranches, Allied planes ensured that Patton's Third Army received a steady flow of supplies. Additionally, Allied pilots prevented the *Luftwaffe* from interfering with American ground units during the fighting at Mortain. Thus, the Americans were able to maintain a tempo of operations that the Germans could not hope to match.

If the 30th Infantry Division had been defeated on 7 August, history may have unfolded in a completely different manner. The loss of Avranches would have undoubtedly slowed or halted Patton's advance, which would have provided *LXXXI Armee Korps* with an opportunity to establish a coherent defensive line. With their southern flank secured, the Germans would have been able to transfer troops north to reinforce *Panzerarmee 5,* and thus when the Canadians launched Operation TRACTABLE on 14 August, they might have faced additional panzer divisions. With the threat to their flanks averted, the Germans could have conducted an orderly withdrawal back to their borders. Given these circumstances, it is not unreasonable to speculate that the war in Europe would not have ended in May 1945 if the Germans had been able to significantly prolong the battle of France. Thanks to the valiant efforts of the American troops defending Mortain on 7 August, this sobering scenario never occurred.

Appendix A: Equivalent Ranks

American Army	German Army	Waffen SS
General	*Generaloberst*	*Oberstgruppenführer*
Lieutenant General	*General der Infanterie, General der Panzertruppen,* and so on	*Obergruppenführer*
Major General	*Generalleutnant*	*Gruppenführer*
Brigadier General	*Generalmajor*	*Brigadeführer*
No equivalent	No equivalent	*Oberführer*
Colonel	*Oberst*	*Standartenführer*
Lieutenant Colonel	*Oberstleutnant*	*Obersturmbannführer*
Major	*Major*	*Sturmbannführer*
Captain	*Hauptmann* *Rittmeister* (Cavalry)	*Hauptsturmführer*
First Lieutenant	*Oberleutnant*	*Obersturmführer*
Second Lieutenant	*Leutnant*	*Untersturmführer*
Master Sergeant/First Sergeant	*Stabsfeldwebel*	*Sturmscharführer*
Technical Sergeant/Staff Sergeant	*Oberfeldwebel/Feldwebel*	*Hauptscharführer*
Sergeant/Technician 3d Grade	*Unterfeldwebel*	*Scharführer*
Corporal/Technician 4th Grade	*Unteroffizier*	*Unterscharführer*
Technician 5th Grade	No equivalent	No equivalent
Private First Class	*Gefreiter/Obergefreiter*	*Rottenführer*
Private	*Soldat*	*SS Mann*

Appendix B: Falaise Pocket

German Divisions in Pocket	Divisions in Pocket Minus Support Elements	Not in Pocket
Fallschirmjäger Division 3	*Infanterie Division 276*	*Fallschirmjäger Division 2*
Fallschirmjäger Division 5	*Infanterie Division 277*	*Infanterie Division 77*
Infanterie Division 84	*SS-Panzer Division 12*	*Luftlande Division 91*
Infanterie Division 85	*SS-Panzer Division 10*	*Infanterie Division 265*
Infanterie Division 89		*Infanterie Division 266*
Infanterie Division 326		*Infanterie Division 271*
Infanterie Division 353		*Infanterie Division 272*
SS-Panzer Division 1		*Infanterie Division 275*
Panzer Division 2		*Infanterie Division 331*
Panzer Division 116		*Infanterie Division 343*
		Infanterie Division 352
		Infanterie Division 363
		Infanterie Division 708
		Infanterie Division 711
		Panzer Lehr
		Panzer Division 9
		Panzer Division 21
		SS-Panzer Division 2
		SS-Panzer Division 9
		SS-Panzergrenadier Division 17

Notes

CHAPTER 1. THE SECOND FRONT OPENS IN NORMANDY

1. *Generalfeldmarschall* Erwin Rommel, for example, was not appointed *Armee Gruppe B* commander until 15 January 1944. As late as April 1944, Hitler still expressed doubt about the "whole thing," i.e., Anglo-American preparations for an invasion by stating that he felt it was "a bare-faced piece of playacting" and a "completely bare-faced bluff." See Walter Warlimont, *Inside Hitler's Headquarters 1939–45,* trans. R. H. Barry (Novato, Calif: Presidio Press, 1990), 408.

2. Hitler ordered the occupation of Hungary by German troops, which took place on 19 March 1944. A number of units employed for this operation, including *Panzer Lehr,* were transferred from France.

3. German defensive strategy was centered on a three-phase concept of operation. The first phase of the defense against an invasion consisted of the prevention of the landing itself. Failing this, a series of local counterattacks designed to set the stage for a decisive assault would constitute the second phase. The third phase consisted of the concentrated counterattack intended to destroy the Allied lodgment. Warlimont, *Inside Hitler's Headquarters,* 433.

4. Von Rundstedt favored the defensive concept of operations described, while Rommel wanted more emphasis placed on phase one and two, e.g., conducting the decisive counterattack much earlier, which essentially did away with phase three. Based on their recent experience at Anzio, Allied planners (who were not aware of the dissension between Rommel and von Rundstedt) anticipated that the Germans would conduct operations in accordance with the concept favored by Rommel.

5. Geoffrey P. Megargee, *Inside Hitler's High Command* (Lawrence: University Press of Kansas, 2000), 216.

6. Gordon A. Harrison, *Cross-Channel Attack* (Washington D.C.: Center for Military History, U.S Government Printing Office, 1989), 465. This information is supported by interrogations of German prisoners in July 1944. Many German POWs related that Rommel had told them "that great masses of troops and tanks were on their way to Normandy

and that the Allies would be thrown back into the sea in 60 days" (from a report entitled "Destruction of the German Armies in Western Europe," Folder 99/12-2.0, 12th Army Group, 6 June 1944–9 May 1945, WWII Operations Reports, 1940–48, RG 407, Records of the Adjutant General's Office, National Archives at College Park, Md. [hereafter cited as NACP]).

7. Harrison, *Cross-Channel Attack,* 176–177.

8. Strategy of the Campaign in Western Europe 1944–45, Study No. 1, General Board, U.S. Forces, European Theater, 15 May 1946, pp. 9–11, Folder 97-USF5-0.3, WWII Operations Reports, 1940–48, RG 407, Records of the Adjutant General's Office, NACP.

9. Forrest C. Pogue interview with Major General Kenneth R. McClean, G-3 Planner for COSSAC and Chief of SHAEF Planning Committee, 13 March 1947, Office of the Chief of Military History Collection–World War II, Supreme Command, U.S. Army Military History Institute, Carlisle Barracks, Pa. (hereafter cited as USAMHI).

10. Strategy of the Campaign in Western Europe, 24.

11. Harrison, *Cross-Channel Attack,* 230.

12. The Germans offset the impact of the air attacks by centralizing their truck transportation assets at corps level and above. These vehicles would move troops and equipment from the Seine and Loire Rivers to the battlefront. The Allied air attacks were primarily intended to slow the German rate of reinforcement in Normandy. The American analysis disclosed that the German supply situation was "assured by well-diversified dumps with an estimated two months supply of gasoline and rations and one year supply of ammunition." The Germans, however, were often unable to efficiently distribute these supplies because they were limited to movement at night. Additionally, a large percentage of their wheeled transport was used to shuttle troops and equipment from rail unloading points to the battlefield. 1st U.S. Army Neptune Plan, copy no. 213, VII Corps files, Office of the G-3, Folder 207-3.5, Operations 20 February–1 June 1944, Box 3934, WWII Operations Reports, 1940–48, RG 407, Records of the Adjutant General's Office, NACP.

13. Entry dated 1 June 1944, George S. Patton Diaries, 1910–1945, Box 3, Folder 6, Annotated Transcripts, 10 February–31 July 1944, George S. Patton Papers, Library of Congress, Washington, D.C.

14. Warlimont, *Inside Hitler's Headquarters,* 428–438.

15. Entries for 15 and 17 June 1944, Chester B. Hansen Diary, February 1943 to October 1944, Folder Diary, 11 June–25 June 1944, Chester B. Hansen Papers, Box 1, USAMHI. Although ULTRA (the Allies' signal intercept operation based in England and run against coded German military radio traffic) provided the Allies with a great deal of operational information, rarely was the maintenance status of the panzer divisions discussed in intercepted messages. Therefore, the Allies were not aware of the relatively poor maintenance status of many German armored units.

16. Notes on the Topography of Lower Normandy and the Cotentin dated April 1944 and compiled by Professor J. D. Bernal, Appendix II, p. 11, Folder European Theater 97-USF1-2.6 to 97-USF1-2.10, Box 349, WWII Operations Reports, 1940–48, RG 407, Records of the Adjutant General's Office, NACP.

17. Report of Terrain Analysis, Annex T, Appendix 4, First Army G-2, 4 January 1944, p. 18; CI-361-A, XIX Corps, Invasion Through the Siegfried Line, Jun–Nov 1944, Folders 360–362 (XVIII and XIX Corps); Combat Interviews; all in WWII Operations

Reports, 1940–48, RG 407, Records of the Adjutant General's Office, NACP. The V Corps terrain analysis, for example, noted that "although not listed as obstacles, the hindering effects of the hedges and walls should not be overlooked. The cultivated fields, which lie inland . . . are bordered by low hedges and earth banks. These hedges and banks are fairly old, and probably sufficiently resistant to constitute definite obstacles to deployment and cross-country movement of motor vehicles and tanks" (Memorandum, "Intelligence Operations ETO V Corps," dated 15 February 1946, Folder 205-2, Intelligence Operations, ETO V Corps, 18 May 1942 to 10 May 1945, Box 3413, WWII Operations Reports, 1940–48, RG 407).

18. Martin Blumenson, *Breakout and Pursuit* (Washington, D.C.: Center for Military History, U.S. Government Printing Office, 1989), 42.

19. Entry for 9 June 1944, Chester B. Hansen Diary.

20. Entry for 17 July 1944, William C. Sylvan Diary, 2 June 1944–7 May 1945, William Sylvan Papers, USAMHI. Major Sylvan was the senior aide-de-camp for Lieutenant General Hodges.

21. FM 100-5, *Field Service Regulations: Operations* (Washington, D.C.: War Department, June 1944), 7.

22. Organization, Equipment, and Tactical Employment of the Infantry Division, Study No. 15, pp. 6–14, Folder 97-USF5-0.3.0 (22515), Report of the General Board, U.S. Forces, European Theater, Box 385, WWII Operations Reports, 1940–48, RG 407, Records of the Adjutant General's Office, NACP.

23. Entry for 3 July 1944, William C. Sylvan Diary.

24. Gordon A. Blaker, *Iron Knights: The United States 66th Armored Regiment* (Shippensburg, Pa.: Burd Street Press, 1999), 223.

25. Cable from Dwight D. Eisenhower to George C. Marshall, dated 27 August 1943, Box 6, Folder Correspondence 1942–1944, WW2 Documents and Reports, Hansen Papers; emphasis added. Interestingly enough, Eisenhower did not tell Patton of his decision until 2 March 1944; see Patton Diaries.

26. Omar N. Bradley, with Clay Blair, *A General's Life: An Autobiography by General of the Army Omar N. Bradley* (New York: Simon and Schuster, 1983), 59.

27. First Army Memorandum entitled "Combined Air and Ground Operations West of St. Lo on Tuesday, 25 July 1944," dated 25 July 1944, Hansen Papers.

28. Strategy of the Campaign in Western Europe, 21.

29. VIII Corps Field Order No. 8, dated 152400B July 1944, 4th Armored Division, Folder 604-3.9.1, Field Orders VIII Corps, July–August 1944, Box 15259, WWII Operations Reports, 1940–48, RG 407, Records of the Adjutant General's Office, NACP. The origins of COBRA can be found in a SHAEF planning document developed in May–June 1944 that called for the employment of strategic bombers in case the Allies were stalemated by German resistance in Normandy.

30. Entry for 15 July 1944, Chester B. Hansen Diary.

31. Blumenson, *Breakout and Pursuit,* 218.

32. James Jay Carafano, *After D-Day: Operation COBRA and the Normandy Breakout* (Boulder, Colo.: Lynne Rienner, 2000), 108.

33. VII Corps Training Memorandum 14, Tanks in Support of Infantry, dated 20 June 1944, Box 1991, WWII Operations Reports, 1940–48, RG 407, Records of the Adjutant General's Office, NACP.

34. First United States Army Battle Experiences, Newsletter Numbers 2–18, dated 13 July 1944 through 12 August 1944, 12th Army Group, Folder 99/12 Hqs 12th Army Grp, July, August, September 1944, Box 1752, WWII Operations Reports, 1940–48, RG 407, Records of the Adjutant General's Office, NACP.

35. It is interesting to note that the VIII Corps field order for COBRA is dated 15 July, only three days after the planning conference took place. The aerial portion of COBRA was canceled by bad weather on 18, 21, and 23 July.

36. Blumenson, *Breakout and Pursuit*, 236. Carafano points out that the casualties resulted primarily from Bradley's insistence on reducing the safety zone to 1,200 yards as opposed to the bombers flying perpendicular to the front lines. Had U.S. troops withdrawn 3,000 yards, as recommended by air commanders, there would have been very few friendly casualties. The evidence suggests Bradley suspected the attacking troops would take casualties from the bombing.

37. Helmut Ritgen, *The Western Front, 1944: Memoirs of a Panzer Lehr Officer*, trans. Joseph Welsh (Winnipeg, Canada: J. J. Fedorowicz, 1995), 102. Although the division commander later claimed that his entire unit had been annihilated, *Panzer Lehr* numbered 11,018 officers and men on 1 August 1944. It still possessed 33 operational tanks, 44 tanks in short-term repair status, 9 artillery pieces, and 391 halftracks. During the entire month of July, *Panzer Lehr* suffered 347 killed, 1144 wounded, and 1480 missing. Compare this to *Panzer Division 21,* which suffered 229 killed, 601 wounded, and 1,019 missing during July. *Panzer Division 21* was involved in Operation GOODWOOD on 18 July, where it was struck by heavy bombers but succeeded in repulsing the British assault.

38. Blumenson, *Breakout and Pursuit*, 249–251.

39. Ibid., 269.

40. Ibid., 287.

41. ULTRA Message XL 4271, dated 010331Z/8/44 [1 August 1944], ULTRA Microfilm Collection, Combined Arms Research Library, Fort Leavenworth, Kans. (hereafter cited as CARL).

CHAPTER 2. THE THIRD ARMY MOVES INTO BRITTANY

1. Martin Blumenson, *Breakout and Pursuit* (Washington, D.C.: Center for Military History, U.S. Government Printing Office, 1989), 344. Montgomery was aware that the creation of an American Army Group would elevate Bradley to a position equivalent to his own. Patton noted that "I told him (Bradley) that Monty sent me an order that I will not go in until we reach Avranches. Brad said he had never seen the order, so I will send him a copy. Monty is doing all he can to stop the formation of an American Army Group as that may cost him his job" (Entry dated 13 July 1944, George S. Patton Diaries, 1910–1945, Box 3, Folder 6, Annotated Transcripts 10 February–31 July 1944, George S. Patton Papers, Library of Congress, Washington, D.C.).

2. Report After Combat, XV Corps, U.S. Army, 31 July 1944 to 31 August 1944, p. 1, Folder 215-0.3 A/A Reports Hqs XV Corps, August 1944, Box 4723, WWII Operations Reports, RG 407, Records of the Adjutant General's Office, NACP.

3. 12th Army Group Letter of Instruction No. 1, dated 29 July 1944, Subject: Operations to Expand the Initial Lodgment Area, G-3 After-Action Reports, 1 August 1944 to

22 February 1945, Folder 99/12-0.1, Box 1749, WWII Operations Reports, RG 407, Records of the Adjutant General's Office, NACP. The divisions, minus VIII Corps, which were to be transferred included the 8th, 80th, 90th, 5th Armored, and French 2d Armored. Both armored divisions as well as the 80th Infantry Division were not actively engaged on 1 August. The 5th, 29th, and 35th Infantry Divisions, however, were scheduled to be placed in Army Group reserve when withdrawn from the line. All three were committed in the Vire sector.

4. A complete account of this incident, at least from Patton's perspective, is found in his numerous diary entries made between 25 April and 3 May 1944.

5. Omar N. Bradley, with Clay Blair, *A General's Life: An Autobiography by General of the Army Omar N. Bradley* (New York: Simon and Schuster, 1983), 285–286. Bradley candidly admitted that he erred by not anticipating that American engineers would restore Cherbourg to its full cargo handling capacity much sooner than predicted.

6. SHAEF Memorandum 13012/Plans Dated 6 August, entitled "Diversion of DRAGOON Forces to OVERLORD Cherbourg or Brittany Ports Between Mid-September and Mid-October 1944," G-3 Division, August 1944, Folder 3, Entry 58, Box 20, Supreme Headquarters Allied Expeditionary Forces Adjutant General Division War Diaries 1943-45, RG 331, Records of Allied Operational and Occupation Headquarters, WW II (SHAEF), NACP.

7. Kent Roberts Greenfield, ed., *Command Decisions* (Washington, D.C.: Center of Military History, 1990), 394.

8. Entries for 30 July and 1 August 1944, George S. Patton Diaries.

9. When Bradley ordered one of Patton's divisions to take up defensive positions on 2 August, Patton told the 12th Army Group commander that "I did not agree with him and feared he was getting the British complex of overcaution." This does not sound like a man who has decided to accept Bradley's judgment without comment, especially given the fact that Patton had not been in command more than forty-eight hours. Entry dated 2 August, George S. Patton Diaries.

10. Entry for 4 August confirming verbal orders issued 1200 hours, 1 August 1944, Third Army G-3 Operations Diary, Section III, Folder for August 1944, Box 2017, WWII Operations Reports, RG 407, Records of the Adjutant General's Office, NACP.

11. Entry for 4 August 1944, George S. Patton Diaries.

12. Report of the VIII Corps After-Action Against Enemy Forces in Normandy and Brittany, France, for the Period 1–31 August 1944, pp. 4–5, Folder 208-0.3 (6879), VIII Corps After-Action Report, August 1944, Box 3958, WWII Operations Reports, RG 407, Records of the Adjutant General's Office, NACP.

13. After-Action Report, Headquarters and Special Troops, 12th Army Group, dated 16 October 1944, p. 8, Folder 99/12-0.3 A/A Reports Hqs 12th Army Grp, August–December 1944, Box 1752, WWII Operations Reports, RG 407, Records of the Adjutant General's Office, NACP.

14. Blumenson, *Breakout and Pursuit,* 370.

15. Report of the VIII Corps After Action Against Enemy Forces in Normandy and Brittany, France, for the Period 1–31 August 1944, p. 5.

16. VIII Corps Sitrep 93 for period 010001B to 011200B August 1944, Folder 208-3.8, VIII Corps G-3 Sitreps, August 1944, Box 4060, WWII Operations Reports, RG 407, Records of the Adjutant General's Office, NACP.

17. Blumenson, *Breakout and Pursuit,* 361. Patton noted that "General 'P' got bull headed and turned east after passing Rennes, and we had to turn him back on his objectives, which are Vannes and Lorient, but his over enthusiasm wasted a day." This diary entry clearly indicates that Patton still supported the Brittany operation; entry dated 4 August 1944, George S. Patton Diaries.

18. 12th Army Group Weekly Intelligence Summary No. 1 for the Week Ending 5 August, dated 7 August 1944, Folder 99/12-2 G-2 A/A Reports, August 1944, Box 1756, WWII Operations Reports, RG 407, Records of the Adjutant General's Office, NACP.

19. 12th Army Group Directive for Current Operations, dated 2 August 1944, First Army G-3 Copy, Folder First Army 101-3.15 to 101-3.17, Box 1991, WWII Operations Reports, RG 407, Records of the Adjutant General's Office, NACP.

20. Report after Combat, XV Corps, U.S. Army, 31 July 1944 to 31 August 1944, p. 2.

21. Entry for 2 August 1944, Third Army G-3 Operations Diary.

22. Entry for 2 August 1944, Chester B. Hansen Diary, February 1943 to October 1944, Folder Diary, 1–15 August 1944, Chester B. Hansen Papers, Box 1, USAMHI.

23. Entry for 2 August 1944, Third Army G-3 Operations Diary. This decision led to the discussion in which Patton informed the 12th Army Group commander that he had disagreed with the decision to send the 79th Infantry Division to Fougeres; entry for 2 August 1944, George S. Patton Diaries.

24. Entry for 2 August 1944, Third Army G-3 Operations Diary.

25. Report After Combat, XV Corps, U.S. Army, 31 July 1944 to 31 August 1944, p. 2.

26. Blumenson, *Breakout and Pursuit,* 430.

27. Report of Operations of the Enemy Terrain and Defense Section of the Intelligence Branch, G-2, 12th Army Group, 1 March 1944 to 8 May 1945, p. 16, Folder 99/12-2.0, Box 1756, WWII Operations Reports, RG 407, Records of the Adjutant General's Office, NACP.

28. Blumenson, *Breakout and Pursuit,* 431; emphasis added.

29. Strategy of the Campaign in Western Europe 1944–45, Study No. 1, p. 32, Folder 97-USF5-0.3, General Board, U.S. Forces, European Theater, 15 May 1946, Box 385, WWII Operations Reports, 1940–48, RG 407, Records of the Adjutant General's Office, NACP.

30. Bradley, *A General's Life,* 290. Bradley's development of this concept is purported to have taken place during the period 2–6 August, although he did not unveil it to his own staff before 6 August.

31. Strategy of the Campaign in Western Europe 1944–45, p. 30.

32. Blumenson, *Breakout and Pursuit,* 430. As early as 10 July, Montgomery suggested a maneuver similar to the COBRA Operation, which would continue to occupy Laval-Mayenne and Alencon–Le Mans once Avranches was captured.

33. 12th Army Group Letter of Instruction No. 2, dated 3 August 1944, G-3 After-Action Reports, 1 August 1944 to 22 February 1945, Folder 99/12-0.1, Box 1749, WWII Operations Reports, RG 407, Records of the Adjutant General's Office, NACP.

34. Letter to Major General Orlando Ward from Major General A. Franklin Kibler, dated 14 June 1952. Kibler, who had been assigned as Bradley's G-3, was responding to questions raised during the preparation of a U.S. Army history entitled *The Supreme Command.* Kibler replied, "It is a fact that all of the momentous decisions connected with the

sweep of the 12th Army Group through the Brittany Peninsula and to the Seine, including the decision to close the pocket at Argentan, were made on the initiative and instigation of General Bradley himself" (Folder "Correspondence and Misc Supreme Command," 2-3.7 CB 8 The Supreme Command, Box 215, Records of the Office of the Chief of Military History, Records of the Historical Service Division, and publications, unpublished manuscripts, and supporting records, 1943-77, RG 319, Records of the Army Staff, Publications, NACP). It should be noted that Kibler specifically uses the word "decision" rather than "plans," which indicated that perhaps he was aware of the similarity between Bradley's plan and Lucky Strike B.

35. Greenfield, *Command Decisions*, 403–404.

36. Report After Combat, XV Corps, U.S. Army, 31 July 1944 to 31 August 1944.

37. Entry for 4 August 1944, Third Army G-3 Operations Diary.

38. John Colby, *War from the Ground Up: The 90th Infantry Division in WWII* (Austin, Tex.: Nortex Press, 1991), 182.

39. Blumenson, *Breakout and Pursuit*, 434; Report After Combat, XV Corps, U.S. Army, 31 July 1944 to 31 August 1944, p. 32.

40. Entry for 5 August 1944, Third Army G-3 Operations Diary.

41. Entry for 5 August, George S. Patton Diaries.

42. Memorandum entitled "Progress on Route of 2d Armored Division (French)," dated 6 August 1944, Folder XX Corps G-3 Journal and File, 1–7 August, WWII Operations Reports, 1940–48, RG 407, Records of the Adjutant General's Office, NACP. Departing from La Haye Du Puits at 2130 hours on 6 August, the lead elements of this division were not expected to reach Avranches prior to 0300 hours on 7 August.

43. Entry for 5 August 1944, Third Army G-3 Operations Diary for 5 August 1944.

44. Blumenson, *Breakout and Pursuit*, 375.

45. Ibid., 365.

46. Report of the VIII Corps After-Action Against Enemy Forces in Normandy and Brittany, France, for the Period 1–31 August 1944, p. 3.

47. This figure was arrived at using the tables of organization for three infantry divisions and three armored divisions found in Shelby Stanton, *Order of Battle, U.S. Army, World War II* (Novato, Calif.: Presidio Press, 1984). VIII Corps troops, calculated using the 15 July 1944 Operations Order, included ten AAA battalions, two separate tank battalions, three TD battalions, and seven corps artillery battalions. XV Corps troops had not completed passing through Avranches, but in terms of vehicles compared roughly to VIII Corps. These figures do not include errant First Army units, other Third Army units, or attached Cavalry Groups. The amount of two-way traffic cannot be calculated.

48. Memorandum entitled "Conflict with XX Corps" dated 5 August 1944, Folder XX Corps G-3 Journal and File, 1–7 August, WWII Operations Reports, 1940–48, RG 407, Records of the Adjutant General's Office, NACP.

49. Letter of instruction dated 3 August 1944 revising boundaries in 12th Army Group Letter of Instruction No. 1.

50. "Report on Liaison Trip," dated 0145 hours on 6 August 1944, Folder XX Corps G-3 Journal and File, 1–7 August, WWII Operations Report, 1940–48, RG 407, Records of the Adjutant General's Office, NACP.

51. ULTRA Message XL 5288, dated 082226Z/8/44 [8 August 1944], ULTRA Microfilm Collection, CARL.

52. Entry for 1 August 1944, George S. Patton Diaries.

53. Report of the VIII Corps After-Action Against Enemy Forces in Normandy and Brittany, France, for the Period 1–31 August 1944, p. 3.

54. Entries for 2 and 3 August 1944, George S. Patton Diaries.

55. S-3 Periodic Report for the 990th Engineer Treadway Company during the periods 010600A August 44 to 020600B August 1944 and 020600B August 1944 to 021800B August 1944, G-3 Journal File, 6th Armored Division, 24 July–16 August 1944, WWII Operations Reports, 1940–48, RG 407, Records of the Adjutant General's Office, NACP.

56. Report After Combat, XV Corps, U.S. Army, 31 July 1944 to 31 August 1944, p. 2. Approximately ten to fifteen FW 190 fighters attacked the XV Corps command post, inflicting two casualties on the 92d Signal Battalion.

57. Blumenson, *Breakout and Pursuit*, 371.

CHAPTER 3. GERMAN PREPARATIONS FOR A COUNTEROFFENSIVE

1. Martin Blumenson, *Breakout and Pursuit* (Washington, D.C.: Center for Military History, U.S. Government Printing Office, 1989), 422.

2. 12th Army Group G-3 Periodic Report, No. 60, dated 4 August, Folder 99/12-2 G-2 A/A Reports, August 1944, Box 1756, WWII Operations Reports, RG 407, Records of the Adjutant General's Office, NACP. This document noted that *Sturmgeschütz Brigade 341* was supporting *LXXXI Armee Korps*.

3. Blumenson, *Breakout and Pursuit*, 421.

4. ULTRA intercept XL 4271, dated 010331Z/7/44 [1 July 1944], ULTRA Microfilm Collection, CARL. The message stated that two tanks had crossed the bridge at 1500 hours, after which fighter-bombers destroyed the structure.

5. Percy E. Schramm, "Oberkommand Wehrmacht Diary (1 Apr–18 Dec 44): The West," Military Study B-034 (1946), in *Guide to Foreign Military Studies, 1945–1954* (Heidelberg: Historical Division, Headquarters, U.S. Army, Europe, 1954), 74–75.

6. Eddy Florentin, *Battle for the Falaise Gap* (New York: Hawthorn Books, 1965), 15.

7. Rudolf Christoff von Gersdorff, "Counterattack Against Avranches," Military Study A-921 (November 1945), in *Guide to Foreign Military Studies, 1945–1954*, 6. This account is significantly at odds with Blumenson, *Breakout and Pursuit*. Given the fact that Gersdorff had nothing to gain by stating that von Kluge was the author of the plan to counterattack Avranches, a view that is supported by Schramm's monograph, I have not lent as much weight to the telephone calls between Berlin and *OB West* quoted in *Breakout and Pursuit*. The *Heeresgruppe B Kriegstagebuch* entries are useful in establishing that von Kluge spent most of 3 August on the telephone trying to acquire resources for Hausser's *7 Armee*. In the tense atmosphere following the attempt against Hitler's life on 20 July, many phone conversations obviously took place purely "for the record." Additionally, von Kluge was apparently not on direct speaking terms with Hitler at this time, which meant his telephone calls to Berlin were limited to *Generalfeldmarschall* Jodl and other staff functionaries who lacked decisionmaking authority.

8. On page 58 of Military Study B-034, it states that *Panzer Division 9* was transferred to *Heeresgruppe B* on 27 July (see note 5). On that same day, *OB West* ordered the

transfer of *84* and *331 Infanterie Divisionen* from *15 Armee, 708 Infanterie Division* from *1 Armee,* and *242 Infanterie Division* from *19 Armee. 1 Armee* sent *708 Infanterie Division* and *9 Panzer Division,* while *15 Armee* dispatched *84, 85, 89, 331,* and *326 Infanterie Divisionen. 6 Fallschirmjäger Division* also received orders for Normandy but did not arrive in time to participate in the campaign.

9. Von Gersdorff, "Counterattack Against Avranches," 1.

10. Blumenson, *Breakout and Pursuit,* 330.

11. Walter Warlimont, "Circumstances of the 20 July 44 Attempt: Was Von Kluge a Traitor?" European Theater Historian Interview No. 5, 12 July 1949, in *Guide to Foreign Military Studies, 1945–1954,* 7.

12. Samuel W. Mitcham Jr., *The Desert Fox in Normandy: Rommel's Defense of Fortress Europe* (Westport, Conn.: Praeger, 1997), 54.

13. Annex No. 1 to 12th Army Group G-2 Periodic Report, No. 71, dated 16 August 1944, Folder 99/12 G-2 A/A Reports August 1944, Box 1756, RG 407, World War II Operations Reports, 1940–48, Records of the Adjutant General's Office, NACP.

14. Blumenson, *Breakout and Pursuit,* 422-423.

15. Schramm, "Oberkommand Wehrmacht Diary," 76.

16. Terry Copp, *Maple Leaf Route: Falaise* (Ontario, Canada: Maple Leaf Route, 1983), 90. *Infanterie Division 89* was reinforced with *Sturmpanzer Abteilung 217,* which was equipped with Sturmpanzer IV's mounting 150mm howitzers.

17. Michael Reynolds, *The Steel Inferno: I SS Panzer Corps in Normandy* (Stapleton, England: Sarpedon, 1997), 214–216. The armored fighting vehicle inventory included fifty-two Panthers, thirty-nine Pzkfw IVs, 8 Tigers, and 27 Jagdpanzer IVs.

18. Rudolf Lehmann and Ralf Tiemann, *The Leibstandarte IV/1,* trans. Nick Olcott (Winnipeg, Canada: J. J. Fedorowicz, 1993), 180–182.

19. *7 Armee Kriegstagebuch,* Entry, 0409 hours, 25 August 1944, conversation between Hausser and von Kluge, entry 58, Special Staff Adjutant General Division War Diaries, 1943–45, German Seventh Army, Box 67, RG 331, Records of Allied Operational and Occupation HQs, WWII (SHAEF), NACP.

20. 12th Army Group G-2 Periodic Report, No. 62, dated 062300B August 1944.

21. 12th Army Group G-2 Periodic Report No. 70, dated 14 August 1944.

22. 12th Army Group G-2 Periodic Report No. 60, dated 4 August 1944 and No. 65, dated 9 August 1944. The lead elements of *Sturmgeschütz Brigade 341* actually arrived in the Avranches-Brecey sector on 1 August. Two companies were immediately committed to combat, losing a combined total of approximately twenty assault guns. Consequently, only one company of fourteen assault guns was readily available to reinforce *LXXXI Armee Korps* (Niklas Zetterling, *Normandy 1944: German Military Organization, Combat Power, and Organizational Effectiveness* [Winnipeg: J. J. Fedorowicz, 2000], 205).

23. Gerhard Graf von Schwerin, "An Interview with Generalleutnant Gerhard Graf von Schwerin: 116 Panzer Division in Normandy," European Theater Historian Interview No. 17, by Kenneth W. Hechler, 1 September 1945, in *Guide to Foreign Military Studies, 1945–1954,* 16.

24. Fritz Kraemer, "Counterattack on Avranches: An Interview with Generalmajor der Waffen-SS Fritz Kraemer," European Theater Historian Interview No. 24, 17 November 1945, in *Guide to Foreign Military Studies, 1945-1954.* Kraemer noted that *Panzer*

Division 116 possessed sixty to seventy tanks while *SS-Panzer Division 1* had sixty tanks available for the counteroffensive. Each division also had a number of unserviceable tanks. Reynolds, *The Steel Inferno,* and the *7 Armee Kriegstagebuch* entry for 302200 July 1944 provide the remainder of the information.

25. ULTRA Message XL5255 dated 1929Z/8/44 [8 August 1944]; ULTRA Microfilm Collection, CARL. *Panzer Division 2* fought against the British until 21 July, when it was relieved by *Infanterie Division 326* (with the exception of *II Abteilung, Panzer Regiment 3,* which remained behind to support the newly arrived infantry division until 27 July).

26. Niklas Zetterling e-mail to author, dated 9 October 2000. The strength figures are found in the *Heersgruppe B Mittagmeldung* for 11 August, with the probable losses suffered at Mortain between 7–10 August added back into the totals. Although frontline units were in good shape, the 1,000-man divisional replacement battalion was short 847 men by the first week of August.

27. Zetterling, *Normandy 1944,* 314.

28. Annex No. 1 to 12th Army Group G-2 Periodic Report, No. 59, dated 032300B August 1944.

29. Ibid.

30. Zetterling, *Normandy 1944,* 379–381.

31. Kraemer, "Counterattack on Avranches."

32. Von Schwerin, "An Interview with Generalleutnant Gerhard Graf von Schwerin," 6.

33. Ibid., 9.

34. ULTRA message XL4176 dated 311417Z August 1944 [3 August 1944], ULTRA Microfilm Collection, CARL. The message stated that "the Allies had penetrated XLVII Panzer Korps lines on the evening of 31 July. On the following day a counterthrust by Panzer Division 116 did not succeed."

35. Ibid. Not including *SS Panzergrenadier Regiment 3, SS-Flak Abteilung 2,* and *III/SS-Artillerie Regiment 2, Das Reich* numbered 12,817 officers and men on 9 August, according to the *Reichsführer-SS Adjutant's* divisional strength report; see Zetterling, *Normandy 1944,* 324.

36. Mark Yerger, *Waffen-SS Commanders: The Army, Corps, and Divisional Commanders of a Legend—Augsberger to Kreutz* (Atglen, Pa.: Schiffer Military History, 1997), 77.

37. Zetterling, *Normandy 1944,* 363.

38. *GVB Meldung,* dated 1 August 1944, found in *Kriegstagebuch Götz von Berlichingen: 30 Oktober 1943 bis 6 Mai 1945,* ed. M. Wind and H. Gunther (Munich: Schild Verlag GmbH, 1993). The order mandating reorganization of remaining units is dated 24 July 1944 and entitled *"Neugruppierung der Kampftruppe der Division."* According to Ia Tgb Nr 485/44, *Kampfgruppe Fick* had an effective combat strength of 19 officers, 54 noncommissioned officers, and 302 men on 5 August 1944.

39. Ibid. Report dated 10 August 1944 by *SS-Panzer Jäger Abteilung 17* entitled *"Gefechtsbericht der Abteilung."* *1 Kompanie* was attached to *Sicherungsregiment 1,* while *2 Kompanie* supported *Infanterie Regiment 748.*

40. "Questions for Heinrich von Luettwitz, Commanding General of the 2d Panzer Division until September 1944," Military Study A-904 (1947), in *Guide to Foreign Military Studies, 1945–1954,* 10.

41. *Divisionsbefehl Nr. 45/44,* dated 1338 hours on 6 August, found in *Kriegstagebuch Götz von Berlichingen.*

42. Von Gersdorff, "Counterattack Against Avranches," 18.

43. SS-Panzer Division 2 "Das Reich" Divisionsbefehl Nr. 43/44 dated 2200 hours on 4 August, found in *Kriegstagebuch Götz von Berlichingen.* The relief in place, which began at 2100 hours on 4 August, was scheduled to conclude at 0600 hours on 5 August.

44. *7 Armee Kriegstagebuch,* entries, 2300 hours on 3 August, 1940 hours on 5 August, and 2400 hours on 5 August 1944.

45. Annex No. 1 to 12th Army G-2 Periodic Report, No. 69, dated 13 August 1944. *Sturmgeschütz Brigade 394* was formed in East Prussia in March 1944 and traveled to Orleans without guns in June 1944. On 10 July, it began moving to Normandy, where it received its assault guns at Tours on 15 July.

46. Reynolds, *the Steel Inferno,* 214. For simplicity's sake, I have noted only one of the many alterations to the *Unternehmen Lüttich* plan. In reality, it was changed almost on a daily basis.

47. Von Gersdorff, "Counterattack Against Avranches," 15.

48. Rudolf Christoff von Gersdorff, "Northern France—Volume IV: Avranches Counterattack (1–11 August 1944)," Military Study B-725 (1946), in *Guide to Foreign Military Studies, 1945–1954.*

49. Von Gersdorff, "Counterattack Against Avranches," 24.

CHAPTER 4. FIRST ARMY MOVES EAST

1. VII Corps Field Order No. 7, dated 1 August 1944, Folder Situation Reports VII Corps, August 1944, Box 3939, WWII Operations Reports, 1940–48, RG 407, Records of the Adjutant General's Office, NACP.

2. Martin Blumenson, *Breakout and Pursuit* (Washington, D.C.: Center of Military History, U.S. Government Printing Office, 1989), 447.

3. Ibid., 448.

4. During a 1997 trip to the battlefield, the author located a roadside sign commemorating the fighting that showed two Pzkfw IVs positioned on the western and northern edges of the village.

5. Message from CG 1ID to CG VII Corps, CG FUSA, CG VIII Corps, CGs 2AD, 90 INF, 4 INF, Sitrep No. 275 dated 032400B August 1944, 1st Infantry Division G-3 Journal, Folder 301-3.2 (22388) G-3 Jnl 1st Inf Div, European Campaign, 1–3 August 1944, Box 5790, WWII Operations Reports, 1940–48, RG 407, Records of the Adjutant General's Office, NACP.

6. J. Lawton Collins, *Lightning Joe: An Autobiography* (Novato, Calif.: Presidio, 1994), 250. Collins actually referred to Mont Joie as Hill 317. These commanding heights have been termed as either Hill 314 or Hill 317. I have chosen to use Hill 314 throughout this book. Although Mont Joie is referred to as Hill 317 in the U.S. Army's official history, this occurred only because the Center of Military History cartographer used modern maps instead of the February 1944 maps.

7. 4th Cavalry Group After-Action Report for August 1944, p. 2, Folder CAVG-4-

0.3 (9218) A/A Rpt, 4th Cavalry Group (M), August 1944, Box 17982, WWII Operations Reports, 1940–48, RG 407, Records of the Adjutant General's Office, NACP.

8. VII Corps Operations Memorandum, No. 57, dated 4 August 1944, Folder "Field Orders—Opns Memos; intell annexes, O'lay VII Corps August 44," Box 3941, WWII Operations Reports, 1940–48, RG 407, Records of the Adjutant General's Office, NACP.

9. 2d AD Field Order No. 6 stated that "VII Corps launches limited attacks early 5 August 44 to seize Gathemo to assist the advance of XIX Corps" (2d Armored Division Field Order No. 6, dated 051400B August 1944, Folder 602-3.9, Box 14969, WWII Operations Reports, 1940–48, RG 407, Records of the Adjutant General's Office, NACP).

10. VII Corps Operations Memorandum, No. 57, dated 4 August 1944.

11. William J. Butler, letter to author, 1998.

12. 1st Infantry Division G-3 Journal, entries, 0015, 0025, 0040, and 0230 hours, 5 August 1944, Folder G-3 Journal and File, 4–6 August 1944, Box 5791, WWII Operations Reports, 1940–48, RG 407, Records of the Adjutant General's Office, NACP.

13. 1st Infantry Division Artillery, S-3 Periodic Report No. 49, for the period 2000 hours on 4 August to 2000 hours on 5 August 1944, Folder G-3 Journal and File, 4–6 August 1944, Box 5791, WWII Operations Reports, 1940–48, RG 407, Records of the Adjutant General's Office, NACP.

14. After-Action Report, August 1944, 26th Field Artillery, 9th Infantry Division, 309-FA (26)-0.7, Journal–France–European Campaign–26th FAB-9th Inf Div, 31 July–31 August 1944, WWII Operations Reports, 1940–48, RG 407, Records of the Adjutant General's Office, NACP.

15. 1st Infantry Division G-3 Journal, entries, 1145, 1340, 1451, and 1610 hours, 5 August 1944.

16. Ibid., entries, 1725, 1742, 1821, 1845, and 1955 hours, 5 August 1944.

17. First Army Field Order No. 5, dated 5 August 1944, Folder 1st Army Field Order No. 5, Box 1881, WWII Operations Reports, 1940–48, RG 407, Records of the Adjutant General's Office, NACP.

18. VII Corps Operations Memorandum, No. 54, dated 1 August 1944.

19. First Army memorandum to 30th Infantry Division, dated 5 August 1944, Folder 1st Army G-3 Jnl File, August 1944, Box 1968, WWII Operations Reports, 1940–48, RG 407, Records of the Adjutant General's Office, NACP.

20. 1st Infantry Division G-3 Journal, entry, 2005 hours, 5 August. There are several references to moving south, but no definitive orders were issued telephonically to Huebner's regiments prior to this time. The original telephone movement order specified division minus one regiment, which was subsequently modified to include the entire 1st Infantry Division.

21. XV Corps After-Action Report for August 1944, p. 3, Folder 215-0.3 A/A Reports Headquarters XV Corps, August 1944, Box 4723, WWII Operations Reports, 1940–48, RG 407, Records of the Adjutant General's Office, NACP.

22. Alvin Beckmann, telephone interview by author, tape recording, 2 February 1993.

23. Carlton P. Russell, telephone interview by author, tape recording, 14 January 1993.

24. Ibid.

25. Ibid.

26. Thomas G. Tousey, letter to author, 1994.

27. Ibid.

28. 1st Infantry Division, G-3 Periodic Report No. 62, and 26th Infantry Regiment Field Order No. 8, dated 6 August 1944, Folder G-3 Journal and File, 4–6 August 1944, Box 5791, WWII Operations Reports, 1940–48, RG 407, Records of the Adjutant General's Office, NACP.

29. 1/39th Infantry S-3 Journal, entry, 6 August 1944, Unit Journal—European Campaign and Occupation of Germany, 1st Bn, 39th Inf Regt, 9th Inf Div, 9 July–31 December 1944, WWII Operations Reports, 1940–48, RG 407, Records of the Adjutant General's Office, NACP.

30. Charles Scheffel, "D-Day to End WWII Europe: Route of the 1st Battalion, 39th Infantry Regiment, 9th Infantry Division, VII Corps, First U.S. Army," unpublished memoir, Oklahoma City, 1986.

31. Heinz Günther Guderian, *Das letze Kriegsjahr im Westen: Die Geschichte der 116. Panzer Division Windhund Division* (Sankt Augustin, Germany: Herbert W. Schallowetz GmbH, SZ Offsetdruck Verlag, 1994), 78.

32. 1/39th Infantry S-3 Journal, entry, 6 August 1944.

33. 899th TD Battalion S-3 Operations Journal entries, 1315, 1850, and 2045 hours, 6 August 1944, TDBN-899-0.7 (5248) Unit Jnl, 899th Tank Destroyer Bn, August–November 1944, WWII Operations Reports, 1940–48, RG 407, Records of the Adjutant General's Office, NACP, and *899th Tank Destroyer Battalion History: Our Battalion* (Munich: Knorr and Hirth, 1945[?]), 38.

34. Daily Operations Summary, 50th Fighter Group, 6 August 1944, Historical Research Agency, Maxwell Air Force Base, Ala. (HRA).

35. First Army memorandum to 30th Infantry Division.

36. 30th Infantry Division Field Order No. 19, dated 050500B August 1944, Folder Field Orders w/supporting papers, "Mortain and Domfront," 5–16 August 1944, Box 8837, WWII Operations Reports, 1940–48, RG 407, Records of the Adjutant General's Office, NACP.

37. Message No. 1 from C.O. Rear Echelon XX Corps, dated 1640 hours on 6 August, Folder XX Corps G-3 Journal and File, 1–7 August 1944, Box 5134, WWII Operations Reports, 1940–48, RG 407, Records of the Adjutant General's Office, NACP.

38. William K. Harrison, *U.S. Army Senior Officer Oral Histories* (Bethesda, Md.: U.S. Army Military History Institute, Oral History Branch, 1989), 35.

39. Joseph Reaser, telephone conversation with author, 18 July 1998.

40. Murray S. Pulver, *The Longest Year* (Freeman, S.D.: Pine Hill Press, 1986), 30.

41. *On the Way: A Historical Narrative of the Two-Thirtieth Field Artillery Battalion, 30th Infantry Division, 16 February 1942 to 8 May 1945* (Poessneck i. Theuringen, Germany: Fr. Gerold Verlag, 1945[?]), 95.

42. Ibid.

43. Guy B. Hagen, telephone interview by author, tape recording, 27 August 1993.

44. Samuel T. MacDowell, John Prejean, and Edward B. Parrish, "The 3d Bn, 117th Inf, in the Counterattack, 7 August," interview by Roland G. Ruppenthal, 18 August 1944, C.I. 96, 30th Inf Div, Mortain Counterattack, 6–12 August 1944, Folders 95–97 Combat Interviews, WWII Operations Reports, 1940–48, RG 407, Records of the Adjutant General's Office, NACP.

45. Study of Organization, Equipment, and Tactical Employment of Tank Destroyer Units, Study No. 60, pp. 8–14, Folder 97-USF5-0.3.0, General Board, U.S. Forces, European Theater, 15 May 1946, Box 398, WWII Operations Reports, 1940–48, RG 407, Records of the Adjutant General's Office, NACP.

46. Thomas Springfield, telephone interview by author, tape recording, 27 February 1994.

47. Allyn R. Vannoy and Jay Karameles, *Against the Panzers: United States Infantry Versus German Tanks, 1944–1945* (Jefferson, N.C.: MacFarland, 1996), 20.

48. 1st Infantry Division Artillery, S-3 Periodic Report No. 50, for the period 052000B August 1944 to 062000B August 1944, Folder G-3 Journal and File, 4–6 August 1944, Box 5791, WWII Operations Reports, 1940–48, RG 407, Records of the Adjutant General's Office, NACP.

49. Summary of telephone conversation between Jayhawk G-2 and Colonel Specht, First Army G-3 Journal, entry no. 45, dated 1410 hours on 6 August, Folder 1st Army G-3 Jnl File, August 1944, Box 1968, WWII Operations Reports, 1940–48, RG 407, Records of the Adjutant General's Office, NACP.

50. *On the Way,* 25.

51. 103d AAA (AW) Daily Action Report, for the period 062100B to 071800B August 1944, in 1st Infantry Division G-3 Journal.

52. Fred R. Harman, letter to author, 8 January 1993.

CHAPTER 5. THE COUNTEROFFENSIVE BEGINS

1. *7 Armee Kriegstagebuch,* entry, 061630 August 1944, entry 58, Special Staff Adjutant General Division War Diaries, 1943–45, German Seventh Army, Box 67, RG 331, Records of Allied Operational and Occupation HQs, WW II (SHAEF), NACP.

2. Gert-Axel Weidemann, *Unser Regiment: Reiter Regiment 2 und Panzer Regiment 24* (Gross Umstadt, Germany: Ernst J. Dohany Druck und Verlag, 1984), 224 –225.

3. Von Funck pointedly mentioned that *Panzer Division 116* "fails practically every time." It is quite evident that great animosity existed between him and von Schwerin. *7 Armee Kriegstagebuch,* entry dated 062200 August 1944.

4. Rudolf Christoff von Gersdorff, "Northern France—Volume IV: Avranches Counterattack (1–11 August 1944)," Military Study B-725 (1946), in *Guide to Foreign Military Studies, 1945-1954* (Heidelberg: Historical Division, Headquarters, U.S. Army, Europe, 1954).

5. ULTRA message XL 4991, 061912Z/8/44 [6 August 1944] and ULTRA message XL 4999 062001Z/8/44 [6 August 1944]; ULTRA Microfilm Collection, CARL.

6. *7 Armee Kriegstagebuch,* entry, 1720 hours, 6 August 1944. The *7 Armee* Chief of Staff Rudolph Gersdorff had telephoned von Funck to relay this theory.

7. ULTRA message XL 5027, 07011Z/8/44 [7 August 1944]. The message further stated that *Jagdkorps 2* would support the attack with all available forces except for *Jagdgeschwader 2.*

8. ULTRA message XL5053, 070429Z/8/44 [7 August 1944].

9. 30th Infantry Division G-3 Operations Journal, entry 95, 7 August 1944, WWII Operations Reports, 1940–48, RG 407, Records of the Adjutant General's Office, NACP.

A verbatim copy is found in 1st Infantry Division Journal and File; see message dated 070010B August 1944.

10. 120th Infantry Regiment S-3 Journal, entry 30, 0356 hours, 7 August 1944, WWII Operations Reports, 1940–48, RG 407, Records of the Adjutant General's Office, NACP. The 120th Infantry Regiment had already been under attack for ninety minutes when it received the warning.

11. Hans Stöber, *Die Sturmflut und das Ende (Band I): Die Invasion–Geschichte der 17.SS-Panzergrenadierdivision "Götz von Berlichingen"* (Munich: Schild Verlag, 2000), 296. Although some American accounts state that a captured Sherman tank participated in this assault, the American vehicle was not acquired by the Germans until late on 7 August. The renegade Sherman, which was probably assigned to A/743d Tank Battalion, was apparently captured near Mortain by the antiaircraft platoon of *SS-Artillerie Regiment 17.* Thinking their vehicle was being strafed by RAF Typhoons, the crew abandoned their vehicle after being fired on by a four-barreled 20mm flak gun. In addition, see 120th Infantry Regiment S-3 Journal, entry 63, 0835 hours, 7 August 1944.

12. James Lucas, *Das Reich: The Military Role of the 2nd SS Division* (London: Arms and Armour Press, 1992), 141. Otto Weidinger also confirms *Leibstandarte*'s Panther battalion delayed the movement of his regiment (*Comrades to the End: The 4th SS-Panzer Grenadier Regiment "Der Führer," 1938–1945*, trans. David Johnston [Atglen, Pa.: Schiffer Military History, 1998], 319).

13. Proctor Eubanks, telephone interview by author, tape recording, 7 October 1993.

14. Robert C. Clark, telephone interview by author, tape recording, 12 December 1993.

15. Stöber, *Die Sturmflut und das Ende,* 291.

16. Grady E. Deal, telephone interview by author, tape recording, 4 April 1993.

17. 120th Infantry Regiment S-3 Journal, entry 17, 0220 hours, 7 August 1944.

18. Ibid., entries 18 and 20, 0220 and 0250 hours, 7 August 1944.

19. Frank Pruitt, telephone interview by author, tape recording, 2 July 1993.

20. Frank E. Moody, telephone interview by author, tape recording, 7 March 1993.

21. 120th Infantry Regiment S-3 Journal, entry 146, 1823 hours, 7 August 1944.

22. Stanley R. Weber, telephone interview by author, tape recording, 26 April 1993.

23. 120th Infantry Regiment S-3 Journal, entry 32, 0440 hours, 7 August 1944.

24. Harry Chocklett, telephone interview by author, tape recording, 10 May 1993.

25. Reginald W. Maybee, "Chapter 3: The Battle of Mortain," abstract from unpublished manuscript, California, 1993[?].

26. Morning Report, A/120th Infantry, 8 August 1944, National Personnel Records Center, St. Louis, Mo. These included two riflemen and three men from the headquarters platoon.

27. Murray S. Pulver, letter to Stephen Lofgren, military historian for Department of the Army Center of Military History, Fort McNair, Washington D.C.,1989.

28. Murray S. Pulver, *The Longest Year* (Freeman, S.Dak.: Pine Hill Press, 1986), 32. The loss of this panzer is also mentioned in Stöber, *Die Sturmflut und das Ende.*

29. Pulver, *The Longest Year,* 32. The Germans were demanding that Pulver and his men surrender.

30. John S. Hanratty, telephone interview by author, tape recording, 21 July 1993.

31. Thomas Springfield, telephone interview by author, 27 February 1994.

32. Lucas, *Das Reich,* 142.

33. Hanratty, interview.

34. Springfield, interview.

35. Tom F. H. Andrew and Hammond D. Birks, "The Counterattack Against the 120th Inf. at Mortain, the Abbaye-Blanche Roadblock," interview by European Theater historian, 18 August 1944, C.I. 96, 30th Inf Div, Mortain Counterattack, 6–12 August 1944, Folders 95–97 Combat Interviews, WWII Operations Reports, 1940–48, RG 407, Records of the Adjutant General's Office, NACP. Curiously enough, no mention is made of Lieutenant Springfield's crucial role at the roadblock.

36. George Simmons, interviews by author, tape recordings, 6 and 22 November 1992.

37. 120th Infantry Regiment S-3 Journal, entry 47, 0650 hours, 7 August 1944.

38. 120th Infantry Regiment S-3 Journal, entry 51, 0712 hours, 7 August 1944.

39. 197th FA Battalion After-Action Report, August 1944, 330-FA-(197)-0.3 (5117) After Battle Report, 197th FA Bn, August 1944, 30th Infantry Division; WWII Operations Reports, 1940–48, RG 407, Records of the Adjutant General's Office, NACP.

40. 298th Engineer Battalion After-Action Report, August 1944, ENBN-298-0.3, A/A Rpt–298th Engr C Bn, June–December 1944, WWII Operations Reports, 1940–48, RG 407, Records of the Adjutant General's Office, NACP.

41. Stöber, *Die Sturmflut und das Ende,* 287. The American machine-gun position in the church was not reduced until approximately 1100 hours.

42. Andrew and Birks, "The Counterattack Against the 120th Inf.," 2.

43. Ibid.

44. 120th Infantry Regiment S-3 Journal, entry 79, 1035 hours, 7 August 1944.

45. Weber, interview.

46. Ibid.

47. *On the Way: A Historical Narrative of the Two-Thirtieth Field Artillery Battalion, 30th Infantry Division, 16 February 1942 to 8 May 1945* (Poessneck i. Theuringen, Germany: Fr. Gerold Verlag, 1945[?]), 95–96.

48. Robert Hewitt, *Workhorse of the Western Front* (Nashville, Tenn.: The Battery Press, 1980), 115.

49. 120th Infantry Regiment S-3 Journal, entry 165, 2215 hours, 7 August 1944.

50. Ibid., Entry 63, 0835 hours, 7 August 1944.

51. Pruitt, interview.

52. 120th Infantry Regiment S-3 Journal, entry 112, 1423 hours, 7 August 1944.

53. Hewitt, *Workhorse of the Western Front,* 115.

54. 120th Infantry Regiment S-3 Journal, entry 92, 1230 hours, 7 August 1944.

55. *On the Way,* 97.

56. James W. Lockett and Ben T. Ammons, "The 2d Bn in the Mortain Counterattack, 7 August," interview by European Theater historian, 18 August 1944, C.I. 96, 30th Inf Div, Mortain Counterattack, 6–12 August 1944, Folders 95–97, Combat Interviews, WWII Operations Reports, 1940–48, RG 407, Adjutant General's Office, NACP, and 120th Infantry Regiment, S-3 Journal, entry 58, 0810 hours, 7 August 1944.

57. 120th Infantry Regiment S-3 Journal, entry 125, 1550 hours, 7 August 1944.

58. Ibid., entries 132 and 136, 1615 and 1710 hours, 7 August 1944.

59. Morning Reports, F/117th Infantry, 7 and 13 August 1944, National Personnel Records Center, St. Louis, Mo. The dead and captured are listed as MIA.

60. 120th Infantry Regiment S-3 Journal, entry 137, 1725 hours, 7 August 1944. This message, which was from the 743d Tank Battalion, noted that "they [F Company] keep yelling for artillery support but we would not give it."

61. 117th Infantry Regiment S-3 Journal, entry, 7 August 1944, Unit Jnl–117th Inf Reg, 15 June–31 August 1944, 30th Infantry Division, WWII Operations Reports, 1940–48, RG 407, Records of the Adjutant General's Office, NACP.

62. Pulver, *The Longest Year,* 33.

63. Ames Broussard, telephone interview by author, tape recording, 12 November 1992.

64. 120th Infantry Regiment S-3 Journal, entry 139, 1750 hours, 7 August 1944.

65. VII Corps Artillery S-3 Journal, entries 3287, 3288, and 3305, 0540 hours, 0700 hours, and 1200 hours, 7 August 1944, Folder VII Corps Artillery Journal, August 1944, Box 3950, WWII Operations Reports, 1940–48, RG 407, Adjutant General's Office, NACP.

66. John O'Hare, telephone interview by author, tape recording, 1 June 1993.

67. Ibid.

68. Lockett and Ammons, "The 2d Bn in the Mortain Counterattack."

69. Kenneth R. Cowan, "Repulse of the Counterattack Aimed at Avranches, 7–12 August," interview by Franklin Ferriss, 6 September 1944, C.I. 96, 30th Inf Div, Mortain Counterattack, 6–12 August 1944, Folders 95–97, Combat Interviews, WWII Operations Reports, 1940–48, RG 407, Adjutant General's Office, NACP. The loss of a Sherman was probably caused by a four-barrel 20mm German flak gun, which prompted the crew to abandon the tank believing it was under attack by strafing fighter-bombers.

70. 120th Infantry Regiment Daily Unit Report No. 52, from 062200 August 1944 to 072200 August 1944, Folder G-3 Supporting Docs 120th Inf Reg to 30 Inf Div, 31 July–14 August 1944, Box 8944, WWII Operations Reports, 1940–48, RG 407, Records of the Adjutant General's Office, NACP.

71. 30th Infantry Division G-3 Journal, entry, 0545 hours, 7 August 1944.

72. Ibid., entry, 0958 hours, 7 August 1944.

73. Ibid., entry, 1048 hours, 7 August 1944.

74. David Korrison, "Repulse of the Counterattack Aimed at Avranches, 7–12 August," interview by Franklin Ferriss, 6 September 1944, C.I. 96, 30th Inf Div, Mortain Counterattack, 6–12 August 1944, Folders 95–97, Combat Interviews, WWII Operations Reports, 1940–48, RG 407, Adjutant General's Office, NACP.

75. CCB 2d Armored Division map overlay with notes, 2200 hours, 7 August 1944, 602-CC(B)-0.7, Jnl and file—Hqs CC "B" 2d Armd Div, 1–8 August 1944,WWII Operations Reports, 1940–48, RG 407, Records of the Adjutant General's Office, NACP.

76. 67th Armored FA Battalion, Attachment to After-Action Report, August 1944, Statement made by Captain Stewart C. Meyer entitled "Action at Barenton," 603-FA(67)-0.7, Jnl—67th Field Arty Bn—3d Arm'd Division, August 1944, WWII Operations Reports, 1940–48, RG 407, Records of the Adjutant General's Office, NACP, and Steward C. Meyer, telephone interview by author, tape recording, 12 January 1993.

77. Ewald Klapdor, *Die Entscheidung: Invasion 1944* (Germany: privately printed, 1984), 370.

CHAPTER 6. STOPPING THE GERMAN ADVANCE ON AVRANCHES

1. Gert-Axel Weidemann, *Unser Regiment: Reiter Regiment 2 und Panzer Regiment 24* (Gross Umstadt, Germany: Ernst J. Dohany Druck und Verlag, 1984), 225.

2. 39th Infantry Regiment S-3 Journal, entry, 0422 hours, 7 August 1944, 309-INF (39)-0.7, Unit Journal–France–European Campaign–39th Infantry Regiment–9th Infantry Division, 1–31 August 1944, WWII Operations Reports, 1940–48, RG 407, Records of the Adjutant General's Office, NACP.

3. Heinz Günther Guderian, *Das letze Kriegsjahr im Westen: Die Geschichte der 116. Panzer Division, Windhund Division* (Sankt Augustin, Germany: Herbert W. Schallowetz GmbH, SZ Offsetdruck Verlag, 1994), 80.

4. Lieutenants Claing, Eddiger, and Mills, "Actions of 4th Division Units Against German Counterattacks, August 7 to 9," interview by William T. Taylor, n.d., p. 2, Combat Interview No. 31, 4th Inf Div, St.-Lô–Mortain, 25 July–8 August 1944, Folders 31–34, Combat Interviews, WWII Operations Reports, 1940–48, RG 407, Records of the Adjutant General's Office, NACP.

5. 2d Armored Division G-3 Journal, entry, 0700 hours, 7 August 1944, 602-3.2, G-3 Journal and file—2d Armd Div, Part I, August 1944, WWII Operations Reports, 1940–48, RG 407, Records of the Adjutant General's Office, NACP.

6. Richard Waller, "Repulse of the German Counterattack Aimed at Avranches, 7–11 August," interview by Franklin Ferriss, 18 August 1944, C.I. 96, 30th Inf Div, Mortain Counterattack, 6–12 August 1944, Folders 95–97, Combat Interviews, WWII Operations Reports, 1940–48, RG 407, Records of the Adjutant General's Office, NACP.

7. 117th Infantry Regiment S-3 Journal, entry, 0239 hours, 7 August 1944, Unit Jnl—117th Inf Reg, 15 Jun–31 August 1944, 30th Infantry Division, WWII Operations Reports, 1940–48, RG 407, Records of the Adjutants General's Officer, NACP. This entry stated that "B Company says that they can hear tanks and infantry approaching toward them."

8. Robert Cushman and Donald F. Renshaw, "Mortain Counterattack, 7 August 44, Action at the Crossroad North of La Fantay [*sic*]," interview by Roland G. Ruppenthal, 17 August 1944, C.I. 96, 30th Inf Div, Mortain Counterattack, 6–12 August 1944, Folders 95–97, Combat Interviews, WWII Operations Reports, 1940–48, RG 407, Adjutant General's Office, NACP. In every account of this battle, la Foutelaye is incorrectly spelled as la Fantay. I have chosen to use the proper French spelling.

9. Emil Raimondi, telephone interview by author, tape recording, 8 April 1993.

10. *History of the 117th Infantry Regiment* (Baton Rouge, La.: Army and Navy Publishing, 1946), 29.

11. Francis Wilts and Lawson Neel, "The TDs in the St. Barthelmy [*sic*] Battle, 7 August 44," interview by Roland G. Ruppenthal, 18 August 1944, C.I. 96, 30th Inf Div, Mortain Counterattack, 6–12 August 1944, Folders 95—97, Combat Interviews, WWII Operations Reports, 1940–48, RG 407, Records of the Adjutant General's Office, NACP. The entire crew was subsequently captured.

12. 117th Infantry Regiment S-3 Journal, entry, 0255 hours, 7 August 1944.

13. Ibid., entry, 0550 hours, 7 August 1944.

14. Wilts and Neel, "The TDs in the St. Barthelmy [*sic*] Battle," 2.

15. Walter M. Johnson et al., "Counterattack at Mortain, 7 August 44," interview by

Roland G. Ruppenthal, 15 August 1944, C.I. 96, 30th Inf Div, Mortain Counterattack, 6–12 August 1944, Folders 95–97, Combat Interviews, WWII Operations Reports, 1940–48, RG 407, Records of the Adjutant General's Office, NACP.

16. George I. Greene, telephone interview by author, tape recording, 6 November 1992.

17. Jones C. Wright et al., "Co A's (117th Inf) Action in the Mortain Counterattack, 7 August," interview by Roland G. Ruppenthal, 17 August 1944, C.I. 96, 30th Inf Div, Mortain Counterattack, 6–12 August 1944, Folders 95–97, Combat Interviews, WWII Operations Reports, 1940–48, RG 407, Records of the Adjutant General's Office, NACP.

18. Joseph Ezehner and D. N. Rockwell, "Anti-Tank Co in the Mortain Counterattack, 7 August 44," interview by Roland G. Ruppenthal, 18 August 1944, C.I. 96, 30th Inf Div, Mortain Counterattack, 6–12 August 1944, Folders 95–97, Combat Interviews, WWII Operations Reports, 1940–48, RG 407, Records of the Adjutant General's Office, NACP, and 117th Infantry, Regiment S-3 Journal, entry, 1146 hours, 7 August 1944. This entry noted that Captain Druckenmiller had showed up at the command post with a machine-gun bullet in his leg.

19. Edmond L. Rachal, telephone conversation with author, 26 September 1998.

20. Wilts and Neel, "The TDs in the St. Barthelmy [sic] Battle." The two men were George Schilling and Liborio Rodriguez. They have been mistakenly identified as George Schiler and Antonio Barrias.

21. Irving Katzman, Joseph H. Klebba, and Clinton W. Robb, "Action of C Co (117th Inf) Counterattack at Mortain, 7 August," interview by Roland G. Ruppenthal, 17 August 1944, C.I. 96, 30th Inf Div, Mortain Counterattack, 6–12 August 1944, Folders 95–97, Combat Interviews, WWII Operations Reports, 1940–48, RG 407, Records of the Adjutant General's Office, NACP.

22. Wilts and Neel, "The TDs in the St. Barthelmy [sic] Battle, and Morning Report, B/823d TD Battalion, 7 August 1944, National Personnel Records Center, St. Louis, Mo.

23. Wilts and Neel, "The TDs in the St. Barthelmy [sic] Battle." This account differs significantly from other published versions of this action.

24. History of the 117th Infantry Regiment, 34.

25. Katzman, Klebba, and Robb, "Action of C Co (117th Inf) Counterattack at Mortain."

26. Ibid.

27. Rachal, telephone conversation.

28. Allyn R. Vannoy and Jay Karameles, Against the Panzers: United States Infantry Versus German Tanks, 1944–1945 (Jefferson, N.C.: MacFarland, 1996), 33.

29. Greene never knew the name of the infantry sergeant; however, William J. Lyman, Curlew History: The Story of the First Battalion, 117th Infantry, 30th Division in Europe during World War II (Chapel Hill, N.C.: Orange Printshop, 1948), noted that Sergeant John Kronik of A/117th Infantry was killed cradling a machine gun that he fired point-blank at a Panther tank.

30. Greene, interview.

31. Katzman, Klebba, and Robb, "Action of C Co (117th Inf) Counterattack at Mortain."

32. 117th Infantry Regiment S-3 Journal, entry, 1121 hours, 7 August 1944.

33. Ibid., entry, 1100 hours, 7 August 1944.

34. Wilts and Neel, "The TDs in the St. Barthelmy [*sic*] Battle," 2.

35. 823d TD Battalion Unit Report, 2200 hours, 6 August 1944 to 2200 hours, 7 August 1944, TDBN-823-0.8 (47684) Jnl File–823d Tank Destroyer Bn, 1–8 August 1944, WWII Operations Reports, 1940–48, RG 407, Records of the Adjutant General's Office, NACP.

36. Thompson Raney, telephone conversation with author, 12 September 1993.

37. Morning Report, L/119th Infantry, 8 August 1944, National Personnel Records Center, St. Louis, Mo.

38. *History of the 67th Armored Regiment* (Brunswick, Germany: George Westermann, GmbH, 1945), 250.

39. 117th Infantry Regiment S-3 Journal, entry, 1256 hours, 7 August 1944.

40. Higgins, interview.

41. Transcript of a tape recording by Frank D. Joseph Jr. that was provided to the author by Frank D. Joseph III, 14 September 2000.

42. Squadron No. 174 and 175 each flew sixteen sorties during this period, with No. 181 flying an additional eight. No. 245 also launched six Typhoons at 1335 hours on 7 August.

43. Form 540 and Form 541 reports for 123 Wing (198, 609, 164, and 183 Squadrons) and 146 Wing (193, 197, 257, 263, and 266 Squadrons), Public Records Office, London.

44. *History of the 67th Armored Regiment*, 30.

45. Morning Report, I/33d Armor, 7 August 1944, National Personnel Records Center, St. Louis, Mo.

46. Weidemann, *Unser Regiment*, 227.

47. Ibid., 228.

48. Hal D. McCown, "Repulse of the Counterattack Aimed at Avranches, 7–12 August," interview by Franklin Ferris[?], 17 August 1944, C.I. 96, 30th Inf Div, Mortain Counterattack, 6–12 August 1944, Folders 95–97, Combat Interviews, WWII Operations Reports, 1940–48, RG 407, Records of the Adjutant General's Office, NACP.

49. Samuel T. MacDowell, John Prejean, and Edward B. Parrish, "The 3d Bn, 117th Inf, in the Counterattack, 7 August," interview by Roland G. Ruppenthal, 18 August 1944, C.I. 96, 30th Inf Div, Mortain Counterattack, 6–12 August 1944, Folders 95–97, Combat Interviews, WWII Operations Reports, 1940–48, RG 407, Records of the Adjutant General's Office, NACP.

50. 117th Infantry Regiment S-3 Journal, entry, 2150 hours, 7 August 1944.

CHAPTER 7. THE LOST BATTALION

1. 230th FA Battalion S-3 Journal Message Log, entries 68 and 86, 7 August 1944, 330-FA (230) 0.7, Jnl and File, 230th FA Bn, 1–31 August 1944, 30th Infantry Division, WWII Operations Reports, 1940–48, RG 407, Records of the Adjutant General's Office, NACP.

2. 30th Infantry Division G-3 Journal, entry, 0110 hours, 8 August 1944, G-3 Jnl— 30th Inf Div, 8–9 August 1944, 330-3.2, 8-8-44 to 8-13-44; 30th Infantry Division, WWII Operations Reports, 1940–48, RG 407, Records of the Adjutant General's Office, NACP.

3. Ibid., entry, 0700 hours, 8 August 1944.

4. 230th FA Battalion S-3 Journal Message Log, entries 3–5, 8 August 1944.

5. Paul W. Nethery, telephone interview with the author, tape recording, 20 March 1993.

6. 230th FA Battalion S-3 Journal Message Log, entry 16, 1015 hours, 8 August 1944.

7. Ibid., entries 28, 30, 32, and 35, 1355, 1415, 1450, and 1645 hours, 8 August 1944.

8. 30th Infantry Division G-3 Journal, entry 190, 2246 hours, 8 August 1944

9. Robert Weiss, telephone conversation with author, 2 March 1998.

10. 230th FA Battalion S-3 Journal Message Log, entry 1, 0215 hours, 8 August 1944.

11. Ken Parker, *Civilian at War* (Traverse City, Mich.: Myers Printing, 1984), 60.

12. Robert Hewitt, *Workhorse of the Western Front* (Nashville, Tenn.: The Battery Press, 1980), 64, and Francis J. Connors, Ashby L. Lohse, and Albert J. Kuster, "The Mortain Counterattack: The 2d Platoon, Co. 'A', 823d TD, at Hill 285, August 6–12," interview by David Garth, 26 September 1944, in C.I. 96, 30th Inf Div, Mortain Counterattack, 6–12 August 1944, Folders 95–97, Combat Interviews, WWII Operations Reports, 1940–48, RG 407, Records of the Adjutant General's Office, NACP.

13. Thomas Springfield, telephone interview by author, tape recording, 27 February 1994.

14. Floyd M. Montgomery, telephone interview by author, tape recording, 29 July 1993.

15. 743d Tank Battalion After-Action Report for August 1944, G-3 Journal—743d Tank Bn, June–August 1944, ARBN-743-3.2 (47694), Armored, WWII Operations Reports, 1940–48, RG 407, Records of the Adjutant General's Office, NACP.

16. 629th TD Battalion S-3 Journal, entry 22, 1330 hours, 8 August 1944 TDBN-629-0.7 Jnl—629th Tank Destroyer Bn, August 1944, WWII Operations Reports, 1940–48, RG 407, Records of the Adjutant General's Office, NACP.

17. Robert E. Herlong, "Repulse of the German Counterattack Aimed at Avranches, 7–11 August," interview by Franklin Ferriss, 18 August 1944 in C.I. 96, 30th Inf Div, Mortain Counterattack, 6–12 August 1944, Folders 95–97, Combat Interviews, WWII Operations Reports, 1940–48, RG 407, Records of the Adjutant General's Office, NACP.

18. David Korrison, "Repulse of the Counterattack Aimed at Avranches, 7–12 August," interview by Franklin Ferriss, 6 September 1944, in ibid.

19. Third Army Memorandum, dated 8 August 1944, Folder 220-3.2 G-3 Journal and File, 7–10 August 1944, Box 5134, XX Corps, WWII Operations Reports, 1940–48, RG 407, Records of the Adjutant General's Office, NACP.

20. XX Corps Message no. 47, dated 2100 hours, 7 August 1944, G-3 Journal and File, 7–10 August 1944, Box 5134, XX Corps, WWII Operations Reports, 1940–48, RG 407, Records of the Adjutant General's Office, NACP.

21. Ibid., 1247 hours, 7 August 1944.

22. 35th Infantry Division G-3 Journal, entry, 1100 hours, 7 August 1944, Journal File 7–8 August 1944, WWII Operations Reports, 1940–48, RG 407, Records of the Adjutant General's Officer, NACP.

23. Ibid., entries 1130, 1140, and 1220 hours, 7 August 1944.

24. Ibid., entry 3, 8 August 1944.

25. Ibid., entry 33, 0920 hours, 8 August 1944.

26. 134th Infantry Regiment S-3 Journal, entry, 0850 hours, 8 August 1944, 335-INF (134)-0.7, Journal–35th Inf Div, 134th Inf Regiment, August 1944, WWII Operations Reports, 1940–48, RG 407, Records of the Adjutant General's Office, NACP.

27. Butler B. Miltonberger and James A. Huston, *134th Infantry Regiment: Combat History of World War II* (Baton Rouge, La.: Army and Navy Publishing, 1946[?]), 56.

28. 4th Cavalry Group After-Action Report for 1–31 August 1944, p. 5, CAVG-4-0.3 (9218) A/A Rpt, 4th Cav Grp (M), August 1944, WWII Operations Reports, 1940–48, RG 407, Records of the Adjutant General's Office, NACP.

29. 35th Infantry Division G-3 Journal, entry 67, 1325 hours, 8 August 1944.

30. 30th Infantry Division G-3 journal entries 105 and 109, 8 August 1944.

31. Fred Cottriel, telephone interview by author, tape recording, 21 February 1993.

32. "History of the 654th Tank Destroyer Battalion" (n.p., n.d.), provided to the author by Everard A. Taylor.

33. 35th Infantry Division G-3 Journal, entry 135, 0225 hours, 8 August 1944.

34. Thomas Groom, telephone interview by author, tape recording, 21 February 1993.

35. Miltonberger and Huston, *134th Infantry Regiment,* 58.

36. Wilhelm Tieke, *In the Firestorm of the Last Years of the War: II. SS-Panzerkorps with the 9. and 10. SS-Divisions "Hohenstaufen" and "Frundsberg,"* trans. Frederick Steinhardt (Winnipeg, Canada: J. J. Fedorowicz, 1999), 179.

37. 67th Armored Regiment After-Action Report for August 1944, p. 3, and Field Order No. 10, 67th Armored Regiment, 0500 hours, 8 August 1944, both in 603-FA (67)-0.7, Jnl—67th Field Arty Bn—3d Arm'd Div, August 1944, WWII Operations Reports, 1940–48, RG 407, Records of the Adjutant General's Office, NACP.

38. 82d Armored Recon Battalion After-Action Report for August 1944; provided by Howard Swonger.

39. CCB 2d Armored Division S-3 Journal, entry, 1205 hours, 8 August 1944, 602-CC (B)-0.7, Jnl and file—Hqs CC "B" 2d Armd Div, 1–8 August 1944, WWII Operations Reports, 1940–48, RG 407, Records of the Adjutant General's Office, NACP.

40. 67th Armored Regiment After-Action Report for August 1944.

41. 230th FA Battalion S-3 Journal Message Log, entry 2, 0640 hours, 9 August 1944.

42. Robert Weiss, *Enemy North, South, East, and West* (Portland, Ore., Strawberry Hill Press, 1998), 102.

43. *On the Way: A Historical Narrative of the Two-Thirtieth Field Artillery Battalion, 30th Infantry Division, 16 February 1942 to 8 May 1945* (Poessneck i. Theuringen, Germany: Fr. Gerold Verlag, 1945[?]), 97.

44. Operation Report "A," Report No. 108, 474th Fighter Group, 10 August 1944, Historical Research Agency, Maxwell Air Force Base, Ala. (HRA).

45. Murray S. Pulver, *The Longest Year* (Freeman, S.D.: Pine Hill Press, 1986), 35.

46. Ibid.

47. 120th Infantry Regiment S-3 Journal, entry 80, 1640 hours, 9 August 1944, 330-INF (120)-0.7, S-3 Jnl–120th Inf Reg—30th Inf Div, 1–31 August 1944, WWII Operations Reports, 1940–48, RG 407, Records of the Adjutant General's Office, NACP.

48. Pulver, *The Longest Year,* 34.

49. Guy B. Hagen, telephone interview by author, tape recording, 27 August 1993.

50. Ibid.

51. *On the Way,* 98. This incident is also discussed in some detail in the unit history of *SS-Panzergrenadier Division 17* written by Hans Stöber, *Die Sturmflut und das Ende (Band 1): Die Invasion—Geschichte der 17. SS-Panzergrenadier Division "Götz von Berlichingen"* (Munich: Schild Verlag, 2000), 300. The surrender emissary was an interrogator assigned to *SS-Panzergrenadier Regiment 37.*

52. Ralph Kerley, "Operations of the 2/120th Infantry at Mortain, France, 7–12 August 1944," USAIS Library Student Monograph, Fort Benning, Ga.: Advanced Officers Class No. 1 (1946–1947), 14.

53. 230th FA Battalion S-3 Journal Message Log, entry 44, 1850 hours, 9 August 1944.

54. Ibid., entries 55 and 56, 2245 and 2350 hours, 9 August 1944.

55. William W. Dwyer, telephone interview by author, tape recording, 26 September 1993.

56. Ilfred D. Leger, telephone interview by author, tape recording, 10 January 1994.

57. Telephone conversation between Hobbs and Birks, 30th Infantry Division G-3 Journal, entry, 1417 hours, 9 August 1944.

58. Thomas Springfield, telephone interview by author, tape recording, 27 February 1994.

59. Morning Report, E/119th Infantry, 11 August 1944, National Personnel Records Center, St. Louis, Mo.

60. *Move Out, Verify: History of the 743rd Tank Battalion* (Frankfurt: 743d Tank Battalion, 1945), 75.

61. Peter L. Henderson, "Repulse of the German Counterattack Aimed at Avranches," interview by Franklin Ferriss, 6 September 1944, in C.I. 96, 30th Inf Div, Mortain Counterattack, 6–12 August 1944, Folders 95–97, Combat Interviews, WWII Operations Reports, 1940–48, RG 407, Records of the Adjutant General's Office, NACP.

62. 30th Infantry Division G-3 Journal, entry 99, 1914 hours, 9 August 1944.

63. Ibid., entry 114, 2029 hours, 9 August 1944.

64. 35th Infantry Division G-3 Journal, entry 7, 0023 hours, 9 August 1944.

65. Ibid., entry 8, 0025 hours, 9 August 1944. The call was from the VII Corps commanding general to the 35th Division CG.

66. 134th Infantry Regiment S-3 Journal, entry 2, 0230 hours, 9 August 1944.

67. Ibid., entry 27, 0705 hours, 9 August 1944.

68. Ibid., entry 3, 0340 hours, 9 August 1944.

69. Ibid, entry 6, 0910 hours, 9 August 1944.

70. 35th Infantry Division G-3 Journal, entry 36, 0950 hours, 9 August 1944.

71. Miltonberger and Huston, *134th Infantry Regiment,* 57, and Morning Report, C/134th Infantry, 15 August 1944, National Personnel Records Center, St. Louis, Mo.

72. 320th Infantry Regiment S-3 Journal, entry, 1235 hours, 9 August 1944, 335-INF(320)-0.7, Opns Journal—35th Inf Div, 320th Inf Reg, August 1944, WWII Operations Reports, 1940–48, RG 407, Records of the Adjutant General's Office, NACP.

73. Ibid., entry, 1400 and 1500 hours, 9 August 1944.

74. Ibid., entry, 1445 hours, 9 August 1944.

75. Ibid., entry, 2200 hours on 9 August 1944.

76. 654th TD Battalion After-Action Report for August 1944, TDBN-654-0.3 (6472) A/A Report–654th Tank Destroyer Bn, 12 July–31 December 1944, WWII Operations Reports, 1940–48, RG 407, Records of the Adjutant General's Office, NACP.

77. 320th Infantry Regiment S-3 Journal, entry, 2150 hours, 9 August 1944.

78. Al Navarette, telephone interview by author, tape recording, 16 December 1992.

79. Bernard A. Byrne, letter to Carlton Thornblom, 24 February 1950; provided to author by Henry Morgan.

80. 320th Infantry Regiment S-3 Journal, entries 2312, 2332, and 2400 hours, 9 August 1944.

81. Byrne letter to Thornblom, 24 February 1950.

82. CCB 2d Armored Division S-3 Journal, entry, 2100 hours, 8 August 1944.

83. Ibid., entry 0955 hours, 9 August 1944.

84. Ibid., entry, 2040 hours, 9 August 1944.

85. *History of the 67th Armored Regiment* (Brunswick, Germany: George Westermann, GmbH, 1945), 251.

86. Ibid.; *History of the 120th Infantry Regiment* (Washington, D.C.: Infantry Journal Press, 1947), 45.

CHAPTER 8. OPPORTUNITY AND COUNTERATTACK

1. Von Funck and Hausser were removed from command (the latter was wounded at Falaise), while von Kluge chose to commit suicide when he was recalled to Berlin.

2. Percy E. Schramm, "Oberkommand Wehrmacht Diary (1 Apr–18 Dec 44): The West," Military Study B-034 (1946), in *Guide to Foreign Military Studies, 1945–1954* (Heidelberg: Historical Division, Headquarters, U.S. Army, Europe, 1954), 83.

3. Ibid., 80.

4. *7 Armee Kriegstagebuch,* entry, 1730 hours, 8 August 1944, entry 58, Special Staff Adjutant General Division War Diaries, 1943–45, Box 67, German Seventh Army War Diary, January–August 1944, RG 331, Records of Allied Operational and Occupation HQs, WWII (SHAEF), NACP.

5. Ibid., entry, 1845 hours, 8 August 1944.

6. Samuel W. Mitcham Jr., *The Desert Fox in Normandy: Rommel's Defense of Fortress Europe* (Westport, Conn.: Praeger, 1997), 149.

7. Heinrich Eberbach, "Panzer Group Eberbach and the Falaise Encirclement: 1 July–20 August 1944," Military Study A-922 (1946), in *Guide to Foreign Military Studies, 1945–1954*, 14.

8. *7 Armee Kriegstagebuch,* entries 1730 and 1745 hours, 8 August 1944.

9. Schramm, "Oberkommand Wehrmacht Diary," 83.

10. *7 Armee Kriegstagebuch,* 1520 hours, 9 August 1944.

11. Eberbach, "Panzer Group Eberbach and the Falaise Encirclement," 15.

12. *7 Armee Kriegstagebuch,* entry, 2035 hours, 7 August 1944.

13. XIX Corps G-2 Estimate of the Situation, provided to XX Corps G-3, 071700 August 1944, Folder 220-3.2 G-3 Journal and File, 7–10 August, Box 5134, XX Corps,

WWII Operations Reports, 1940–48, RG 407, Records of the Adjutant General's Office, NACP.

14. 12th Army Group Plans Log, 0001–2400 7 August 1944, entries 1100 hours and 1600 hours, Folder G-3 Jnl (vol. II to enclosure 20), 12th Army Grp, 1–31 August 1944, Box 1770, WWII Operations Reports, 1940–48, RG 407, Records of the Adjutant General's Office, NACP.

15. Third Army G-3 Operations Diary, Section III, entry for 7 August 1944, Folder for August 1944, Box 2017, and XX Corps telephone conversation records for 7 August Folder G-3 Journal and File, 7–10 August 1944, Box 5134, both in WWII Operations Reports, 1940–48, RG 407, Records of the Adjutant General's Office, NACP.

16. Omar N. Bradley, with Clay Blair, *A General's Life: An Autobiography by General of the Army Omar N. Bradley* (New York, Simon and Schuster, 1983), 293.

17. XV Corps After-Action Report for August 1944, p. 3, Folder 215-0.3 A/A Reports Hqrs XV Corps, August 1944, Box 4723, WWII Operations Reports, 1940–48, RG 407, Records of the Adjutant General's Office, NACP.

18. Ibid., p. 4.

19. Bradley, *A General's Life,* 294.

20. Third Army G-3 Operations Diary, entry, 8 August 1944.

21. Bradley, *A General's Life,* 294.

22. Memorandum from Lieutenant General Patton to Major General Gaffey, dated 8 August 1944, Folder G-3 Journal and File, 7–10 August 1944, Box 5234, XX Corps, WWII Operations Reports, 1940–48, RG 407, Records of the Adjutant General's Office, NACP.

23. Bradley, *A General's Life,* 295.

24. Letter of Instruction No. 4, dated 8 August 1944, 12th Army Group G-3 After-Action Report, 1 August 1944 to 22 February 1945, vol. V, Box 1749, WWII Operations Reports, 1940–48, RG 407, Records of the Adjutant General's Office, NACP.

25. Ibid.

26. VII Corps Operations Memorandum No. 60, dated 8 August 1944, Folder "Field Orders—Opns Memos, intell annexes, O'lay VII Corps August 44," Box 3941, WWII Operations Reports, 1940–48, RG 407, Records of the Adjutant General's Office, NACP.

27. Morning Report, C/39th Infantry, 8 August 1944, National Personnel Records Center, St. Louis, Mo.

28. A. Eaton Roberts, *Five Stars to Victory: The Exploits of Task Force Lovelady, 2nd Bn. (Reinf), 33rd Arm'd Regt, 3rd Arm'd Div, U.S. Army in the War Against Germany* (Birmingham, Ala.: Atlas Printing and Engraving, 1949), 30–31.

29. 629th TD Battalion S-3 Journal, entries 1–7, 0030 through 0326 hours, 8 August 1944, TDBN-629-0.7 Jnl–629th Tank Destroyer Bn, August 1944, WWII Operations Reports, 1940–48, RG 407, Records of the Adjutant General's Office, NACP.

30. 12th Infantry Regiment S-3 Operations Journal, entry, 1934 hours, 7 August 1944, 304-INF(12)-0.7 (23227) Jnl—12th Inf Regt—4th Inf Div, August 1944, WWII Operations Reports, 1940–48, RG 407, Records of the Adjutant General's Office, NACP.

31. 30th Infantry Division G-3 Journal, entry, 2200 hours, 7 August 1944, G-3 Jnl—30th Inf Div 5–7 August, WWII Operations Reports, 1940–48, RG 407, Records of the Adjutant General's Office, NACP.

32. 117th Infantry Regiment S-3 Journal, entry, 0222 hours, 8 August 1944, Unit

Jnl—117th Inf Reg, 15 June–31 August 1944, 30th Infantry Division, WWII Operations Reports, 1940–48, RG 407, Records of the Adjutant General's Office, NACP.

33. Kenneth R. Lindner, telephone interview by author, tape recording, 5 June 1994.

34. 117th Infantry Regiment S-3 Journal, entry, 0730 hours, 8 August 1944.

35. William J. Lyman, *Curlew History: The Story of the First Battalion, 117th Infantry, 30th Division in Europe During World War II* (Chapel Hill, N.C.: Orange Printshop, 1948), 32–33.

36. 12th Infantry Regiment S-3 Operations Journal, entry, 0520 hours, 8 August 1944.

37. Combat Team 12, Field Order Number 48, 12th Infantry Regiment S-3 Operations Journal, entry, 0900 hours, 8 August 1944.

38. 12th Infantry Regiment S-3 Operations Journal, entry, 1732 hours, 8 August 1944.

39. William L. Anderson and James C. Piper, interview by Lieutenant Fife, 18 August 1944, C.I. 31, 4th Inf Div, St.-Lô–Mortain, 25 July–8 August 1944, Folder 31–34, Combat Interviews, WWII Operations Reports, 1940–48, RG 407, Records of the Adjutant General's Office, NACP.

40. 12th Infantry Regiment After-Action Report, 12th Infantry Regiment S-3 Operations Journal, August 1944.

41. Glenn W. Thorne, telephone interview by author, tape recording, 20 March 1994.

42. 119th Infantry Regiment S-3 Journal, entry, 0958 hours, 8 August 1944, 30th Infantry Division, WWII Operations Reports, 1940–48, RG 407, Records of the Adjutant General's Office, NACP.

43. Juan D. Haines, interview by European Theater historian, 19 August 1944[?], C.I. 261, 3d Arm Div, Fromental, 7–28 August 1944, Folders 259–261, Combat Interviews, WWII Operations Reports, 1940–48, RG 407, Records of the Adjutant General's Office, NACP.

44. F. J. Strauss et al., *Friedens und Kriegserlebnisse einer Generation: Ein Kapitel Weltgeschichte aus der Sicht der Panzerjäger-Abteilung 38 (SF) in der ehemaligen 2. (Wiener) Panzerdivision* (Schweinfurt, Germany: Schweinfurter Tagblatt, 1961[?]), 171.

45. 36th Armored Infantry Regiment S-3 Journal, entry, 1955 hours, 8 August 1944, 603-INF(36)-3.2, S-3 Jnl—36th Armd Inf Regt—3d Armored Div, August 1944, WWII Operations Reports, RG 407, Records of the Adjutant General's Officer, NACP.

46. 119th Infantry Regiment S-3 Journal, entry, 1900 hours, 8 August 1944.

47. Ibid., entries, 2125 and 2150 hours, 8 August 1944.

48. 39th Infantry Regiment S-3 Journal, entry, 1945 hours, 8 August 1944, 309-INF(39)-0.7, Unit Journal–France–European Campaign–39th Infantry Regiment–9th Infantry Division, 1–31 August 1944, WWII Operations Reports, 1940–48, RG 407, Records of the Adjutant General's Office, NACP.

49. 1/39th Infantry S-3 Journal, entry, 0038 hours, 9 August 1944, Unit Journal—European Campaign and Occupation of Germany, 1st Bn, 39th Inf Regt, 9th Inf Div, 9 July–31 December 1944, WWII Operations Reports, 1940–48, RG 407, Records of the Adjutant General's Office, NACP. The ETO historian's interview with Lieutenant Scheffel dated 21 August 1944 describes the incident in which the Germans drove sheep through a minefield.

50. 39th Infantry Regiment S-3 Journal, entry, 0315 hours, 9 August 1944.

51. Ibid., entry, 0425 hours, 9 August 1944.

52. Ibid., entry, 0930 hours, 9 August 1944. The 39th Infantry journal noted that the 26th FA would be required to mark the targets before the attack took place.

53. Operation Report, 492d Fighter Squadron, 9 August 1944, HRA.

54. 39th Infantry Regiment S-3 Journal, entry, 1630 hours, 9 August 1944.

55. 12th Infantry Regiment S-3 Operations Journal, entry, 0730 hours, 9 August 1944.

56. Ibid., entry, 0910 hours, 9 August 1944.

57. Glenn W. Thorne, telephone interview by author, tape recording, 20 March 1994.

58. 30th Infantry Division G-3 Journal, entry 16, 0822 hours, 9 August 1944.

59. 117th Infantry Regiment S-3 Journal, entry, 1910 hours, 9 August 1944, Unit Jnl—117th Inf Reg, 15 June–31 August 1944, WWII Operations Reports, 1940–48, RG 407, Records of the Adjutant General's Office, NACP.

60. 12th Infantry Regiment After-Action Report for August 1944, Appendix No. 4, "Losses in Action: Officer and Men," 304-INF(12)-0.7 (23227) Jnl—12th Inf Regt—4th Inf Div, August 1944, WWII Operations Reports, 1940–48, RG 407, Records of the Adjutant General's Office, NACP.

61. 30th Infantry Division G-2 Periodic Report 090001 to 092400 August 1944, 330-FA(230)-0.7 Jnl and File 230th FA Bn, August 1944, Box 8883, WWII Operations Reports, 1940–48, RG 407, Records of the Adjutant General's Office, NACP.

62. 30th Infantry Division G-3 Journal, entry 22, 1000 hours, 9 August 1944.

63. 36th Armored Infantry Regiment S-3 Journal, entry 9, 1230 hours, 9 August 1944.

64. 30th Infantry Division G-3 Journal, entry 54, 1440 hours, 9 August 1944.

65. 119th Infantry Regiment S-3 Journal, entry, 1700 hours, 9 August 1944.

66. 36th Armored Infantry Regiment S-3 Journal, entry 22, 1730 hours, 10 August 1944.

67. 119th Infantry Regiment S-3 Journal, entry, 1110 hours, 9 August 1944.

CHAPTER 9. HOLDING THE HIGH GROUND

1. 120th Infantry Regiment S-3 Journal, entry, 0055 hours, 10 August 1944, 330-INF(120)-0.7, 120th Inf Regt 1–31 August 1944, 30th Infantry Division, WWII Operations Reports, 1940–48, RG 407, Records of the Adjutant General's Office, NACP.

2. Ibid., entry, 1345 hours, 12 August 1944. Three of the panzers were left behind when the Germans retreated, while the other four were retrieved by the SS, although two were on fire as they were being towed out of the area.

3. Ibid., entry, 1335 hours, 10 August 1944.

4. 230th FA Battalion S-3 Journal, entry, 1420 hours, 10 August 1944, 330-FA(230)0.7, Jnl and File, 230th FA Bn, 1–31 August 1944, 30th Infantry Division, WWII Operations Reports, 1940–48, RG 407, Records of the Adjutant General's Office, NACP.

5. Operation Report "A," 492d Fighter Squadron, 10 August 1944, HRA.

6. DZ Europe: History of the 440th Troop Carrier Group (Germany: privately printed, 1945), 117.

7. Robert Weiss, telephone conversation with author, 2 March 1998.

8. *History of the 120th Infantry Regiment* (Washington, D.C.: Infantry Journal Press, 1947), 55.

9. 30th Infantry Division G-3 Journal, entry 145, 1645 hours, 10 August 1944, G-3 Jnl—30th Infantry Div, 10–13 August 1944, WWII Operations Reports, 1940–48, RG 407, Records of the Adjutant General's Office, NACP.

10. 230th Field Artillery S-3 Journal, entry, 1825 hours, 10 August 1944.

11. 30th Infantry Division G-3 Journal, entry, 2145 hours, 10 August 1944.

12. Floyd M. Montgomery, telephone interview by author, tape recording, 29 July 1993.

13. *Combat History of the 119th Infantry Regiment* (Baton Rouge, La.: Army and Navy Publishing, 1946), 36.

14. 120th Infantry Regiment S-3 Journal, entry, 1315 hours, 10 August 1944.

15. Ibid., entry, 0900 hours, 10 August 1944.

16. Thomas Springfield, telephone interview by author, tape recording, 27 February 1994.

17. Tom F. H. Andrew and Hammond D. Birks, "The Counterattack Against the 120th Inf. at Mortain, the Abbaye-Blanche Roadblock," interview by European Theater historian, 18 August 1944, p. 5, C.I. 96, 30th Inf Div, Mortain Counterattack, 6–12 August 1944, Folders 95–97, Combat Interviews, WWII Operations Reports, 1940–48, RG 407, Records of the Adjutant General's Office, NACP.

18. Hans Stöber, *Die Sturmflut und das Ende: Die Invasion—Geschichte der 17. SS-Panzergrenadier Division "Götz von Berlichingen"* (Munich: Schild Verlag, 2000), 298.

19. 30th Infantry Division G-3 Journal, entry, 1255 hours, 10 August 1944, and 629th TD Battalion S-3 Journal, entry, 1305 hours, 10 August 1944, TDBN-629-0.7 Jnl–629th Tank Destroyer Bn, August 1944, WWII Operations Reports, 1940–48, RG 407, Records of the Adjutant General's Office, NACP.

20. 230th FA Battalion S-3 Journal, entry, 1240 hours, 10 August 1944.

21. Morning Reports, G/119th Infantry, 10 to 12 August 1944, National Personnel Records Center, St. Louis, Mo.

22. Emmett W. Tripp, telephone interviews by author, tape recordings, 11 and 18 December 1992.

23. Edward C. Arn and Thomas H. Kirkman, "Activities of the 2d Battalion, 119th Infantry, August 9–12," interview by David Garth, 5 September 1944, C.I. 96, 30th Inf Div, Mortain Counterattack, 6–12 August 1944, Folders 95–97, Combat Interviews, WWII Operations Reports, 1940–48, RG 407, Records of the Adjutant General's Officer, NACP.

24. *Combat History of the 119th Infantry Regiment,* 35.

25. Thomas E. Magness, telephone interview by author, tape recording, 4 April 1993.

26. 320th Infantry Regiment S-3 Journal, entries, 0400 and 0527 hours, 10 August 1944, 335-INF(320)-0.7, Opns Journal—35th Inf Div, 320th Inf Regt, August 1944, WWII Operations Reports, 1940–48, RG 407, Records of the Adjutant General's Office, NACP.

27. 35th Infantry Division G-3 Journal, entry, 0740 hours, 10 August 1944, Journal file, 9–10 August 1944, WWII Operations Reports, 1940–48, RG 407, Records of the Adjutant General's Office, NACP.

28. War Diary Entry, D/32d Armored Regiment, 10 August 1944; copy provided to author by Alvin Beckmann.

29. Bernard A. Byrne, letter to Carlton Thornblom, 24 February 1950; provided to author by Henry Morgan.

30. 737th Tank Battalion S-3 "Report of Action against the Enemy, Unit: 737th Tank Battalion on 10 August 1944," A/A Rpt–737th Amph Tractor Bn, ARBN-737-0.3 (6144), Armored, WWII Operations Reports, 1940–48, RG 407, Records of the Adjutant General's Office, NACP.

31. Ben W. Hackman, telephone interview by author, 18 November 1992.

32. C Company had sixteen tanks, while A and B Companies of the 737th possessed eleven apiece. D/32d Armor also had eleven operational tanks. See 737th Tank Battalion S-3, "Report of Action," August 1944.

33. Junior K. Lambert, telephone interview by author, tape recording, 13 December 1992.

34. 320th Infantry Regiment S-3 Journal Entries dated 1525 and 1550 hours, 10 August 1944, see note 26.

35. Carlton C. Thornblom, "Operations of the 1/320th Infantry at Mortain, 7–12 August 1944," USAIS Library Student Monograph, Fort Benning, Ga., Advanced Officers Class No (1950), 13.

36. 30th Infantry Division G-3 Journal, entry, 1613 hours, 10 August 1944.

37. 120th Infantry Regiment S-3 Journal, entry, 1558 hours, 10 August 1944.

38. Henry Morgan, letter to author, 27 November 1992.

39. Stöber, *Die Sturmflut und das Ende,* 303.

40. Robert Kluttz, telephone interview by author, tape recording, 2 December 1992.

41. Thornblom, "Operations of the 1/320th Infantry at Mortain," 15.

42. Morgan, letter to author.

43. Thornblom, "Operations of the 1/320th Infantry at Mortain," 16–17. I was able to ascertain that it was Captain Conde by Thornblom's description of the tank company commander in his monograph. Thomas Eller, the 3d Platoon leader of A/737th Tank Battalion, later confirmed that this description matched his company commander.

44. Art Newman, telephone interview by author, tape recording, 12 May 1993.

45. Samuel Belk, telephone conversation with author, 10 July 1998.

46. Ibid.

47. Thornblom, "Operations of the 1/320th Infantry at Mortain," 18.

48. 320th Infantry Regiment S-3 Journal, entry, 2230 hours, 10 August 1944.

49. 120th Infantry Regiment S-3 Journal Entries, 1730 and 1731 hours, 10 August 1944.

50. Walter Krueger, "LVIII Panzer Corps: 24 July–15 September 1944," Military Study B-445, in *Guide to Foreign Military Studies, 1945–1954* (Heidelberg: Historical Division, Headquarters, U.S. Army, Europe, 1954), 15.

51. James A. Huston, *Biography of a Battalion: Being the Life and Times of an Infantry Battalion in Europe in World War II* (Gering, Nebr.: Courier Press, 1950), 248.

52. Fred R. Harman, telephone interview by author, tape recording, 21 December 1992, and Thomas G. Tousey, telephone interview by author, tape recording, 26 January 1993.

53. VII Corps G-2 Log Entry, 10 August 1944, 207-2.2, G-2 Jrnl and file, VII Corps,

10–11 August 1944, WWII Operations Reports, 1940–48, RG 407, Records of the Adjutant General's Office, NACP.

54. Tousey, interview, and 35th Infantry Division G-3 Journal, entry, 0745 hours, 10 August 1944. VII Corps G-3 Journal, entries, 0700 and 1800 hours, 10 August 1944, WWII Operations Reports, 1940–48, RG 407, Records of the Adjutant General's Office, NACP.

55. 230th FA Battalion S-3 Journal Entries, 0851 and 0955 hours, 11 August 1944.

56. George R. Poulson, telephone interview by author, tape recording, 4 November 1993.

57. John O'Hare, telephone interview by author, tape recording, 1 June 1993.

58. Murray S. Pulver, *The Longest Year* (Freeman, S.D.: Pine Hill Press, 1986), 37.

59. Robert E. Herlong, "Repulse of the German Counterattack Aimed at Avranches, 7–11 August," interview by Franklin Ferriss, 18 August 1944, C.I. 96, 30th Inf Div, Mortain Counterattack, 6–12 August 1944, Folders 95–97, Combat Interviews, WWII Operations Reports, 1940–48, RG 407, Records of the Adjutant General's Office, NACP.

60. 30th Infantry Division G-3 Journal, entry, 0857 hours, 11 August 1944.

61. Ibid., entries, 0930 and 0940 hours, 11 August 1944, see note 9.

62. 35th Infantry Division G-3 Journal, entry, 0900 hours, 11 August 1944.

63. 743d Tank Battalion After-Action Report for August 1944, p. 4, G-3 Jnl743d Tank Bn, June–August 1944, ARBN-743-3.2 (47694), Armored, WWII Operations Reports, 1940–48, RG 407, Records of the Adjutant General's Office, NACP.

64. Samuel M. Hogan, "Activities of Team No. 3, 3d Armored Division, August 7–12, 1944," interview by European Theater historian, 19 August 1944, C.I.-261, 3d Arm Div, Fromental, 7–28 August 1944, Folders 259–261, Combat Interviews, WWII Operations Reports, 1940–48, RG 407, Records of the Adjutant General's Office, NACP.

65. *Combat History of the 119th Infantry Regiment,* 36, and Morning Report, H/119th Infantry, 12 August 1944, National Personnel Records Center, St. Louis, Mo.

66. Hogan, "Activities of Team No. 3."

67. Morgan, letter to author.

68. Thornblom, "Operations of the 1/320th Infantry at Mortain."

69. 320th Infantry Regiment S-3 Journal, entries, 0635 and 0850 hours, 11 August 1944.

70. 35th Infantry Division G-3 Journal, entry, 1450 hours, 11 August 1944.

71. 35th Infantry Division G-3 Journal, entry, 1725 hours, 11 August 1944.

72. 320th Infantry Regiment S-3 Journal, entry, 2000 hours, 11 August 1944.

73. Kurt Forster's account is found in *Das Regiment Deutschland 1934–1945,* written by the Veterans Association of the Deutschland Regiment (Freinsheim, Germany: Gerhard Eichelmann, Gesamtherstellung und Verlag, 1993), 247–251.

74. 320th Infantry Regiment S-3 Journal, entry, 1615 hours, 11 August 1944. The note is attached to the journal.

75. 35th Infantry Division G-3 Journal, entry, 1145 hours, 11 August 1944, and 320th Infantry Regiment S-3 Journal, entry, 1115 hours, 11 August 1944.

76. 320th Infantry Regiment S-3 Journal, entry, 1703 hours, 11 August 1944.

77. Ibid., entry 113, 1850 hours, 11 August 1944.

78. Thornblom, "Operations of the 1/320th Infantry at Mortain," 25.

79. Joseph L. Vignes, telephone interview by author, tape recording, 23 November 1992, and Jack Sabata, letter to author, 5 September 1992.

80. Morgan, letter to author, and Thornblom, "Operations of the 1/320th Infantry at Mortain."

81. Homer W. Kurtz, telephone interview by author, tape recording, 30 November 1992.

82. Ewald Klapdor, *Die Entscheidung: Invasion 1944* (Germany: privately printed, 1984), 371.

83. Donald E. Houston, *Hell on Wheels: The 2d Armored Division* (Novato, Calif.: Presidio, 1977), 249.

84. CCB, 2d Armored Division S-3 Journal, entry, 1905 hours, 11 August 1944, 602-CC(B)-0.7, Jnl and file—Hqs CC "B" 2d Armd Div, 9–16 August 1944, WWII Operations Reports, 1940–48, RG 407, Records of the Adjutant General's Office, NACP, and *History of the 67th Armored Regiment* (Brunswick, Germany: George Westermann, GmbH, 1945), 252.

85. CCB, 2d Armored Division S-3 Journal, entry, 1545 hours, 11 August 1944.

86. *History of the 67th Armored Regiment,* 183.

CHAPTER 10. IMPENDING DEFEAT

1. Walter Krueger, "LVIII Panzer Corps: 24 July–15 September 1944," Military Study B-445, in *Guide to Foreign Military Studies, 1945–1954* (Heidelberg: Historical Division, Headquarters U.S. Army, Europe, 1954), 6.

2. Ibid., 9.

3. Martin Blumenson, *Breakout and Pursuit* (Washington, D.C., Center for Military History, U.S. Government Printing Office, 1989), 482.

4. Ibid., 484.

5. Percy E. Schramm, "Oberkommand Wehrmacht Diary (1 Apr–18 Dec 44): The West," Military Study B-034 (1946), in *Guide to Foreign Military Studies, 1945–1954*, 83.

6. Ibid., 84.

7. *7 Armee Kriegstagebuch,* entry (undated), 1944, entry 58, Special Staff Adjutant General Division War Diaries, 1943–45, German Seventh Army Box 67, RG 331, Records of Allied Operational and Occupation HQs, WW II (SHAEF), NACP. The follow-on to this conversation is found on page 23a of the *Kriegstagebuch.*

8. XV Corps Report After Combat, U.S. Army, 31 July to 31 August 1944, p. 5, Folder 215-0.3 A/A Reports Hqs XV Corps, August 1944, Box 4723, WWII Operations Reports, 1940–48, RG 407, Records of the Adjutant General's Office, NACP.

9. Omar N. Bradley, *A Soldier's Story* (New York: Henry Holt, 1951), 370.

10. Diary entry for 9 August 1944, William C. Sylvan Diary 2 June 1944–May 7, 1945, Personal Papers of William Sylvan, U.S. Army Military History Institute, Carlisle, Pennsylvania.

11. Omar N. Bradley, with Clay Blair, *A General's Life: An Autobiography by General of the Army Omar N. Bradley* (New York: Simon and Schuster, 1983), 296.

12. Third Army G-2 Estimate No. 6, dated 10 August 1944, Folder 103-2.1 Third Army G-2 Periodic Reports (Nos. 33–81), 13 July–30 August 1944, Box 2037, WWII Operations Reports, 1940–48, RG 407, Records of the Adjutant General's Office, NACP.

13. Diary entry for 10 August, George S. Patton Diaries, 1910–1945, Box 3, Fold-

ers 7–8, Annotated Transcripts, 1 August 1944–29 November 1944, George S. Patton Collection, Library of Congress, Washington, D.C.

14. Entry for 10 August 1944, Chester B. Hansen Diary, February 1943 to October 1944, Folder Diary, 1 August–15 August 1944, Chester B. Hansen Papers, Box 1, USAMHI.

15. 21 Army Group Directive M 518, dated 11 August 1944, Folder 99-21-3.1 G-3 Periodic Reports 21st Army Group, 9 June–16 September 1944, Box 1817, WWII Operations Reports, 1940–48, RG 407, Records of the Adjutant General's Office, NACP.

16. VII Corps Operations Memo 63, dated 11 August 1944, Folder "Field Orders—Opns Memos, intell annexes, O'lay VII Corps August 1944," Box 3941, VII Corps 207-3.9, May to November 1944, WWII Operations Reports, 1940–48, RG 407, Records of the Adjutant General's Office, NACP. Field Order 19 from the 4th Infantry Division stated that "4th Inf Div (Reinf) (less CT 12 and 8) moves by motor 10 Aug 1944 to vicinity Buais–le Teilleul to prevent enemy penetration from the east within its zone of action."

17. Hans Eberbach, "Panzer Group Eberbach and the Falaise Encirclement: 1 July–20 August 1944," Military Study A-922 (1946), in *Guide to Foreign Military Studies, 1945–1954*, 18.

18. Blumenson, *Breakout and Pursuit*, 484.

19. *7 Armee Kriegstagebuch*, estimate of the situation, 10 August 1944.

20. Schramm, "Oberkommand Wehrmacht Diary," 83.

21. Ibid., 85.

22. Ibid., 84–85.

23. Blumenson, *Breakout and Pursuit*, 495.

24. Entry for 11 August 1944, Chester B. Hansen Diary.

25. Blumenson, *Breakout and Pursuit*, 501.

26. Entry for 11 August 1944, George S. Patton Diaries.

27. Third Army G-3 Operations Diary, entry 11 August 1944, Folder for August 1944, Box 2017, WWII Operations Reports, RG 407, Records of the Adjutant General's Office, NACP. In his diary that evening, Patton noted that he "got home to find out that Gaffey had not yet got the VIII Corps going, so we can release the 4th Armored. I was quite angry."

28. 39th Infantry Regiment S-3 Journal, entry 12, 0915 hours, 10 August 1944, 309-INF(39)-0.7, Unit Journal–France–European Campaign–39th Infantry Regiment-9th Infantry Division, 1–31 August 1944, WWII Operations Reports, 1940–48, RG 407, Records of the Adjutant General's Office, NACP.

29. 1/39th Infantry S-3 Journal, entry, 1030 hours, 10 August 1944, Unit Journal–European Campaign and Occupation of Germany, 1st Bn, 39th Inf Regt, 9th Inf Div, 9 July–31 December 1944, WWII Operations Reports, 1940–48, RG 407, Records of the Adjutant General's Office, NACP.

30. OPFLASH Report No.1 for mission 133, 50th Fighter Group, 81st Fighter Squadron, 1150 hours, Historical Research Agency, Maxwell Air Force Base, Ala. (HRA).

31. 39th Infantry Regiment S-3 Journal, entry 14, 1045 hours, 10 August 1944.

32. 39th Infantry Regiment S-3 Journal, entry 16, 1210 hours, 10 August 1944.

33. Operations Report A, 365th Fighter Group, 10 August 1944, HRA.

34. 39th Infantry Regiment S-3 Journal, entry 18, 1250 hours, 10 August 1944.

35. 119th Infantry Regiment S-3 Journal, entry, 0940 hours, 10 August 1944, 30th

Infantry Division, WWII Operations Reports, 1940–48, RG 407, Records of the Adjutant General's Office, NACP.

36. Ibid., entry, 1105 hours, 10 August 1944.

37. Ibid., entry, 1315 hours, 10 August 1944.

38. 1/39th Infantry S-3 Journal, entries, 1919 and 2056 hours, 10 August 1944.

39. *7 Armee Kriegstagebuch,* Report No. 682/44, *7 Armee* Headquarters Advanced Command Post, to *Heeresgruppe B,* 10 August 1944.

40. 117th Infantry Regiment S-3 Journal, entry, 0745 hours, 10 August 1944, Unit Jnl—117th Inf Reg, 15 June–31 August 1944, 30th Infantry Division, WWII Operations Reports, 1940–48, RG 407, Records of the Adjutant General's Office, NACP.

41. 12th Infantry Regiment After-Action Report for August 1944, Appendix No. 4, "Losses in Action: Officer and Men," 12th Infantry Regiment, September 1944, 304-INF(12)-0.7 (23227) Jnl—12th Inf Regt—4th Inf Div, August 1944, WWII Operations Reports, 1940–48, RG 407, Records of the Adjutant General's Office, NACP.

42. 117th Infantry S-3 Journal, entry, 1100 hours, 10 August 1944.

43. 30th Infantry Division G-3 Journal, entry 139, 1559 hours, 10 August 1944, G-3 Jnl—30th Inf Div, 10–13 August 1944, WWII Operations Reports, 1940–48, RG 407, Records of the Adjutant General's Office, NACP.

44. Ibid., entry, 0710 hours, 10 August 1944.

45. Ibid., entry, 0820 hours, 10 August 1944.

46. 12th Infantry Regiment S-3 Journal, entry, 0947 hours, 10 August 1944, 304-INF(12)-0.7 (23227) Jnl—12th Inf Regt—4th Inf Div, August 1944, WWII Operations Reports, 1940–48, RG 407, Records of the Adjutant General's Office, NACP.

47. 12th Infantry Regiment After-Action Report for August 1944.

48. 12th Infantry Regiment S-3 Journal, entry, 1209 hours, 10 August 1944.

49. Ibid., entries, 1225 and 1254 hours, 10 August 1944.

50. 30th Infantry Division G-3 Journal, entry 91, 1225 hours, 10 August 1944.

51. Ibid., entry 103, 1315 hours, 10 August 1944.

52. 12th Infantry Regiment S-3 Journal, entry, 1530 hours, 10 August 1944.

53. Ibid., entry, 1800 hours, 10 August 1944.

54. Gerald P. Harrington, telephone interview by author, tape recording, 19 April 1994.

55. 30th Infantry Division Letter of Instruction, dated 102200 August 1944, Folder Field Orders w/supporting papers "Mortain and Domfront," 30th Infantry Division, 5–16 August 1944, Box 8837, 30th Infantry Division 330-3.9, WWII Operations Reports, 1940–48, RG 407, Records of the Adjutant General's Office, NACP.

56. 39th Infantry Regiment S-3 Journal, entries, 0030 and 0610 hours, 11 August 1944. The details for the 3d Battalion patrols were found in 1/39th Infantry S-3 Journal, entry, 0002 hours on 11 August 1944.

57. 1/39th Infantry S-3 Journal, entries dated 0936, 1032, 1050, and 1120 hours, 11 August 1944.

58. Ibid., entries, 1538 and 1548 hours, 11 August 1944.

59. 26th FA Battalion After-Action Report for August 1944, p .5, 309-FA(26)-0.1, Narrative Report–France–Belgium–Germany–European Campaign–26th Field Artillery Battalion–9th Infantry Division, 3 July–31 December 1944, WWII Operations Reports, 1940–48, RG 407, Records of the Adjutant General's Office, NACP.

60. William J. Butler, "The Combat Cage," unpublished memoir, Kalamazoo, Mich., November 1998, 102.

61. 39th Infantry Regiment S-3 Journal, entry, 2230 hours, 11 August 1944.

62. 119th Infantry Regiment S-3 Journal, entry, 0945 hours, 11 August 1944.

63. Michel Coupard and Jack Lecoq, *Le Mortainais: Mortain et Juvigny le-Tertre—Memoire en Images* (Joue les Tours, France: Editions Alan Sutton, 1997), 76. A monument to Guerinel is located in the present-day town square of St.-Barthelemy.

64. 117th Infantry Regiment S-3 Journal Entries, 0100, 1205, and 1545 hours, 11 August 1944.

65. Ibid., entries dated 1710, 1755, and 1800 hours. 11 August 1944.

66. Casualty figures are from the 12th Infantry Regiment After-Action Report for August 1944. Mention of the knocked-out panzer was made in the 117th Infantry S-3 Journal, entry, 2145 and 2220 hours on 11 August.

67. Charles Scheffel, telephone conversation with author, 19 September 1998.

68. 117th Infantry Regiment S-3 Journal, entry, 1950 hours, 11 August 1944.

69. 30th Infantry Division G-3 Journal, entry 46, 1205 hours, 11 August 1944.

70. 12th Infantry Regiment S-3 Journal, entry 19, 1455 hours, 11 August 1944. The S-3 Journal entry notes the progress of the 1/12th Infantry, and the after-action report provides the source for the casualties.

71. Gerald P. Harrington, telephone interview by author, tape recording, 19 April 1994.

72. All casualty figures are from the 12th Infantry Regiment After-Action Report for August 1944.

73. Kenneth E. Lay, telephone interview by author, tape recording, 1 November 1994. Although some accounts mention the fact that fragments from a mortar round hit Johnson, I believe that he was one of the first casualties inflicted by the panzer counterattack that started at 1800 hours that afternoon. The August 1944 interview of Lieutenants Piper and Anderson specifically states that the battalion command group was hit by tank fire.

74. William L. Anderson and James C. Piper, interview by Lieutenant Fife, 18 August 1944, C.I. 31, 4th Inf Div, St.-Lô–Mortain, 25 July–8 August 1944, Folders 31–34, Combat Interviews, WWII Operations Reports, 1940–48, RG 407, Records of the Adjutant General's Office, NACP. Anderson and Piper mistakenly attribute this incident to the evening of 8 August, but the 12th Infantry Regiment S-3 Journal clearly indicates that it occurred on 11 August 1944. Entry 29 states that "the counterattack started when the half-tracks were knocked out."

75. 12th Infantry Regiment S-3 Journal, entry 24, 1636 hours, 11 August 1944.

76. Anderson and Piper, interview. Anderson and Piper confused both his rank and the date for this incident, which actually took place during the panzer counterattack on 11 August. Private Burik is listed in the casualty roster for E Company as KIA on 13 August.

77. Marvin Jensen, *Strike Swiftly!: The 70th Tank Battalion from North Africa to Normandy to Germany* (Novato, Calif.: Presidio, 1997), 196.

78. 30th Infantry Division G-3 Journal, entry, 2050 hours, 11 August 1944.

79. 12th Infantry Regiment S-3 Journal, entry 35, 2141 hours, 11 August 1944, and 30th Infantry Division, G-3 Journal, entry 123, 2224 hours, 11 August 1944.

CHAPTER 11. TIGHTENING THE NOOSE

1. Percy E. Schramm, "Oberkommand Wehrmacht Diary (1 Apr–18 Dec 44): The West," Military Study B-034, 1946, in *Guide to Foreign Military Studies, 1945–1954* (Heidelberg: Historical Division, Headquarters, U.S. Army, Europe, 1954), 85.

2. Ibid., 84–85.

3. Ibid., 86.

4. Walter Krueger, "LVIII Panzer Corps: 24 July–15 September 1944," Military Study B-445, in *Guide to Foreign Military Studies, 1945-1954*, 16–17.

5. Heinz Günther Guderian, *Das letze Kriegsjahr im Westen: Die Geschichte der 116. Panzer Division Windhund Division* (Sankt Augustin, Germany: Herbert W. Schallowetz GmbH, SZ Offsetdruck Verlag, 1994), 87. *Panzer Division 116*, for example, was notified of the withdrawal orders in "the late afternoon." It would take even longer to get the word down to battalions and companies.

6. 1/39th Infantry S-3 Journal, entry, 0510 hours, 12 August 1944, Unit Journal—European Campaign and Occupation of Germany, 1st Bn, 39th Inf Regt, 9th Inf Div, 9 July–31 December 1944, WWII Operations Reports, 1940–48, RG 407, Records of the Adjutant General's Office, NACP.

7. 39th Infantry Regiment S-3 Journal, entries, 0915, 1025, and 1050 hours, 12 August, 309-INF(39)-0.7, Unit Journal–France–European Campaign–39th Infantry Regiment–9th Infantry Division, 1–31 August 1944, WWII Operations Reports, 1940–48, RG 407, Records of the Adjutant General's Office, NACP.

8. 30th Infantry Division G-3 Journal, entry, 0735 hours, 12 August 1944, G-3 Jnl—30th Inf Div, 10–13 August 1944, WWII Operations Reports, 1940–48, RG 407, Records of the Adjutant General's Office, NACP.

9. Ibid., entry, 0155 hours, 12 August 1944.

10. Ibid., entry, 0720 hours, 12 August 1944.

11. 119th Infantry Regiment S-3 Journal, entry, 1200 hours, 12 August 1944, 330-INF(119) 0.7, August 1944, 30th Infantry Division, WWII Operations Reports, 1940–48, RG 407, Records of the Adjutant General's Office, NACP.

12. 366th Fighter Group Operations Report "A," No. 134, Historical Research Agency, Maxwell Air Force Base, Ala. (HRA).

13. Dunbar Whitman, "Interview with Capt Dunbar Whitman, EO, 1st Bn, 12th Inf, Mortain Battle," interview by European Theater historian, 18 August 1944[?], p. 4, C.I. 31, 4th Inf Div, St.-Lô–Mortain, 25 July–8 August 1944, Folders 31–34, Combat Interviews, WWII Operations Reports, 1940–48, RG 407, Records of the Adjutant General's Office, NACP.

14. William L. Anderson and James C. Piper, interview by Lieutenant Fife, 18 August 1944, C.I. 31, 4th Inf Div, St.-Lô–Mortain, 25 July–8 August 1944, Folders 31–34, Combat Interviews, WWII Operations Reports, 1940–48, RG 407, Records of the Adjutant General's Office, NACP.

15. Marc Dillard, telephone interview by author, tape recording, 19 March 1994.

16. 12th Infantry Regiment S-3 Journal, entries 3–12, 12 August 1944, 304-INF(12)-0.7 (23227) Jnl—12th Infantry Regt—4th Infantry Division, August 1944, WWII Operations Reports, 1940–48, RG 407, Records of the Adjutant General's Office, NACP.

17. Emmett W. Tripp, telephone interviews by author, tape recordings, 11 and 18 December 1992.

18. Message from TF 3 to CCB, 3d Armored Division, 1300 hours, 12 August 1944, 603-CC(B)-0.7, Jnl and file—Hqs CC "B" 3d Armd Div, 9–16 August 1944, WWII Operations Reports, 1940–48, RG 407, Records of the Adjutant General's Office, NACP.

19. 117th Infantry Regiment S-3 Journal, entry, 1235 hours, 12 August 1944, Unit Jnl—117th Inf Reg, 15 June–31 August 1944, 30th Infantry Division, WWII Operations Reports, 1940–48, RG 407, Records of the Adjutant General's Office, NACP.

20. Kenneth R. Lindner, telephone interview by author, tape recording, 5 June 1994.

21. 117th Infantry Regiment S-3 Journal, entry, 1714 hours, 12 August 1944.

22. Ibid., entry 24, 1525 hours, 12 August 1944.

23. 320th Infantry Regiment S-3 Journal, entries, 0530 and 0625 hours, 12 August 1944, 335-INF(320)-0.7, Opns Journal—35th Inf Div, 320th Inf Reg, August 1944, WWII Operations Reports, 1940–48, RG 407, Records of the Adjutant General's Office, NACP.

24. Homer W. Kurtz, telephone interview by author, tape recording, 30 November 1992.

25. 35th Infantry Division G-3 Journal, entry, 1105 hours, 12 August 1944, Journal file, 11–12 August 1944, WWII Operations Reports, 1940–48, RG 407, Records of the Adjutant General's Office, NACP.

26. 30th Infantry Division G-3 Journal, entry, 2320 hours, 11 August 1944.

27. Interview with veteran of the 30th Infantry Division who did not wish to be named, telephone interview by author, tape recording, 22 September 1993.

28. Guy B. Hagen, telephone interview by author, tape recording, 27 August 1993, and Hodges, interview.

29. 35th Infantry Division G-3 Journal, entry, 2325 hours, 12 August 1944.

30. Leonard T. Murray, telephone interview by author, tape recording, 1 December 1992, and Morning Report, K Company, 320th Infantry, 16 August 1944, National Personnel Records Center, St. Louis, Mo.

31. James A. Huston, *Biography of a Battalion: Being the Life and Times of an Infantry Battalion in Europe in World War II* (Gering, Nebr.: Courier Press, 1950), 69.

32. 35th Infantry Division G-3 Journal, entry, 0855 hours, 12 August 1944.

33. CCB 2d Armored Division Operations Journal, entry 2, 0130 hours, 12 August 1944, 602-CC (B)-0.7, Jnl and file—Hqs CC "B" 2d Armd Division, 9–16 August 1944, WWII Operations Reports, 1940–48, RG 407, Records of the Adjutant General's Office, NACP.

34. VII Corps G-3 Journal, entry, 1100 hours, 12 August 1944, 207-3.2, G-3 Jrnl and file, VII Corps, 12 August 1944, WWII Operations Reports, 1940–48, RG 407, Records of the Adjutant General's Office, NACP.

35. *History of the 67th Armored Regiment* (Brunswick, Germany: George Westermann, GmbH, 1945), 252.

36. VII Corps G-2 Journal, entry, 0330 hours, 13 August 1944, 207-2.2, G-2 Jrnl and file, VII Corps, 12–13 August 1944, WWII Operations Reports, 1940–48, RG 407, Records of the Adjutant General's Office, NACP.

37. Wilhelm Tieke, *In the Firestorm of the Last Years of the War: II. SS-Panzerkorps with the 9. and 10. SS-Divisions "Hohenstaufen" and "Frundsberg,"* trans. Frederick Steinhardt (Winnipeg: J. J. Fedorowicz, 1999), 185.

38. British 30 Corps Intelligence Summary No. 475, undated, Folder 1st Army G-3 Jnl File, August 1944, Box 1968, WWII Operations Reports, 1940–48, RG 407, Records of the Adjutant General's Office, NACP.

39. VII Corps Field Order No. 8, dated 13 August 1944, Folder Situation Reports VII Corps, August 1944, Box 3939, WWII Operations Reports, 1940–48, RG 407, Records of the Adjutant General's Office, NACP.

40. Third Army G-3 Operations Diary, Section III, entry, 12 August, Folder for August 1944, Box 2017, WWII Operations Reports, 1940–48, RG 407, Records of the Adjutant General's Office, NACP.

41. "Questions for Heinrich von Luettwitz, Commanding General of the 2d Panzer Division until September 1944, Normandy Campaign of 2 Panzer Division, 26 July–6 September 1944," Military Study A-904, in *Guide to Foreign Military Studies, 1945–1954*, 20–21.

42. Martin Blumenson, *Breakout and Pursuit* (Washington, D.C.: Center for Military History, U.S. Government Printing Office, 1989), 503. However, Blumenson incorrectly identifies *Kampfgruppe Wahl* as belonging to *SS-Panzer Division 2*. See M. Wind and H. Gunther, eds., *Kreigstagebuch vom 30. Oktober 1943 bis 6. Mai 1945; 17-SS Panzergrenadier Division "Götz Von Berlichingen"* (Munich: Schild Verlag GmbH, 1993), unit report by *Divisionskommandeur* Otto Binge to *Divisionskommandeur, SS-Panzer Division 2*, dated 15 August 1944. Additionally, *Kampfgruppe von Hauser* from *Panzer Lehr* reinforced *Infanterie Division 331*. See Jean-Claude Perrigault, *La Panzer Lehr Division: Le Choc Des Allies Brise L'Arme D'Elite De Hitler Normandie–Lorraine–Ardennes* (Bayeux, France: Editions Heimdal, 1995), 307–308.

43. Gerhard Graf von Schwerin, "An Interview with Generalleutnant Gerhard Graf von Schwerin: 116 Panzer Division in Normandy," European Theater historian Interview No. 17, by Kenneth W. Hechler, 1 September 1945, in *Guide to Foreign Military Studies, 1945–1954*, 21.

44. Guderian, *Das letze Kriegsjahr im Westen*, 91–92.

45. *Paths of Armor: The Fifth Armored Division in World War II*, (Nashville, Tenn.: Battery Press, 1950), 63.

46. Guderian, *Das letze Kriegsjahr im Westen*, 92–93.

47. Blumenson, *Breakout and Pursuit*, 505.

48. Martin Blumenson, *Command Decisions: General Bradley's Decision at Argentan (13 August 1944)*, Center for Military History pub. No. 70-7-17, (Washington, D.C.: U.S. Government Printing Office, 1990), 414.

49. Blumenson, *Breakout and Pursuit*, 510–511.

50. Third Army G-3 Operations Diary, entry for 12 August.

51. XV Corps Report After Combat, U.S. Army, 31 July to 31 August 1944, p. 6, WWII Operations Reports, RG 407, Records of the Adjutant General's Office, NACP.

52. *Paths of Armor: The Fifth Armored Division in World War II*, 64.

53. Blumenson, *Breakout and Pursuit*, 517.

54. Ibid., 518.

55. Hans Eberbach, "Panzer Group Eberbach and the Falaise Encirclement: 1 July–20 August 1944," Military Study A-922 (1946), in *Guide to Foreign Military Studies, 1945–1954*, 29.

56. Ibid., 30.

57. Ibid., 27.

58. Blumenson, *Breakout and Pursuit,* 528.

59. Ibid., 522.

60. Tieke, *In the Firestorm of the Last Years of the War,* 187.

61. XV Corps Report After Combat, p. 7.

62. Third Army G-3 Operations Diary, entries, 16 and 17 August.

63. Fritz Bayerlein, "An Interview with Gen Lt Fritz Bayerlein: Critique of Normandy Breakthrough—Panzer Lehr Division from St.-Lô to the Ruhr," European Theater historian interview no. 67, 15 August 1945, in *Guide to Foreign Military Studies, 1945–1954,* 14.

64. Tieke, *In the Firestorm of the Last Years of the War,* 195.

65. Ibid., 194.

66. John Colby, *War from the Ground Up: The 90th Division in WW II* (Austin, Tex.: Nortex Press, 1991), 235.

67. Von Luettwitz, "Normandy Campaign of 2 Panzer Division," 22.

68. Tieke, *In the Firestorm of the Last Years of the War,* 196.

69. Rudolf Lehmann and Ralf Tiemann, *The Leibstandarte IV/1,* trans. Nick Olcott (Winnipeg: J. J. Fedorowicz, 1993), 224.

70. Ian Gooderson, *Air Power at the Battlefront: Allied Close Air Support in Europe, 1943–45* (London: Frank Cass, 1998), 116–119.

CHAPTER 12. *UNTERNEHMEN LÜTTICH*—A FINAL ASSESSMENT

1. Heinz Günther Guderian, *Das letze Kriegsjahr im Westen: Die Geschichte der 116. Panzer Division Windhund Division* (Sankt Augustin, Germany: Herbert W. Schallowetz GmbH, SZ Offsetdruck Verlag, 1994), 83–84.

2. Geoffrey P. Megargee, *Inside Hitler's High Command* (Lawrence: University Press of Kansas, 2000), 122–123.

3. "Problems of Combined Command," lecture delivered by General Dwight D. Eisenhower at the National War College, Washington, D.C., 18 June 1948, in Matthew B. Ridgeway Papers, U.S. Army Military History Institute, Carlisle Barracks, Pa.

4. *7 Armee Kriegstagebuch,* entry, 1500 hour, 7 August 1944, Entry 58, Special Staff Adjutant General Division War Diaries, 1943–45, German Seventh Army Box 67, RG 331, Records of Allied Operational and Occupation HQs, WW II (SHAEF), NACP. This entry is the record of a telephone conversation between *Oberst* Walter Reinhard, *XLVII Panzer Korps* chief of staff, and *Oberst* von Gersdorff, *7 Armee* chief of staff. The *7 Armee* chief of staff telephoned *Heeresgruppe B* twenty minutes later and relayed the same information. However, he also rather optimistically claimed that *Leibstandarte* advanced to within two kilometers of Juvigny le Tertre.

Bibliography

PRIMARY SOURCES

Allen, Floyd G. Telephone interview by author. Tape recording. 6 November 1992.

Alloway, Curtis H. Telephone interview by author. Tape recording. 17 December 1992.

Anderson, William L., and James C. Piper. Interview by Lieutenant Fife. 18 August 1944. Combat Interviews No. 31, 4th Inf Div, St.-Lô–Mortain, 25 July–8 August 1944; Folders 31–34; Combat Interviews. WWII Operations Reports, 1940–48, RG 407, Records of the Adjutant General's Office, NACP.

Andrew, Tom F. H., and Hammond D. Birks. "The Counterattack Against the 120th Inf. at Mortain, the Abbaye-Blanche Roadblock." Interview by European Theater historian. 18 August 1944. C.I. 96, 30th Inf Div, Mortain Counterattack, 6–12 August 1944, Folders 95–97, Combat Interviews. WWII Operations Reports, 1940–48. RG 407, Records of the Adjutant General's Office, NACP.

Arn, Edward C., and Thomas H. Kirkman. "Activities of the 2d Battalion, 119th Infantry, August 9–12." Interview by David Garth. 5 September 1944. C.I. 96, 30th Inf Div, Mortain Counterattack, 6–12 August 1944, Folders 95–97, Combat Interviews. WWII Operations Reports, 1940–48, RG 407, Records of the Adjutant General's Office, NACP.

Bayerlein, Fritz. "An Interview with Gen Lt Fritz Bayerlein: Critique of Normandy Breakthrough—Panzer Lehr Division from St.-Lô to the Ruhr." European Theater Historian Interview No. 67, 15 August 1945. In *Guide to Foreign Military Studies, 1945–1954*. Heidelberg: Historical Division, Headquarters, U.S. Army, Europe, 1954.

Beckmann, Alvin. Telephone interview by author. Tape recording. 2 February 1993.

Belk, Samuel. Telephone conversation with author. 10 July 1998.

———. Telephone interview by author. Tape recording. 14 March 1995.

Bell, Charles W. Telephone interview by author. Tape recording. 17 December 1992.

Bisesto, Pasquale. Telephone interview by author. Tape recording. 17 November 1993.

Bradley, Omar N. *A Soldier's Story*. New York: Henry Holt, 1951.

Bradley, Robert B. Telephone interview by author. Tape recording. 16 January 1994.

Broussard, Ames. Telephone interview by author. Tape recording. 12 November 1992.

Butler, William J. "The Combat Cage." Unpublished memoir. Kalamazoo, Mich., November 1998.

———. Letter to author. 1998.

Byrne, Bernard A. Letter to Carlton Thornblom. 24 February 1950. Provided to author by Henry Morgan.

Cardinale, Antonio. Telephone interview by author. Tape recording. 13 March 1993.

Carroll, Merrill R. Telephone interview by author. Tape recording. 4 January 1994.

Cervantes. Leonard T. Telephone interview by author. Tape recording. 22 September 1993.

Chocklett, Harold. Telephone interview by author. Tape recording. 16 June 1993.

Chocklett, Harry. Telephone interview by author. Tape recording. 10 May 1993.

Clabough, Roy A. Telephone interview by author. Tape recording. 14 January 1993.

Claing, Lieutenant, Lieutenant Eddiger, and Lieutenant Mills. "Actions of 4th Division Units Against German Counterattacks, August 7 to 9." Interview by William T. Taylor. N.d. C.I. 31, 4th Inf Div, St.-Lô–Mortain, 25 July–8 August 1944; Folders 31–34, Combat Interviews. WWII Operations Reports, 1940–48. RG 407, Records of the Adjutant General's Office, NACP.

Clark, Robert C. Telephone interview by author. Tape recording. 12 December 1993.

Collins, J. Lawton, *Lightning Joe: An Autobiography*. Novato, Calif.: Presidio, 1994.

Connors, Francis J., Ashby L. Lohse, and Albert J. Kuster. "The Mortain Counterattack: The 2d Platoon, Co. 'A', 823d TD, at Hill 285, August 6–12." Interview by David Garth. 26 September 1944. C.I. 96, 30th Inf Div, Mortain Counterattack, 6–12 August 1944; Folders 95–97, Combat Interviews. WWII Operations Reports, 1940–48.; RG 407, Records of the Adjutant General's Office, NACP.

Cooper, Belton. Telephone interview by author. Tape recording. 21 February 1993.

Corbin, Charles R. Telephone interview by author. Tape recording. 20 January 1993.

Cordell, Robert A. Telephone interview by author. Tape recording. 19 June 1993.

Cottriel, Fred. Telephone interview by author. Tape recording. 21 February 1993.

Cowan, Kenneth R. "Repulse of the Counterattack Aimed at Avranches, 7–12 August." Interview by Franklin Ferriss. 6 September 1944. C.I. 96, 30th Inf Div, Mortain Counterattack, 6–12 August 1944; Folders 95–97, Combat Interviews. WWII Operations Reports, 1940–48. RG 407, Records of the Adjutant General's Office, NACP.

Cushman, Robert, and Donald F. Renshaw. "Mortain Counterattack, 7 August 1944, Action at the Crossroad North of la Fantay." Interview by Roland G. Ruppenthal. 17 August 1944. C.I. 96, 30th Inf Div, Mortain Counterattack, 6–12 August 1944, Folders 95–97, Combat Interviews, WWII Operations Reports, 1940–48. RG 407, Records of the Adjutant General's Office, NACP.

Davies, Wilfred. Telephone interview by author. Tape recording. 11 December 1994.

Deal, Grady E. Telephone interview by author. Tape recording. 4 April 1993.

Dillard, Marc. Telephone interview by author. Tape recording. 19 March 1994.

Dugan, Haynes. "Death of Col. Cornog." Unpublished manuscript. Shreveport, La., n.d.

Dunlap, Jack. Letter to Charles Scheffel. 18 June 1997.

Dunleavy, John J. Telephone interview by author. Tape recording. 17 November 1992.

Dwyer, William. Telephone interview by author. Tape recording. 26 September 1993.

Eberbach, Hans. "Panzer Group Eberbach and the Falaise Encirclement: 1 July–20 August 1944." Military Study A–922. 1946. In *Guide to Foreign Military Studies, 1945–1954.* Heidelberg: Historical Division, Headquarters, United States Army, Europe, 1954.

Eller, Thomas A. Telephone interview by author. Tape recording. 6 December 1992.

Eubanks, Proctor. Telephone interview by author. Tape recording. 7 October 1993.

Ezehner, Joseph, and D. N. Rockwell. "Anti–Tank Co in the Mortain Counterattack, 7 August 1944." Interview by Roland G. Ruppenthal. 18 August 1944. C.I. 96, 30th Inf Div, Mortain Counterattack, 6–12 August 1944, Folders 95–97, Combat Interviews, WWII Operations Reports, 1940–48. RG 407, Records of the Adjutant General's Office, NACP.

Fowler, Robert. Telephone interview by author. Tape recording. 19 July 1993.

Freeman, Arthur. Telephone interview by author. Tape recording. 25 January 1993.

Greene, George I. Telephone interview by author. Tape recording. 6 November 1992.

Groom, Thomas. Telephone interview by author. Tape recording. 21 February 1993.

Hackman, Ben W. Telephone interview by author. Tape recording. 18 November 1992.

Hagen, Guy B. Telephone interview by author. Tape recording. 27 August 1993.

Haines, Juan D. Interview by European Theater historian. 19 August 1944[?]. C.I.–261, 3d Arm Div, Fromental, 7–28 August 1944, Folders 259–261, Combat Interviews, WWII Operations Reports, 1940–48. RG 407, Records of the Adjutant General's Office, NACP.

Hanratty, John S. Telephone interview by author. Tape recording. 21 July 1993.

Hansen, Chester B. Diary, February 1943 to October 1944. Box 1. Chester B. Hansen Papers. U.S. Army Military History Institute, Carlisle Barracks, Pa.

Harman, Fred R. Letter to author. 8 January 1993.

———. Telephone interview by author. Tape recording. 21 December 1992.

Harrington, Gerald P. Telephone interview by author. Tape recording. 19 April 1994.

Harrison, Gordon A. *Cross-Channel Attack.* Washington, D.C.: Center for Military History, U.S. Government Printing Office, 1989.

Harrison, William K. *U.S. Army Senior Officer Oral Histories.* Bethesda, Md.: U.S. Army Military History Institute, Oral History Branch, 1989.

Henderson, Peter L. "Repulse of the German Counterattack Aimed at Avranches." Interview by Franklin Ferriss. 6 September 1944. C.I. 96, 30th Inf Div, Mortain Counterattack, 6–12 August 1944, Folders 95–97, Combat Interviews, WWII Operations Reports, 1940–48.; RG 407, Records of the Adjutant General's Office, NACP.

Henderson, Peter, Millard A. Glantz, and Theodore A. Baumeister. "Action at Barenton, 6–7 August." Interview by European Theater historian. 11 September 1944[?]. C.I. 96, 30th Inf Div, Mortain Counterattack, 6–12 August 1944, Folders 95–97, Combat Interviews, WWII Operations Reports, 1940–48. RG 407, Records of the Adjutant General's Office, NACP.

Herlong, Robert E. "Repulse of the German Counterattack Aimed at Avranches, 7–11 August." Interview by Franklin Ferriss. 18 August 1944. C.I. 96, 30th Inf Div, Mortain Counterattack, 6–12 August 1944, Folders 95–97, Combat Interviews, WWII Operations Reports, 1940–48. RG 407, Records of the Adjutant General's Office, NACP.

Higgins, Bill. Telephone interview by author. Tape recording. 8 April 1993.

Hogan, Samuel M. "Activities of Team No. 3, 3d Armored Division, August 7–12, 1944." Interview by European Theater historian. 19 August 1944. C1–261, 3d Arm Div, Fromental, 7–28 August 1944, Folders 259–261, Combat Interviews, WWII Operations Reports, 1940–48. RG 407, Records of the Adjutant General's Office, NACP.

Hughes, G. Dayton. Telephone interview by author. Tape recording. 23 July 1993.

Infantry Field Manual—Rifle Regiment, February 9, 1942, Washington, D.C.: United States Government Printing Office, 1942.

Interview with veteran of the 30th Infantry Division who did not wish to be named. Telephone interview by author. Tape recording. 22 September 1993.

Jackson, Charles L. Telephone interview by author. Tape recording. 28 February 1994.

Johnson, Walter M., et al. "Counterattack at Mortain, 7 August 1944." Interview by Roland G. Ruppenthal. 15 August 1944. C.I. 96, 30th Inf Div, Mortain Counterattack, 6–12 August 1944, Folders 95–97, Combat Interviews, WWII Operations Reports, 1940–48. RG 407, Records of the Adjutant General's Office, NACP.

Katzman, Irving, Joseph H. Klebba, and Clinton W. Robb. "Action of C Co (117th Inf) Counterattack at Mortain, 7 Aug." Interview by Roland G. Ruppenthal. 17 August 1944. C.I. 96, 30th Inf Div, Mortain Counterattack, 6–12 August 1944. Folders 95–97, Combat Interviews, WWII Operations Reports, 1940–48. RG 407, Records of the Adjutant General's Office, NACP.

Kerley, Ralph. "Operations of the 2/120th Infantry at Mortain, France, 7–12 August 1944." USAIS Library Student Monograph. Fort Benning, Ga.: Advanced Officer's Class no. 1, USAIS, 1946–1947.

Kluttz, Robert. Telephone interview by author. Tape recording. 2 December 1992.

Korrison, David. "Repulse of the Counterattack Aimed at Avranches, 7–12 August." Interview by Franklin Ferriss. 6 September 1944. C.I. 96, 30th Inf Div, Mortain Counterattack, 6–12 August 1944, Folders 95–97, Combat Interviews, WWII Operations Reports, 1940–48. RG 407, Records of the Adjutant General's Office, NACP.

Kraemer, Fritz. "Counterattack on Avranches: An Interview with Generalmajor der Waffen–SS Fritz Kraemer," European Theater Historian interview No. 24. 17 November 1945. In *Guide to Foreign Military Studies, 1945–1954*. Heidelberg: Historical Division, Headquarters, U.S. Army, Europe, 1954.

Kriegstagebuch 30. Oktober 1943 bis 6. Mai 1945: 17-SS Panzergrenadier Division "Götz von Berlichingen." Edited by M. Wind and H. Gunther. Munich: Schild Verlag GmbH, 1993.

Krueger, Walter. "LVIII Panzer Corps: 24 July–15 September 1944." Military Study B-445. In *Guide to Foreign Military Studies, 1945–1954*. Heidelberg: Historical Division, Headquarters, U.S. Army, Europe, 1954.

Kurtz, Homer W. Telephone interview by author. Tape recording. 30 November 1992.

Lambert, Junior K. Telephone interview by author. Tape recording. 13 December 1992.

Lay, Kenneth E. Telephone interview by author. Tape recording. 1 November 1994.

Leger, Ilfred D. Telephone interview by author. Tape recording. 10 January 1994.

Lindner, Kenneth R. Telephone interview by author. Tape recording. 5 June 1994.

Lockett, James W., and Ben T. Ammons. "The 2d Bn in the Mortain Counterattack, 7 Aug." Interview by European Theater Historian. 18 August 1944. C.I. 96, 30th Inf Div, Mortain Counterattack, 6–12 August 1944, Folders 95–97, Combat Interviews, WWII Operations Reports, 1940–48. RG 407, Records of the Adjutant General's Office, NACP.

MacDowell, Samuel T., John Prejean, and Edward B. Parrish. "The 3d Bn, 117th Inf, in the Counterattack, 7 Aug." Interview by Roland G. Ruppenthal. 18 August 1944. C.I. 96, 30th Inf Div, Mortain Counterattack, 6–12 August 1944, Folders 95–97, Combat Interviews, WWII Operations Reports, 1940–48. RG 407, Records of the Adjutant General's Office, NACP.

Magness, Thomas E. Telephone interview by author. Tape recording. 4 April 1993.

Malloy, Frank. Telephone interview by author. Tape recording. 8 December 1993.

May, William W. Letter to Haynes Dugan. 11 November 1991.

———. Letter to Waverly H. Cousins. 18 January 1946.

Maybee, Reginald. "Chapter 3: The Battle of Mortain." (Abstract from unpublished manuscript. 1993[?].

———. Telephone interview by author. Tape recording. 19 May 1993.

McCown, Hal D. "Repulse of the Counterattack Aimed at Avranches, 7–12 August." Interview by Franklin Ferris[?]. 17 August 1944. C.I. 96, 30th Inf Div, Mortain Counterattack, 6–12 August 1944, Folders 95–97, Combat Interviews, WWII Operations Reports, 1940–48. RG 407, Records of the Adjutant General's Office, NACP.

Memorandum entitled "Notes on the Operations of XIX Corps (8 June–24 June) by Capt. Franklin Ferriss." CI 361–A, XIX Corps, Invasion Through the Siegfried Line, June–November 1944; Folders 360–362 (XVIII and XIX Corps), Combat Interviews, WWII Operations Reports, 1940–48. RG 407, Records of the Adjutant General's Office, NACP.

Meyer, Stewart C. Telephone interview by author. Tape recording. 12 January 1993.

Montgomery, Floyd M. Telephone interview by author. Tape recording. 29 July 1993.

Moody, Frank E. "Mortain, France, August 5–12, 1944." Unpublished manuscript.

———. Telephone interview by author. Tape recording. 7 March 1993.

Morgan, Henry. Letter to author. 27 November 1992.

Murray, Leonard T. Telephone interview by author. Tape recording. 1 December 1992.

Navarette, Al. Telephone interview by author. Tape recording. 16 December 1992.

Nethery, Paul W. Telephone interview by author. Tape recording. 20 March 1993.

Newman, Art. Telephone interview by author. Tape recording. 12 May 1993.

Offer, Royal A. Telephone interview by author. Tape recording. 30 December 1992.

O'Hare, John. Telephone interview by author. Tape recording. 1 June 1993.

Parker, Ken. *Civilian at War*. Traverse City, Mich.: Myers Printing, 1984.

Patton, George S. Diaries, 1910–1945. Boxes 1–3, Annotated Transcripts. Library of Congress, Washington, D.C.

Pearson, Alton. Letter to author. 1 April 1994.

———. Telephone interview by author. Tape recording. 7 April 1994.

Phillips, Edmund F. Telephone interview by author. Tape recording. 20 March 1994.

Plezia, Frank. Telephone interview by author. Tape recording. 12 April 1993.

Poulson, George R. Telephone interview by author. Tape recording. 4 November 1993.

Pruitt, Frank. Telephone interview by author. Tape recording. 2 July 1993.

Pulver, Murray S. Letter to Stephen Lofgren, military historian for Department of the Army Center of Military History, Fort McNair, Washington, D.C., 1989.

———. *The Longest Year*. Freeman, S.D.: Pine Hill Press, 1986.

"Questions for Heinrich von Luettwitz, Commanding General of the 2d Panzer Division until September 1944, Normandy Campaign of 2 Panzer Division, 26 July–6 September

1944." Military Study A–904. 1947. In *Guide to Foreign Military Studies, 1945–1954*. Heidelberg: Historical Division, Headquarters, U.S. Army, Europe, 1954.

Rachal, Edmond L. Telephone conversation with author. 26 September 1998.

Raimondi, Emil. Telephone interview by author. Tape recording. 8 April 1993.

Raney, Thompson. Telephone conversation with author. 12 September 1993.

Reaser, Joseph. Telephone conversation with author. 18 July 1998.

Richardson, James. "The Operations of the 1st Battalion, 39th Infantry (9th Infantry Division) at Cherence le Roussel, France, 4–10 August 1944." USAIS Library Student Monograph. Fort Benning, Ga.: Advanced Officer's Class no. 1, USAIS, 1946–1947.

Ritgen, Helmut. *The Western Front, 1944: Memoirs of a Panzer Lehr Officer*. Translated by Joseph Welsh. Winnipeg: J. J. Fedorowicz, 1995.

Ruback, Albert J., et al. "Activities of the 120th Regiment, 30th Division, August 6–12." Interview by European Theater historian. 26 August 1944[?]. C.I. 96, 30th Inf Div, Mortain Counterattack, 6–12 August 1944, Folders 95–97, Combat Interviews, WWII Operations Reports, 1940–48. RG 407, Records of the Adjutant General's Office, NACP.

Russell, Carlton P. Telephone interview by author. Tape recording. 14 January 1993.

Sabata, Jack. Letter to author. 5 September 1992.

Scala, Nick. Telephone conversation with author. 14 March 1995.

Scheffel, Charles. "D–Day to End WWII Europe: Route of the 1st Battalion, 39th Infantry Regiment, 9th Infantry Division, VII Corps, First U.S. Army." Unpublished memoir. Oklahoma City, Okla., 1986.

———. Letter to author. 1996.

———. Telephone conversation with author. 7 July and 19 September 1998.

Schramm, Percy E. "Oberkommand Wehrmacht Diary (1 Apr–18 Dec 44): The West." Military Study B–034. 1946. In *Guide to Foreign Military Studies, 1945–1954*. Heidelberg: Historical Division, Headquarters, U.S. Army, Europe, 1954.

Schumacher, Marcus. Telephone interview by author. Tape recording. 23 May 1993.

Scott, Albert E. Telephone interview by author. Tape recording. 21 July 1993.

Simmons, Buster D. Letter to author. 26 April 1998.

Simmons, George. Telephone interviews by author. Tape recordings. 6 and 22 November 1992.

Spector, Jean. "Repulse of the Counterattack Aimed at Avranches, 7–12 August." Interview by Franklin Ferriss. 18 August 1944. C.I. 96, 30th Inf Div, Mortain Counterattack, 6–12 August 1944, Folders 95–97, Combat Interviews, WWII Operations Reports, 1940–48. RG 407, Records of the Adjutant General's Office, NACP.

Springfield, Thomas. Telephone interview by author. Tape recording. 27 February 1994.

Stong, Evert. Letter to Charles Scheffel. 18 February 1991.

Street, Thomas E. *How to Survive Combat as a Point Man If You're Lucky . . . and Lose Friends If They Aren't*. Bennington, Vt.: Merriam Press, 1997.

Sylvan, William C. Diary, 2 June 1944–7 May 1945. Papers of William C. Sylvan. U.S. Army Military History Institute, Carlisle Barracks, Pa.

Tedesco, Frank R. Telephone interview by author. Tape recording. 28 October 1994.

Thomas, Edwin. Telephone interview by author. Tape recording. 27 August 1993.

Thornblom, Carlton C. "Operations of the 1/320th Infantry at Mortain, 7–12 August

1944." USAIS Library Student Monograph. Fort Benning, Ga.: Advanced Officers' Class no. 1, USAIS, 1950.

Thorne, Glenn W. Telephone interview by author. Tape recording. 20 March 1994.

Tousey, Thomas. Letter to author. 1994.

——. Telephone interview by author. Tape recording. 26 January 1993.

Tripp, Emmett W. Telephone interviews by author. Tape recordings. 11 and 18 December 1992.

ULTRA Microfilm Collection. Reel numbers 29–39. Combined Army Research Library (CARL), Fort Leavenworth, Kans.

Vignes, Joseph L. Telephone interview by author. Tape recording. 23 November 1992.

Von Gersdorff, Rudolf Christoff. "Counterattack Against Avranches." Military Study A-921. November 1945. In *Guide to Foreign Military Studies, 1945–1954*. Heidelberg: Historical Division, Headquarters, U.S. Army, Europe, 1954.

——. "Northern France—Volume IV: Avranches Counterattack (1–11 August 1944)." Military Study B–725. 1946. In *Guide to Foreign Military Studies, 1945–1954*. Heidelberg: Historical Division, Headquarters, U.S. Army, Europe, 1954.

Von Schwerin, Gerhard Graf. "An Interview with Generalleutnant Gerhard Graf von Schwerin: 116 Panzer Division in Normandy," European Theater Historian Interview No. 17. By Kenneth W. Hechler. 1 September 1945. In *Guide to Foreign Military Studies, 1945–1954*. Heidelberg: Historical Division, Headquarters, U.S. Army, Europe, 1954.

Walker, Emet. "As I Remember." Unpublished memoir. 1994[?].

Waller, Richard. "Repulse of the German Counterattack Aimed at Avranches, 7–11 August." Interview by Franklin Ferriss. 18 August 1944. C.I. 96, 30th Inf Div, Mortain Counterattack, 6–12 August 1944. Folders 95–97, Combat Interviews, WWII Operations Reports, 1940–48. RG 407, Records of the Adjutant General's Office, NACP.

Warlimont, General Walter. "Circumstances of the 20 July 44 Attempt: Was von Kluge a Traitor?" European Theater Historian Interview No. 5. 12 July 1949. In *Guide to Foreign Military Studies, 1945–1954*. Heidelberg: Historical Division, Headquarters, U.S. Army, Europe, 1954.

Weber, Stanley R. Telephone interview by author. Tape recording. 26 April 1993.

Weiss, Robert. *Enemy North, South, East West.* Portland, Ore.: Strawberry Hill Press, 1998.

——. Telephone conversation with author. 2 March 1998.

Westmoreland, William C. "Mortain Counterattack, 7–10 August 1944, 9th Division Artillery." Interview by Kenneth W. Hechler. 11 June 1945. C.I. 54, 9th Inf. Div, Mortain Counterattack, 7–10 August 1944, Folders 51–54; Combat Interviews, WWII Operations Reports, 1940–48. RG 407, Records of the Adjutant General's Office, NACP.

Whitman, Dunbar. "Interview with Capt Dunbar Whitman, EO, 1st Bn, 12th Inf, Mortain Battle." Interview by European Theater Historian. 18 August 1944[?]. Combat Interview No. 31, 4th Inf Div, St.-Lô–Mortain, 25 July– 8 August 1944, Folders 31–34; Combat Interviews, WWII Operations Reports, 1940–48. RG 407, Records of the Adjutant General's Office, NACP.

Whitsett, John. Telephone interview by author. Tape recording. 18 November 1993.

Wilkinson, Dudley C. Telephone interview by author. Tape recording. 1 April 1993.
Willis, Daniel. Telephone interview by author. Tape recording. 2 January 1993.
Wilts, Francis, and Lawson Neel. "The TDs in the St. Barthelmy [sic] Battle, 7 August 1944."
    Interview by Roland G. Ruppenthal. 18 August 1944. C.I. 96, 30th Inf Div, Mortain
    Counterattack, 6–12 August 1944, Folders 95–97, Combat Interviews, WWII Opera-
    tions Reports, 1940–48. RG 407, Records of the Adjutant General's Office, NACP.
Wineberger, Roy C. Telephone interview by author. Tape recording. 21 December 1992.
Workman, Grady. "The Attack of 8 August 1944." Interview by Roland G. Ruppenthal.
    18 August 1944. C.I. 96, 30th Inf Div, Mortain Counterattack, 6–12 August 1944,
    Folders 95–97, Combat Interviews, WWII Operations Reports, 1940–48. RG 407,
    Records of the Adjutant General's Office, NACP.
Wright, Jones C., et al. "Co A's (117th Inf) Action in the Mortain Counterattack, 7 Aug."
    Interview by Roland G. Ruppenthal. 17 August 1944. C.I. 96, 30th Inf Div, Mortain
    Counterattack, 6–12 August 1944, Folders 95–97, Combat Interviews, WWII Oper-
    ations Reports, 1940–48. RG 407, Records of the Adjutant General's Office, NACP.

SECONDARY SOURCES

899th Tank Destroyer Battalion History: Our Battalion. Munich: Knorr and Hirth,
    1945[?].
Blaker, Gordon A. Iron Knights: The United States 66th Armored Regiment. Shippens-
    burg, Pa.: Burd Street Press, 1999.
Blumenson, Martin. Breakout and Pursuit. Washington, D.C.: Center for Military History,
    U.S. Government Printing Office, 1989.
——. Command Decisions: General Bradley's Decision at Agentan (13 August 1944).
    Center for Military History Pub. No. 70-7-17. Washington, D.C.: U.S. Government
    Printing Office, 1990.
Bradley, Omar N., with Clay Blair. A General's Life: An Autobiography by General of the
    Army Omar N. Bradley. New York: Simon and Schuster, 1983.
Bradley, Robert B. Aidman! New York: Vantage Press, 1970.
Carafano, James Jay. After D-Day: Operation Cobra and the Normandy Breakout. Boul-
    der, Colo.: Lynne Rienner Publishers, 2000.
Carrell, Paul. Invasion: They're Coming. Atglen, Pa.: Schiffer Publishing, 1995.
Colby, John. War from the Ground Up: The 90th Division in WWII. Austin, Tex.: Nortex
    Press, 1991.
Combat History of the 119th Infantry Regiment. Baton Rouge, La.: Army and Navy Pub-
    lishing, 1946.
Copp, Terry. Maple Leaf Route: Falaise. Ontario: Maple Leaf Route Publishers, 1983.
Coupard, Michel, and Jack Lecoq. Le Mortainais: Mortain et Juvigny-le-Tertre—Memoire
    en Images. Joue les Tours, France: Editions Alan Sutton, 1997.
Das Regiment Deutschland 1934–1945. Written by the Veterans Association of the
    Deutschland Regiment. Freinsheim, Germany: Gerhard Eichelmann, Gesamther-
    stellung und Verlag, 1993.
D'Este, Carlo. Decision in Normandy. New York: Harper Perennial, 1995.
DZ Europe: History of the 440th Troop Carrier Group. N.p. Privately printed, 1945.

Faubus, Orval Eugene. *In This Faraway Land: A Personal Journey of Infantry Combat in World War II*. Conway, Ark.: River Road Press, 1971.

Fay, Norman F., and Charles M. Kincaid. *History of the Thirtieth Division Artillery*. N.p., 1945[?].

Featherston, Alwyn. *Saving the Breakout: The 30th Division's Heroic Stand at Mortain, August 7–12, 1944*. Novato, Calif.: Presidio Press, 1993.

Florentin, Eddy. *Battle for the Falaise Gap*. New York: Hawthorn Books, 1965.

Folkestad, William B. *The View from the Turret: The 743d Tank Battalion During World War II*. Shippensburg, Pa.: Burd Street Press, 1996.

Greenfield, Kent Roberts, ed. *Command Decisions*. Washington, D.C.: Center of Military History, 1990.

Guderian, Heinz Günther. *Das letze Kriegsjahr im Westen: Die Geschichte der 116. Panzer Division Windhund Division*. Sankt Augustin, Germany: Herbert W. Schallowetz GmbH, SZ Offsetdruck Verlag, 1994.

Gunter, Helmut. *Das Auge der Division: Die Aufklärungsabteilung der SS-Panzergrenadier Division "Götz Von Berlichingen."* Preuss, Germany: Verlag K.W. Schutz KG, 1985.

Hewitt, Robert. *Workhorse of the Western Front*. Nashville, Tenn.: Battery Press, 1980.

Historical Department. *St.-Lô: 7 July–19 July 1944, American Forces in Action Series*. Washington, D.C.: War Department, 1946.

History of the 67th Armored Regiment. Brunswick, Germany: George Westermann, GmbH, 1945.

History of the 117th Infantry Regiment. Baton Rouge, La.: Army and Navy Publishing, 1946.

History of the 120th Infantry Regiment. Washington, D.C.: Infantry Journal Press, 1947.

"History of the 654th Tank Destroyer Battalion." Unpublished manuscript. Provided to author by Everard A. Taylor, 1993.

Houston, Donald E. *Hell on Wheels: The 2d Armored Division*. Novato, Calif.: Presidio Press, 1977.

Huston, James A. *Biography of a Battalion: Being the Life and Times of an Infantry Battalion in Europe in World War II*. Gering, Nebr.: Courier Press, 1950.

Ingersoll, Ralph, *Top Secret*. New York: Harcourt, Brace, 1946.

Jensen, Marvin. *Strike Swiftly! The 70th Tank Battalion from North Africa to Normandy to Germany*. Novato, Calif.: Presidio Press, 1997.

Johnson, Gerden F. *History of the 12th Infantry Regiment in World War II*. Boston: privately printed, 1947.

Klapdor, Ewald. *Die Entscheidung: Invasion 1944*. Germany: privately printed, 1984.

Kurowski, Franz. *Infantry Aces*. Winnipeg: J. J. Fedorowicz Publishing, 1994.

Lefevre, Eric. *Panzers in Normandy: Then and Now*. London: Battle of Britain Prints International Limited Publishers, 1983.

Lehmann, Rudolf, and Ralf Tiemann. *The Leibstandarte IV/1*. Translated by Nick Olcott. Winnipeg: J. J. Fedorowicz, 1993.

Lucas, James. *Das Reich: The Military Role of the 2d SS Division*. London: Arms and Armour Press, 1992.

Lyman, William J. *Curlew History: The Story of the First Battalion, 117th Infantry, 30th Division in Europe During World War II*. Chapel Hill, N.C.: Orange Printshop, 1948.

Megargee, Geoffrey. *Inside Hitler's High Command*. Lawrence: University Press of Kansas, 2000.

Messenger, Charles. *Hitler's Gladiator: The Life and Times of Oberstgruppenführer and Panzergeneral-Oberst der Waffen SS Sepp Dietrich*. London: Brassey's Defence Publishers, 1988.

Meyer, Hubert. *The History of 12. SS-Panzerdivision Hitlerjugend*. Translated by H. Harri Henschler. Winnipeg: J. J. Fedorowicz, 1994.

Miltonberger, Butler B., and James A. Huston. *134th Infantry Regiment: Combat History of World War II*. Baton Rouge, La.: Army and Navy Publishing, 1946[?].

Mitcham, Samuel W., Jr. *The Desert Fox in Normandy: Rommel's Defense of Fortress Europe*. Westport, Conn.: Praeger Publishers, 1997.

Move Out, Verify: History of the 743d Tank Battalion. Frankfurt: 743d Tank Battalion, 1945.

Munoz, Antonio J. *The Iron Fist Division: A Combat History of the 17th SS-Panzer Grenadier Division "Götz Von Berlichingen," 1943–1945*. Bennington, Vt.: Merriam Press, 1998.

On the Way: A Historical Narrative of the Two-Thirtieth Field Artillery Battalion, 30th Infantry Division, 16 February 1942 to 8 May 1945. Poessneck i. Theuringen, Germany: Fr. Gerold Verlag, 1945[?].

Paths of Armor: The Fifth Armored Division in World War II. Nashville, Tenn.: Battery Press, 1950.

Perrigault, Jean-Claude. *La Panzer Lehr Division: Le Choc Des Allies Brise L'Arme D'Elite De Hitler Normandie–Lorraine–Ardennes*. Bayeux, France: Editions Heimdal, 1995.

Reynolds, Michael. *The Steel Inferno: I SS Panzer Corps in Normandy*. Stapleton, England: Sarpedon Publishers, 1997.

Roberts, A. Eaton. *Five Stars to Victory: The Exploits of Task Force Lovelady, 2d Bn. (Reinf), 33d Arm'd Regt, 3d Arm'd Div, U.S. Army in the War Against Germany*. Birmingham, Ala.: Atlas Printing and Engraving, 1949.

Stöber, Hans. *Die eiserne Faust: Bildband und Chronik der 17. SS-Panzergrenadier Division "Götz von Berlichingen."* Neckargemund, Germany: Kurt Vowinckel Verlag, 1966.

——. *Die Sturmflut und das Ende (Band 1): Die Invasion—Geschichte der 17. SS-Panzer Grenadier Division "Götz von Berlichingen."* Munich: Schild Verlag, 2000.

Strauss, F. G., et al. *Friedens und Kriegserlebnisse einer Generation: Ein Kapitel Weltgeschichte aus der Sicht der Panzerjäger-Abteilung 38 (SF) in der ehemaligen 2. (Wiener) Panzerdivision*. Schweinfurt, Germany: *Schweinfurter Tageblatt*, 1961[?].

Tieke, Wilhelm. *In the Firestorm of the Last Years of the War: II. SS-Panzerkorps with the 9. and 10. SS-Divisions "Hohenstaufen" and "Frundsberg."* Translated by Frederick Steinhardt. Winnipeg: J. J. Fedorowicz, 1999.

Vannoy, Allyn R., and Jay Karameles. *Against the Panzers: United States Infantry Versus German Tanks, 1944–1945*. Jefferson, N.C.: MacFarland, 1996.

Warlimont, Walter. *Inside Hitler's Headquarters, 1939–45*. Translated by R. H. Barry. Novato, Calif.: Presidio Press, 1990.

Weidemann, Gert-Axel. *Unser Regiment: Reiter Regiment 2 und Panzer Regiment 24*. Gross Umstadt, Germany: Ernst J. Dohany Druck und Verlag, 1984.

Weidinger, Otto. *Comrades to the End: The 4th SS-Panzer Grenadier Regiment "Der*

Führer," 1938–1945. Translated by David Johnston. Atglen, Pa.: Schiffer Military History, 1998.

Yerger, Mark C. *Knights of Steel: The Structure, Development, and Personalities of the 2. SS-Panzer Division.* Vol. 1. Hershey, Pa.: Michael J. Horetsky Publishers, 1989.

———. *Knights of Steel: The Structure, Development, and Personalities of the 2. SS-Panzer Division.* Vol. 2. Lancaster, Pa.: privately printed, 1994.

———. *Waffen-SS Commanders: The Army, Corps, and Divisional Leaders of a Legend—Augsberger to Kreutz.* Atglen, Pa.: Schiffer Military History, 1997.

Zetterling, Niklas. *Normandy 1944: German Military Organization, Combat Power, and Organizational Effectiveness.* Winnipeg: J. J. Fedorowicz, 2000.

Index